# welcc



'Understanding is the bedrock to everything we do. The more we know, the more we value what we've got. And appreciating it means we take care of it and enjoy it.'

I love discovering new things about the past so I take a particular interest in the research that English Heritage does into the historic places you will find in the following pages. Did you know, for example, that we recently discovered that the oldest door in the country was in the Pyx Chapel of the Chapter House in Westminster Abbey? Or that King Henry VIII's Calshot Castle, at the end of Southampton Water was adapted to modern second world war military tactics with quick firing guns, searchlights, a flying-boat station and a battery disguised as a seaside bungalow?

England's rich heritage never ceases to surprise and inspire. At the beginning of this new season, we think we have more than ever before to offer you and your family. At Battle Abbey in East Sussex we are opening a new exhibition and restaurant. This tells the story of one of the most important events in British history, using stunning film footage and computer-generated imagery, depicting the battle itself. A new shop, ticket office and exhibition are also opening at Goodrich Castle, Herefordshire.

In addition, 2007 will see two new temporary exhibitions. *Picture House* will continue the tradition of contemporary art installations at Belsay Hall in Northumberland. An exhibition at Kenwood House, London, will explore Lord Mansfield's efforts towards the abolition of the slave trade in England.

Every year, in this column, I am able to tell you how much we are investing in our properties – this year, a massive £7m. Of course, financial investment of this kind is crucial, but English Heritage also believes passionately in investing in intellectual investigation and revelation. Understanding is the bedrock to everything we do. The more we know, the more we value what we've got. And appreciating it means we take care of it and enjoy it. And guess what? The more we enjoy it, the more we'll want to know about it and thus a virtuous circle is complete.

We now have more than 630,000 members supporting our vital work. As always we look forward to welcoming you to show you what we've been doing and to giving you a great and unforgettable day out.

SIMON THURLEY

**Chief Executive of English Heritage**

Photo: Hugo Burnand

Sculpture at Bolsover Castle

# contents



## Opening Times

**1 April 2007 to 20 March 2008**
All information is correct at the time of going to press – some opening times may change, especially in bad weather. Please call Customer Services or check our website before you visit.

At some of our properties, visitors cannot be admitted less than one hour before closing time. Please call in advance to confirm individual policies. Where properties have a keykeeper, please contact them before setting off. For those open at 'any reasonable time', please visit during daylight hours, for safety reasons and to avoid causing a disturbance.

Properties showing this symbol may be closed at certain times for private events, please check in advance.

Some of our smaller staffed properties may close between 1pm and 2pm. Contact Customer Services for more information.

**Details of OS map references** are provided for easy location of each property, with specific map numbers and co-ordinates (OS Explorer maps).

## Contact

**Customer Services**
English Heritage
PO Box 569
Swindon
SN2 2YP
England

**Telephone** 0870 333 1181
**Facsimile** 01793 414926
**Email** customers@english-heritage.org.uk
**Website** www.english-heritage.org.uk

Above: (left) Waterloo Gallery doorway, Apsley House, (top right) Appuldurcombe House and (bottom right) Byland Abbey.



# membership

English Heritage looks after over **400 properties**, and as a membe you are entitled to visit them all for free as many times as you wish You are also entitled to free or reduced-price entry to a wide range of events, and you will receive our award-winning quarterly magazine, *Heritage Today*.

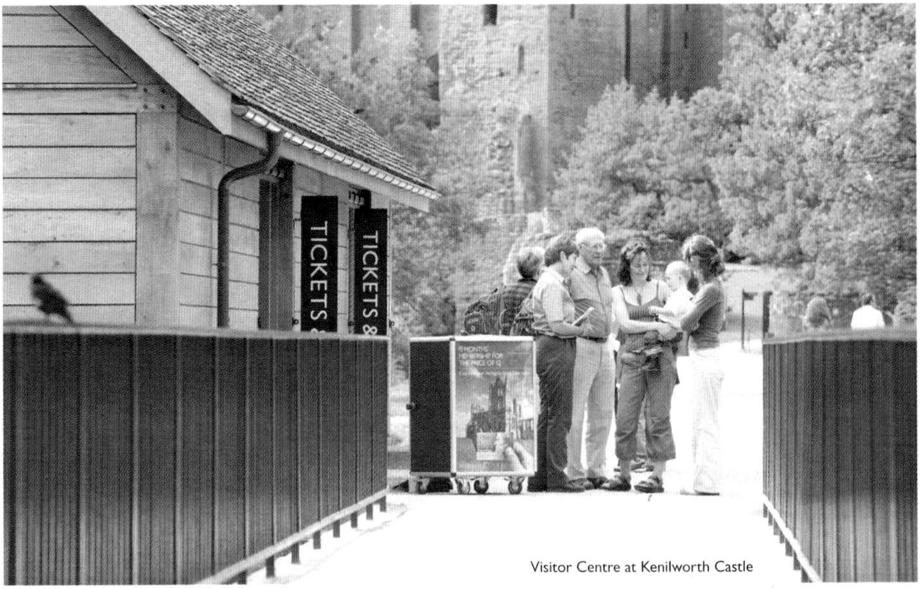


Visitor Centre at Kenilworth Castle

### Children Go Free

English Heritage believes in encouraging an enjoyment of history early, and this is reflected in our Children Go Free policy. This allows free entry for up to six accompanying children (under 19) per member, within the family group. Children should be carefully supervised, as historic sites can be hazardous. For non-members, discounted family tickets are available.

### More places in England

Your membership card will also give you free or discounted entry to many other sites in England. See the Other Historic Attractions section in each region.

**Please note:** discounts will not apply on days when events are held at these properties.

Walmer Castle & Gardens

### Enjoy Britain's heritage

You can also use your membership card to visit over 100 historic properties in Scotland, Wales and the Isle of Man. During your first year of English Heritage membership, you pay just half-price entry to properties in the care of Cadw (Welsh Historic Monuments), Historic Scotland and Manx National Heritage. Each year after that entry is completely free. For listings of these properties, see pages 256-259.

## Contact us

If you have comments or views to share, contact Customer Services on 0870 333 1181.

Please note that national call charges apply. Alternatively, write to us at:
English Heritage
Customer Services
PO Box 569, Swindon SN2 2YP
**customers@english-heritage.org.uk**

**www.english-heritage.org.uk/membership**

Every penny from your membership helps us to conserve our historic sites. We appreciate your support, and urge you to continue helping us preserve England's heritage for future generations. In return, we hope you'll gain enjoyment from your membership.

*English Heritage membership makes the perfect gift.*

*Call 0870 333 1182 or visit www.english-heritage.org.uk/gift*

# planning your visit

## Essential tips before you visit.

### Access

We are committed to ensuring that our properties are enjoyed by and are accessible to all. In this handbook we have used the ♿ symbol to indicate that at least some areas are accessible by wheelchair.

For a more thorough guide to accessibility at many of our properties, please refer to our *Access Guide*, which is free. This offers an honest assessment of which of our landscapes and buildings have the most to offer visitors with disabilities. These include sites with alternative routes for wheelchair users, or with features like scented gardens, tactile objects/displays and specially created audio tours. Information on parking and drop-off points is also included, with an indication of some of the obstacles you may encounter around each site, such as steep steps, or grounds which may become water-logged in wet weather.

Some of these features and facilities will also be of interest to families and carers with young children, or those who like to include both children and grandparents in their days out.

If you have any questions about a particular site, please do call in advance. The companion of a visitor with disabilities is admitted free to all English Heritage properties (free entry for one companion only).

Information on our sites can also be obtained by fax. For individual site fax numbers, please telephone or email Customer Services.

The Access Guide is available in large type, braille, on tape and on disc by region, or on our website. Visit **www.english-heritage.org.uk/accessguide** to download your free copy. Alternatively, please call 0870 333 1181 or minicom 01793 414878, or email **customers@english-heritage.org.uk**

Look out for **special displays, exhibitions and visitor centres** at many of our sites.

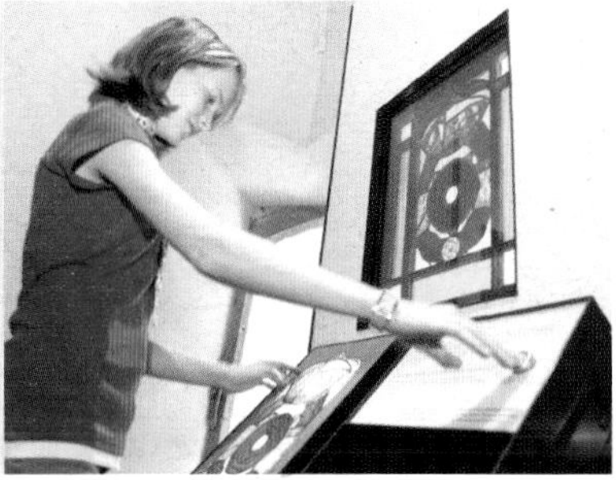

### Catering and picnics

Refreshments are available at restaurants and tearooms at some sites, many located within historic buildings. Visitors are also welcome to picnic in the grounds of many sites. Please check individual listings for details.

### Dogs

Dogs on leads are welcome where possible. Please see individual listings for details. Guide and hearing dogs are welcome everywhere.

### Educational

Visiting historic sites is an important way of inspiring school children and adult learners about history. We actively encourage these visits by providing free entry to our sites for pre-booked educational groups. We also provide a range of resources to enable teachers and students to get the most out of their visit.

We follow the Department for Education and Skills' Guidelines on Health and Safety on Educational Visits, and require at least one adult to every six children in a group containing pupils of school years one to three. The ratio may go down to one to 15 for years seven and above. For more information visit **www.english-heritage.org.uk/learning**

**Families and children**
We welcome families with children of all ages. Many of our sites include special features, exhibitions or educational facilities suitable for children. Some offer baby-changing facilities. For safety reasons, babies cannot be carried in back carriers at certain properties. You are responsible for the children's supervision and safety at all times: please ensure a sensible number of adults in relationship to the number of children.

**Family learning**
Look out for the exciting range of resources we are developing at many of our sites. Already featured at over 50 sites, these range from free children's activity sheets and back packs to book boxes, and 'Very Big Books' for younger children – as well as interactive Discovery Centres. Properties with these resources are marked with a .

**Guides and tours**
Audio guides are available at over 50 of our sites. In exceptional circumstances, for instance when an event is taking place or for larger groups of visitors, audio guides may not be available. To check for special events see the Events section of *Heritage Today* magazine, visit **www.english-heritage.org.uk/events** or call Customer Services. Guidebooks are also on sale at staffed properties or through our postal service – call 0870 429 6658.

**Photography**
Non-commercial photography is welcome in all our grounds. For conservation reasons, it is not permitted inside some properties.

**Public transport and cycling**
All public transport information is correct at time of going to press. If you have any comments or suggestions, please call Barry Doe on 01202 528707. Details of all bus travel in England is available from Traveline on 0870 608 2608 or online at **www.traveline.org.uk**

Call Sustrans on 0117 929 0888 or visit the website **www.sustrans.org.uk** for cycle route information.

**Safety**
Due to their historic nature, some of our sites have features which could be hazardous – steep slopes, sheer drops, slippery or uneven surfaces, steep/uneven steps and deep/fast-flowing water. Please pay attention to all safety notices.

These sites are marked ⚠ in this handbook, but if you are in any doubt about hazards, please call the property in advance. Please take care when you visit, and remember to wear suitable footwear. Always prevent fires and do not climb on the monuments at any of our sites.

We encourage children to have fun, but please ensure they are supervised at all times. Our staff are always willing to advise on safety issues.

**Smoking**
Smoking is not permitted inside any English Heritage property.

**Toilets**
Toilets are available at or near many English Heritage sites. Please check individual listings.

# admission

Entry to English Heritage sites is free to all members on presentation of your named valid membership card. You are also entitled to free or reduced entry at a range of events and other historic attractions.



### Children

All children under five are admitted free to our properties. Members can also take up to six children (under 19), within the family group, into our properties free. Unaccompanied children aged 16 or over obtain free entry on production of their parents' membership card. (There may be a charge for children at some events and at the non-English Heritage properties listed in this guide.)

### Events

Please note you may be charged a supplementary fee when events are being held at a property (check in *Heritage Today* or on our website for details of events). Opening times may also vary when a public or private event is held: please check with the property before you travel.

### Non-members

There are three levels of charges for non-members shown in the handbook.

**For example:**

| | |
|---|---|
| Adult | **£2.50** |
| Concession | **£1.90** |
| Children (under 16) | **£1.30** |

The concessions apply to senior citizens, jobseekers and students with relevant ID. Prices may vary from the example shown above.

### Families

Family tickets are available at some of our larger properties: in most cases family tickets admit two adults and three children. This may vary at sites not managed by English Heritage; please call in advance to confirm their policy.

Wrest Park

### Groups

Discounts of 15% (10% at Stonehenge) are available for groups of eleven or more visitors paying together.

Call Customer Services on 0870 333 1181 for a copy of our *Group Visits Guide*. We recommend that groups book in advance.

### Overseas Visitor Pass

An Overseas Visitor Pass (OVP) allows unlimited free access to over 100 of our properties for one or two weeks.

With your OVP you enjoy free entry to all English Heritage properties listed in this handbook marked with the OVP symbol, plus free or reduced entry to hundreds of exciting events.

There may be a charge for some events at our properties (check the events leaflet available at our sites). The OVP does not entitle you to free admission at sites not managed by English Heritage and not marked with the OVP symbol.

For more information please call 0870 333 1181 or visit **www.english-heritage.org.uk/ovp**

Osborne House woodland

Beeston Castle

Yarmouth Castle

Etal Castle

# support us



We depend increasingly on donations from individuals and voluntary support from the private sector and the Lottery. We are very grateful to all our members and supporters; last year you raised £35 million to help us conserve and restore some of this country's most culturally important and iconic sites. Thank you.

Donations and bequests from members and visitors have helped us to make significant improvements to many of our properties over recent years.

One of last year's impending projects was the woodland restoration at Osborne House. This has conserved a vital habitat for endangered wildlife such as red squirrels and dormice, giving English Heritage the opportunity to open the area to visitors in the future.

There are many ways you can help; from making a donation to leaving a gift in your Will for the future. You can make a donation when you renew your membership, at any of our sites or online at **www.english-heritage.org.uk/supportus**

Visit the Membership and Support Us pages on our website at **www.english-heritage.org.uk**, telephone our Development Department on 0207 973 3798 or email us at **development@ english-heritage.org.uk** to discuss how your gift can support our priority projects.

## Projects currently being supported by donations and bequests

### Beeston Castle, Cheshire

Restoration of the designed landscape, conservation of remaining archaeology, on-site interpretation, creation of a handling collection, and greater accessibility for visitors.

### Yarmouth Castle, Isle of Wight

Reinterpretation of the Tudor fort, with a new exhibition and displays including audio-visual material and objects.

### Cleeve Abbey, Somerset

New graphics-based displays installed throughout the site.

### Etal Castle, Northumberland

Design and interpretation panels within the existing exhibition.

### Free sites

Forty new interpretative panels for free sites around the country.

### NMR

Acquisition of aerofilms archive for NMR – a collection of hundreds of thousands of aerial photographs taken since 1919, which will be kept together and made available for public access and research.

### Osborne House, Isle of Wight

Purchase of Durbar Room chairs: the acquisition and interpretation of four of the original chairs from the Durbar Room.

Above: (left) Kirkham Priory, (top centre) Rievaulx Abbey, (top right) Whitby Abbey, (bottom centre) Richmond Castle and (bottom right) Dover Castle.



# about us

It is our job at English Heritage to make sure that the historic environment of England is properly maintained and cared for. By employing some of the country's very best architects, archaeologists and historians, we aim to help people understand and appreciate why the historic buildings and landscapes around them matter.

## Who are we?

English Heritage was established in 1983 as the Historic Buildings and Monuments Commission for England. We are the Government's leading adviser on the historic environment, and are sponsored by the Department for Culture, Media & Sport (DCMS).

We also operate with other Government departments, including the Office of the Deputy Prime Minister (ODPM) and the Departments for the Environment, Food & Rural Affairs (DEFRA) and Trade & Industry (DTI).

## What do we do?

The history of England is preserved in the many ancient buildings and sites throughout the country – our job is to protect and promote this historic environment. From the earliest traces of human settlement to the most significant buildings of our own time, we want every important historic site to get the care and attention it deserves. By employing the best architects, archaeologists and historians, we help people understand and appreciate why the historic environment matters.

## Who are the people?

Chief Executive Simon Thurley works alongside our Chairperson, and they are assisted by a team of 16 commissioners who come from a wide variety of backgrounds, and change every four years.

If you want to find out more about what happens at our Commission meetings, you can look up the minutes at **www.english-heritage.org.uk/minutes**

Kirby Hall

## How are we funded?

We are funded partly by the Government, and partly by revenue earned from our historic properties. Over a quarter of our income comes from membership, donations, fundraising and the Lottery. Every penny counts, and there are many ways in which you can support us.

Choose to pay your membership by direct debit, as this keeps administration costs low. Sign up to Gift Aid, which enables us to recoup 28 pence from every pound given at **www.english-heritage.org.uk/giftaid**. Purchase a gift of membership as a wonderful present, or introduce a friend by taking them along to a site or enjoying one of our many events together.

## Why is our work important?

We believe that future generations should have the opportunity to enjoy England's historic environment. This can only happen if we begin to preserve and protect our historic sites now. As well as undertaking the work ourselves, we are able to provide assistance to others.

We hope that the information we provide at our sites, as well as through our Learning programmes, will encourage people to value the importance of England's historic environment.

Through our role in the planning system, we are able to ensure that any changes made to England's architectural heritage serve to enhance and protect it.

## How do we differ from The National Trust?

We are partly funded by the government and have a wider remit than The National Trust, including national and local government responsibilities.

We give conservation grants and provide advisory and education services. We identify buildings, monuments and landscapes for protection and make our research available through publications and on our website.

Rochester Castle

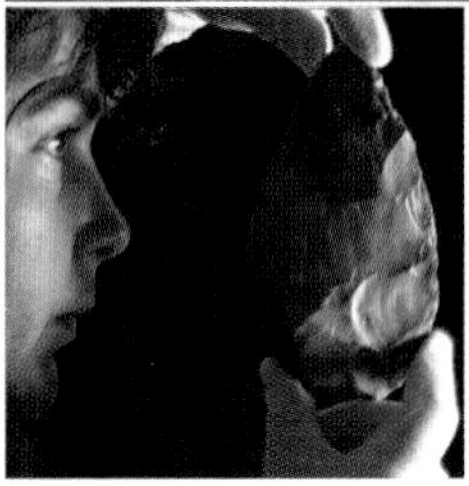

# at work

English Heritage exists to make the past part of our future. We aim to create a cycle of understanding, valuing, caring for and enjoying our historic environment.

## Enjoying

### Our properties

We currently look after over 400 historic sites, which are open to the public. Our properties include historic country houses, palaces, ruined abbeys, prehistoric settlements, burial sites, castles, statues and Roman remains. There is no better way to find out about history than when it is brought to life before your eyes at an English Heritage event. See page 20 for highlights of our events for the forthcoming year.

Our property list includes Stonehenge, Hadrian's Wall, Dover Castle, Apsley House and Rievaulx Abbey. At many of these sites we provide visitor centres, exhibitions and educational resources.

## Understanding

### Research

Our research and training programmes increase understanding of the historic environment, helping us to guide its management in an informed and sustainable way. We concentrate our fieldwork and analysis on poorly understood building types, as well as on specific sites and areas. For more information email **buildingshistory@english-heritage.org.uk**

### Training: Craft & Skills

Traditional skills are at risk of dying out in the UK, and there are currently only 86,000 craftspeople with the specialist skills to maintain our historic buildings. English Heritage is developing training in these essential skills, including thatching and stonemasonry.

This means there will be a continuing source of crafts-people to maintain England's half million listed historic buildings and Buildings at Risk.

### Learning

Our Learning programmes encourage people of all ages and abilities to understand, value and enjoy the historic environment. Each year, we stage a variety of activities for schools, families, adult learners and hard-to-reach communities. Together with our publishing programmes, these help us to inspire current and future generations with a lifetime's passion for their heritage.

### Education volunteering

In order to help us increase our range of learning activities, we have recently launched a new programme of education volunteering. Our Education Volunteers will, for example, provide support for Discovery Visits, conduct guided tours, undertake research and demonstrate handling collections. For the volunteer, the benefits of participating in the programme include learning new skills, meeting new people and helping to ensure that the historic environment is understood and enjoyed by our visitors. To find out more, contact Kate Davies, Education Volunteers Manager on 01793 414438 or **kate.davies@english-heritage.org.uk**

### Education

Each year we welcome over 500,000 pupils and school teachers to our sites completely free of charge. To enliven their visit, we have also recently launched a new programme of 'Discovery Visits' at 50 sites across the country. These include costumed workshops and guided tours led by specialist educators and staff. We have also expanded our range of educational publications, including a new series of *Ghastly Guides* for children.

### Outreach

Our team of Outreach Officers leads a range of exciting, creative projects with hard-to-reach audiences across the country including young people, ethnic communities and people with disabilities. We are committed to engaging new audiences through projects ranging from oral history to community archaeology digs, youth theatre and creating community heritage gardens. The team also works with the Civic Trust to broaden participation in Heritage Open Days. In addition, we recently staged a major national conference – Your Place or Mine? – on engaging new audiences with heritage. To find out more or to have your say, go to: **www.yourplaceormine.org.uk**

For more details, visit our website **www.english-heritage.org.uk/learning**

### Publishing

We publish a wide range of books on a variety of subjects – including general history, gardening, cookery, architecture, photography and children's books. To order a New Titles catalogue call Customer Services on 0870 333 1181 or view all our books at **www.english-heritage.org.uk/books**. Also see p22 for more information.

Educational visit to Kenilworth Castle

## Valuing

### Grants

We give grants to individuals, Local Authorities and voluntary organisations to undertake urgent repairs and to conserve and enhance the historic environment. We also advise the Heritage Lottery Fund on the allocation of money to worthwhile schemes which do not fit our own grant criteria. Find out more at **www.english-heritage.org.uk/grants**

### Statutory advice

We advise Local Planning Authorities on listed building planning applications. Buildings need to change to thrive, and we work proactively with Local Authorities to ensure that any changes recognise the historic potential of the building.

We publish an annual Buildings at Risk Register, with information on listed buildings and scheduled monuments 'at risk' from neglect and decay. We also award grants to Local Authorities to undertake urgent repairs to these buildings.

### Policies

Among our key responsibilities is developing robust policies to enable national and local decision makers to protect and promote the historic environment. The evidence to support these policies is published annually as Heritage Counts, and can be viewed at **www.heritagecounts.org.uk.** We play an important role in international conservation, advising on the designation and management of World Heritage Sites in the UK, and campaigning in Brussels and Strasbourg on behalf of the historic environment.

## Caring

### Archaeology

As the national archaeology service for England, we set standards, promote innovation and provide detailed archaeological knowledge of the historic environment. More information on our archaeological work can be found at **www.english-heritage.org.uk/archaeology**

### England's Historic Wreck Sites

English Heritage now has responsibilities for all English maritime archaeological sites, from low water to a 12-nautical mile territorial limit.

Containing the remains of vessels and their contents, wreck sites may merit legal protection if they contribute significantly to our understanding of our maritime past. The law protects important sites against uncontrolled disturbance and allows heritage agencies to develop research, education and access initiatives, raising awareness of them. The Designated Wrecks around England range from Late Bronze Age cargoes to early submarines. Sites range from sandy beaches to rocky seabeds. English Heritage advises the Government on designations, manages the licencing scheme enabling access to sites, and facilitates the Government's Advisory Committee for Historic Wreck Sites. Further information is available from English Heritage's Maritime Archaeology Team.

### Listed buildings

We recommend buildings of special architectural or historic interest to the Secretary of State for Culture, Media and Sport for listing. Listing means that any changes made to either the internal or external structure of a building are subject to stricter planning regulations.

Most listed buildings date from before 1840, but we also recommend some later buildings. Modern buildings need to be of significant importance, and normally over 30 years old before they are likely to be listed.

There are three categories of listing: Grade I, Grade II* and

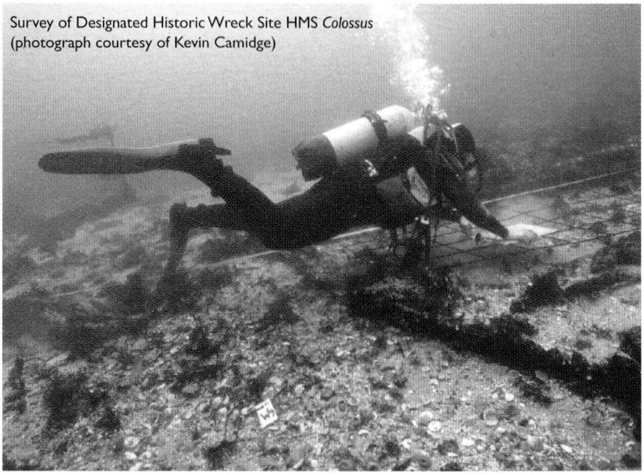

Survey of Designated Historic Wreck Site HMS *Colossus* (photograph courtesy of Kevin Camidge)

Grade II. Grade I and Grade II* buildings are of outstanding architectural or historic interest, and of particular importance to the nation's built heritage.

For more information on current listed buildings and how to suggest a building for listing, see **www.english-heritage.org.uk/listing**

View details and images of England's listed buildings at **www.imagesofengland.org.uk**

### Conservation

In addition to listing buildings, we also designate monuments and landscapes for protection. For example, ruins, earthworks or burial sites may be scheduled as monuments and subject to special control.

We also work with Local Authorities on designating Conservation Areas. These are usually areas characterised by architectural and historic features worth preserving or enhancing. England is fortunate to possess a number of World Heritage Sites, including Stonehenge and Hadrian's Wall. We work with UNESCO to devise management plans for these unique places.

Ikon Gallery Brindley Place, Birmingham. A converted School

Battlefields are also important sources of archaeological and historic interest. There are over 40 on the English Heritage Register of Historic Battlefields. We keep a similar register of parks and gardens, including the country's most important green spaces, from country house gardens to hospital grounds.

Find out more about our conservation work at **www.english-heritage.org.uk/conservation**

## Blue Plaques

English Heritage has been operating the Blue Plaque scheme since 1986, and in May 2006 brought the total number of London plaques to 800.

To qualify for a Blue Plaque, a person must have been dead for 20 years or have passed the centenary of their birth, and a building associated with them must survive.

If you would like to know how to nominate someone for a Blue Plaque, go to **www.english-heritage.org.uk/blueplaques**

# NMR

## The archive of English Heritage, the National Monuments Record (NMR) holds over 10 million photographs, plans, drawings, reports, records and publications covering England's archaeology, architecture, social and local history.



The quickest and easiest way to view our collections is via our website: **www.english-heritage.org.uk/NMR** There you'll find more detailed information about what we offer, and links to our main online resources:

**www.english-heritage.org.uk/viewfinder** – view historic images of England, from the 1840s to the present.

**www.imagesofengland.org.uk** – discover over 270,000 contemporary photographs of England's historic buildings and monuments.

**www.english-heritage.org.uk/pastscape** – for information on England's ancient sites, monuments and old buildings.

For access to our wider archive, not just the material available online, you can call, write or visit us in person. At our offices in Swindon, we handle individual enquiries and carry out searches of our collections on your behalf – our standard service is free.

Alternatively you can pop in and do your own research, although it's best to make an appointment so that we can help you make the most of your visit. To find out more call us on 01793 414600 or visit us online at **www.english-heritage.org.uk/NMR**

### OPENING TIMES

**Public search room:**
Tue-Fri 9.30am-5pm
(Tel 01793 414600 for details)

### HOW TO FIND US

Kemble Drive
Swindon SN2 2GZ
**Train:** Swindon ¼ mile

Hoover Building, London
© English Heritage Photo Library

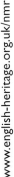

Ranger's House – The Wernher Collection

# hiring a property

## Create a memorable occasion for your historic day.

What could be a more stunning setting for a wedding, birthday celebration, anniversary dinner or corporate event than an historic English Heritage property?

Celebrations can now be arranged at selected English Heritage properties.

Experienced staff are on hand to help fine-tune arrangements and ensure your event will provide special memories for years to come.

Properties available for hire are marked with a [hire symbol] throughout the handbook. Those also licensed for civil ceremonies are marked with a [civil ceremony symbol].

For more information on exclusive hire, please contact the Hospitality Manager for the property on the phone number to the right, or visit the website: **www.english-heritage.org.uk/hospitality**

## Properties available for hire

### East of England

Audley End House & Gardens, Essex. Tel: 01799 529403

### West

Kenilworth Castle, Warwickshire. Tel: 01926 852078

### East Midlands

Bolsover Castle, Derbyshire Tel: 01246 856456

### London

Chiswick House Tel: 0207 973 3292

Eltham Palace Tel: 0208 294 2577

Marble Hill House Tel: 0207 973 3416

Ranger's House – The Wernher Collection Tel: 0208 294 2577

Wellington Arch Tel: 0207 973 3292

### South East

Bishop's Waltham Palace, Hampshire. Tel: 01424 775705

Deal Castle, Kent Tel: 01304 209889

Dover Castle, Kent Tel: 01304 209889

Osborne House & Gardens, Isle of Wight. Tel: 01983 203055

Walmer Castle & Gardens, Kent. Tel: 01304 209889

### South West

Old Wardour Castle, Wiltshire Tel: 01305 820868

Pendennis Castle, Cornwall Tel: 01326 310106

Portland Castle, Dorset Tel: 01305 820868

St Mawes Castle, Cornwall Tel: 01326 310106

# events

There is no better way to find out about history than when it is brought to life before your eyes at the very sites that helped shape it.

Battle of Hastings re-enactment

Children will love the children's festival at Dover Castle and our new Battle Abbey Boot Camp!

From big battle spectaculars and medieval jousts to family fun days, our historical events programme is the largest in Europe, and offers you hundreds of events to choose from.

**Family fun**

This year's events programme offers even more hands-on fun for families and children, including a children's history festival at Dover Castle and a boot camp at Battle Abbey. Popular favourites such as medieval jousts, treasure trails and have-a-go archery also return.

**Festival of History 2007**

Now in its fifth year, our annual two-day spectacular, Festival of History, is the biggest event of its kind in Europe. Over 1,000 top historical performers bring you over 2,000 years of history, from the Roman Empire to the Swinging Sixties.

For more information and tickets, visit **www.festivalofhistory.org.uk**

**History brought to life**

Fans of historical action will also enjoy our series of battle re-enactments, played out at sites across the country, including the most famous of all, the **Battle of Hastings** in October.

The famous battlefields can be further explored with the help of one of our historical experts, on a **Battlefield Hike.**

For a more leisurely encounter with the past, our fully-guided **Tours Through Time** include luxury coach travel and expert commentary, with bed, breakfast and dinner for overnight trips.

For more information on Tours Through Time telephone 0845 121 2863 or visit **www.brooklandtravel.com**

For a full events listing check the latest copy of *Heritage Today*, visit www.english-heritage.org.uk/events or call Customer Services on 0870 333 1183.

# books and gifts



At many of our historic sites, you will find visitor centres packed with a range of gifts and books to enhance your visit. You can also order many items over the phone, by post or online.

## Books

We publish a wide range of books on a variety of subjects – including general history, gardening, cookery, architecture, photography and children's books.

To order our new titles catalogue call Customer Services on 0870 333 1181 or view all our books at **www.english-heritage.org.uk/books**

## Guidebooks

We also publish a series of guidebooks for many of our properties. These contain more historical information, combined with the most up-to-date research and a tour of the site.

Properties which have a guidebook are marked with a 🕮 symbol throughout this handbook.

## Gifts

Many properties have a gift shop selling a wide range of great gifts, books, toys and souvenirs. The range reflects the location, style and history of the property – whether it's a castle, an abbey or an art deco palace. Properties with gift shops are marked with a 🛍 symbol throughout this handbook.

Many of our products can be found online – visit **www.english-heritage.org.uk/shopping** – and you can also buy through our mail order service on 01761 452966.

## New ranges

**Mugs**
Look out for our brand new range of mugs for properties including Stonehenge, Tintagel Castle, Kenwood and Whitby Abbey.

**Stationery**
Working with our extensive photographic library, we have produced a stunning range of greetings cards showing **Stonehenge** in all its moods, from archival historic shots, paintings and engravings to contemporary photographic images.

For children, there is a great new range of **Princess and Knight** stationery – perfect for would-be knights and princesses everywhere.

## Members' offers

We work with a wide range of commercial partners to bring special offers to members and great retail deals to the High Street.

Our partners make a donation for every booking or sale made, which helps us to continue to protect the historic environment. Offers include the fantastic period paint range that we launched with The Little Greene Paint Company which brings in much-needed revenue to English Heritage.

For more information on current offers and deals, visit our website, or look out for the latest offers in *Heritage Today*.

Above: (top right) Pavilion Cottage, Osborne House, (centre bottom) Refectory Cottage, Rievaulx Abbey.



# holiday cottages

Location is one of the key principles behind the development of our holiday cottages, which are all positioned at the heart of an historic property – where history, discovery and enjoyment are just on the doorstep.

Not only are the locations unsurpassed, they also offer the unique opportunity to experience a very special place in peace and privacy. At most of our cottages and apartments, when the property closes for the day and the public go home, you will have the joy of knowing that the major part of the gardens and grounds are there just for you to enjoy.

All our cottages and apartments are located within easy reach of the best of England's countryside, bustling market towns, historic houses, cathedrals, churches and glorious gardens. Many also have well-marked walking and cycling trails close by.

## Properties available with holiday cottages

**Dover Castle**
The Sergeant Major's House

**Osborne House**
Pavilion Cottage

**St Mawes Castle**
Fort House

**Pendennis Castle**
The Custodian's House

**Rievaulx Abbey**
Refectory Cottage

For a reservation call 0870 333 1187

## New for 2007

**Battle Abbey**
South Lodge Cottage

**Carisbrooke Castle**
Apartment

**North Leigh Roman Villa**
Cottage

**Walmer Castle**
Cottage and Apartment

**Audley End House**
Cambridge Lodge

**Witley Court**
Pool House Cottage

**Mount Grace Priory**
Cottage

Link Building Room and Sphinx, Chiswick House – see page 33

# London

‘O fruitful Genius! that bestoweth here
An everlasting plenty, year by year
O place! O people! Manners! framed to please
All nations, customs, kindreds, languages!’

From *His Return to London*, by Robert Herrick (1591-1674)

# Properties See individual listings for details

**Camden**
Kenwood House

**Greenwich**
Eltham Palace
Ranger's House – the Wernher Collection

**Hounslow**
Chiswick House

**Kingston-upon-Thames**
Coombe Conduit

**Richmond**
Marble Hill House

**Southwark**
Winchester Palace

**Tower Hamlets**
London Wall

**Westminster**
Apsley House
Chapter House and Pyx Chamber
Jewel Tower
Wellington Arch

Comprehensive map of our sites
Pages 266-267

For bus and public transport information, call Transport for London on **0207 222 1234**

Above: (left) Apsley House, (top and bottom centre) Kenwood, (top right) Eltham Palace and (bottom right) Jewel Tower.



# Treasure Houses of London

London's world-famous galleries and museums make it a paradise for art-lovers. What is perhaps not so commonly recognised, is that many of English Heritage's great London houses – in themselves magnificent buildings, often set in green oases of parkland – also display some of England's finest art collections. Moreover these paintings, sculptures and other rich treasures are displayed not in a museum or gallery context, but rather (as they were meant to be seen) within original, restored or recreated rooms.

Thus at **Chiswick House**, the Palladian villa designed by the architect and connoisseur Lord Burlington as a combination of home and private gallery, loans of more than 30 Old Master paintings – including a newly discovered Rubens, never seen in public before – grace the Red Velvet Room. They enhance, and are enhanced by, the sumptuously painted and gilded ceilings designed and produced for the house by William Kent. **Kenwood**, remodelled by Robert Adam for the great judge Lord Mansfield, houses among its richly decorated interiors not only the famous Iveagh Bequest of paintings, but also the Suffolk Collection with its magnificent full-length portraits of fashionably-dressed Elizabethan and Jacobean courtiers. Here too, in 2007, an exhibition marks the bicentenary of the Abolition of the Slave Trade in the British Empire, and Lord Mansfield's influence on bringing this about.

The elegant Georgian interiors of **Ranger's House**, in Greenwich Park, serve as an elegant setting for the amazing Wernher Collection of nearly 700 medieval and Renaissance works of art. Richmond's **Marble Hill House**, perhaps the most charming of all 'London fringe' villas, displays not only a fine collection of early Georgian paintings associated with the learned society hostess Henrietta Howard, but also newly-hung recreations of the fashionable hand-painted Chinese wallpapers she installed. This autumn there will be an exhibition here to celebrate a new biography of this remarkable woman.

By complete contrast **Eltham Palace**, home of the millionaire Courtauld family, shows off the finest and most glamorous 1930s Art Deco interiors in Britain. And, right at the centre of London, the Duke of Wellington's landmark Regency town mansion, **Apsley House**, displays amid its opulent Regency staterooms the duke's own outstanding international art collection, as well as the impressive range of trophies accumulated by the great man, including a colossal nude statue of his opponent Napoleon.

# Apsley House Hyde Park – W1J 7NT

Apsley House, home of the first Duke of Wellington and his descendants, stands right in the heart of London at Hyde Park Corner. For over 200 years, this great metropolitan mansion has been known colloquially as 'Number 1 London', because it was the first house encountered after passing the tollgates at the top of Knightsbridge.

Waterloo Gallery doorway

Apsley House was originally designed and built by Robert Adam between 1771 and 1778 for Baron Apsley – from whom it takes its name. It passed to the Wellesley family in 1807, being first owned by Richard and then his younger brother Arthur Wellesley – the Duke of Wellington.

Wellington is most famous for defeating Napoleon at the Battle of Waterloo in 1815, but this was only the culmination of a brilliant military career. He was also a major politician, rising from representing a small Irish constituency in 1790 to Prime Minister in 1828.

The current appearance of Apsley House is the result of alterations made by the Wellesley family, who twice extended the brick Adam house and encased it in stone. The Corinthian portico and two bays of the west wing were added in 1828. Perhaps more importantly, many rooms were redesigned to reflect the Duke of Wellington's rising status, and remain important survivals of Regency interiors. They provided the perfect backdrop for entertaining, particularly at the annual Waterloo Banquets which commemorated the great victory.

Inside Apsley House you will see many aspects of the first duke's

The Empress Josephine by Robert Lefèvre

life and work, outstandingly his amazing art collection. Paintings by many famous artists are hung throughout the first floor, many of them part of the Spanish Royal Collection which came into Wellington's possession after the Battle of Vitoria in 1813. A colossal nude statue of Napoleon by Canova dominates the stairwell at the centre of the house.

Throughout his military career, the duke was presented with a vast collection of silver plate and unique porcelain as trophies from grateful nations. Many of these can be seen in the Plate and China Room. Wellington's victories are celebrated in the fine British craftsmanship of the magnificent Wellington Shield, designed by Thomas Stothard, and the impressive candelabra presented by the Merchants and Bankers of the City of London.

When the seventh Duke of Wellington gave the house to the nation in 1947, the family retained the private rooms, which they still use today. This makes Apsley House not only the last surviving great London town house open to the public, but also the only property managed by English Heritage in which the original owner's family still live.

A comfortable seating area has now been created in the Inner Hall, where visitors can browse through leather-bound albums of images of Wellington, his descendants, and Apsley House. The new 'Wellington Boot' activity pack, for children aged 5-11, is filled with activity sheets and puzzles.

Wellington enthusiasts may also be interested in visiting the spectacular Wellington Arch opposite Apsley House (see p.41), and elegant Walmer Castle (see p.80), the duke's residence when he was Lord Warden of the Cinque Ports.

**www.english-heritage.org.uk/apsleyhouse**

## NON-MEMBERS

| | |
|---|---|
| **Apsley House** | |
| Adult | £5.30 |
| Concession | £4.00 |
| Child | £2.70 |
| **Joint ticket with Wellington Arch** | |
| Adult | £6.90 |
| Concession | £5.20 |
| Child | £3.50 |
| Family | £17.30 |

## OPENING TIMES

| | |
|---|---|
| 1 Apr-31 Oct, Tue-Sun & Bank Hols | 10am-5pm |
| 1 Nov-20 Mar, Tue-Sun | 10am-4pm |
| Closed | 24-26 Dec and 1 Jan |

## HOW TO FIND US

**Direction:** 149 Piccadilly, Hyde Park Corner

**Train:** Victoria ½ mile

**Bus:** From surrounding areas

**Tube:** Hyde Park Corner, adjacent

**Tel:** 0207 499 5676

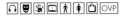

MAP Page 266 (4E)
OS Map 161/173 (ref TQ 284799)

## Chapter House and Pyx Chamber
Westminster Abbey

Built by the royal masons in 1250, the Chapter House of Westminster Abbey was originally used in the 13th century by Benedictine monks for their daily meetings. It later became a meeting place of the King's Great Council and the Commons, predecessors of today's Parliament.

A beautiful octagonal building with a vaulted ceiling and delicate central column, it offers rarely seen examples of medieval sculpture, an original floor of glazed tiles and spectacular wall paintings. A door within the vestibule dating from c. 1050 is thought to be the oldest in England. The 11th-century Pyx Chamber also has a medieval tiled floor, and was used as a monastic and royal treasury. It contains a 13th-century stone altar that survived the Reformation.

**Chapter House free to EH members. Under the care and management of the Dean and Chapter of Westminster.**

### OPENING TIMES

Throughout the year;
Mon-Sun 10am-4pm

Closed Good Fri, 24-26 Dec & 1 Jan

May be closed at short notice on state and religious occasions

### HOW TO FIND US

**Direction:** Through the cloister from Dean's Yard if you only want to visit the Chapter House. Turn into Dean's Yard off Broad Sanctuary. Turn left along the square and go through the entrance-way into the cloister

**Train:** Victoria and Charing Cross both ¾ mile, Waterloo 1 mile

**Bus:** From surrounding areas

**Tube:** Westminster and St James' Park stations both ¼ mile

**Tel:** 0207 654 4900

MAP Page 267 (4F)
OS Map 161/173 (ref TQ 299795)

Chiswick House
See feature opposite

## Coombe Conduit
Kingston-upon-Thames

Coombe Conduit is made up of two small Tudor buildings connected by an underground passage. Water was once supplied to Hampton Court Palace via this tunnel.

Managed by the Kingston-upon-Thames Society.

### OPENING TIMES

Apr-Sep,
every 2nd Sun 2pm-4pm

### HOW TO FIND US

**Direction:** Coombe Lane on the corner of Lord Chancellor's Walk

**Train:** Norbiton ¾ mile

**Bus:** Tfl 57 Kingston – Streatham

**Tel:** 0208 942 1296

MAP Page 266 (4E)
OS Map 161 (ref TQ 204698)

Eltham Palace
See feature – Page 34

# Chiswick House Chiswick – W4 2RP

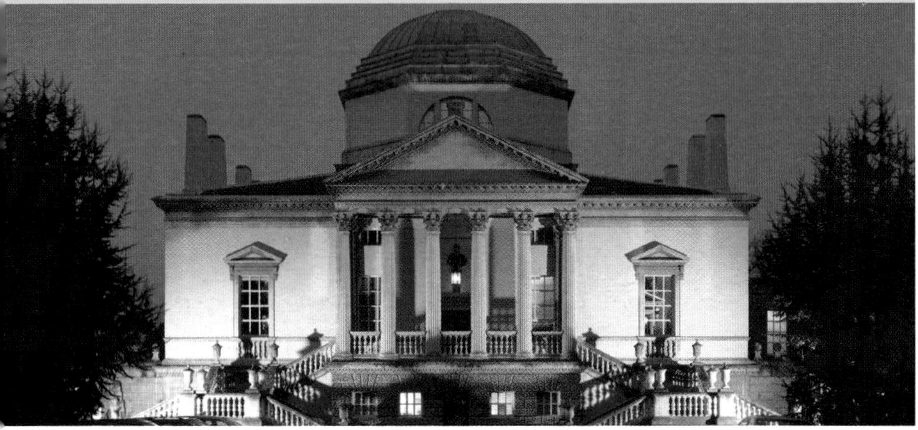



:hiswick House is one of the ıost glorious examples of 8th-century British ·chitecture. The third Earl of urlington (1694-1753), who esigned this elegant Classical lla, drew inspiration from his rand tours' of Italy.

. promoter of the Palladian :yle originally pioneered in ritain by Inigo Jones, Burlington ɔught to create the kind of lla and garden found in the ıburbs of ancient Rome. To ɔ so, he employed William ent to create sumptuous ıteriors to contrast with ıe pure exterior.

he intimate Bedchamber 'loset has now been ɛdecorated, with paintings and rints providing an insight into ıe Burlington family. A double ɔrtrait of Lord and Lady ırlington, by William Aikman, angs alongside charming aintings of their two young aughters. Further exciting ɔans of Old Master paintings, cluding a recently discovered ubens, are displayed to enhance the pictures in the Red and Green Velvet rooms. They emphasise the artistic diversity which characterised Burlington's combination of home and private gallery.

The Classical gardens are a perfect complement to the house. There is level access to most of the grounds (except for Terrace Walk, owing to a gradient). Wander among the statues in the Italianate gardens, and look out for the buildings hidden in the trees.

The Chiswick House & Gardens Trust (reg. charity 1109239) has been set up to lead a major restoration project to restore the historic gardens and improve visitor facilities. Visit www.chgt.org.uk for details.

**www.english-heritage.org.uk/chiswickhouse**

Available for corporate and private hire.

Licensed for civil wedding ceremonies.

## NON-MEMBERS

| | |
|---|---|
| Adult | £4.20 |
| Concession | £3.20 |
| Child | £2.10 |
| Family | £10.50 |

## OPENING TIMES

| | |
|---|---|
| 1 Apr-31 Oct, Wed-Sun & Bank Hols | 10am-5pm |
| Closes at 2pm on Sat | |
| 1 Nov-23 Dec and 1 Mar-20 Mar Pre-booked tours by appointment on certain days only, please contact site for details | |
| Closed | 24 Dec-29 Feb |

## HOW TO FIND US

**Direction:** Burlington Lane, W4

**Train:** Chiswick ½ mile

**Bus:** TfL 190 Hammersmith – Richmond; E3 Greenford – Chiswick

**Tube:** Turnham Green ¾ mile

**Tel:** 0208 995 0508

P OVP

Disabled access (ground floor; wheelchair stair-climber to first floor, please call to confirm use prior to visit).

Dogs on leads (restricted areas only).

Parking (off westbound A4).

**MAP Page 266 (4E)**

**OS Map 161 (ref TQ 424740)**

# Eltham Palace Greenwich – SE9 5QE

When textile magnates Stephen and Virginia Courtauld built their 1930s Art Deco mansion by the Great Hall of medieval Eltham Palace, they created a masterpiece of 20th-century design.

Virginia Courtauld's bathroom

Completed in 1936, the exterior of the house was built in sympathy with the older building, using a red brick design inspired by Hampton Court Palace. But the interior was and remains a showpiece of glamorous 1930s design. Visitors can revel in the eclectic mix of French-influenced Art Deco, ultra-smart ocean-liner style and cutting-edge Swedish design.

The dining room is a tour-de-force, with pink leather-upholstered chairs, bird's-eye maple veneered walls and a silver ceiling. It is entered through black-and-silver doors portraying animals and birds, drawn from life at London Zoo.

Even more exotic is Virginia Courtauld's vaulted bathroom, lined with onyx and gold mosaic, complete with gold-plated bath taps and a statue of the goddess Psyche. Luxury also emanates from the centrally heated sleeping quarters of the Courtaulds' pet ring-tailed lemur, Mah-Jongg.

A house with all the latest modern conveniences, the Courtaulds' home came with underfloor heating, a centralised vacuum cleaner and a built-in audio system.

The entrance hall

The Spotlight display brings together discoveries from the Courtauld era, including original furniture and family photographs. Stephen Courtauld was a director of the famous Ealing Film Studios. Now, for the first time, visitors can also enjoy an original 10-minute Courtauld home movie, restored using the latest technology. It gives an intimate glimpse of the millionaire's family swimming, admiring their gardens, and relaxing with their lemur and other pets.

As you leave the opulent 1930s house and enter the medieval palace, the interior presents a striking contrast. The Great Hall was built for Edward IV in the 1470s, and Henry VIII spent much of his childhood here.

The 19 acres of beautiful gardens surrounding the palace include both 20th-century and medieval elements. These include a rock garden sloping down to the moat, a medieval bridge, herbaceous borders inspired by modern designer Isabelle Van Groeningen, a sunken rose garden and plenty of picnic areas. The garden is special at any time of year, but visitors will delight in the spring bulbs display and the wisteria cascading over the classical pergola in summer.

*The Gathering Storm* and Stephen Fry's *Bright Young Things.*

**www.english-heritage.org.uk/elthampalace**

Available for corporate and private hire.

Licensed for civil wedding ceremonies.

## NON-MEMBERS

| **House and Garden** | |
|---|---|
| Adult | £7.90 |
| Concession | £5.90 |
| Child | £4.00 |
| Family | £19.80 |
| **Garden only** | |
| Adult | £4.90 |
| Concession | £3.70 |
| Child | £2.50 |

## OPENING TIMES

| | |
|---|---|
| 1 Apr-31 Oct, Sun-Wed | 10am-5pm |
| 1 Nov-23 Dec, Sun-Wed | 11am-4pm |
| Closed | 24 Dec-2 Feb |
| 3 Feb-20 Mar, Sun-Wed | 11am-4pm |

## HOW TO FIND US

**Direction:** Off Court Rd SE9, Junction 3 on the M25, then A20 to Eltham

**Train:** Eltham and Mottingham, both ½ mile

**Bus:** From surrounding areas

**Tel:** 0208 294 2548

P OVP

Disabled access (and parking via Court Yard entrance).

Parking (signed off Court Rd).

Pushchairs and large rucksacks need to be left at reception.

MAP Page 267 (4F)
OS Map 162 (ref TQ 424740)

# Kenwood Hampstead – NW3 7JR

Set in leafy grounds beside Hampstead Heath, this outstanding house was remodelled by Robert Adam between 1764 and 1779. He transformed the original brick building into a majestic villa for the great judge, Lord Mansfield. The richly decorated library is one of Adam's great masterpieces, a feast for the eyes.

Above: The library

Brewing magnate Edward Cecil Guinness, first Earl of Iveagh, bought Kenwood House and gardens in 1925. When he died in 1927, he bequeathed the house, estate and part of his collection of pictures to the nation. The Iveagh Bequest includes important paintings by many great artists, including Rembrandt, Vermeer, Turner, Reynolds and Gainsborough. Recently they have been joined by Constable's oil sketch *Hampstead Heath.* The paintings beautifully complement Kenwood's sumptuous interiors.

The first floor displays a very different array of paintings. The Suffolk Collection includes magnificent portraits of Elizabethan and Stuart men and women by William Larkin, Van Dyck and Lely, given by the Hon. Mrs Greville Howard in 1974.

The parkland surrounding Kenwood was particularly influenced by the great English landscape gardener, Humphry Repton. Set high on a hill, the views of London from these tranquil grounds are stunning. Visitors can also enjoy the lakeside walks and meandering woodland paths, which provide a superb backdrop for the famous summer concerts.

Most of the grounds are accessible by gravel path and grass, but wheelchair users will need strong pushers to manage the slopes. The Brew House Restaurant and Café is a great place to stop for lunch or a cup of tea.

A variety of guided tours are available for a small charge: please call the house for details.

**NEW FOR 2007**

24 May to 2 Sep 2007. 'Mansfield, Slavery and Justice, A public and private legacy'

Display to commemorate the 2007 Bicentenary of the Abolition of the Slave Trade in the British Empire.

Kenwood, once the home of William Murray, 1st Earl of Mansfield, will examine the important slavery cases which came before him, as one of the 18th century's most senior Judges. We will explore how far each case influenced attitudes towards Abolition, who the described people were, and their circumstances living and surviving in London. The private story of Kenwood involves a young girl of dual heritage, Mansfield's great-niece, Dido Elizabeth Belle. Born after her father's liaison with a slave, she was brought up at Kenwood and occupied a curious and ambiguous role within the Mansfield's household and affections.

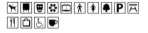

*Notting Hill, Mansfield Park* and recent films including *Venus* and *Scenes of a Sexual Nature.*

A portrait detail of Dido Elizabeth Belle and Lady Elizabeth Finch Hatton, from the Collection of The Earl of Mansfield at Scone Palace, Perth, Scotland

**www.english-heritage.org.uk/kenwoodhouse**

## OPENING TIMES

| | |
|---|---|
| 1 Apr-31 Oct, daily | 11am-5pm |
| 1 Nov-20 Mar, daily | 11am-4pm |
| Closed | 24-26 Dec and 1 Jan |

The Park stays open later, please see site notices. House and grounds free; donations welcome. Pre-booked group tours available

## HOW TO FIND US

**Direction:** Hampstead Lane, NW3

**Train:** Hampstead Heath 1½ miles

**Bus:** Tfl 210 Finsbury Park – Golders Green

**Tube:** Archway and Golders Green, then 210 bus.

**Tel:** 0208 348 1286

Disabled access (ground floor only; toilets).

Dogs on leads (restricted areas only).

Garden shop and house shop.

Parking (charge. Disabled bays. Mobility service available on request).

Restaurant (The Brew House Café open all year; serves home-made food throughout the day).

Please note: Kenwood hosts regular events, garden tours and acclaimed summer concerts.

**MAP Page 266 (3E)**
**OS Map 173 (ref TQ 271874)**

## Jewel Tower
Westminster – SW1P 3JX

The Jewel Tower, or 'King's Privy Wardrobe', was built c. 1365 to house Edward III's treasures. One of only two buildings of the original Palace of Westminster to survive the fire of 1834, the tower features a 14th-century ribbed vault. It displays 'Parliament Past and Present', a fascinating exhibition about the history of Parliament.

The second floor now includes new illustrated panels, telling the story of this small but important building.

The remains of a moat and medieval quay are still visible outside.

### NON-MEMBERS

| | |
|---|---|
| Adult | £2.90 |
| Concession | £2.20 |
| Child | £1.50 |

### OPENING TIMES

| | |
|---|---|
| 1 Apr-31 Oct, daily | 10am-5pm |
| 1 Nov-20 Mar, daily | 10am-4pm |
| Closed | 24-26 Dec & 1 Jan |

### Jewel Tower

### HOW TO FIND US

**Direction:** Located on Abingdon Street, opposite the southern end of the Houses of Parliament (Victoria Tower)

**Train:** Charing Cross ¾ mile, Victoria and Waterloo, both 1 mile

**Bus:** From surrounding areas

**Tube:** Westminster ¼ mile

**Tel:** 0207 222 2219

OVP

**MAP Page 267 (4F)**
**OS Map 161/173 (ref TQ 301793)**

## Kenwood House
See feature – Page 36

## London Wall
Tower Hill

This is the best-preserved remnant of the Roman wall which once formed part of the eastern defences of Roman Londinium. Built c. AD 200, the wall defined the shape and size of London for over a millennium.

### OPENING TIMES

Free access

### HOW TO FIND US

**Direction:** Located outside Tower Hill Underground station, EC3

### London Wall

**Train:** Fenchurch Street ¼ mile

**Bus:** From surrounding areas

**Tube:** Tower Hill, adjacent

**MAP Page 267 (3F)**
**OS Map 173 (ref TQ 336807)**

## Marble Hill House
See feature – Page 39

## Ranger's House – The Wernher Collection
See feature – Page 40

## Wellington Arch
See feature – Page 41

## Winchester Palace
Southwark

Part of the great hall of Winchester Palace, built in the early 13th century as the London house of the Bishops of Winchester, including the striking rose window which adorns the west gable. Most of the palace was destroyed by fire in 1814.

### OPENING TIMES

Free access

### HOW TO FIND US

**Direction:** Next to Southwark Cathedral and the Golden Hinde replica ship; corner of Clink St and Storey St, SE1

**Train/Tube:** London Bridge ¼ mile

**Bus:** From surrounding areas

**MAP Page 267 (4F)**
**OS Map 173 (ref TQ 325803)**

# Marble Hill House Richmond – TW1 2NL

Marble Hill is the last complete survivor of the elegant villas and gardens which bordered the Thames between Richmond and Hampton Court in the 18th century. It was begun in 1724 for the remarkable Henrietta Howard, mistress of King George II when he was Prince of Wales, and friend of some of the cleverest men in England. The house and gardens were planned by a coterie of fashionable connoisseurs, including Lord Herbert and Mrs Howard's neighbour, the poet Alexander Pope.

A lovely Palladian villa still set in 66 acres of riverside parkland, Marble Hill was intended as an Arcadian retreat from crowded 18th-century London. It became renowned as a salon of literary wits, gathered round their learned hostess. The compact but carefully planned interior is focused on the first-floor 'Great Room' where Mrs Howard held court. Beside it are her own columned showpiece bedchamber with a charming long gallery above and dining and breakfast parlours below.

Marble Hill's decoration and furnishings have been exquisitely restored and recreated, and some of its original contents, dispersed in 1824, have been re-assembled from as far afield as Philadelphia and Melbourne, Australia. There is also a fine collection of early Georgian paintings, including portraits of Mrs Howard and her circle. There can be few places in England which better recall the atmosphere of Georgian fashionable life.

A new display recreates the Chinese wallpaper Henrietta Howard hung in the dining room in 1751. Using historical references and motifs, a unique paper has been designed to fit the room, each sheet different and, like the originals, hand painted by Chinese artists.

**NEW FOR 2007** Celebrate a new biography and display on Henrietta, Lady Suffolk.

**8 Sep–28 Oct**

Available for corporate and private hire.

Licensed for civil wedding ceremonies.

### NON-MEMBERS

| | |
|---|---|
| Adult | £4.20 |
| Concession | £3.20 |
| Child | £2.10 |
| Family | £10.50 |

### OPENING TIMES

| | |
|---|---|
| 1 Apr-31 Oct | |
| Sat | 10am-2pm |
| Sun & Bank Hols | 10am-5pm |
| Tours on Tue & Wed | 12pm & 3pm |
| 1 Nov-23 Dec and 1 Mar-20 Mar Pre-booked tours by appointment on certain days only, please contact site for details | |
| Closed | 24 Dec-29 Feb |

### HOW TO FIND US

**Direction:** Richmond Rd, Twickenham

**Train:** St Margarets ½ mile

**Bus:** From surrounding areas

**Tube:** Richmond 1 mile

**Tel:** 0208 892 5115

OVP

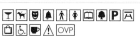

Café (Coach House Café, April-Oct).

Disabled access (exterior & ground floor only; toilets).

Dogs (restricted areas only).

MAP Page 266 (4E)

OS Map 161 (ref TQ 173736)

# Ranger's House – The Wernher Collection

Greenwich Park – SE10 8QX

Ranger's House is an elegant Georgian villa built in 1723, which became the official residence of the 'Ranger of Greenwich Park' after 1815, when the post was held by Princess Sophia Matilda, niece of George III. It remained an aristocratic and then royal home until 1902.

The house stands on the borders of Greenwich Park, and the Meridian Line passes through its grounds. Today it houses the Wernher Collection – an astounding display of medieval and Renaissance works of art, all purchased by the diamond magnate Sir Julius Wernher (1850-1912).

Arranged within the panelled interiors of this graceful mansion, the Wernher Collection presents a glittering spectacle – a sumptuous arrangement of silver and jewels, paintings and porcelain.

Nearly 700 works of art are on display, including early religious paintings and Dutch Old Masters, minute carved Gothic ivories, fine Renaissance bronzes and silver treasures. Together these pieces reveal the genius of medieval craftsmen, and the unparalleled quality of Renaissance decorative arts.

With the Cutty Sark, Greenwich and Blackheath all nearby, Ranger's House makes a great day out.

**www.english-heritage.org.uk/rangershouse**

Available for corporate and private hire.

Licensed for civil wedding ceremonies.

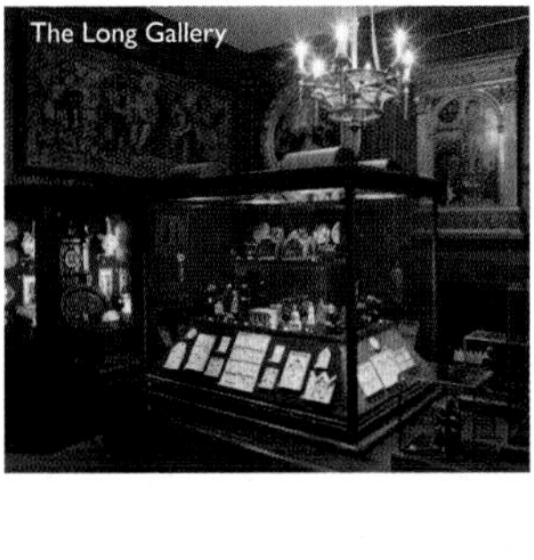

The Long Gallery

## NON-MEMBERS

| | |
|---|---|
| Adult | £5.50 |
| Concession | £4.10 |
| Child | £2.80 |

## OPENING TIMES

1 Apr-30 Sep,
Sun-Wed 10am-5pm
Prebooked groups on Thursdays

1 Oct-21 Dec and 1 Mar-20 Mar
Pre-booked tours by appointment on certain days only, please contact site for details

Closed 22 Dec-29 Feb

## HOW TO FIND US

**Direction:** Chesterfield Walk, Blackheath SE10

**DLR:** Cutty Sark

**Train:** Blackheath, Greenwich, Lewisham and Maze Hill, all ¾ mile

**Bus:** Tfl 53 Trafalgar Sq – Plumstead

**River:** Greenwich Pier

**Tel:** 0208 853 0035

OVP

Toilets (including disabled).

MAP Page 267 (4F)
OS Map 161/162 (ref TQ 388769)

# Wellington Arch Hyde Park – W1J 7JZ

Set in the heart of Royal London at Hyde Park Corner, Wellington Arch is a landmark for Londoners and visitors alike. George IV originally commissioned this massive monument as a grand outer entrance to Buckingham Palace. It was completed in 1830 by architect Decimus Burton, and moved to its present site in 1882.

Take a lift to the balconies just below the spectacular bronze sculpture which tops the imposing monument, for glorious views over London's Royal Parks and the Houses of Parliament. The statue is the largest bronze sculpture in Europe, and depicts the angel of peace descending on the chariot of war.

Inside the Arch, three floors of exhibits tell its fascinating history, including its time as London's smallest Police Station.

The Arch's Viewing Gallery offers unique views of the Household Cavalry passing beneath on their way to and from the Changing of the Guard at Horse Guards Parade.

Apsley House (see p.30), opposite the Wellington Arch, was the London home of the Duke of Wellington.

**www.english-heritage.org.uk/wellingtonarch**

Available for corporate and private hire.

Display inside the Arch

## NON-MEMBERS

| | |
|---|---|
| Adult | £3.20 |
| Concession | £2.40 |
| Child | £1.60 |

## OPENING TIMES

| | |
|---|---|
| 1 Apr-31 Oct, Wed-Sun & Bank Hols | 10am-5pm |
| 1 Nov-20 Mar, Wed-Sun | 10am-4pm |
| Closed | 24-26 Dec and 1 Jan |

The property may close at short notice, please ring in advance for details

## HOW TO FIND US

**Direction:** Hyde Park Corner, W1J

**Train:** Victoria ¾ mile

**Bus:** From surrounding areas

**Tube:** Hyde Park Corner, adjacent

**Tel:** 0207 930 2726

E OVP

**Please note:** Exclusive group tours are available every Mon, with talk, slide presentation and refreshments on request (small charge).

MAP Page 266 (4E)
OS Map 161/173 (ref TQ 284798)

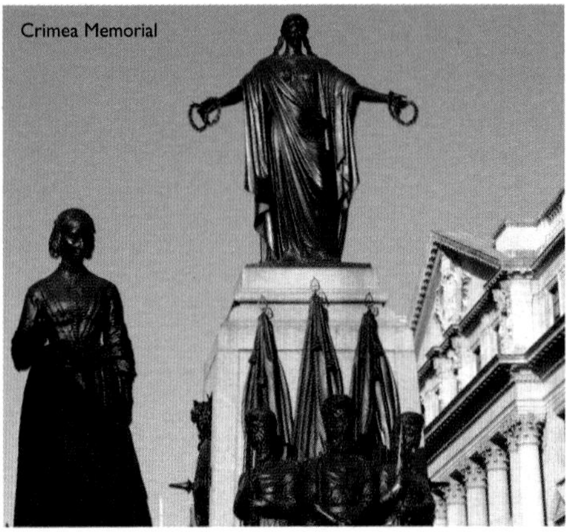
Crimea Memorial

# London Statues



In 1999 English Heritage assumed responsibility for the maintenance of 47 statues and monuments within central London, including the Wellington Arch, which you are invited to explore (see p.41).

Statues provide a fascinating insight into the preoccupations of the period. Many of them are associated with wars and military campaigns, such as the Napoleonic Wars, the Boer War and the two World Wars. Royalty is also well represented, with examples throughout the city from Charles I, 1633, to Edward VII, 1921.

A leaflet giving more information about the intriguing history of London's statues and memorials is available free of charge from English Heritage. To obtain a copy of Kings and Queens: Royal Statues & Memorials in London, call English Heritage on 0870 333 1181.

Thomas Cubitt Statue

## The Capital's Monuments

| | |
|---|---|
| Viscount Alanbrooke | Whitehall, SW1 |
| Queen Anne | Queen Anne's Gate, SW1 |
| Belgian War Memorial | Victoria Embankment |
| Simon Bolivar | Belgrave Square, SW1 |
| Duke of Cambridge | Whitehall, SW1 |
| Colin Campbell | Waterloo Place, SW1 |
| Carabiniers Memorial | Chelsea Embankment, SW3 |
| Edith Cavell | St Martin's Place, WC2 |
| Cenotaph | Whitehall, SW1 |
| King Charles I | Whitehall, SW1 |
| Queen Charlotte | Queen Square, WC1 |
| Clive of India | King Charles St, SW1 |
| Christopher Columbus | Belgrave Square, SW1 |
| Crimea Memorial | Waterloo Place, SW1 |
| Thomas Cubitt | St George's Drive, Pimlico, SW1 |
| Lord Curzon | Carlton House Terrace, SW1 |
| Duke of Devonshire | Whitehall, SW1 |
| Edward VII | Waterloo Place, SW1 |
| General Eisenhower | Grosvenor Square, W1 |
| Sir John Franklin | Waterloo Place, SW1 |
| General de Gaulle | Carlton Gardens, SW1 |
| King George II | Golden Square, W1 |
| King George III | Cockspur St, SW1 |
| General Gordon | Victoria Embankment |
| Earl Haig | Whitehall, SW1 |
| Sir Arthur Harris | St Clement Danes, WC2 |
| Lord Herbert | Waterloo Place, SW1 |
| King James II | National Gallery, Trafalgar Square, WC2 |
| Duke of Kent | Crescent Gardens (locked), Portland Place, W1 |
| Baron Lawrence | Waterloo Place, SW1 |
| Machine Gun Corps | Apsley Way, W1 |
| Montgomery | Whitehall, SW1 |
| Lord Napier of Magdala | Queen's Gate, SW7 |
| Marble Arch | W1 |
| Florence Nightingale | Waterloo Place, SW1 |
| Samuel Plimsoll | Victoria Embankment |
| Lord Portal | Victoria Embankment |
| Sir Walter Raleigh | Old Royal Naval College, Greenwich, SE10 |
| Royal Artillery Memorial | Apsley Way, SW1 |
| General de San Martin | Belgrave Square, SW1 |
| Captain Scott | Waterloo Place, SW1 |
| Viscount Slim | Whitehall, SW1 |
| Lord Trenchard | Victoria Embankment |
| George Washington | Trafalgar Square, WC2 |
| Duke of Wellington | Apsley Way, W1 |
| Wellington Arch and Quadriga | Apsley Way, W1 |
| King William III | St James's Square, SW1 |

# Other historic attractions

Discounted entry to our members (discounts may not apply on event days)

## The Albert Memorial
Kensington – SW1

Her Majesty the Queen reopened the Albert Memorial in 1998, after one of the most ambitious conservation projects ever undertaken by English Heritage. It took four years to repair structural damage to the memorial, which involved stripping the monument to its cast-iron core and rebuilding it with all the original elements conserved. A fully-guided tour provides exclusive access behind the railings of the site.

Managed by the Royal Parks.

### ENTRY

Tour (EH members) £4.00

Discount does not extend to EH Corporate Partners

### OPENING TIMES

Mar-Dec, guided tours only on 1st Sun of every month at 2pm & 3pm

Booking necessary only for 10+. Group bookings at other times by prior arrangement

### HOW TO FIND US

**Train:** Paddington 1¼ miles, Victoria 1½ miles

**Bus:** From surrounding areas

**Tube:** Knightsbridge ½ mile, South Kensington ½ mile

**Tel:** 0207 495 0916

MAP Page 266 (4E)
OS Map 161/173 (ref TQ 265797)

## Danson House
Kent – DA6 8HL

The most significant building at risk in London in 1995, now restored for the nation by English Heritage and opened to the public for the first time in 30 years by Bexley Heritage Trust. Built for Sir John Boyd, this is one of Sir Robert Taylor's finest villas, with additions by Sir William Chambers. The restored 1760s interiors include a magnificent dining room scheme of 19 paintings by Charles Pavilion, and a rare George England organ.

### ENTRY

| | |
|---|---|
| Adult | £5.00 |
| Concession | £4.50 |
| Child (accompanied) | Free |

25% discount to English Heritage Members

Discount does not extend to EH Corporate Partners

### OPENING TIMES

21 Mar-4 Nov
Wed, Thu, Sun & Bank Hol Mons
11am-5pm (last entry 4.15pm)

Pre-booked guided tours at other times subject to availability
Tel: 0208 298 6951

### HOW TO FIND US

**Train:** Welling Station 1 mile

**Bus:** TfL B13 from New Eltham, B16 from Kidbrooke, 89 from Lewisham, 486 from Greenwich

**Tel:** 0208 303 6699

www.historicdanson.com

MAP Page 267 (4F)
OS Map 162 (ref TQ 473752)

## Kensal Green Cemetery
Kensal Green – W10

Kensal Green Cemetery is one of seven cemeteries established to cope with the huge population explosion which London experienced at the height of the Industrial Revolution. It houses some spectacular pieces of Victorian Gothic mausoleum architecture and some illustrious residents, including Prince Augustus Frederick, Duke of Sussex (the sixth son of King George III) and his sister Princess Sophia. English Heritage helped to restore the Dissenters' Chapel in 1997. There are plans to restore the Anglican Chapel and some of the monuments. Tours, arranged by the Friends of Kensal Green Cemetery, are given every Sunday at 2pm. These include a visit to the catacombs on the first and third Sunday of every month (under 12s not admitted to the catacombs).

### ENTRY

Tour (EH members) £4.00

Discount does not extend to EH Corporate Partners

### OPENING TIMES

Daily

### HOW TO FIND US

**Train/Tube:** Kensal Green, adjacent

**Tel:** 07951 631001

MAP Page 266 (3E)
OS Map 173 (ref TQ 231825)

Osborne House – see page 70

# South East

'See you our stilly woods of oak
And the dread ditch beside?
O that was where the Saxons broke
On the day that Harold died'

From *Puck's Song* by Rudyard Kipling, 1906

# Properties See individual listings for details

## West Berkshire
Donnington Castle

## Hampshire
Bishop's Waltham Palace
Calshot Castle
Flowerdown Barrows
Fort Brockhurst
Fort Cumberland
Hurst Castle
Itchen Abbas Roman Villa
King James's and Landport Gates
Medieval Merchant's House
Netley Abbey
Northington Grange
Portchester Castle
Royal Garrison Church
Silchester Roman City Walls and Amphitheatre
Southwick Priory
Titchfield Abbey
Wolvesey Castle (Old Bishop's Palace)

## Kent
Bayham Old Abbey
Deal Castle
Dover Castle and the Secret Wartime Tunnels
Dymchurch Martello Tower
Eynsford Castle
Faversham Stone Chapel
The Home of Charles Darwin (Down House)
Horne's Place Chapel
Kit's Coty House and Little Kit's Coty House
Knights Templar Church
Lullingstone Roman Villa
Maison Dieu
Milton Chantry
Old Soar Manor
Richborough Roman Amphitheatre
Richborough Roman Fort
Reculver Towers and Roman Fort
Rochester Castle
St Augustine's Abbey and Conduit House
St Augustine's Cross
St John's Commandery
St Leonard's Tower
Sutton Valence Castle
Temple Manor
Upnor Castle
Walmer Castle and Gardens
Western Heights

## Oxfordshire
Abingdon County Hall
Deddington Castle
Minster Lovell Hall and Dovecote
North Hinksey Conduit House
North Leigh Roman Villa
Rollright Stones
Wayland's Smithy
Uffington Castle
White Horse and Dragon Hill

## Surrey
Farnham Castle Keep
Waverley Abbey

## East Sussex
1066 Battle of Hastings, Abbey and Battlefield
Camber Castle
Pevensey Castle

## West Sussex
Boxgrove Priory
Bramber Castle

## Isle of Wight
Appuldurcombe House
Carisbrooke Castle
Osborne House
St Catherine's Oratory
Yarmouth Castle

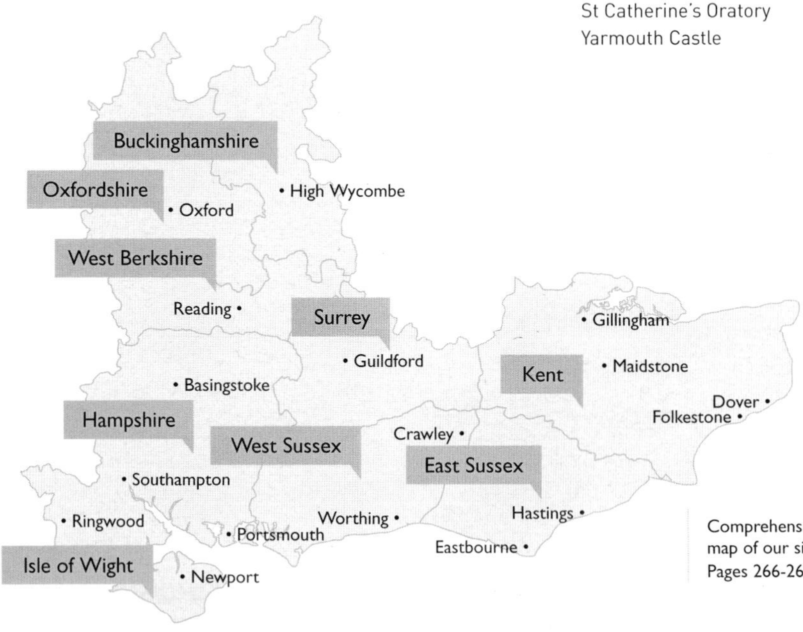


Comprehensive map of our sites Pages 266-267

Above: (left) Battle Abbey, (top left) Dover Castle, (top right) Osborne House, (bottom left) Carisbrooke Castle, (bottom centre) Minster Lovell Hall, (bottom left) Carisbrooke Castle.



# A Trail of Conquest

The South East of England, the region nearest the European mainland, has long been the area where both invaders and new ideas made their first impact on Britain. Among English Heritage's varied sites in the region are many reminders of the two most successful conquerors, the Romans and the Normans. In 2007, with the opening of a major new exhibition at **1066 Battle of Hastings, Abbey and Battlefield**, attention focuses especially on the Normans.

Everyone knows the date 1066, when William of Normandy defeated Harold of England at the place near Hastings now known as Battle. And even now, as ever since 1066, many people identify strongly either with the victors or the vanquished of that literally fateful conflict. For some, the Normans are the enforcers of much-needed order on a chaotic land, bringing England into the mainstream of European culture and laying the foundations of its later greatness. For others, they are fascistic bullies who set their oppressive 'Norman Yoke' on the brave and freedom-loving English. Neither view, of course, is either completely right or totally wrong – history is never that simple. **1066: the Battle for England**, the new interactive exhibition, explores the backgrounds of both sides in the conflict, as well as the dramatic events which led up to the clash of armies 'at the hoar apple tree' on 14 October 1066.

Whatever our view of them, there is no doubt that the Normans have left their mark on south-east England – often in the form of castles, their most effective instrument of conquest. A 'Norman trail' of the region might include such early Norman earthwork castles as those in **Bramber** in Sussex, **Eynsford** in Kent and **Deddington** in Oxfordshire, the first two (like many Norman strongholds) later refortified in stone. At **Pevensey** and **Portchester**, already ancient Roman forts were adapted as Norman castles, and both castles in **Carisbrooke** and **Dover** – the region's most impressive, and among the finest in all England – have Norman origins. But perhaps most characteristically Norman of all, with their keynote 'Norman' round arches, are the great early 12th-century stone keep of **Rochester Castle**, and the lesser-known but fascinating **St Leonard's Tower**, both built by Norman bishops. For as at **Battle Abbey** itself, founded to commemorate their victory, the Normans set their distinctive stamp – for better or worse – on the English church as well as the English nation.

## Abingdon County Hall
Oxfordshire – OX14 3HG

This splendid 17th-century baroque building housed a courtroom for Assizes, raised on arches over a market space. It now houses the Abingdon Museum. Entry is free.

Managed by Abingdon Town Council.

### OPENING TIMES

| | |
|---|---|
| Daily | 10.30am-4pm |

**Closed 24-26 Dec, 1 Jan, Bank Hols (except during Aug Bank Hols) and during exhibition changeovers**

**Roof-top visits – spring to autumn, Sats only. Adult £2.00, Child £0.50. Only children over 6 years admitted**

### HOW TO FIND US

**Direction:** In Abingdon, 7 miles south of Oxford; in Market Place

**Train:** Radley 2½ miles

**Bus:** Oxford Bus 35/A/B from Oxford (passes ≷ Radley)

**Tel:** 01235 523703

**MAP Page 266 (3C)**
**OS Map 170 (ref SU 498971)**

## Appuldurcombe House
Isle of Wight – PO38 3EW

The shell of Appuldurcombe, once the grandest house on the Isle of Wight and still an important example of English

Appuldurcombe House

baroque architecture: the 1701 south front has now been restored. It stands in 'Capability' Brown-designed grounds. An exhibition of photographs and prints depict the house and its history.

You can also visit the Freemantle Gate (part of the 1770s neo-Classical addition to the estate) on the nearby public footpath, and the adjacent Falconry Centre (not under the care of English Heritage).

Managed by Mr and Mrs Owen.

### NON-MEMBERS

| | |
|---|---|
| Adult | £3.25 |
| Concession | £3.00 |
| Child | £2.25 |
| Family | £10.00 |

**Please note there is an additional charge for members and non-members for the Falconry Centre**

### OPENING TIMES

| | |
|---|---|
| 1 Apr-30 Sep, daily | 10am-4pm |
| Closed | 1 Oct-16 Mar |
| 17-20 Mar, daily | 10am-4pm |

Last entry 1 hour before closing

### HOW TO FIND US

**Direction:** Wroxall ½ mile, off B3327

**Train:** Shanklin 3½ miles

**Bus:** Southern Vectis 3 Ryde – Newport

**Ferry:** Ryde 11 miles (Wightlink 0870 582 7744; Hovercraft 01983 811000); West Cowes 12 miles, East Cowes 12 miles (both Red Funnel – 0870 444 8898)

**Tel:** 01983 852484

**MAP Page 266 (7C)**
**OS Map 29 (ref SZ 543800)**

## 1066 Battle of Hastings, Abbey and Battlefield
See feature – Page 50

## Bayham Old Abbey
Kent – TN3 8DE

The impressive ruins of an abbey of Premonstratensian 'white canons', on the Kent-Sussex border. They include much of the 13th to 15th-century church, the chapter house, and a picturesque 14th-century gatehouse. Now set in an 18th-century landscape designed by Humphry Repton, the famous landscape gardener who also planned the grounds of Kenwood House in London. Rooms in the 'Georgian Gothick' dower house are also open to visitors.

### NON-MEMBERS

| | |
|---|---|
| Adult | £3.60 |
| Concession | £2.70 |
| Child | £1.80 |

### OPENING TIMES

| | |
|---|---|
| 1 Apr-30 Sep, daily | 11am-5pm |

### HOW TO FIND US

**Direction:** 1¾ miles W of Lamberhurst, off B2169

**Train:** Frant 4 miles

**Bus:** Arriva 256 Tunbridge Wells – Wadhurst (passes ≷ Tunbridge Wells)

**Tel:** 01892 890381

OVP

Disabled access (grounds only).

**MAP Page 267 (5G)**
**OS Map 136 (ref TQ 650365)**

## Bishop's Waltham Palace
Hampshire – SO32 1DH

The ruins of a medieval palace (together with later additions) used by the bishops and senior clergy of Winchester as they travelled through their diocese. Winchester was the richest diocese in England, and its properties were grandiose and extravagantly appointed. Much of what can be seen today is the work of William Wykeham, who was bishop from 1367. There is an exhibition on the Winchester bishops on the first floor of the farmhouse.

Other palaces of the Bishops of Winchester include Farnham Castle Keep and Wolvesey Castle (Old Bishop's Palace).

Available for corporate and private hire.

Licensed for civil wedding ceremonies.

### OPENING TIMES

**Grounds:**
1 May-30 Sep, Sun-Fri 10am-5pm

**Farmhouse**
Open by request

**Guided Tours**
Sun during Aug 11am

### HOW TO FIND US

**Direction:** In Bishop's Waltham

**Train:** Botley 3½ miles

**Bus:** Stagecoach in Hampshire 69 Winchester-Fareham (passes close to Winchester and

## Bishop's Waltham Palace

Fareham); Solent Blue Line 8 from Eastleigh (passes Botley)

**Tel:** 01489 892460

OVP

Disabled access (grounds only).

Dogs on leads (restricted areas only).

MAP Page 266 (6C)
OS Map 119 (ref SU 552174)

## Boxgrove Priory
West Sussex

The guest house and other remains of a Benedictine priory: much of the fine 12th to 14th-century monastic church survives as the parish church.

### OPENING TIMES

Any reasonable time

### HOW TO FIND US

**Direction:** N of Boxgrove; 4 miles E of Chichester, on minor road off A27

**Train:** Chichester 4 miles

**Bus:** Stagecoach in the South Downs 55 from Chichester

MAP Page 266 (6D)
OS Map 121 (ref SU 908076)

## Bramber Castle
West Sussex

The remains of a Norman castle on the banks of the River Adur, founded by William de Braose c. 1075. The earthworks are dominated by a towering wall of the keep gatehouse.

### OPENING TIMES

Any reasonable time

### HOW TO FIND US

**Direction:** On W side of Bramber village, off A283

**Train:** Shoreham-by-Sea 4½ miles

**Bus:** Brighton & Hove 2A Brighton – Steyning (passes Shoreham-by-Sea)

## Bramber Castle

Parking (limited).

MAP Page 266 (6E)
OS Map 122 (ref TQ 185107)

## Calshot Castle
Hampshire – SO4 1BR

This artillery fort, built by Henry VIII to defend the sea passage to Southampton, was recently used as a Navy and RAF base.

Managed by Hampshire County Council.

### NON-MEMBERS

| | |
|---|---|
| Adult | £2.50 |
| Concession | £1.80 |
| Child | £1.50 |
| Family | £6.00 |

### OPENING TIMES

31 Mar-31 Oct, daily 10am-4pm

### HOW TO FIND US

**Direction:** On spit, 2 miles SE of Fawley, off B3053

**Bus:** Solent Blue Line Bluestar 9 Southampton – Calshot (passes Southampton), to within 1 mile

**Tel:** 02380 892023; when castle is closed, please call 02380 892077

Disabled access (Keep: ground floor only; toilets).

MAP Page 266 (6C)
OS Map 22/29/119 (ref SU 489025)

# 1066 Battle of Hastings, Abbey and Battlefield

East Sussex – TN33 0AD

Everyone knows at least one date in English history – 1066, the year the invading Normans defeated the English at the Battle of Hastings. In fact the conflict took place some 7 miles north of Hastings, at a place then called Senlac. Here, William the Conqueror later founded 'Battle' Abbey to commemorate the event: and on the site of its high altar, you can stand on the very spot where King Harold of England fell. Now an imaginative new exhibition: **1066: The Battle for England**, brings the background and impact of the famous battle vividly to life.

The Great Gatehouse

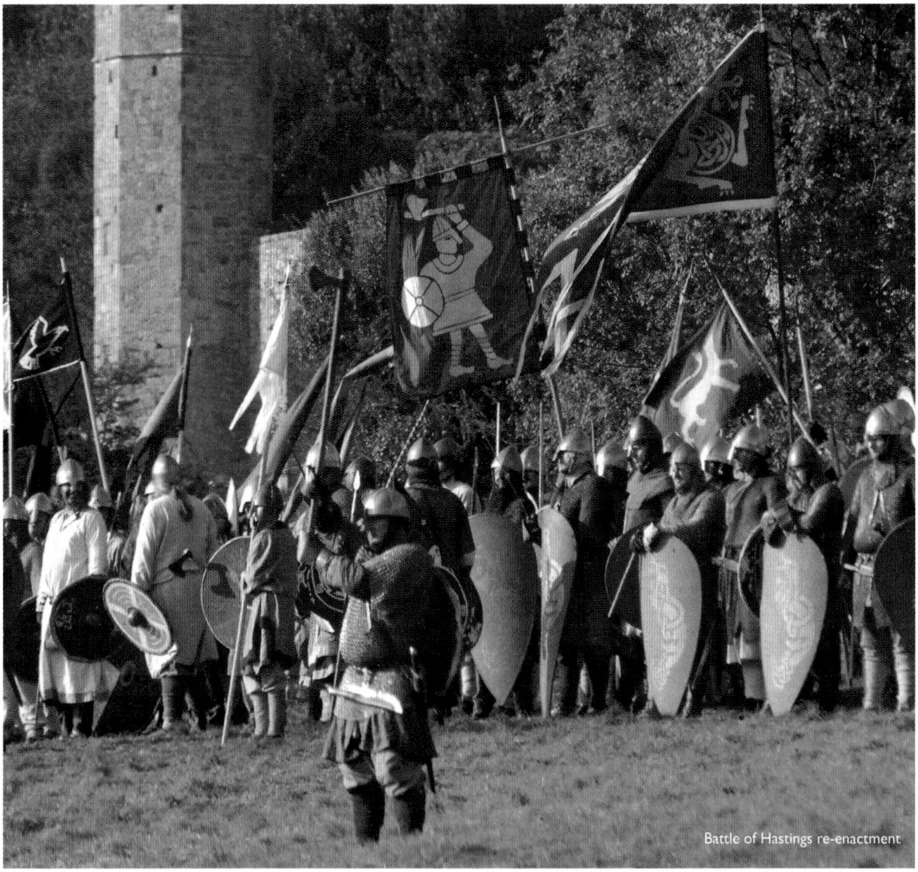
Battle of Hastings re-enactment



As the symbol of Norman victory, Battle Abbey enjoyed great wealth and special privileges. Little of the original Norman structure survives, but you can still see many later monastic buildings, including the dormitory range with its fine vaulted novices' chamber. The west range, incorporating the abbots' Great Hall, was converted into a mansion after Henry VIII's Dissolution of the Monasteries, and is now a school. Best preserved and most impressive of all is the Great Gatehouse, rebuilt c. 1338 and perhaps the finest surviving monastic entrance in Britain.

The battlefield – later part of the abbey's Great Park – and abbey were purchased for the nation in 1976.

A new audio tour re-creates the sounds of the battle, as you stand where the Saxon army's ridge-top 'shield wall' watched the Normans advancing towards them. After about an hour of fighting, the Normans panicked and fled, but William rallied them and successfully counter-attacked. Several 'pretended retreats' followed, luring the Saxons into breaking ranks in pursuit, but then cutting them down. After some ten hours of fighting, the Normans launched an assault which finally broke the fatally weakened Saxon shield wall. At this time King Harold was killed, perhaps struck in the eye by an arrow as depicted in the famous Bayeux Tapestry. By nightfall the Norman victory was complete. The new family tour uses 'interviews' with soldiers, monks and key figures from the time to retell the story of this fateful event.

Visit the abbey museum which explores the history of the abbey and includes artefacts found on site during excavations. The Discovery ▶

## 1066 Battle of Hastings, Abbey and Battlefield

The interpretation area of the new exhibition

NEW FOR 2007 The exciting new exhibition: **1066: The Battle for England**, uses the latest technology and interactive displays to draw a vivid picture of the social and political events, both for Saxons and Normans, of the years which led up to the conflict, and illustrates the impact this pivotal battle had on shaping English history. Listening points, graphic presentations, hands-on interactives and touch-screen displays look at how life was for the opposing sides. Central to this is a short film which dramatically explains the events leading up to this bloody struggle, culminating in the events of 14 October 1066 – when *'the fields were covered in corpses, and all around the only colour to meet the gaze was blood-red'*. [The Chronicle of Battle Abbey]. The new building which houses the exhibition, carefully designed to reflect the building materials and surroundings of this historic site, houses a stylish café serving light lunches and all day refreshments.

Centre, housing an activity-based exhibition, is available to pre-booked school parties and open to families at weekends and throughout the school holidays. There is also a themed children's outdoor play area.

Following your visit, why not while away a pleasant afternoon in Battle town: it has a Town Trail, museum, plenty of antique shops, and hosts events and farmers' markets. From Battle you can take the 1066 Walk to Pevensey Castle (one of Britain's oldest strongholds) where William first landed before moving to Hastings (see p.68).

Find out about other places in the area by visiting the tourist information centre in the site shop, which is accessible from Battle High Street. Don't miss one of the highlights of the national events calendar, a spectacular re-enactment of the Battle of Hastings on the weekend of 13 & 14 October 2007.

**For more details call 01424 773792 or visit www.english-heritage.org.uk/events**

www.english-heritage.org.uk/battleabbeyandbattlefield

Holiday cottage available to let.

## NON-MEMBERS

| | |
|---|---|
| Adult | £6.30 |
| Concession | £4.70 |
| Child | £3.20 |
| Family | £15.80 |

## OPENING TIMES

| | |
|---|---|
| 1 Apr-30 Sep, daily | 10am-6pm |
| 1 Oct-20 Mar, daily | 10am-4pm |
| Closed | 24-26 Dec and 1 Jan |

## HOW TO FIND US

**Direction:** In Battle, at south end of High St. Take the A2100 off the A21

**Train:** Battle ½ mile. Inclusive rail and admission tickets package available; ask at any Southeastern station

**Bus:** Arriva Kent & Sussex 4/5 Maidstone – Hastings

**Tel:** 01424 773792

**Local Tourist Information:** Battle (01424 773721) and Hastings (01424 781111)

OVP

Audio tours (interactive, also available for families, the visually impaired, those in wheelchairs or with learning difficulties, and in French, Spanish, German, Dutch, and Japanese; braille guides in English only). Audio tours will not be issued on special events days.

Disabled access (grounds and visitor centre).

Dogs on leads (restricted areas only).

Parking (charge payable for members and non-members).

New guidebook.

MAP Page 267 (6G)
OS Map 124 (ref TQ 749157)

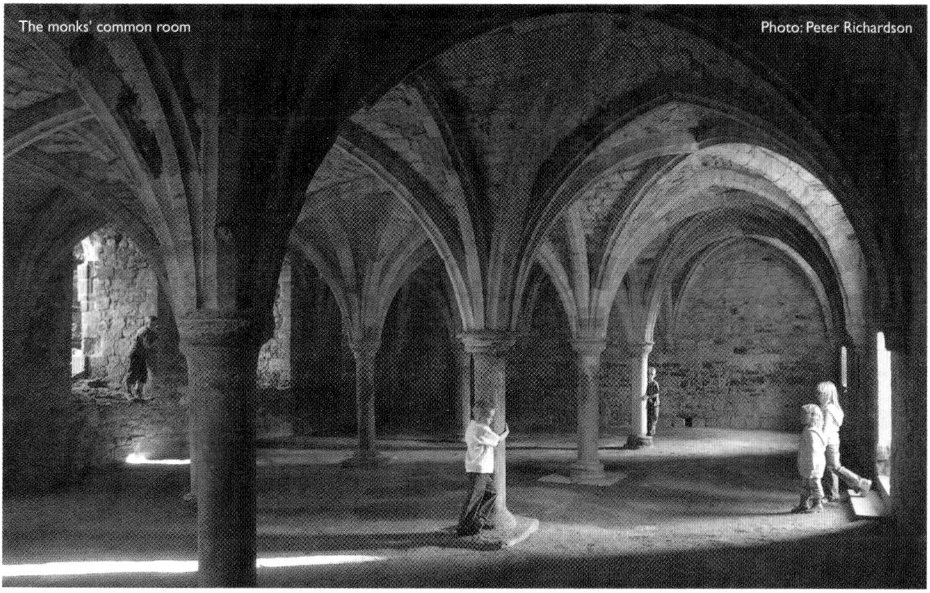

The monks' common room

Photo: Peter Richardson

## Camber Castle
East Sussex

The ruins of an unusually unaltered artillery fort, built by Henry VIII to guard the port of Rye. There are monthly guided walks round Rye Harbour Nature Reserve, including the castle. Contact the Reserve Manager for further details.

www.wildrye.info

Managed by Rye Harbour Nature Reserve.

### NON-MEMBERS

| | |
|---|---|
| Adult | £2.00 |
| Concession | £1.00 |
| (Accompanied children free) | |

Subject to change

### OPENING TIMES

| | |
|---|---|
| 1 Jul-30 Sep, Sat-Sun (last entry 4.30pm) | 2pm-5pm |

Opening times subject to change

### HOW TO FIND US

**Direction:** 1 mile walk across fields, off the A259; 1 mile S of Rye, off Harbour Road. No vehicle access

**Train:** Rye 1¼ miles

**Bus:** From surrounding areas to Rye, then 1¼ miles

**Tel:** 01797 223862

MAP Page 267 (6H)
OS Map 125 (ref TQ 922185)

## Carisbrooke Castle
See feature – Page 56

## Deal Castle
Kent – CT14 7BA

## Deal Castle

Deal Castle is one of the finest Tudor artillery castles in England. It is among the earliest and most elaborate of a chain of coastal forts, which also includes Calshot, Camber, Walmer and Pendennis Castles. Most were built at great speed between 1539 and 1542 by order of King Henry VIII, who feared an invasion by the Catholic powers of Europe. Its squat, rounded turrets were designed to deflect incoming cannon balls, and acted as platforms from which to fire barrages from increasingly sophisticated artillery pieces. The fort guarded the sheltered anchorage of 'the Downs' – the stretch of water between the shore and the hazardous Goodwin Sands, a graveyard of ships. Today you can explore the whole of the castle from the storerooms to the first-floor captain's residence. A pleasant cycle path links Deal and Walmer Castles along the beachfront.

Available for corporate and private hire.

Licensed for civil wedding ceremonies.

### NON-MEMBERS

| | |
|---|---|
| Adult | £4.00 |
| Concession | £3.00 |
| Child | £2.00 |

### OPENING TIMES

| | |
|---|---|
| 1 Apr-30 Sep, daily (Closes 5pm Sats) | 10am-6pm |

### HOW TO FIND US

**Direction:** SW of Deal town centre

**Train:** Deal ½ mile

**Bus:** From surrounding areas

## Deal Castle

**Tel:** 01304 372762

OVP

Audio tours (also available in French, German and Dutch).

Disabled access (courtyards and ground floor only, parking available).

MAP Page 267 (5J)
OS Map 150 (ref TR 378522)

## Deddington Castle
Oxfordshire

Extensive earthworks marking the site of an 11th-century motte and bailey castle.

Managed by Deddington Parish Council.

### OPENING TIMES

Any reasonable time

### HOW TO FIND US

**Direction:** S of B4031 on E side of Deddington; 17 miles N of Oxford

**Train:** King's Sutton 5 miles

**Bus:** Stagecoach in Oxfordshire 59/A/B Oxford – Banbury, to within ½ mile

MAP Page 266 (2C)
OS Map 191 (ref SP 472316)

## Donnington Castle
West Berkshire

## Donnington Castle

The striking twin-towered 14th-century gatehouse of this castle, later the focus of a Civil War siege and battle, survives amid impressive earthworks.

### OPENING TIMES

**Any reasonable time; exterior viewing only**

### HOW TO FIND US

**Direction:** 1 mile N of Newbury, off B4494

**Train:** Newbury 1¼ miles

**Bus:** Newbury Buses 6, 118, Four Valleys 99, 107 from ⇌ Newbury

Disabled access (steep slopes within grounds).

MAP Page 266 (4C)
OS Map 158 (ref SU 461692)

## Dover Castle and the Secret Wartime Tunnels

See feature – Page 58

## Down House – see the Home of Charles Darwin

See feature – Page 62

## Dymchurch Martello Tower

Kent – TN29 0TJ

Fully restored and re-equipped with its cannon, this is one of 103 ingeniously-designed artillery towers, built at vulnerable points around the south and east coasts to resist threatened Napoleonic invasion.

## Dymchurch Martello Tower

### OPENING TIMES

**Open August Bank Hol and Heritage Open Days (6-9 Sep)**

### HOW TO FIND US

**Direction:** In Dymchurch, from High St only

**Train:** Sandling 7 miles; Dymchurch (Romney, Hythe and Dymchurch Railway) adjacent

**Bus:** Stagecoach in East Kent 12, Stagecoach in Hastings 711 Dover – Hastings (passes close to ⇌ Folkestone Central)

OVP

MAP Page 267 (5H)
OS Map 125/138 (ref TR 102292)

## Eynsford Castle

Kent – DA4 0AA

The remains of one of the earliest Norman stone castles, built c. 1100 and little changed afterwards, including the full-height motte wall and part of the hall.

### OPENING TIMES

| | |
|---|---|
| 1 Apr-30 Sep, daily | 10am-6pm |
| 1 Oct-30 Nov, daily | 10am-4pm |
| 1 Dec-31 Jan, Wed-Sun | 10am-4pm |
| 1 Feb-20 Mar, daily | 10am-4pm |
| Closed | 24-26 Dec and 1 Jan |

### HOW TO FIND US

**Direction:** In Eynsford, off A225

**Train:** Eynsford 1 mile

**Bus:** Arriva, 413/5 ⇌ Eynsford – Dartford

MAP Page 267 (4F)
OS Map 162 (ref TQ 542658)

## Farnham Castle Keep

Surrey – GU9 0JA

The impressive motte, shell-keep, bailey wall and other defences of a castle founded in 1138 and redeveloped by Henry II after 1155. Long a residence of the wealthy bishops of Winchester, the fortress itself was abandoned after Civil War service: later attendant buildings remain in private occupation.

### NON-MEMBERS

| | |
|---|---|
| Adult | £2.90 |
| Concession | £2.20 |
| Child | £1.50 |

### OPENING TIMES

6-9 Apr (Easter), May Bank Hols & 1 Jul-31 Aug, Fri-Sun 1pm-5pm

**Guided tour**
Sun during Aug 2.30pm

### HOW TO FIND US

**Direction:** ½ mile N of Farnham town centre, on A287

**Train:** Farnham ¾ mile

**Bus:** From surrounding areas

**Tel:** 01252 713393

OVP

MAP Page 266 (5D)
OS Map 145 (ref SU 837473)

# Carisbrooke Castle Isle of Wight – PO30 1XY

Crowning a hilltop south of Newport, Carisbrooke Castle has held the dominant defensive position on the Isle of Wight for over 900 years.

With its keep, battlements and working well house, Carisbrooke Castle is an exciting site for the whole family to explore. There has been a fortress here since at least Saxon times, but the present castle was built on this site in c. 1100, when the island was granted to the de Redvers family.

When the Spanish Armada passed alarmingly close in 1588, Carisbrooke became enormously significant for the defence of the realm. It was suspected that the Spanish might attempt to seize the island, and in response the castle was transformed into an artillery fortress.

Charles I was imprisoned here in 1647. He was comfortably accommodated in the Constable's Lodging, and a bowling green was constructed for his recreation.

Nevertheless he made two attempts to escape: the first was foiled only when he became wedged in the window bars. Today the Charles I room is furnished as a typical bedroom of the Stuart period.

The well house and tread wheel are still in working order and open to visitors. Prisoners may have originally worked the wheel, but from the late 17th century donkeys were used. These happy, hard-working animals can now be found giving demonstrations.

The on-site Carisbrooke Museum (managed by the Carisbrooke Museum Trust) provides more historical information about the castle, as well as memorabilia and artefacts relating to Charles I.

**www.english-heritage.org.uk/carisbrookecastle**

Holiday cottage available to let.

## NON-MEMBERS

| | |
|---|---|
| Adult | £5.60 |
| Concession | £4.20 |
| Child | £2.80 |
| Family | £14.00 |

## OPENING TIMES

| | |
|---|---|
| 1 Apr-30 Sep, daily | 10am-5pm |
| 1 Oct-20 Mar, daily | 10am-4pm |
| Closed | 24-26 Dec and 1 Jan |

## HOW TO FIND US

**Direction:** 1¼ miles SW of Newport. Follow signs for Carisbrooke village and then the castle

**Train:** Ryde Esplanade 9 miles; Wootton (Isle of Wight Steam Railway) 5 miles

**Bus:** Southern Vectis 6, 7, 38 from Newport, West Wight and Ventnor, all to within ¼ mile

**Ferry:** West Cowes 5 miles, East Cowes 6 miles (Red Funnel – 0870 444 8898); Fishbourne 6 miles, Ryde 8 miles, Yarmouth 9 miles (Wightlink 0870 582 7744; Hovercraft Ryde 01983 811000)

**Tel:** 01983 522107

**Local Tourist Information:** 01983 813813

E OVP

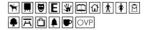

Disabled access (grounds and lower levels only).

Tearooms (open Apr-Oct).

MAP Page 266 (7C)
OS Map 29 (ref SZ 486878)

# Dover Castle and the Secret Wartime Tunnels

Kent – CT16 1HU

Pivotal to the defence of England's shores right into the 20th century, Dover Castle tells the tale of the evolution of a fortress.

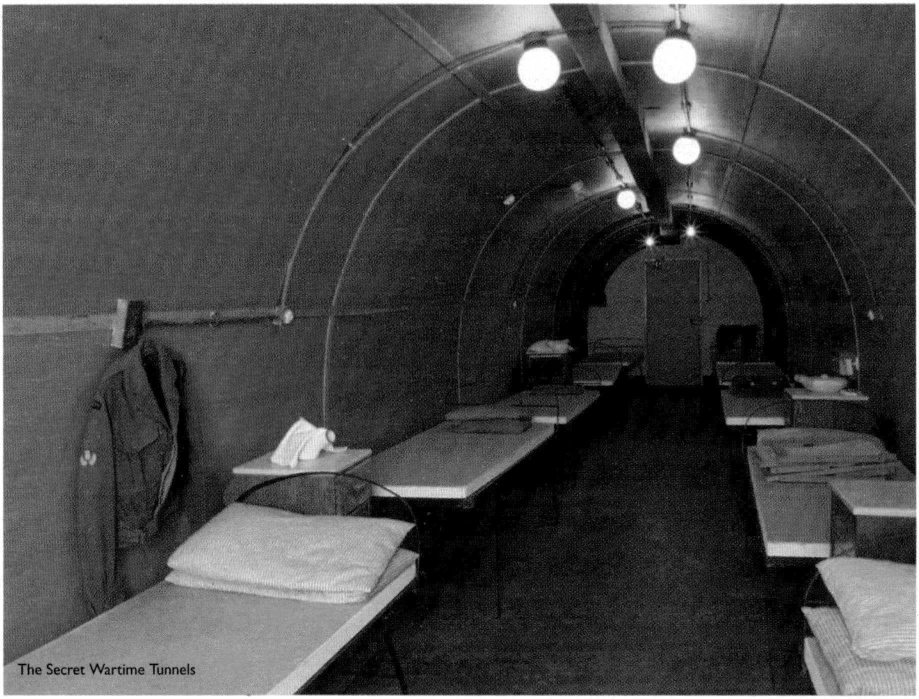
The Secret Wartime Tunnels

No fortress in England boasts a longer history than Dover Castle. Commanding the shortest sea crossing between England and the continent, the site has served as a vital strategic centre since Roman times.

William the Conqueror strengthened the existing Anglo-Saxon fort in 1066, both Henry II and Henry VIII made their own additions, and Vice Admiral Ramsay famously oversaw the Dunkirk evacuations from the tunnels built into the cliffs beneath the castle.

### Dover's wartime secret

The White Cliffs are one of England's most celebrated sights, yet hidden inside them is a fascinating and secret world. Deep underground lies an extensive network of tunnels – some first dug during the Napoleonic Wars, but so strategically useful that they continued to be used right through to the 20th century.

### Dunkirk evacuation – Operation Dynamo

In May 1940 these tunnels provided the nerve centre for Vice Admiral Ramsay to plan Operation Dynamo – the evacuation of British and allied troops from the Dunkirk beaches of northern France.

This evacuation proved crucial in saving the British army from total defeat and capture. The best estimate was that only 45,000 troops could be evacuated, yet on 4 June Sir Winston Churchill announced to the House of Commons that 338,000 troops had been saved, despite the operation itself coming under fierce attack.

Today you can tour the Secret Wartime Tunnels and experience life as it was lived by the 700 personnel based here in the worst days of World War II. You can see the Command Centre where Sir Winston Churchill viewed the Battle of Britain, and relive the drama as a surgeon

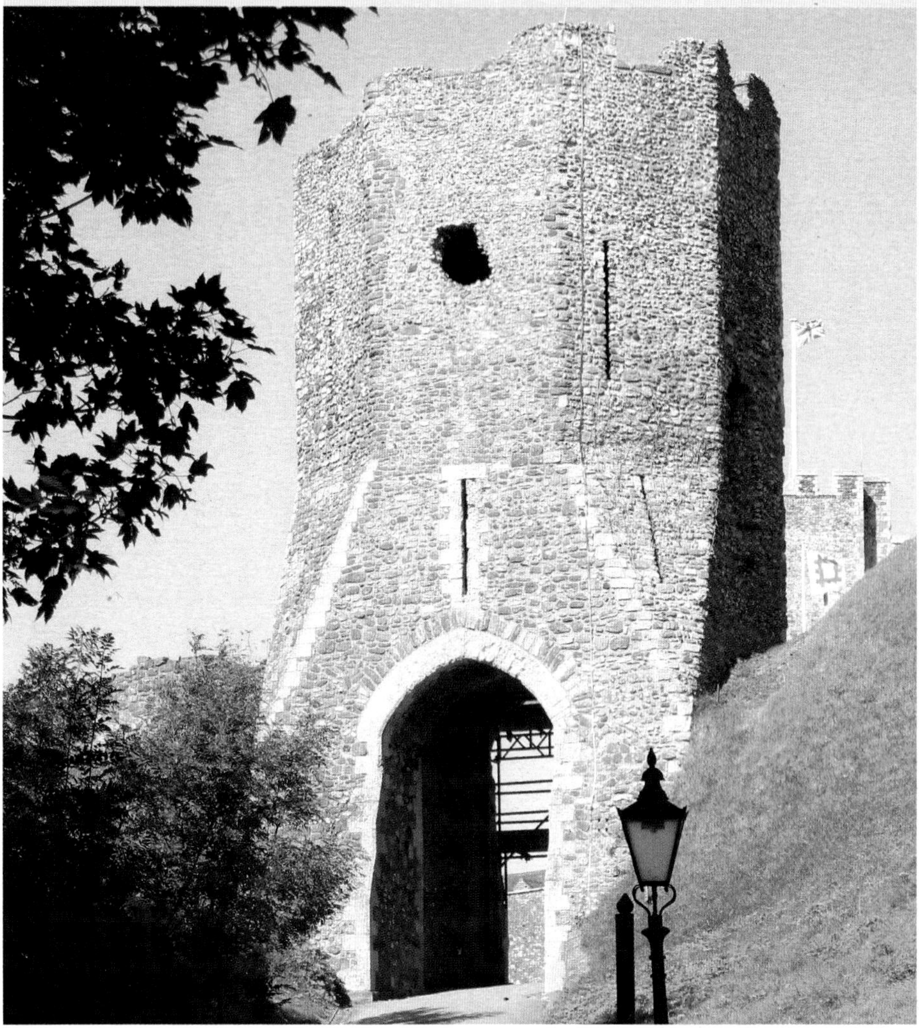

struggles to save the life of an injured pilot in the underground hospital. Sounds, smells and film clips from the time realistically recreate the atmosphere of wartime Britain.

Outside, Admiralty Look-out stands on the edge of the cliff, offering a tremendous view of the White Cliffs and across to France. (No public access to viewing platform until early summer 2007, due to conservation works.) To the west of the look-out you can see a statue of Vice Admiral Ramsay, and read about his key role in both the Dunkirk evacuations and the 1944 Normandy landings.

**The key to medieval England**
The Norman castle was built by Henry II during the 1180s. Around the core of his massive new keep, he raised a double circuit of concentric and strongly-towered walls, creating a fortress then unparalleled in western Europe. The Avranches Tower was purpose-built to control an angle in the eastern defences. Originally it had three floors with three triple loops per floor, a total of 27 loops. From some of the survivors of these you can still view the outer ditch defences. Tours are available on the first Friday of every month (additional charge payable).

The 1216 Siege Experience, a stunning presentation using light, film and sound technology, highlights the stronghold's key role in resisting invasion. It recounts the epic sieges of 1216-17, when Dover Castle held out almost alone for King John against rebel barons and their French ally Prince Louis.

### Henry VIII's visit

Following the annulment of his marriage to Catherine of Aragon, his excommunication by the Pope and the 1538 peace treaty between France and Spain, Henry VIII was isolated in Europe and a Catholic invasion of England seemed inevitable. The King commissioned a great chain of coastal artillery forts, coming to Dover in 1539 to inspect the work personally. An exciting exhibition at the castle offers a tableau of the preparations for Henry VIII's visit. Very close to Dover you will find two more of Henry's coastal defences, Deal Castle and Walmer Castle.

Also of interest at the site are the Princess of Wales' Royal Regiment Museum; one of the best-preserved Roman lighthouses in Europe; and the most complete Saxon church in Kent.

The Stone Hut, originally built in 1912 for the Royal Garrison Artillery, has now been converted and is being used as an archaeological store for the South East. On the first Friday of every month (or by pre-arranged booking), visitors can view changing exhibitions of treasures from across the region, including Roman coins and pots, as well as artefacts from both World War II and the Cold War.

Zeffirelli's *Hamlet*, starring Mel Gibson, *To Kill a King*, starring Dougray Scott and *The Other Boleyn Girl*, starring Scarlett Johansson.

**www.english-heritage.org.uk/dovercastle**

Available for corporate and private hire.

Licensed for civil wedding ceremonies.

Holiday cottage available to let.

Land train

## NON-MEMBERS

| | |
|---|---|
| Adult | £9.80 |
| Concession | £7.40 |
| Child | £4.90 |
| Family | £24.50 |

Includes Secret Wartime Tunnels tour. Additional charges for members and non-members may apply on event days

## OPENING TIMES

| | |
|---|---|
| 1 Apr-31 Jul, daily | 10am-6pm |
| 1-31 Aug, daily | 9.30am-6pm |
| 1-30 Sep, daily | 10am-6pm |
| 1-31 Oct, daily | 10am-5pm |
| 1 Nov-31 Jan, Thu-Mon | 10am-4pm |
| 1 Feb-20 Mar, daily | 10am-4pm |

The keep closes at 5pm on Sat if a hospitality event is booked. Last admission ½ hr before closing time. Secret Wartime Tunnel tour: timed ticket system in operation; last tour 1 hour before closing

Closed 24-26 Dec and 1 Jan

## HOW TO FIND US

**Direction:** E of Dover town centre

**Train:** Dover Priory 1½ miles

**Bus:** Stagecoach in East Kent, 15/X, Kent Passenger Services 593 from Dover (pass close Dover Priory)

**Tel:** 01304 211067

**Local Tourist Information:** Dover 01304 205108

E P

OVP

Disabled access (courtyard, grounds and basement. There is good access for wheelchair users to the tunnels, although entry is down a steep slope. Mobility scooters, wheelchair routes and guides are available on site).

Dogs on leads (restricted areas only).

New guidebook.

MAP Page 267 (5J)

OS Map 138 (ref TR 325419)

# The Home of Charles Darwin

Kent – BR6 7JT

It was at Down House that Charles Darwin worked on his scientific theories, and wrote *On the Origin of Species by Means of Natural Selection* – the book which both scandalised and revolutionised the Victorian world when published in 1859.

The house remains much as it was when Darwin lived here. The rooms on the ground floor have been furnished to reflect the domestic life of the family, while the study holds his writing desk, chair and numerous objects connected with his work. The first floor offers an interactive exhibition on his life, research and discoveries.

Charles Darwin

English Heritage has restored the gardens to their appearance in Darwin's time. Some of his outdoor experiments on natural selection are recreated in the garden and the greenhouse, with its orchids and carnivorous plants. The newly installed observation beehive will enable visitors to see honeybees at work building honeycombs, just as Darwin did almost 150 years ago when trying to prove his theory of evolution. Visitors can also stroll around the famous Sandwalk, the path Darwin paced as he worked out his ideas.

Discover more about Darwin and his family from our inclusive audio tour, narrated by Sir David Attenborough.

Down House and the surrounding landscape is the UK's 2006 nomination for World Heritage Site status, potentially ranking it alongside iconic sites like the Pyramids and Stonehenge: the result of the bid will be known in Summer 2007.

**www.english-heritage.org.uk/downhouse**

## NON-MEMBERS

| | |
|---|---|
| Adult | £7.20 |
| Concession | £5.40 |
| Child | £3.60 |
| Family | £18.00 |

## OPENING TIMES

| | |
|---|---|
| 1 Apr-30 Jun, Wed-Sun and Bank Hols | 11am-5pm |
| 1 Jul-31 Aug, daily (grounds close 6pm) | 11am-5pm |
| 1 Sep-31 Oct, Wed-Sun | 11am-5pm |
| 1 Nov-16 Dec, Wed-Sun | 11am-4pm |
| Closed | 17 Dec-29 Feb |
| 1-20 Mar, Wed-Sun | 11am-4pm |

Some building works may be undertaken during 2007/8.

## HOW TO FIND US

**Direction:** Luxted Rd, Downe; off A21or A233

**Train:** Orpington 3¾ miles

**Bus:** 146 from Bromley North and South railway station; R8 from Orpington

**Tel:** 01689 859119

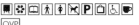

OVP

Audio tours.

Parking (plus space for one coach).

MAP Page 267 (4F)
OS Map 147 (ref TQ 431611)

## Faversham Stone Chapel (Our Lady of Elverton)
Kent

The remains of the small medieval parish church of Stone-next-Faversham – the only one in England to incorporate within its fabric the remains of a 4th-century Romano-British pagan mausoleum. It lay close to the probable site of the small Roman town of Durolevum and its Roman cemetery at Ospringe, finds from which can be seen at the Maison Dieu (see page 65).

Managed by The Faversham Society.

www.faversham.org/society

### OPENING TIMES
Any reasonable time

### HOW TO FIND US
**Direction:** In field immediately North of A2 just West of Ospringe and opposite Faversham Road

**Train:** Faversham 1½ miles

**Bus:** Arriva 333, Jaycrest 335 Maidstone – Faversham (passes Faversham)

**Tel:** 01795 534542

**E-mail:** ticfaversham@btconnect.com

**MAP Page 267 (4H)**
**OS Map 149 (ref TQ 992613)**

## Flowerdown Barrows
Hampshire

Three Bronze Age burial mounds, including the largest and finest 'disc barrow' in Hampshire, once part of a larger 'barrow cemetery'.

### OPENING TIMES
Any reasonable time

## Flowerdown Barrows

### HOW TO FIND US
**Direction:** Off B3049, out of Winchester to Littleton; at crossroads in centre of village

**Train:** Winchester 2 miles

**Bus:** Stagecoach in Hampshire 86 from Winchester (passes Winchester)

**MAP Page 266 (5C)**
**OS Map 132 (ref SU 459320)**

## Fort Brockhurst
Hampshire – PO12 4DS

One of a number of forts built in the 1860s to protect Portsmouth and its vital harbour. Largely unaltered, the parade ground, gun ramps and moated keep can all be viewed. The fort currently stores a treasure trove of objects from English Heritage's extensive reserve collections. Objects on display have been excavated from sites in the South East and South West and include stonework, textiles, jewellery, and furniture from many periods.

Portchester Castle – which acted as a prison during the Napoleonic Wars – is nearby.

### NON-MEMBERS
Please call for details.

### OPENING TIMES
The fort opens 12pm-3pm on the second Fri of every month, Feb to Oct, for guided tours and handling sessions, Heritage Open Days (6-9 Sep), and is available for private hire. Please call 02392 581059 for details

### HOW TO FIND US
**Direction:** Off A32, in Gunner's Way, Elson; on N side of Gosport

**Train:** Fareham 3 miles

**Bus:** First 81-7 Fareham – Gosport Ferry (passes Fareham; also Gosport Ferry links with Portsmouth & Southsea)

**Tel:** 02392 581059

Disabled access (grounds and ground floor only).

Dogs on leads (restricted areas only).

**MAP Page 266 (6C)**
**OS Map 119/29 (ref SU 596021)**

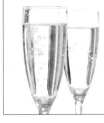

## Fort Cumberland
Hampshire – PO4 9LD

Perhaps England's most impressive piece of 18th-century defensive architecture, Fort Cumberland was reconstructed in pentagonal form by the Duke of Cumberland between 1785 and 1810, and designed to protect Langstone Harbour. Southsea beach is nearby.

### OPENING TIMES

The fort opens occasionally for pre-booked guided tours and Heritage Open Days (6-9 Sep). Call 02392 378291 for opening details

### HOW TO FIND US

**Direction:** In Portsmouth's Eastney district on the estuary approach, via Henderson Rd off Eastney Rd, or from the Esplanade

**Train:** Fratton 2 miles

**Bus:** First 15, 16/A Portsmouth Harbour – Hayling Ferry

**MAP Page 266 (6C)**
**OS Map 119/120 (ref SZ 683993)**

## The Home of Charles Darwin, Down House
See feature – Page 62

## Horne's Place Chapel
Kent

A rare survival of a fine domestic chapel, built for William Horne in 1366 and attached to his timber-framed manor house, which was attacked during the Peasants' Revolt of 1381. The house and chapel are privately owned.

### OPENING TIMES

By arrangement; please call 01304 211067

## Horne's Place Chapel

### HOW TO FIND US

**Direction:** 1½ miles N of Appledore

**Train:** Appledore 2½ miles

Parking (nearby).

**MAP Page 267 (5H)**
**OS Map 125 (ref SZ 683993)**

## Hurst Castle
Hampshire – SO41 0TP

One of the most advanced of the artillery fortresses built by Henry VIII: used as a prison for eminent 17th-century captives, and later strengthened during the 19th and 20th centuries. It commands the narrow entrance to the Solent.

Managed by Hurst Castle Services.

### NON-MEMBERS

| | |
|---|---|
| Adult | £3.20 |
| Concession | £2.80 |
| Child | £1.80 |

### OPENING TIMES

| | |
|---|---|
| 6 Apr-31 Oct, daily | 10.30am-5.30pm |
| Closed | 1 Nov-20 Mar |

### HOW TO FIND US

**Direction:** 1½ mile walk on shingle spit from Milford-on-Sea. Best approached by ferry from Keyhaven – call 01590 642500 for ferry details and fares

**Train:** Lymington Town 4½ miles to Keyhaven, 6½ miles to site

## Hurst Castle

**Bus:** Wilts & Dorset 123 Bournemouth – Lymington (passes New Milton), to within 2½ miles, or 1 mile to ferry

**Tel:** 01590 642344

Dogs on leads (restricted areas only).

Tearoom/restaurant (Castle Café, not managed by EH. Open Apr-May weekends only, Jun-Sep daily).

Parking (charge payable, at Milford seafront or Keyhaven).

**MAP Page 266 (7B)**
**OS Map 22/29 (ref SZ 318897)**

## Itchen Abbas Roman Villa
Itchen, Hampshire

The remains of a prehistoric settlement and a Roman villa, including enclosures, ditches and trackways visible in the form of cropmarks. Pottery dating from the Iron Age and a Roman hypocaust system for underfloor heating have been found here.

### OPENING TIMES

No public access. For more information call 01424 775705

**MAP Page 266 (5C)**
**OS Map 132 (ref SU 528343)**

## King James's and Landport Gates, Portsmouth
Hampshire – PO1 2EJ

Two ornamental gateways, once part of Portsmouth's defences. King James's Gate (of 1687) has been moved, but Landport Gate, designed by Hawksmoor (1760) as the principal entrance to Portsmouth, remains in its original position.

### OPENING TIMES

Any reasonable time; exterior viewing only

King James's and Landport Gates

## HOW TO FIND US

**Direction:** King James's Gate forms the entrance to United Services Recreation Ground (officers), Burnaby Rd; Landport Gate as above, men's entrance on St George's Road

**Train:** Portsmouth Harbour ¼ mile

**Bus:** From surrounding areas

MAP Page 266 (6C)
OS Map 29/119
(King James's Gate ref SZ 636999, Landport Gate ref SZ 634998)

## Kit's Coty House and Little Kit's Coty House
Kent

The remains of two megalithic 'dolmen' burial chambers. Impressive Kit's Coty has three uprights and a massive capstone: Little Kit's Coty, alias the Countless Stones, is now a jumble of sarsens.

### OPENING TIMES

Any reasonable time

### HOW TO FIND US

**Direction:** W of A229 2 miles N of Maidstone

**Train:** Aylesford 2½ miles

**Bus:** Arriva 101 ⇌ Maidstone East – Gillingham

MAP Page 267 (4G)
OS Map 148 (Kit Coty's House ref TQ 745608, Little Kit Coty's House ref TQ 744604)

## Knights Templar Church, Dover
Kent

The foundations of a small medieval church, traditionally the site of King John's submission to the Papal Legate in 1213.

### OPENING TIMES

Any reasonable time

Knights Templar Church, Dover

### HOW TO FIND US

**Direction:** On the Western Heights above Dover

**Train:** Dover Priory ¾ mile

**Tel:** 01304 211067

Dogs on leads (restricted areas only).

MAP Page 267 (5J)
OS Map 138 (ref TR 313407)

## Lullingstone Roman Villa
Kent – DA4 0JA

A most exciting archaeological find. The villa was built c. AD 75, and extended several times during 300 years of Roman occupation: it includes a room decorated with Christian symbols, among the earliest evidence for Christianity in Britain. Much is still visible today, including mosaic-tiled floors, wall paintings, and the extensive 4th-century bath complex, built when the villa was at its most prosperous. There is also a display of the skeletal remains found on site.

### NON-MEMBERS

| | |
|---|---|
| Adult | £4.00 |
| Concession | £3.00 |
| Child | £2.00 |

### OPENING TIMES

| | |
|---|---|
| 1 Apr-30 Sep, daily | 10am-6pm |
| 1 Oct-30 Nov, daily | 10am-4pm |
| 1 Dec-31 Jan, Wed-Sun | 10am-4pm |
| 1 Feb-20 Mar, daily | 10am-4pm |
| Closed | 24-26 Dec and 1 Jan |

**May be closed for part of 2007/8 due to building works. Please call in advance to avoid disappointment**

Lullingstone Roman Villa

### HOW TO FIND US

**Direction:** ½ mile SW of Eynsford; off A225; off junction 3 of M25

**Train:** Eynsford ¾ mile

**Tel:** 01322 863467

**Local Tourist Information:** Clacket Lane 01959 565063

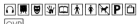

OVP

Audio tours – subject to availability (also available for the visually impaired and for those with learning difficulties, and in French and German).

MAP Page 267 (4F)
OS Map 162 (ref TQ 530651)

## Maison Dieu
Kent – ME13 8NS

Originating as a 13th-century wayside hospital, this flint and timber-framed building now displays Roman artefacts from nearby sites.

Managed by The Faversham Society.

**www.faversham.org/society**

### NON-MEMBERS

| | |
|---|---|
| Adult | £1.00 |
| Concession | £0.80 |
| Child | £0.50 |
| Subject to change | |

Group visits at other times by appointment

### OPENING TIMES

| | |
|---|---|
| 6 Apr-31 Oct, Sat-Sun, and Bank Hols | 2pm-5pm |
| Closed | 1 Nov-20 Mar |

### HOW TO FIND US

**Direction:** On main A2 on W corner of Water Lane in village of Ospringe. Public car park 300yds W

**Train:** Faversham ¾ mile

**Bus:** Arriva 333, Jaycrest 335 Maidstone – Faversham (passes ⇌ Faversham)

**Tel:** 01795 534542

**E-mail:** ticfaversham@btconnect.com

E

MAP Page 267 (4H)
OS Map 149 (ref TR 313407)

## Medieval Merchant's House
Hampshire – SO1 0AT

John Fortin, a merchant who traded with Bordeaux, started building this house c. 1290. A residence and place of business, it stood on one of the busiest streets in medieval Southampton. Now restored to its mid-14th-century appearance by the removal of later additions, it is equipped with replica period furnishings. It stands near the medieval town wall, built to defend Southampton against seaborne attacks. Netley Abbey, Calshot Castle and Hurst Castle are all within reasonable travelling distance.

### NON-MEMBERS

| | |
|---|---|
| Adult | £3.60 |
| Concession | £2.70 |
| Child | £1.80 |

### OPENING TIMES

1 Apr-30 Sep, Fri-Sun and Bank Hols 12pm-6pm

### HOW TO FIND US

**Direction:** 58 French St, ¼ mile S of city centre, just off Castle Way (between High St and Bugle St)

**Train:** Southampton ¾ mile

**Bus:** First 17/A from Southampton

## Medieval Merchant's House

**Tel:** 02380 221503

OVP

Audio tours (also available for the visually impaired and those with learning difficulties).

Disabled access (one step).

MAP Page 266 (6B)
OS Map 22 (ref SU 419112)

## Milton Chantry
Kent – DA12 2BH

Mainly encased in brick but still retaining its 14th-century timber roof, this was in turn part of a hospital, a chantry chapel, a public house, and a Georgian barracks, before its basement became a World War II gas decontamination chamber. The building is within Gravesham's Heritage Quarter and currently exhibits a fascinating insight into the borough's heritage.

Managed by Gravesham Borough Council.

### OPENING TIMES

1 Apr-30 Sep, Sat, Sun and Bank Hols 12pm-5pm

Admission outside these times by appointment

Opening times subject to change – please call to avoid disappointment

### HOW TO FIND US

**Direction:** In New Tavern Fort Gardens; E of central Gravesend, off A226

**Train:** Gravesend ¾ mile

**Bus:** From surrounding areas

**Tel:** 01474 321520

MAP Page 267 (4G)
OS Map 162/163 (ref TQ 653743)

## Minster Lovell Hall and Dovecote
Oxfordshire

The extensive and picturesque ruins of a 15th-century riverside manor house, including a fine hall, south-west tower, and complete nearby dovecote. The home of Richard III's henchman Lord Lovell.

### OPENING TIMES

Any reasonable time.
Dovecote – exterior only

### HOW TO FIND US

**Direction:** Adjacent to Minster Lovell church; 3 miles W of Witney, off A40

**Train:** Charlbury 7 miles

**Bus:** Stagecoach in Oxford 102/3 Witney – Carterton with connections from Oxford

MAP Page 266 (2B)
OS Map 180 (ref SP 325113)

## Netley Abbey
Hampshire

The most complete surviving Cistercian monastery in southern England, with almost all the walls of its 13th-century church still standing, along with many monastic buildings. After the Dissolution, the buildings were converted into the mansion

## Netley Abbey

house of Sir William Paulet. Even in ruins, the abbey continued to be influential, inspiring Romantic writers and poets.

### OPENING TIMES

| | |
|---|---|
| 6 Apr-30 Sep, daily | 10am-6pm |
| 1 Oct-20 Mar, Sat-Sun | 10am-3pm |
| Closed | 24-26 Dec and 1 Jan |
| **Guided tour** Sats during Aug | 11am |

### HOW TO FIND US

**Direction:** In Netley; 4 miles SE of Southampton, facing Southampton Water

**Train:** Netley 1 mile

**Bus:** First 16 ⇌ Southampton – Hamble; Solent Blue Line 9A Eastleigh – Hamble (passing ⇌ Southampton Airport Parkway)

**Tel:** 02392 378291

Toilets (nearby, across the road near the estuary).

MAP Page 266 (6C)
OS Map 22 (ref SU 453090)

## North Hinksey Conduit House
Oxfordshire

Roofed conduit for Oxford's first water mains, constructed during the early 17th century.

### OPENING TIMES

| | |
|---|---|
| Exterior viewing only 6 Apr-30 Sep, Thu-Sun and Bank Hols | 10am-4pm |

### HOW TO FIND US

**Direction:** In North Hinksey off A34; 1½ miles W of Oxford. Located off track leading from Harcourt Hill; use the footpath from Ferry Hinksey Lane (near railway station)

**Train:** Oxford 1½ mile

MAP Page 266 (3C)
OS Map 180 (ref SP 495050)

## North Leigh Roman Villa
Oxfordshire

The remains of a large, well-built Roman courtyard villa. The most important feature is a near complete mosaic tile floor, patterned in reds and browns.

Holiday cottage available to let.

### OPENING TIMES

Grounds – any reasonable time. There is a viewing window for the mosaic tile floor. Pedestrian access only from main road – 550 metres (600 yards)

### HOW TO FIND US

**Direction:** 2 miles N of North Leigh; 10 miles W of Oxford, off A4095

**Train:** Hanborough 3½ miles

**Bus:** Stagecoach in Oxford 11 Oxford – Witney, to within 1½ miles

Parking (lay-by, not in access lane).

MAP Page 266 (2B)
OS Map 180 (ref SP 397154)

## Northington Grange
Hampshire

Set like a lakeside temple in a landscaped park, Northington Grange is the foremost example of the Greek Revival style in England. Created between 1804 and 1809 when William Wilkins encased an earlier house in Classical facades, most strikingly the temple front supported on eight gigantic columns. It provides a stunning backdrop for the opera evenings which take place here in the summer; call 01962 868600 for details.

The 1999 film, *Onegin*, with Ralph Fiennes.

### OPENING TIMES

| | |
|---|---|
| Exterior only: 1 Apr-31 May, daily | 10am-6pm |
| 1 Jun-31 Jul, daily | 10am-3pm |
| 1 Aug-30 Sep, daily | 10am-6pm |
| 1 Nov-20 Mar, daily | 10am-4pm |
| Closes 3pm June and July for opera evenings | |
| Closed | 24-26 Dec and 1 Jan |

### HOW TO FIND US

**Direction:** Located 4 miles N of New Alresford, off B3046 along a farm track – 450 metres (493 yards)

**Train:** Winchester 8 miles

**Bus:** Cango C41/2 Basingstoke-Alresford (booked on 0845 602 4135)

**Tel:** 01424 775705

Disabled access (with assistance, steep steps to terrace).

MAP Page 266 (5C)
OS Map 132 (ref SU 562362)

Don't forget your membership card when you visit a property.

## Old Soar Manor
Kent – TN15 0QX

A small but complete portion of a stone manor house built c. 1290. The first floor 'solar' private chamber, with attendant chapel and garderobe, stands over a vaulted undercroft.

Maintained, managed and owned by The National Trust.

### OPENING TIMES

| | |
|---|---|
| 6 Apr-28 Sep, Sat-Thu and Bank Hols | 10am-6pm |

### HOW TO FIND US

**Direction:** 1 mile E of Plaxtol

**Train:** Borough Green and Wrotham 2½ miles

**Bus:** Autocar 222 Tonbridge – Borough Green; New Enterprise 404 from Sevenoaks. On both, alight at the E end of Plaxtol, then ¾ mile by footpath

**Tel:** 01732 810378

P

Parking (limited).

MAP Page 267 (5G)
OS Map 147/148 (ref TR 228693)

## Osborne House
See feature – Page 70

## Pevensey Castle
East Sussex – BN24 5LE

With a history stretching back over 16 centuries, Pevensey Castle chronicles more graphically than any other fortress the story of Britain's south coast defences. Beginning in the 4th century as one of the last and strongest of the Roman 'Saxon Shore' forts – two-thirds of whose towered walls still stand – it was the landing place of William the Conqueror's army in 1066.

During the decades after the Conquest the fort was converted into a full-scale Norman castle, with a great stone keep and towered bailey wall occupying one corner. Later a twin-towered gatehouse was added, and later still it was strengthened and modernised to face the threat of the Armada in 1588. This was not Pevensey's last military service: during World War II, pillboxes and machine gun posts were cunningly camouflaged among its ancient walls.

An exhibition with artefacts found on site and an audio tour tell the story of the castle.

### NON-MEMBERS

| | |
|---|---|
| Adult | £4.00 |
| Concession | £3.00 |
| Child | £2.00 |

### OPENING TIMES

| | |
|---|---|
| 1 Apr-30 Sep, daily | 10am-6pm |
| 1-31 Oct, daily | 10am-4pm |
| 1 Nov-20 Mar, Sat-Sun | 10am-4pm |
| Closed | 24-26 Dec and 1 Jan |

### HOW TO FIND US

**Direction:** In Pevensey off A259

**Train:** Pevensey & Westham or Pevensey Bay, both ½ mile

**Bus:** Stagecoach in Hastings 710 from Eastbourne

**Tel:** 01323 762604

P OVP

## Pevensey Castle

Dogs on leads (restricted areas only).

Parking (charge payable).

Tearooms (call 01424 775705 for opening arrangements).

Toilets (nearby).

MAP Page 267 (6G)
OS Map 123/124 (ref TQ 645048)

## Portchester Castle
See feature – Page 74

## Reculver Towers and Roman Fort
Kent – CT6 6SS

An imposing landmark, the twin 12th-century towers of the ruined church stand amid the remains of an important Roman 'Saxon Shore' fort and a Saxon monastery. Richborough Roman Fort is within easy travelling distance.

### OPENING TIMES

Any reasonable time; external viewing only

### HOW TO FIND US

**Direction:** At Reculver; 3 miles E of Herne Bay

**Train:** Herne Bay 4 miles

**Bus:** Stagecoach in East Kent 7 from Herne Bay

**Tel:** 01227 740676

P

Disabled access (grounds only – long slope up from car park).

MAP Page 267 (4J)
OS Map 150 (ref TR 228693)

## Richborough Roman Fort and Amphitheatre
Kent – CT13 9JW

## Richborough Roman Fort and Amphitheatre

Evocatively sited amid the East Kent marshes, Richborough is perhaps the most symbolically important of all Roman sites in Britain, witnessing both the beginning and almost the end of Roman rule here. The site is now two miles from the sea; in AD 43 it overlooked a sheltered lagoon harbour. Here, all but certainly, the invading Roman forces first landed and established a bridgehead. This event was later commemorated by a mighty triumphal arch, whose cross-shaped foundations still survive here. Proclaiming that the Roman conquest of Britain was complete, this also provided an impressive gateway for arrivals at what became the province's main entry port.

By the mid-3rd century, however, Roman Britain was under attack by sea-borne Saxon and other raiders. The once-prosperous commercial port of Rutupiae was hastily fortified, first by the digging of the great triple ditches and ramparts still visible round the site of the arch. But within a decade or so the defences were completely revamped, and Richborough was provided with its circuit of towered stone walls and outer ditches, becoming one of the most important of the 'Saxon Shore' forts. It was also among the last to be regularly occupied: there is evidence of a large Roman population here in the early 5th century, some of them worshipping in the little Early Christian church discovered in one corner of the fort.

You can choose to reach the fort as the Romans would have done, by boat. Boats sail from

## Richborough Roman Fort and Amphitheatre

Sandwich, but not every day: please contact the site to check times.

### NON-MEMBERS

| | |
|---|---|
| Adult | £4.00 |
| Concession | £3.00 |
| Child | £2.00 |

### OPENING TIMES

**Fort:**

1 Apr-30 Sep, daily 10am-6pm

**Amphitheatre:** Any reasonable time, access across grazed land from footpath; please call 01304 612013 for details

### HOW TO FIND US

**Direction:** At the A256/A257 roundabout, take the road for Sandwich and then turn left at the fire station

**Train:** Sandwich 2 miles

**Tel:** 01304 612013

Dogs on leads (restricted areas only).

**MAP Page 267 (4J) OS Map 150 (Fort ref TR 324602) (Ampitheatre ref TR 321598)**

## Rochester Castle

Kent – ME1 1SW

Strategically placed astride the London Road, guarding an important crossing of the River Medway, this imposing fortress has a complex history of destruction and rebuilding. Its mighty Norman tower-keep of Kentish ragstone was built c. 1127 by William of Corbeil, Archbishop of Canterbury, with the encouragement of Henry I. Consisting of three floors above a basement, it still stands 113 feet high. Attached is a tall protruding forebuilding, with its own set of defences to pass through before the keep itself could be entered at first floor level.

## Rochester Castle

In 1215, garrisoned by rebel barons, the castle endured an epic siege by King John. Having first undermined the outer wall, John used the fat of 40 pigs to fire a mine under the keep, bringing its southern corner crashing down. Even then the defenders held out within the building, until they were eventually starved out after a resistance of nearly two months.

Rebuilt under Henry III and Edward I, the castle remained a viable fortress in the 15th century, but a century later it was decaying. Today it stands repaired as a proud reminder of the history of Rochester, along with the nearby cathedral and Dickensian cobbled streets.

Managed by Medway Council.

### NON-MEMBERS

| | |
|---|---|
| Adult | £4.00 |
| Concession | £3.00 |
| Child | £3.00 |
| Family | £11.00 |

### OPENING TIMES

31 Mar-31 Oct, daily 10am-6pm

1 Nov-20 Mar, daily 10am-4pm

Last admission 45 mins before closing

Closed 24-26 Dec and 1 Jan

**During 2007 Rochester Castle may be undergoing conservation work. To avoid disappointment, please call in advance of visit**

### HOW TO FIND US

**Direction:** By Rochester Bridge (A2); junction 1 of M2 and junction 2 of M25

**Train:** Rochester ½ mile

**Bus:** From surrounding areas

**Tel:** 01634 402276

Audio tours (small charge).

Toilets (in castle grounds).

**MAP Page 267 (4G) OS Map 148/163 (ref TQ 741686)**

# Osborne House Isle of Wight – PO32 6JX

After her marriage to Prince Albert in 1840, Queen Victoria felt the need for a family residence in the country. To use her words, 'a place of one's own – quiet and retired'.

The Billiard Room

Queen Victoria knew and liked :he Isle of Wight after visiting as ι child, and she and the Prince Consort were both determined :o buy a property there.

It is impossible to imagine a ›rettier spot,' wrote the Queen ιfter a visit to Osborne House. n 1845 the royal couple ›urchased the property with ιn estate of 342 acres, plus the ιdjacent Barton Manor to ιouse equerries and grooms ιnd to serve as the home farm.

Before the deeds had even :hanged hands, architect Thomas Cubitt had been approached – rstly to build a new wing and hen to demolish the old house and add further wings. Once all the work was complete, an exquisite pair of Italianate towers dominated the landscape and looked out over passing ships in the nearby Solent.

## Artistic interiors

The interiors of Osborne House abound with opulence in both architectural design and decoration. Marble sculptures, commissioned by Victoria and Albert, line the classically designed Grand Corridor of the house and recall the royal couple's love of the arts. Portraits and frescos adorn the walls, serving as a reminder of the family's links to the crowned heads of Europe, and of the unrivalled

Horse-drawn carriage

supremacy of the British Empire. Family photographs on the desks of Queen Victoria and Prince Albert offer a further insight into the way they lived.

Queen Victoria's role as Empress of India is celebrated in the richly decorated Durbar Room. Constructed from 1890-91, the room served as an elaborate banqueting hall and every surface, from floor to ceiling, is ornately embellished.

The walls are decorated with symbols from India, including Ganesh – the elephant god of good fortune – and the deeply coffered ceiling is composed of fibrous plaster. The completion of the room coincided with the introduction of electricity, so the Indian-influenced lamp stands were designed to take full advantage of this emerging technology.

### Italianate gardens

Prince Albert worked with Cubitt on the Italianate designs for the terraced formal gardens which complement the house. Visitors can now enjoy the Walled Garden much as Victoria and Albert did, since English Heritage has restored it as part of the Contemporary Heritage Gardens Scheme.

The grounds also contain a children's play area, a summerhouse, a museum, and a miniature fort and barracks, as well as the Swiss Cottage, originally built as an educational tool where the royal children could learn domestic skills. There is a beautiful wild flower meadow near the Swiss Cottage, and rare red squirrels can be seen throughout the gardens. There is a courtesy minibus, with wheelchair access, to Swiss Cottage.

Queen Victoria loved to stroll through the gardens, and the primroses in the woods were

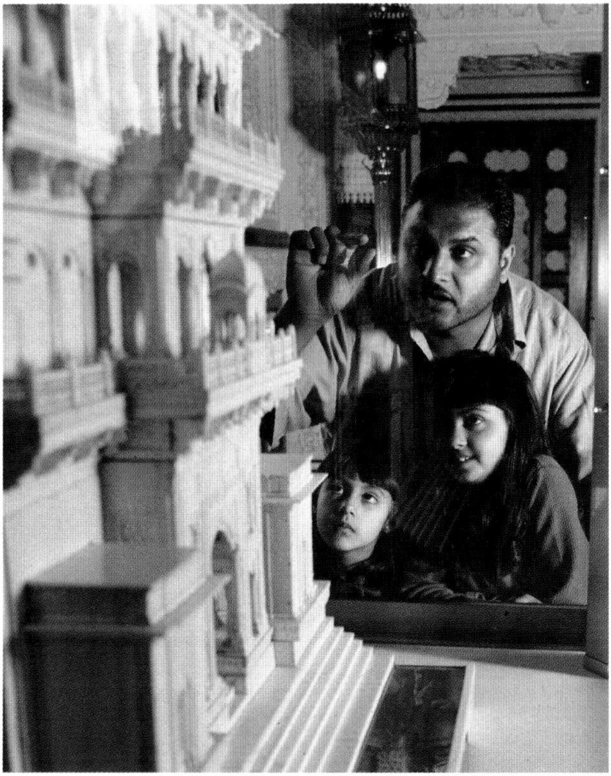

her particular favourites. Most of the gardens are accessible on tarmac and compacted gravel paths. Horse and carriage rides are also available (extra charge).

The Terrace Restaurant has wonderful views across the terrace gardens down to the Solent. It has waiter-served lunches and afternoon teas. (Please note: for non-members, a minimum grounds charge applies for access to the Terrace Restaurant.)

The exhibition in the newly opened Petty Officers Quarters is the best place to start any visit. It covers various aspects of the sumptuously furnished house and magnificent grounds, as well as the lives and personalities of the Victorian royal family and the servants who cared for them. Here you will also find a café serving refreshments and light lunches, and a large shop.

### Guided Tours

From Nov to Mar, the house is open for pre-booked guided tours, allowing visitors to enjoy a selection of rooms at a quieter time of year in the company of one of our expert guides. For details of our annual Christmas tours and events please call the house or visit **www.english-heritage.org.uk/osbornehouse**

Available for corporate and private hire.

Holiday cottage available to let.

## NON-MEMBERS

**House and Grounds**

| | |
|---|---|
| Adult | £9.80 |
| Concession | £7.40 |
| Child | £4.90 |
| Family | £24.50 |

## NON-MEMBERS

**Grounds Only**

| | |
|---|---|
| Adult | £5.90 |
| Concession | £4.40 |
| Child | £3.00 |
| Family | £14.80 |

## OPENING TIMES

| | |
|---|---|
| 1 Apr-30 Sep, daily (house closes 5pm) | 10am-6pm |
| 1-31 Oct, daily | 10am-4pm |
| 1 Nov-20 Mar, Wed-Sun Prebooked guided tours (last tour is 2.30pm. Christmas tour season 10 Nov-6 Jan) | 10am-4pm |
| Closed | 24-26 Dec and 1 Jan |

On 20-21 Jul, 27-28 Jul & 6 Aug, the house will close at 3pm (grounds 4pm) for special events

## HOW TO FIND US

**Direction:** 1 mile SE of East Cowes

**Bus:** Southern Vectis 4, Ryde – E Cowes; 5 Newport – E Cowes

**Train:** Ryde Esplanade 7 miles; Wootton (Isle of Wight Steam Railway) 3 miles

**Ferry:** East Cowes 1½ mile (Red Funnel – 0870 4448898); Fishbourne 4 miles; Ryde 7 miles (Wightlink 0870 5827744; Hovercraft: Ryde 01983 811000)

**Tel:** 01983 200022

**Local Tourist Information:** Cowes and Newport 01983 813818

E P OVP

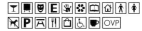

Disabled access (Access for wheelchair users to the first floor, by an existing lift. Whilst we endeavour to provide this service whenever the house is open, there will be occasions when wheelchair access to the first floor is not available).

New guidebook.

**MAP Page 266 (7C)**
**OS Map 29 (ref SZ 516948)**

# Portchester Castle Hampshire – PO16 9QW

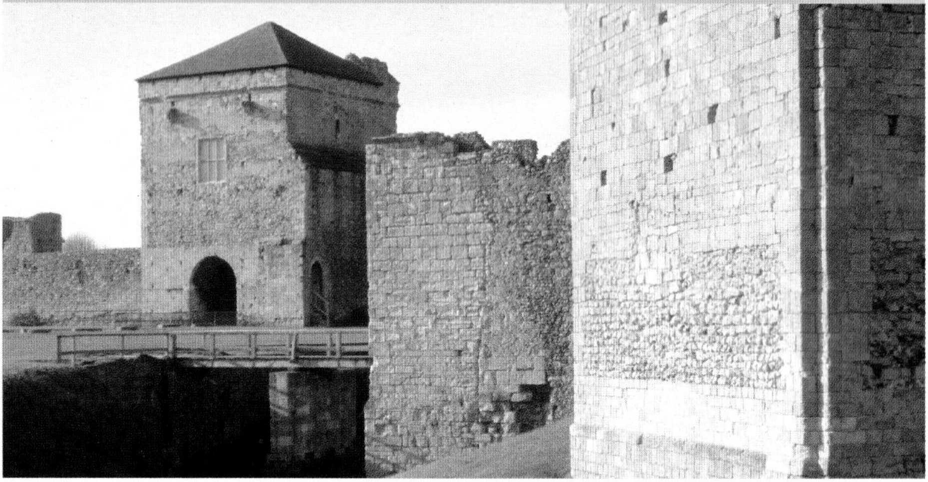

Portchester Castle's commanding location has made it a major factor in the Solent's defences for hundreds of years.

The most impressive and best-preserved of the Roman 'Saxon Shore' forts, Portchester was originally built in the late 3rd century. It is the only Roman stronghold in northern Europe whose walls still mainly stand to their full height. Subsequently housing a Saxon settlement, the huge waterside fortress became a Norman castle in the 12th century, when a formidable tower-keep was built in one corner.

Portchester was in the front line throughout the Hundred Years War, serving as a staging-post for expeditions to France and repelling cross-Channel raids. Richard II transformed part of the castle into a palace in 1396 and Henry V used it as a departure point for the Agincourt campaign in 1415. Thereafter it saw little action, but was used to house troops in the Civil War, and prisoners of war during the Dutch and Napoleonic Wars.

An exhibition in the keep interprets the history of the castle and Portchester village, and displays finds excavated on site. The inclusive audio tour explains life in the castle over the centuries, from the point of view of some of the people who worked or were incarcerated there.

Roman intaglio of Mercury

www.english-heritage.org.uk/portchestercastle

## NON-MEMBERS

| | |
|---|---|
| Adult | £4.00 |
| Concession | £3.00 |
| Child | £2.00 |

## OPENING TIMES

| | |
|---|---|
| 1 Apr-30 Sep, daily | 10am-6pm |
| 1 Oct-20 Mar, daily | 10am-4pm |
| Closed | 24-26 Dec and 1 Jan |

## HOW TO FIND US

**Direction:** On the S side of Portchester off A27; Junction 11 on M27

**Train:** Portchester 1 mile

**Bus:** First 1/A, 5 Fareham – Southsea to within ¼ mile

**Tel:** 02392 378291

OVP

Disabled access (grounds and lower levels only).

Dogs on leads (restricted areas only).

Toilets (facilities are in the car park, operated by Fareham District Council).

MAP Page 266 (6C)
OS Map 29/119 (ref SU 625046)

## Rollright Stones
Oxfordshire

Traditionally a monarch and his courtiers petrified by a witch, the Rollright Stones consist of three groups: the King's Men stone circle; the Whispering Knights burial chamber; and the single King Stone. They span nearly 2,000 years of Neolithic and Bronze Age development.

Managed by The Rollright Trust.

### OPENING TIMES
All the stones are accessible sunrise to sunset, 'The Whispering Knights' and 'The King Stone' via a footpath; entry to 'The King's Men' is courtesy of the owner, who may levy a small charge (Adult 50p, Child 25p, subject to change)

### HOW TO FIND US
**Direction:** Off unclassified road between A44 and A3400; 3 miles NW of Chipping Norton, near villages of Little Rollright and Long Compton

**Train:** Moreton-in-Marsh 6½ miles

**Tel:** 01608 642299

Parking (in lay-by).

MAP Page 266 (2B)
OS Map 45/191 (ref SP 297309)

## Royal Garrison Church, Portsmouth
Hampshire – PO1 2NJ

### Royal Garrison Church
Royal Garrison Church was constructed c. 1212 as a hospital. Although the church was badly damaged in a 1941 fire-bomb raid on Portsmouth, the chancel was saved.

Managed by the Friends of the Royal Garrison.

### OPENING TIMES
| | |
|---|---|
| 6 Apr-30 Sep, Mon, Tue, Thu-Sat | 11am-4pm |
| (contact the keykeeper in winter 02392 378291) | |
| Closed | Sun and Wed |

### HOW TO FIND US
**Direction:** In Portsmouth; on Grand Parade S of High St

**Train:** Portsmouth Harbour ¾ mile

**Bus:** From surrounding areas

**Tel:** 02392 378291

Parking (nearby).

MAP Page 266 (6C)
OS Map 29/119 (ref SZ 633992)

## St Augustine's Abbey
Kent – CT1 1TF

This great abbey, marking the rebirth of Christianity in southern England, was founded in AD 597 by St Augustine. Originally created as a burial place for the Anglo-Saxon kings of Kent, it is part of the Canterbury World Heritage Site, along with the cathedral and St Martin's Church.

### St Augustine's Abbey
The impressive abbey is situated outside the city walls and is sometimes missed by visitors. At the abbey, you can also enjoy the museum and free audio tour.

### NON-MEMBERS
| | |
|---|---|
| Adult | £4.00 |
| Concession | £3.00 |
| Child | £2.00 |

### OPENING TIMES
| | |
|---|---|
| 1 Apr-30 Jun, Wed-Sun | 10am-5pm |
| 1 Jul-31 Aug, daily | 10am-6pm |
| 1 Sep-20 Mar, Sun | 11am-5pm |
| Open Mon for education groups, by request | |
| Closed | 24-26 Dec and 1 Jan |



### HOW TO FIND US
**Direction:** In Canterbury, ¼ mile E of Cathedral Close

**Train:** Canterbury East and West, both ¾ mile

**Bus:** From surrounding area

**Tel:** 01227 767345

**Local Tourist Information:** Canterbury 01227 766567

Audio tours (interactive).

Disabled access (all site can be viewed, but some steps).

Parking (nearby).

MAP Page 267 (4J)
OS Map 150 (ref TR 155578)

## St Augustine's Abbey Conduit House
Kent

The Conduit House is part of the monastic waterworks which supplied nearby St Augustine's Abbey.

### OPENING TIMES
Any reasonable time; exterior viewing only

St Augustine's Abbey Conduit House

### HOW TO FIND US

**Direction:** In King's Park. Approx. 5-10 min walk from St Augustine's Abbey. Please call or ask at the abbey for directions

**Train:** Canterbury East or West, both 1½ miles

MAP Page 267 (4J)
OS Map 150 (ref TR 159580)

## St Augustine's Cross
Kent

This 19th-century cross of Saxon design marks what is traditionally thought to have been the site of St Augustine's landing on the shores of England in AD 597. Accompanied by 30 followers, Augustine is said to have held a mass here before moving on.

### OPENING TIMES

Any reasonable time

### HOW TO FIND US

**Direction:** 2 miles E of Minster off B29048

**Train:** Minster 2 miles

**Bus:** Stagecoach in East Kent 37, Eastonways E42 from Ramsgate

MAP Page 267 (4J)
OS Map 150 (ref TR 340642)

## St Catherine's Oratory
Isle of Wight

A tall medieval octagonal tower, allegedly a lighthouse, built here in 1328 as penance for stealing church property from a wrecked ship. Affectionately known as the Pepperpot, it stands on one of the highest parts of the Isle of Wight.



It is part of the Tennyson Heritage Coast, a series of linked cliff-top monuments. A later lighthouse can be seen nearby.

Maintained and managed by The National Trust.

### OPENING TIMES

Any reasonable time

### HOW TO FIND US

**Direction:** E of Blackgang roundabout, off A3055

**Train:** Shanklin 9 miles

**Bus:** Southern Vectis 6 Ventnor – Newport, to within 1 mile

**Ferry:** West Cowes 14 miles, East Cowes 14 miles (both Red Funnel – 0870 444 8898); Yarmouth 15 miles (Wightlink – 0870 582 7744)

P

MAP Page 266 (7C)
OS Map 29 (ref SZ 494773)

## St John's Commandery
Kent

The flint-walled 13th-century chapel and hall of a 'Commandery' of Knights Hospitallers, later converted into a farmhouse. It has a fine moulded-plaster ceiling and a remarkable timber roof.

### OPENING TIMES

Any reasonable time for exterior viewing. Internal viewing by appointment only; please call 01304 211067

### HOW TO FIND US

**Direction:** 2 miles NE of Densole, off A260

**Train:** Kearsney 4 miles

**Bus:** Stagecoach in East Kent 16/A Folkestone Central – Canterbury, to within 1 mile



**Tel:** 01553 631330

MAP Page 267 (5J)
OS Map 138 (ref TR 232440)

## St Leonard's Tower
Kent

An early and well-preserved example of a small free-standing Norman tower keep, surviving almost to its original height. It was probably built c. 1080 by Gundulf, Bishop of Rochester, and takes its name from a chapel of St Leonard which once stood nearby.

Managed by West Malling Parish Council.

### OPENING TIMES

Any reasonable time for exterior viewing. Internal viewing by appointment only; please call 01732 870872

### HOW TO FIND US

**Direction:** Nr West Malling, on unclassified road W of A228

**Train:** West Malling 1 mile

**Bus:** Arriva 70 from Maidstone, 151 from Chatham

Disabled access (grounds only).

MAP Page 267 (4G)
OS Map 148 (ref TQ 676571)

## Silchester Roman City Walls and Amphitheatre
Hampshire

Originally a tribal centre of the Iron Age Atrebates, Silchester became the large and important Roman town of Calleva Atrebatum. Unlike most Roman towns, it was never re-occupied or built over after its abandonment in the 5th century, so that archaeological investigations give an unusually complete picture of its development. The complete circuit of its 3rd-century walls, among the best-preserved Roman town defences in England and 1½ miles (2½ km) long, can still be traced, although none of the buildings within them survive above ground. Outside them are the remains of a Roman amphitheatre, which provided seating for over 4,500 spectators.

### OPENING TIMES
Any reasonable time

### HOW TO FIND US
**Direction:** On a minor road, 1 mile E of Silchester

**Train:** Bramley or Mortimer, both 2¾ miles

**Bus:** Reading Buses 143 from Reading to within ½ mile

**MAP Page 266 (4C)**
**OS Map 159 (ref SU 639624)**

## Southwick Priory
Hampshire

Scanty remains of a wealthy priory of Augustinian canons, transferred from Portchester: once a famous place of pilgrimage.

### OPENING TIMES
Any reasonable time

## Southwick Priory

**MAP Page 266 (6C)**
**OS Map 119 (ref SU 628084)**

## Sutton Valence Castle
Kent

The ruins of a small 12th-century Norman keep, with panoramic views over the Weald.

### OPENING TIMES
Any reasonable time

### HOW TO FIND US
**Direction:** 5 miles SE of Maidstone; in Sutton Valence village, on A274

**Train:** Headcorn 4 miles, Hollingbourne 5 miles

**Bus:** Arriva 12 Maidstone – Tenterden (passes Headcorn)

**MAP Page 267 (5G)**
**OS Map 137 (ref TQ 815491)**

## Temple Manor
Kent

Part of a manor house of the Knights Templar, built in about 1240, with a fine first floor hall displaying traces of wall paintings.

Managed by Medway Council.

### OPENING TIMES
31 Mar-31 Oct, Sat-Sun 11am-3pm

Closed 1 Nov-20 Mar

(For group visits please call 01634 402276)

### HOW TO FIND US
**Direction:** Located in Strood (Rochester), off A228

**Train:** Strood ¾ mile

**Bus:** From surrounding areas

Disabled access (grounds only).

**MAP Page 267 (4G)**
**OS Map 148/163 (ref TQ 733685)**

## Titchfield Abbey
Hampshire – PO15 5RA

The ruins of a 13th-century Premonstratensian abbey, part of its church converted into a grand turreted Tudor gatehouse.

### OPENING TIMES
| | |
|---|---|
| 6 Apr-30 Sep, daily | 10am-5pm |
| **Guided tours** | |
| Sat during Aug | 3pm |
| 1 Oct-20 Mar, daily | 10am-4pm |
| Closed | 24-26 Dec and 1 Jan |

### HOW TO FIND US
**Direction:** Located ½ mile N of Titchfield, off A27

**Train:** Fareham 2 miles

**Bus:** First 26 Fareham-Hedge End (passing Fareham)

**Tel:** 01424 775705

**MAP Page 266 (6C)**
**OS Map 119 (ref SU 542067)**

## Uffington Castle, White Horse and Dragon Hill
Oxfordshire

These atmospheric sites lie along the Ridgeway. Uffington 'Castle' is a large Iron Age hillfort, Dragon Hill a natural mound associated in legend with St George. The famous and enigmatic White Horse is the oldest chalk-cut hill figure in Britain, and may be more than 2,500 years old.

Owned and managed by The National Trust.

## Uffington Castle, White Horse and Dragon Hill

### OPENING TIMES

Any reasonable time

### HOW TO FIND US

**Direction:** S of B4507, 7 miles W of Wantage

MAP Page 266 (3B)
OS Map 170 (ref SU 301866)

## Upnor Castle
Kent – ME2 4XG

Set in tranquil grounds adjoining a riverside village, this rare example of an Elizabethan artillery fort was begun in 1559 and redeveloped in 1599-1601, to protect warships moored at Chatham dockyards. Despite a brave attempt it entirely failed to do so in 1667, when the Dutch sailed past it to burn or capture the English fleet at anchor.

Managed by Medway Council.

### NON-MEMBERS

| | |
|---|---|
| Adult | £4.50 |
| Concession | £3.50 |
| Child | £3.50 |
| Family | £12.50 |

## Upnor Castle

### OPENING TIMES

| | |
|---|---|
| 31 Mar-30 Sep, daily | 10am-6pm |
| 1-31 Oct, daily | 10am-4pm |
| Last admission 45 mins before closing | |
| Closed | 24-26 Dec and 1 Jan |

### HOW TO FIND US

**Direction:** At Upnor, on unclassified road off A228

**Train:** Strood 2 miles

**Bus:** ASD 197 from Chatham; otherwise Arriva/Nu-Venture 191-3 Chatham – Hoo, alight Wainscott, then 1 mile

**Tel:** 01634 718742 or 01634 338110 when castle is closed

Audio guide (small charge).

Disabled access (grounds only).

Dogs on leads (restricted areas only).

Parking (at a slight distance from castle – park before village).

MAP Page 267 (4G)
OS Map 163 (ref TQ 759706)

## Walmer Castle and Gardens
See feature – Page 80

## Waverley Abbey
Surrey

Fragments of the church and monastic buildings of the first Cistercian abbey in England, founded in 1128.

### OPENING TIMES

| | |
|---|---|
| 6 Apr-30 Sep, daily | 10am-5pm |
| **Guided tour** | |
| Sun during Aug | 10.30am |

## Waverley Abbey

### HOW TO FIND US

**Direction:** 2 miles SE of Farnham, off B3001; off Junction 10 of M25

**Train:** Farnham 2 miles

**Bus:** Stagecoach in Hants & Surrey 46 Guildford – Aldershot (passing Farnham)

Parking (limited).

MAP Page 266 (5D)
OS Map 145 (ref SU 868453)

## Wayland's Smithy
Oxfordshire

A fine and atmospheric Neolithic chambered long barrow 2km along the Ridgeway from the Uffington White Horse: it was once believed to be the habitation of the Saxon smith-god Wayland.

Managed by The National Trust.

### OPENING TIMES

Any reasonable time

### HOW TO FIND US

**Direction:** On the Ridgeway; ¾ mile NE of B4000, Ashbury – Lambourn Road

Parking (may be a charge).

MAP Page 266 (3B)
OS Map 170 (ref TQ 759706)

## Western Heights, Dover
Kent

A huge fortification begun during the Napoleonic Wars and completed in the 1860s, designed to protect Dover from French invasion. Only the moat can be visited.

Part of the White Cliffs Countryside Project.

## Western Heights, Dover

### OPENING TIMES
Any reasonable time

### HOW TO FIND US
**Direction:** Above Dover town on W side of harbour

**Train:** Dover Priory ¾ mile

**Tel:** 01304 211067

**MAP Page 267 (5J)**
**OS Map 138 (ref TR 312408)**

## Wolvesey Castle (Old Bishop's Palace)
Hampshire

Begun as a 12th-century Norman keep and bailey castle, the palace was the chief residence of the Bishops of Winchester. Situated next to Winchester Cathedral, its extensive ruins reflect their importance and wealth. The last great occasion at Wolvesey was on 25 July 1554, when Queen Mary and Philip of Spain held their wedding breakfast in the East Hall.

### OPENING TIMES

| | |
|---|---|
| 6 Apr-30 Sep, daily | 10am-5pm |
| **Guided tour** Sun during Aug | 2pm |

## Wolvesey Castle

### HOW TO FIND US
**Direction:** ¾ mile SE of Winchester Cathedral, next to the Bishop's Palace; access from College St

**Train:** Winchester ¾ mile

**Bus:** From surrounding areas

**Tel:** 02392 378291

**MAP Page 266 (5C)**
**OS Map 132 (ref SU 484291)**

## Yarmouth Castle
Isle of Wight – PO41 0PB

© Skyscan Balloon Photography

This last and most sophisticated addition to Henry VIII's coastal defences was completed after his death in 1547, with the first new-style 'arrowhead' artillery bastion built in England. Also a magnificent picnic spot, with views over the Solent.

Other artillery forts built by Henry VIII include Deal Castle, Hurst Castle and Pendennis Castle.

**NEW FOR 2007** New displays opening at Easter 2007 evoke Yarmouth's past, and tell the story of the 16th-century ship wrecked near the castle.

## Yarmouth Castle

### NON-MEMBERS

| | |
|---|---|
| Adult | £2.90 |
| Concession | £2.20 |
| Child | £1.50 |

### OPENING TIMES
1 Apr-30 Sep, Sun-Thu 11am-4pm

### HOW TO FIND US
**Direction:** In Yarmouth, adjacent to car ferry terminal

**Bus:** Southern Vectis 7 from Newport

**Ferry:** Wightlink – 0870 582 7744 (Lymington-Yarmouth)

**Tel:** 01983 760678

Disabled access (ground floor only).

Parking (coaches and cars 200 metres (220 yards) limited to 1 hour only).

**MAP Page 266 (7B)**
**OS Map 22/29 (ref SZ 354898)**

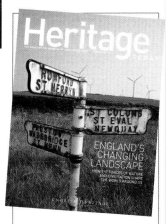

# Walmer Castle and Gardens Kent – CT14 7LJ

Originally built during the reign of Henry VIII as part of a chain of coastal artillery defences against Catholic attack from Europe, Walmer Castle has evolved over time into an elegant residence.

Aerial view of Walmer Castle and Queen Mother's Garden

The Dining Room

Walmer Castle became the official residence of the Lord Warden of the Cinque Ports in 1708. It is easy to imagine why the Duke of Wellington, who held the post of Lord Warden for 23 years, enjoyed his time here so much.

Wellington's spirit still lives on at Walmer Castle, where the armchair in which he died on 14 September 1852 can still be seen. His campaign bed also remains on display as a testament to his spartan tastes, along with a pair of original 'Wellington boots' and a great many personal effects in the fascinating on-site Wellington museum.

Successive Lords Warden have left their mark on Walmer Castle's buildings and gardens. Thus Lady Hester Stanhope used local militia to create new landscaping as a surprise for her uncle, Lord Warden William Pitt: while Lord Warden W.H. Smith – member of the famous stationer's family – saved many of the valuable furnishings now on display.

Wellington Boots

In recent years, Lords Warden have been provided with private apartments above the gatehouse, and both Sir Robert Menzies (former Australian Prime Minister) and Her Majesty Queen Elizabeth the Queen Mother made regular visits to the castle. Some of the rooms used by the Queen Mother are open to visitors, as is her magnificent garden, given to Her Majesty on her 95th birthday.

The beautiful gardens surrounding the house also include a commemorative lawn, woodland walk, croquet lawn and a working kitchen garden. The remainder of the grounds are mostly wildlife gardens, a great place to spot birds.

Home-made lunches and teas are available at the Lord Warden's Tearoom, and the well-stocked gift shop is well worth a visit. An audio tour is available and plants are on sale.

There is a pleasant cycle path along the beachfront between Deal and Walmer Castles.

Available for corporate and private hire.

Licensed for civil wedding ceremonies.

Holiday cottage available to let.

www.english-heritage.org.uk/walmercastle

## NON-MEMBERS

| | |
|---|---|
| Adult | £6.30 |
| Concession | £4.70 |
| Child | £3.20 |
| Family | £15.80 |

## OPENING TIMES

| | |
|---|---|
| 1 Apr-30 Sep, daily (closes at 4pm Sat) | 10am-6pm |
| 1-31 Oct, Wed-Sun | 10am-4pm |
| Closed | 1 Nov-29 Feb |
| 1-20 Mar, Wed-Sun | 10am-4pm |

Closed 13-14 Jul and to 1pm 15 Jul when Lord Warden in residence

## HOW TO FIND US

**Direction:** On coast S of Walmer, on A258; Junction 13 of M20 or from M2 to Deal

**Train:** Walmer 1 mile

**Bus:** From surrounding areas

**Tel:** 01304 364288

**Local Tourist Information:** Deal 01304 369576 and Dover 01304 205108

OVP

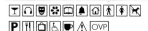

Audio tours (also in French, Dutch and German).

Disabled access (courtyard and garden only; parking available).

Parking (near approach to castle).

**MAP Page 267 (5J)**
**OS Map 138 (ref TR 378501)**

# Other historic attractions

Discounted entry to our members (discounts may not apply on event days)

## Anne of Cleves House
Lewes, East Sussex – BN7 1JA

This 15th-century timber framed Wealden hall-house was given to Anne as part of her divorce settlement from Henry VIII.

Managed by Sussex Past.

### ENTRY

| | |
|---|---|
| Adult | £3.50 |
| Concession | £3.00 |
| Child | £1.60 |
| Family (2+2) | £8.00 |
| Family (1+4) | £6.50 |

50% discount for EH members

### OPENING TIMES

| | |
|---|---|
| Mar-Oct, Tue-Sat | 10am-5pm |
| Sun, Mon & Bank Hols | 11am-5pm |
| Remainder of year, Tue-Sat | 10am-5pm |
| Closed | 24-26 Dec |

**Tel:** 01273 474610

www.sussexpast.co.uk

MAP Page 267 (6F)
OS Map 122 (ref TQ 411096)

## Dover Museum and Bronze Age Boat Gallery
Dover, Kent – CT16 1PB

This modern interactive museum tells the story of Dover's rich history, and displays the world's oldest prehistoric seagoing boat, discovered nearby.

Managed by Dover District Council.

### ENTRY

| | |
|---|---|
| Adult | £2.50 |
| Concession and Child | £1.50 |

50% discount for EH members

### OPENING TIMES

| | |
|---|---|
| Mon-Sat | 10am-5.30pm |
| Sun (Apr-Sep only) | 1pm-5pm |
| Closed | 25-26 Dec & 1 Jan |

**Tel:** 01304 201066

www.dovermuseum.co.uk

MAP Page 267 (5J)
OS Map 138 (ref TR 319414)

## Fishbourne Roman Palace
Chichester, West Sussex – PO19 3QR

In the first century AD, this Roman palace was probably the largest domestic building in Britain. Today, the remains of its north wing, with many fine mosaic floors, can be seen. Behind the scenes tours are available in the Collections Discovery Centre.

Managed by Sussex Past.

### ENTRY

| | |
|---|---|
| Adult | £6.80 |
| Concession | £5.80 |
| Child | £3.60 |
| Family (2+2) | £17.40 |

50% discount for EH members

### OPENING TIMES

| | |
|---|---|
| 1 Mar-31 Jul | 10am-5pm |
| 1-31 Aug | 10am-6pm |
| 1 Sep-31 Oct | 10am-5pm |
| 1 Nov-15 Dec | 10am-4pm |
| 16 Dec-21 Jan Sat-Sun | 10am-4pm |
| 25 Dec | Closed |
| 22 Jan-28 Feb | 10am-4pm |

**Tel:** 01243 785859

www.sussexpast.co.uk

MAP Page 266 (6D)
OS Map 120 (ref SU 839048)

## The Historic Dockyard
Chatham, Kent – ME4 4TZ

Discover over 400 years of maritime history as you explore the many galleries and attractions which are guaranteed to excite and entertain – whatever your age! See where HMS *Victory* was built and tread the well-worn cobbles – following the footsteps of Nelson. For centuries the Dockyard walls kept many closely guarded secrets safe. Visit The Historic Dockyard Chatham today and see them revealed.

Managed by Chatham Historic Dockyard Trust.

### ENTRY

Admission charges apply.
Please call for details.
20% reduction for EH members.
Ticket is valid for 12 months from date of first visit

### OPENING TIMES

| | |
|---|---|
| 10 Feb-28 Oct, daily | 10am-6pm |

Closes 6pm or dusk if earlier

Weekends only in November

**Tel:** 01634 823807

www.thedockyard.co.uk

MAP Page 267 (4G)
OS Map 163/148 (ref TQ 75969)

## Leeds Castle
Nr Maidstone, Kent – ME17 1PL

Listed in the Domesday Book, Leeds Castle has been a Norman stronghold, a royal residence for six of England's medieval queens and a palace of Henry VIII. The castle's attractions include a dog collar museum, aviary, maze and grotto, vineyard, toddlers' play area and seasonal falconry displays.

Managed by Leeds Castle Enterprises Ltd.

### ENTRY

| | |
|---|---|
| Adult | £14.00 |
| Concession | £11.00 |
| Child | £8.50 |

10% discount for EH members

### OPENING TIMES

Daily from 10am.
Please check website for up-to-date opening times and special ticketed events before you visit

**Tel:** 01622 765400

www.leeds-castle.com

MAP Page 267 (5G)
OS Map 137/148 (ref TQ 837533)

## Lewes Castle and Barbican House Museum
Lewes, East Sussex – BN7 1YE

This imposing Norman castle offers magnificent views across the town of Lewes and surrounding downland. The adjacent Barbican House Museum holds displays of

## Lewes Castle and Barbican House Museum

Sussex archaeology and the Lewes town model.

Managed by Sussex Past.

### ENTRY

| | |
|---|---|
| Adult | £4.70 |
| Concession | £4.20 |
| Child | £2.40 |
| Family (2+2) | £12.20 |
| Family (1+4) | £9.50 |

50% discount for EH members

### OPENING TIMES

Daily, except 24-26 Dec and Mondays in Jan

| | |
|---|---|
| Tue-Sat | 10am-5.30pm |
| Sun, Mon & Bank Hols | 11am-5.30pm |

Last admission ½ hour before closing

**Tel:** 01273 486290

www.sussexpast.co.uk

MAP Page 267 (6F)
OS Map 122/123 (ref TQ 413101)

## Marlipins Museum
Shoreham-By-Sea, West Sussex – BN43 5DA

A c. 12th-century building with a knapped flint and Caen stone chequer-work façade, containing a fully accessible museum with many exhibits of local interest.

Managed by Sussex Past.

### ENTRY

| | |
|---|---|
| Adult | £2.50 |
| Concession | £2.00 |
| Child | £1.50 |

50% discount for EH members

### OPENING TIMES

| | |
|---|---|
| 1 May-31 Oct, Tue-Sat | 10.30am-4.30pm |

**Tel:** 01273 462994/01323 441279

www.sussexpast.co.uk

MAP Page 266 (6E)
OS Map 122 (ref TQ 215050)

## Michelham Priory
Nr Hailsham, East Sussex – BN27 3QS

Explore the Tudor mansion that evolved from the former Augustinian Priory, set on a tranquil island encircled by England's longest water-filled medieval moat.

Managed by Sussex Past.

### ENTRY

| | |
|---|---|
| Adult | £6.00 |
| Concession | £5.00 |
| Child | £3.00 |
| Family (2+2) | £15.20 |

50% discount for EH members

### OPENING TIMES

1 Mar-31 Jul, Tue-Sun & Bank Hols 10.30am-4.30pm (5pm Apr-Jul)

| | |
|---|---|
| 1-31 Aug daily | 10.30am-5.30pm |
| 1-30 Sep Tue-Sun | 10.30am-5pm |
| 1-31 Oct Tue-Sun | 10.30am-4.30pm |

**Tel:** 01323 844224

www.sussexpast.co.uk

MAP Page 267 (6F)
OS Map 123 (ref TQ 559093)

## Penshurst Place and Gardens
Penshurst, Kent – TN11 8DG

### Penshurst Place and Gardens

Magnificent ancestral home of the Sidney family since 1552, set amidst tranquil Tudor gardens and parkland. Medieval Barons' Hall dating from 1341, and Staterooms containing a wonderful collection of furniture, tapestries, portraits, porcelain and armour. Venture playground, toy museum, woodland trail, garden tearoom and gift shop.

#### ENTRY

| | |
|---|---|
| **House & Grounds** | |
| Adult | £7.50 |
| Concession | £7.00 |
| Child | £5.00 |
| **Grounds only** | |
| Adult | £6.00 |
| Concession | £5.50 |
| Child | £4.50 |

EH members get free entry to the house when purchasing a grounds only ticket

Discount does not extend to EH Corporate Partners

#### OPENING TIMES

Please call or check website for details

**Tel:** 01892 870307

www.penshurstplace.com

MAP Page 267 (5F)
OS Map 147 (ref TQ 528440)

### The Priest House
West Hoathly, West Sussex – RH19 4PP

Standing in the beautiful surroundings of a traditional cottage garden on the edge of Ashdown Forest, The Priest House is an early 15th-century timber-framed hall-house with a dramatic roof of Horsham stone. Inside the house are many interesting exhibits, while outside is a delightful fragrant herb garden.

Managed by Sussex Past.

#### ENTRY

| | |
|---|---|
| Adult | £2.90 |
| Concession | £2.60 |
| Child | £1.45 |

50% discount for EH members

#### OPENING TIMES

| | |
|---|---|
| 1 Mar-31 Jul, Tue-Sat & Bank Hols | 10.30am-5.30pm |
| Sun | 12pm-5.30pm |
| 1-31 Aug, Mon-Sat | 10.30am-5.30pm |
| Sun | 12pm-5pm |
| 1 Sep-31 Oct, Tue-Sat | 10.30am-5.30pm |
| Sun | 12pm-5.30pm |

**Tel:** 01342 810479

www.sussexpast.co.uk

MAP Page 267 (5F)
OS Map 135 (ref TQ 362325)

### Royal Pavilion
Brighton, East Sussex – BN1 1EE

This Regency palace was the magnificent seaside residence of King George IV. The exterior, which was inspired by Indian architecture, contrasts with interiors decorated in Chinese taste.

Managed by Brighton and Hove City Council.

#### ENTRY

| | |
|---|---|
| Adult | £7.50 |
| Concession | £5.75 |
| Child (age 5-15) | £5.00 |

Prices subject to change. Adult EH members are entitled to £1 off adult admission

#### OPENING TIMES

| | |
|---|---|
| Apr-Sep, daily | 9.30am-5.45pm |
| Oct-Mar, daily | 10am-5.15pm |

Last admission 45 mins before closing

| | |
|---|---|
| Closed | 25-26 Dec (closes 24 Dec 2.30pm) |

**Tel:** 01273 290900

www.royalpavilion.org.uk

MAP Page 267 (6F)
OS Map 122 (ref TQ 313042)

### Rycote Chapel
Oxfordshire – OX9 2PE

This 15th-century chapel has original furniture, including exquisitely carved and painted woodwork.

Owned by Mr and Mrs Bernard Taylor and managed by the Rycote Buildings Charitable Foundation.

#### ENTRY

| | |
|---|---|
| Adult | £3.50 |
| Concession | £2.50 |
| Child | £1.50 |

Prices subject to change

## Rycote Chapel

### OPENING TIMES

1 Apr-30 Sep, Fri-Sun 2pm-6pm
Times may change at short notice – please ring for details

**Directions:** 3 miles SW of Thame off A329

**Bus:** Arriva 280 Oxford – Aylesbury (passes ⇌ Haddenham and Thame Parkway), to within ½ mile

**Train:** Haddenham and Thame Parkway 5 miles

**Tel:** 01844 210210/07742 925512

**MAP Page 266 (3C)**
**OS Map 180 (ref TQ 362325)**

## Weald and Downland Open Air Museum

Nr Chichester, West Sussex – PO18 0EU

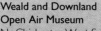

England's leading museum of historic buildings, set in 50 acres of beautiful Sussex countryside.

Managed by the Weald and Downland Open Air Museum.

### ENTRY

| | |
|---|---|
| Adult | £8.25 |
| Concession | £7.25 |
| Child | £4.40 |

50% discount for EH members

Discount does not extend to EH Corporate Partners

### OPENING TIMES

Open throughout the year. Please call or check website for details

Tel: 01243 811348

www.wealddown.co.uk

**MAP Page 266 (6D)**
**OS Map 120 (ref SU 874128)**

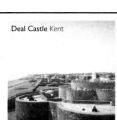

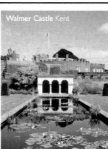

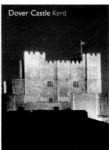

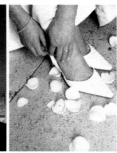

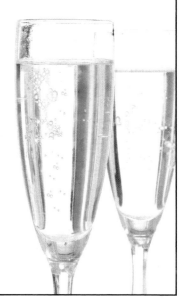

Stonehenge – see page 112

# South West

'More than in gardened Surrey, nature spills
A wealth of heather, kidney-vetch and squills
Over these long-defended Cornish hills

A gun-emplacement of the latest war
Looks older than the hill fort built before
Saxon or Norman headed for the shore.'

From *Cornish Cliffs*, by John Betjeman, 1966

# Properties
See individual listings for details

## Bristol & Bath
Sir Bevil Grenville's Monument
Stanton Drew Circles and Cove
Stoney Littleton Long Barrow
Temple Church

## Cornwall
Ballowall Barrow
Carn Euny Ancient Village
Chysauster Ancient Village
Dupath Well
Halliggye Fogou
Hurlers Stone Circles
King Doniert's Stone
Launceston Castle
Pendennis Castle
Penhallam Manor
Restormel Castle
St Breock Downs Monolith
St Catherine's Castle
St Mawes Castle
Tintagel Castle
Tregiffian Burial Chamber
Trethevy Quoit

## Devon
Bayard's Cove Fort
Berry Pomeroy Castle
Blackbury Camp
Dartmouth Castle
Grimspound
Hound Tor Deserted Medieval Village
Kirkham House
Lydford Castle and Saxon Town
Merrivale Prehistoric Settlement
Okehampton Castle
Royal Citadel (Plymouth)
Totnes Castle
Upper Plym Valley

## Dorset
Abbotsbury Abbey Remains
Christchurch Castle and Norman House
Fiddleford Manor
Jordan Hill Roman Temple
Kingston Russell Stone Circle
Knowlton Church and Earthworks
Maiden Castle
The Nine Stones
Portland Castle
St Catherine's Chapel
Sherborne Old Castle
Winterbourne Poor Lot Barrows

## Gloucestershire
Belas Knap Long Barrow
Blackfriars
Cirencester Amphitheatre
Great Witcombe Roman Villa
Greyfriars
Hailes Abbey
Kingswood Abbey Gatehouse
Notgrove Long Barrow
Nympsfield Long Barrow
Odda's Chapel
Offa's Dyke
Over Bridge
St Briavel's Castle
St Mary's Church
Uley Long Barrow (Hetty Pegler's Tump)
Windmill Tump Long Barrow

## Isles of Scilly
Bant's Carn Burial Chamber and Halangy Down Ancient Village
Cromwell's Castle
Garrison Walls
Harry's Walls
Innisidgen Lower and Upper Burial Chambers
King Charles's Castle
Old Blockhouse
Porth Hellick Down Burial Chamber

## Somerset
Butter Cross
Cleeve Abbey
Farleigh Hungerford Castle
Gallox Bridge
Glastonbury Tribunal
Meare Fish House
Muchelney Abbey
Nunney Castle
Yarn Market

## Wiltshire
Alexander Keiller Museum
Avebury
Avebury Stone Circles
Bradford-on-Avon Tithe Barn
Bratton Camp and White Horse
Chisbury Chapel
Hatfield Earthworks
Ludgershall Castle and Cross
Netheravon Dovecote
Old Sarum
Old Wardour Castle
The Sanctuary
Silbury Hill
Stonehenge
West Kennet Avenue
West Kennet Long Barrow
Windmill Hill
Woodhenge

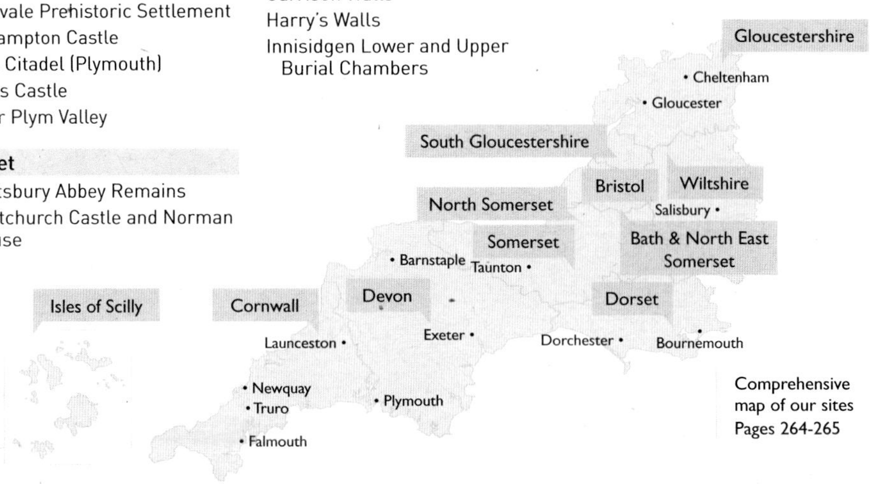


Comprehensive map of our sites Pages 264-265

Above: (left) Farleigh Hungerford Castle, (top) Stonehenge, (bottom left to right) Tintagel Castle, Dartmouth Castle and Pendennis Castle.



# Famous Sites, Mythical Delights

Extending from the Cotswolds, through Gloucestershire, Wiltshire, Somerset , Dorset and Devon to Land's End and the Isles of Scilly, the South West is one of English Heritage's largest regions, including more individual sites than any other. Among this rich variety of places to visit are many deservedly renowned 'stars': but also a wealth of quieter, lesser-known delights, well worth seeking out.

Oldest as well as most internationally famous of all are the great prehistoric monuments of **Stonehenge** and **Avebury**, a World Heritage Site. But the South West's unrivalled collection of prehistoric sites also range from **Stanton Drew Circles** – the third largest assembly of prehistoric standing stones in England, to remoter, atmospheric monuments like Cornwall's **Balowall Barrow** or **Trethevy Quoit**. Here too are mighty Iron Age hillforts like **Maiden Castle**: but also **Blackbury Camp**, now almost hidden by woodland.

For lovers of romantic and picturesquely-sited castles, it would be hard to match **Tintagel Castle** or **Berry Pomeroy Castle**: but the region is also notable for its trio of distinctive round keeps, at **Launceston**, **Restormel** and **Totnes Castles**. Among later coastal 'artillery fortresses', **Dartmouth**, **Pendennis**, **Portland** and **St Mawes Castles** are outstanding, easily accessible and much visited. The smaller **St Catherine's Castle** near Fowey and **Cromwell's Castle** in the Scillies, by contrast, reward explorers who reach them via winding scenic footpaths. **Cleeve**, **Hailes** and **Muchelney Abbeys** are all major monastic sites, each with its own special attractions and especially well-preserved features. Lesser-known Christian – or at least nominally Christian – sites include charming **Dupath Well** and rather eerie **Knowlton Church and Earthworks**, a ruined church within a prehistoric 'henge'.

The South West is outstanding, too, for the medieval and later wall paintings in its English Heritage sites. A 'themed tour' of these might include **Cleeve Abbey** and the parish churches near **Muchelney** and **Hailes Abbeys**; **Farleigh Hungerford Castle's** remarkable painted chapel and **Berry Pomeroy Castle**'s gatehouse; and undoubtedly **St Mary's Church, Kempley**, with one of the most complete and well-preserved sets of medieval wall-paintings in all England.

Everyone will have (or develop) favourites among these minor as well as major delights of the South West. Exploring as many of them as possible, with the aid of this handbook and English Heritage's three *Heritage Unlocked* booklets for the region, is the best way to find out which is yours.

# Avebury Wiltshire

© www.britainonview.com

Avebury rivals – some would say exceeds – Stonehenge as the largest, most impressive and complex prehistoric site in Britain. Built and altered over many centuries from about 2850 BC to 2200 BC, it now appears as a huge circular bank and ditch, enclosing an area of 28½ acres (11½ hectares), including part of Avebury village. Within this 'henge' ditch is an inner circle of great standing stones, enclosing two more stone circles, each with a central feature.

The site's present appearance owes much to the marmalade-heir Alexander Keiller, who excavated and re-erected many stones during the 1930s, and whose archaeological collections are displayed in the nearby museum. Associated with pagan devil-worship, many stones had been broken or buried in medieval and later times, one crushing its destroyer as it fell.

Avebury is part of a wider Neolithic landscape, with many other ritual sites in English Heritage care. West Kennet Avenue (p.116) joined it to The Sanctuary (p.111), and another stone avenue connected it with Beckhampton. West Kennet Long Barrow (p.116) and Windmill Hill (p.117) are also nearby, as is the huge and mysterious Silbury Hill (p.111). This extraordinary assemblage of sites seemingly formed a huge 'sacred landscape', whose use and purpose can still only be guessed at. Avebury and its surroundings have, with Stonehenge, achieved international recognition as a World Heritage Site.

Avebury Stone Circle, West Kennet Avenue and Long Barrow, The Sanctuary and Windmill Hill are managed by The National Trust on behalf of English Heritage.

### OPENING TIMES

Any reasonable time

Usual facilities may not be available around the Summer Solstice 20-22 June. Please check before you visit

### HOW TO FIND US

See Alexander Keiller Museum

Parking (Visitor car park free to EH members. S of Avebury off A4361. Free disabled visitors' parking in village car park).

MAP Page 265 (3J)
OS Map 157 (ref SU 099700)

## Avebury, Alexander Keiller Museum

Wiltshire – SN8 1RF

One of the most important prehistoric archaeological collections in Britain.
The admission fee includes access to both the Stables and Barn Galleries. The Barn Gallery contains an interactive display and CD-ROMs which tell the story of this awe-inspiring landscape and the people associated with it over the last 6,000 years.

Museum managed by The National Trust.

### NON-MEMBERS

| | |
|---|---|
| Adult | £4.20 |
| Child | £2.10 |
| Family (2+2) | £10.50 |
| Family (1+3) | £7.50 |

Reduced rate when arriving by cycle or public transport

### OPENING TIMES

| | |
|---|---|
| 1 Apr-31 Oct | 10am-6pm |
| 1 Nov-20 Mar | 10am-4pm |
| Closed | 24-25 Dec |

Closes at dusk if earlier

### HOW TO FIND US

**Direction:** In Avebury, 7 miles W of Marlborough

**Train:** Pewsey 10 miles; Swindon 11 miles

**Bus:** Stagecoach in Swindon/ First 49 Swindon – Trowbridge; Wilts & Dorset 5/6 Salisbury – Swindon (all services pass close to Swindon)

E

Parking £5 (redeemable against museum entry).

MAP Page 265 (3J)
OS Map 157 (ref SU 099700)

## Abbotsbury Abbey Remains
Dorset

Part of a monastic building, perhaps the abbot's lodging, of Benedictine Abbotsbury Abbey. St Catherine's Chapel is within half a mile.

### OPENING TIMES
Any reasonable time

### HOW TO FIND US
**Direction:** Located in Abbotsbury, off B3157, near the churchyard

**Train:** Upwey 7½ miles

**Bus:** First X53 Poole – Exeter (passes close to Weymouth)

Parking (charged).

MAP Page 265 (5H)
OS Map 15 (ref SY 578852)

## Abbotsbury, St Catherine's Chapel
Dorset

Set high on a hilltop overlooking Abbotsbury Abbey, this sturdily buttressed and barrel-vaulted 14th-century chapel was built by the monks as a place of pilgrimage and retreat.

### OPENING TIMES
Any reasonable time

### HOW TO FIND US
**Direction:** ½ mile S of Abbotsbury; by path from village, off B3157. Path leads off signposted lane to Swannery

**Train:** Upwey 7 miles

**Bus:** First X53 Poole – Exeter

MAP Page 265 (5H)
OS Map 15 (ref SY 573848)

## Bayard's Cove Fort:
see Dartmouth, Bayard's Cove Fort – Page 94

## Ballowall Barrow
Cornwall

In a spectacular cliff-edge position, this large Bronze Age chambered tomb had a long and complex history as a sacred site. Seen as excavated by the Victorians.

Managed by The National Trust.

### OPENING TIMES
Any reasonable time

### HOW TO FIND US
**Direction:** 1 mile W of St Just, near Carn Gloose

**Train:** Penzance 8 miles

**Bus:** First 17/A Penzance – St Just, then 1 mile

MAP Page 264 (7A)
OS Map 102 (ref SW 355312)

## Belas Knap Long Barrow
Gloucestershire

A particularly fine example of a Neolithic long barrow of c. 3000 BC, with the mound restored and surrounded by a stone wall. The tomb chambers, where the remains of 31 Stone Age people were found, have been opened up for visitors to view.

Managed by Gloucestershire County Council.

### OPENING TIMES
Any reasonable time

### HOW TO FIND US
**Direction:** Near Charlton Abbots; ½ mile on Cotswold Way

**Train:** Cheltenham 9 miles

**Bus:** Castleways from Cheltenham, to within 1¾ miles of site

MAP Page 265 (1J)
OS Map 45 (ref SP 021254)

## Berry Pomeroy Castle
Devon – TQ9 6NJ

Tucked away in a steep wooded valley, Berry Pomeroy Castle is the perfect romantic ruin. Within the 15th-century defences of the Pomeroy family castle, still displaying a wall painting of the Three Kings in its gatehouse chamber, looms the dramatic ruined shell of its successor, the great Elizabethan mansion of the Seymours. Begun in c.1560 and ambitiously enlarged from c.1600, their mansion was intended to become the most spectacular house in Devon, a match for Longleat and Audley End.Never completed, and abandoned by 1700, it became the focus of spooky ghost stories, recounted in the audio tour. Woodland walks from the car park (including steep tracks) provide fine views of the ruins from below.

New ticket office and shop for 2007.

### NON-MEMBERS

| | |
|---|---|
| Adult | £3.80 |
| Concession | £2.90 |
| Child | £1.90 |

### OPENING TIMES

| | |
|---|---|
| 1 Apr-30 Jun, daily | 10am-5pm |
| 1 Jul-31 Aug, daily | 10am-6pm |
| 1-30 Sep, daily | 10am-5pm |
| 1-31 Oct, daily | 10am-4pm |
| Closed | 1 Nov-20 Mar |

## Berry Pomeroy Castle

### HOW TO FIND US

**Direction:** 2½ miles E of Totnes off A385

**Train:** Totnes 3½ miles

**Bus:** Stagecoach in Devon 111 Torquay – Dartmouth (passes Totnes)

**Tel:** 01803 866618

OVP

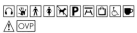

Disabled access (grounds and ground floor only).

Parking (no coach access), at end of long drive (approx ¾ mile).

Tearoom (not managed by EH).

MAP Page 265 (6F)
OS Map 20/110 (ref SX 839623)



## Blackbury Camp
Devon

An Iron Age hillfort with impressive ramparts, now surrounded by woodland.

### OPENING TIMES

Any reasonable time

### HOW TO FIND US

**Direction:** Off B3174/A3052

**Train:** Honiton 6½ miles

MAP Page 265 (5G)
OS Map 115 (ref ST 823604)

## Blackfriars, Gloucester:
see Gloucester, Blackfriars – Page 97

## Bradford-on-Avon Tithe Barn
Wiltshire

## Bradford-on-Avon Tithe Barn

A spectacular 14th-century monastic stone barn, 51 metres (168 ft) long, with an amazing timber-cruck roof.

### OPENING TIMES

| | |
|---|---|
| Daily | 10.30am-4pm |
| Closed | 25 Dec |

### HOW TO FIND US

**Direction:** Located ½ mile S of town centre off B3109

**Train:** Bradford-on-Avon ¼ mile

**Bus:** First/Wilts & Dorset X4/5 Bath – Salisbury

Parking (adjacent, not managed by EH – charge applies).

MAP Page 265 (3H)
OS Map 156 (ref ST 823604)

## Bratton Camp and White Horse
Wiltshire

Below an Iron Age hillfort, enclosing a much earlier long barrow, stands the Westbury White Horse. Cut into the hillside in 1778, this replaced an older horse, possibly commemorating King Alfred's nearby victory over the Vikings.

### OPENING TIMES

Any reasonable time

### HOW TO FIND US

**Direction:** 2 miles E of Westbury off B3098, 1 mile SW of Bratton

**Train:** Westbury 3 miles

**Bus:** First 87/8 Trowbridge – Devizes (passes Westbury)

MAP Page 265 (3J)
OS Map 143 (ref ST 823604)

## Butter Cross, Dunster:
see Dunster, Butter Cross – Page 94

## Carn Euny Ancient Village
Cornwall

Among the best preserved ancient villages in the South-West, occupied from Iron Age until late Roman times. It includes the foundations of stone houses, and an intriguing 'fogou' underground passage.

Managed by the Cornwall Heritage Trust.

### OPENING TIMES

Any reasonable time

### HOW TO FIND US

**Direction:** 1¼ miles SW of Sancreed off A30

**Train:** Penzance 6 miles

**Bus:** First 17/A Penzance – St Just, to within 2 miles of the site

Parking (600 metres (660 yards) away in Brane).

MAP Page 264 (7A)
OS Map 102 (ref SW 402288)

## Chisbury Chapel
Wiltshire

A pretty thatched and flint-walled 13th-century chapel, later used as a barn.

### OPENING TIMES

Any reasonable time

### HOW TO FIND US

**Direction:** Off unclassified road, ¼ mile E of Chisbury, off A4; 6 miles E of Marlborough

**Train:** Bedwyn 1 mile

MAP Page 265 (3K)
OS Map 157 (ref SU 280660)

## Christchurch Castle and Norman House
Dorset

The remains of Christchurch Castle include parts of the mound-top keep, and more

Christchurch Castle and Norman House

unusually the 12th-century riverside chamber block or 'Constable's House'. This very early example of domestic architecture includes a rare Norman chimney.

### OPENING TIMES

Any reasonable time

### HOW TO FIND US

**Direction:** Located in Christchurch, near the Priory

**Train:** Christchurch ¾ mile

**Bus:** From surrounding areas

**MAP Page 265 (5K)**
**OS Map 22 (ref SZ 160927)**

## Chysauster Ancient Village
Cornwall – TR20 8XA

This Iron Age settlement was originally occupied almost 2,000 years ago. The village consisted of eight stone-walled homesteads known as 'courtyard houses', found only on the Land's End peninsula and the Isles of Scilly. The houses line a 'village street', and each had an open central courtyard surrounded by a number of thatched rooms. There are also the remains of an enigmatic 'fogou' underground passage.

### NON-MEMBERS

| | |
|---|---|
| Adult | £2.40 |
| Concession | £1.80 |
| Child | £1.20 |

Chysauster Ancient Village

### OPENING TIMES

| | |
|---|---|
| 1 Apr-30 Jun, daily | 10am-5pm |
| 1 Jul-31 Aug, daily | 10am-6pm |
| 1-30 Sep, daily | 10am-5pm |
| 1-31 Oct, daily | 10am-4pm |
| Closed | 1 Nov-20 Mar |

### HOW TO FIND US

**Direction:** Located 2½ miles NW of Gulval, off B3311

**Train:** Penzance 3½ miles

**Bus:** First 16 Penzance – St Ives, to within 1½ miles

**Tel:** 07831 757934

P OVP

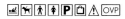

**MAP Page 264 (7B)**
**OS Map 102 (ref SW 472350)**

## Cirencester Amphitheatre
Gloucestershire

The earthwork remains of one of the largest Roman amphitheatres in Britain, built in the early 2nd century. It served the Roman city of Corinium (now Cirencester), then second only in size and importance to London, and had a capacity of around 8,000 spectators. Later fortified against Saxon invaders.

### OPENING TIMES

Any reasonable time

### HOW TO FIND US

**Direction:** Located W of Cirencester, next to the bypass. Access from the town, or along Chesterton Lane from the W end of the bypass, on to Cotswold Ave

**Train:** Kemble 4 miles

**Bus:** Stagecoach in the Cotswolds 881, Pulham's 855 from Kemble; Pulham's 855 from Moreton-in-Marsh

**MAP Page 265 (2J)**
**OS Map 45/169 (ref SP 020014)**

## Cleeve Abbey
Somerset – TA23 0PS

The picturesque Cistercian abbey of Cleeve boasts the most impressively complete and unaltered set of monastic cloister buildings in England, standing roofed and two storeys high. They include the gatehouse, the 15th-century refectory with its glorious angel roof, an unusual 'painted chamber', and the floor of an earlier refectory, decked from end to end with 13th-century heraldic tiles, the protection of which is the subject of an ongoing high profile project. The great dormitory is one of the finest examples in the country. Beneath it are the newly vaulted warming room, and the sacristy with more early 13th-century tilework and decoration.

The exhibition 'Our Painted Past' illustrates wall-paintings from around the country.

**NEW FOR 2007** From summer 2007, new information and displays guide you around the abbey and illustrate daily monastic life.

www.english-heritage.org.uk/cleeve

### NON-MEMBERS

| | |
|---|---|
| Adult | £3.50 |
| Concession | £2.60 |
| Child | £1.80 |

### OPENING TIMES

| | |
|---|---|
| 1 Apr-30 Jun, daily | 10am-5pm |
| 1 Jul-31 Aug, daily | 10am-6pm |
| 1-30 Sep, daily | 10am-5pm |
| 1-31 Oct, daily | 10am-4pm |
| Closed | 1 Nov-20 Mar |

## Cleeve Abbey

### HOW TO FIND US

**Direction:** Located in Washford, ¼ mile S of A39

**Train:** Washford ½ mile (West Somerset Railway)

**Bus:** First 28 Taunton – Minehead; 38 from Minehead

**Tel:** 01984 640377

E P OVP

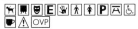

Disabled access (grounds and ground floor only, plus toilet).

Dogs on leads (in grounds only).

MAP Page 265 (4F)
OS Map 9 (ref ST 047407)



## Dartmouth Castle

See feature opposite

## Dartmouth, Bayard's Cove Fort
Devon

A small early Tudor artillery fort, built to defend Dartmouth harbour entrance.

### OPENING TIMES

Any reasonable time

### HOW TO FIND US

**Direction:** Located in Dartmouth, on the riverside

**Train:** Paignton, 7 miles; Kingswear (Paignton and Dartmouth Railway) few minutes walk, both by ferry

**Bus:** Stagecoach in Devon 120 Paignton – Kingswear, then ferry to Dartmouth; 111 Torquay – Dartmouth

MAP Page 265 (6F)
OS Map 20 (ref SX 879509)

## Dunster, Butter Cross
Somerset

The transplanted stump of a medieval stone cross, once a meeting-place for butter-sellers.

Managed by The National Trust.

### OPENING TIMES

Any reasonable time

### HOW TO FIND US

**Direction:** Beside minor road to Alcombe, 350 metres (400 yards) NW of Dunster parish church

**Train:** Dunster (West Somerset Railway) 1 mile

**Bus:** First 28 Taunton – Minehead; 38 from Minehead to within ½ mile

MAP Page 265 (4F)
OS Map 9 (ref ST 823604)

## Dunster, Gallox Bridge
Somerset

This ancient stone bridge – originally 'gallows bridge'– once carried packhorses bringing fleeces to Dunster market.

Managed by The National Trust.

### OPENING TIMES

Any reasonable time

### HOW TO FIND US

**Direction:** Located off A396 at the S end of Dunster village

**Train:** Dunster ¾ mile (West Somerset Railway)

**Bus:** First 28 Taunton – Minehead, also 38 from Minehead, to within ¼ mile of site

MAP Page 265 (4F)
OS Map 9 (ref SS 989432)

## Dunster, Yarn Market
Somerset

This fine 17th-century timber-framed octagonal market hall is a monument to Dunster's once-flourishing cloth trade.

Managed by The National Trust.

### OPENING TIMES

Any reasonable time

### HOW TO FIND US

**Direction:** In Dunster High St

**Train:** Dunster (West Somerset Railway) ½ mile

**Bus:** First 28 Taunton – Minehead, to within ¼ mile; 38 from Minehead

MAP Page 265 (4F)
OS Map 9 (ref SS 989432)

## Dupath Well
Cornwall

This charming well-house of c. 1500 stands over an ancient spring, believed to cure whooping cough. Built by the Augustinian canons of nearby St Germans priory, it houses the remains of an immersion bath for cure-seekers.

Managed by the Cornwall Heritage Trust.

### OPENING TIMES

Any reasonable time

### HOW TO FIND US

**Direction:** 1 mile E of Callington off A388

**Train:** Gunnislake 4½ miles

**Bus:** First 76 Plymouth – Launceston, then 1 mile

MAP Page 264 (6D)
OS Map 201 (ref SX 375692)

# Dartmouth Castle Devon – TQ6 0JN

This well-preserved and beautifully sited castle juts out into the narrow entrance of the Dart estuary.

Begun in the late 14th century, a defence called 'the Fortalice' was intended to protect the homes of Dartmouth merchants from shipborne attack. By 1491 it had been reinforced by a gun tower, probably the very first fortification in England purpose-built to mount heavy cannon.

It is said that Chaucer based the 'Shipman' character in his *Canterbury Tales* on John Hawley – the colourful merchant and Mayor of Dartmouth who began the first castle. Today, you can enjoy other tales of the castle as you journey through time from the Tudor period and the Civil War to World War II. Displays on the castle's 600-year history add to the experience.

Why not make it a full day out and take a boat trip from the quayside at Dartmouth, which lands you just a short walk from the castle entrance.

**www.english-heritage.org.uk/dartmouthcastle**

## NON-MEMBERS

| | |
|---|---|
| Adult | £3.90 |
| Concession | £2.90 |
| Child | £2.00 |

## OPENING TIMES

| | |
|---|---|
| 1 Apr-30 Jun, daily | 10am-5pm |
| 1 Jul-31 Aug, daily | 10am-6pm |
| 1-30 Sep, daily | 10am-5pm |
| 1-31 Oct, daily | 10am-4pm |
| 1 Nov-20 Mar, Sat-Sun | 10am-4pm |
| Closed | 24-26 Dec and 1 Jan |

## HOW TO FIND US

**Direction:** 1 mile SE of Dartmouth off B3205, narrow approach road

**Train:** Paignton 8 miles via ferry

**Bus:** Stagecoach in Devon 120 Paignton – Kingswear, then a ferry to Dartmouth; Stagecoach in Devon 111 Torquay – Dartmouth (passing ⇌ Totnes). On both, alight Dartmouth, then 1 mile walk or ferry to site

**Tel:** 01803 833588

**Local Tourist Information**
Dartmouth: 01803 834224

OVP

Parking (not owned by EH, small charge).

Tearooms (not managed by EH).

Toilets (not managed by EH).

MAP Page 265 (6F)
OS Map 20 (ref SX 887503)

## Farleigh Hungerford Castle
Somerset – BA2 7RS

Farleigh Hungerford was begun in the 1370s by Sir Thomas Hungerford, Speaker of the Commons, and extended in the 15th century by his son Walter, Lord Hungerford, Agincourt veteran and distinguished medieval statesman. The remains of their fortress, built in the most up-to-date and fashionable quadrangular style of the time, includes two tall corner towers, along with a walled outer court incorporating a complete castle Chapel and attendant Priest's House.

Crowded with fine family monuments and bedecked with wall-paintings, the chapel stands above a crypt where the lead coffins of 16th and 17th-century Hungerfords are still visible. These have 'death masks' of the deceased indented into them, and are probably the best examples of their type in Britain. The colourful Hungerford family included two members executed during the Wars of the Roses and another – who imprisoned his wife here for four years – beheaded for alleged treason and witchcraft by Henry VIII. One Lady Hungerford was hanged for murdering her first husband and burning his body in the castle's kitchen oven, another was

Farleigh Hungerford Castle

charged with adultery and attempted poisoning.

The chequered history of Farleigh and its owners is told in interpretation panels, extensive displays in the Priest's House, and an audio tour. Much improved facilities for disabled visitors include a touch-screen virtual tour, while family and educational facilities include a 'book box', a schools base and examples of historic costumes.

**www.english-heritage.org.uk/farleighhungerford**

### NON-MEMBERS

| | |
|---|---|
| Adult | £3.50 |
| Concession | £2.60 |
| Child | £1.80 |

### OPENING TIMES

| | |
|---|---|
| 1 Apr-30 Jun, daily | 10am-5pm |
| 1 Jul-31 Aug, daily | 10am-6pm |
| 1-30 Sep, daily | 10am-5pm |
| 1-31 Oct, daily | 10am-4pm |
| 1 Nov-20 Mar, Sat & Sun | 10am-4pm |
| Closed | 24-26 Dec & 1 Jan |

### HOW TO FIND US

**Direction:** In Farleigh Hungerford, 9 miles SE of Bath; 3½ miles W of Trowbridge on A366

**Train:** Avoncliffe 2 miles; Trowbridge 3½ miles

**Bus:** Bodmans 96 from Trowbridge (passes close to Trowbridge) then 1½ mile

**Tel:** 01225 754026

Disabled access (Chapel and Priest's House, ground floor only. Disabled toilet).

MAP Page 265 (3H)
OS Map 143/156 (ref ST 801576)

## Fiddleford Manor
Dorset

The principal parts of a small stone manor house, probably begun c. 1370 for William Latimer, Sheriff of Somerset and Dorset. The hall and solar chamber display outstandingly fine timber roofs.

**Please note:** The adjoining building is a private residence and is not open to visitors.

### OPENING TIMES

| | |
|---|---|
| 1 Apr-30 Sep, daily | 10am-6pm |
| 1 Oct-31 Mar, daily | 10am-4pm |
| Closed | 24-26 Dec and 1 Jan |

### HOW TO FIND US

**Direction:** 1 mile E of Sturminster Newton off A357

**Bus:** Damory 310 from Blandford

Disabled access (ground floor only – with 1 step).

Parking (no coach access).

MAP Page 265 (4H)
OS Map 129 (ref ST 801136)

## Gallox Bridge, Dunster
See Dunster, Gallox Bridge – Page 94

## Glastonbury Tribunal
Somerset – BA6 9DP

A fine late 15th-century stone town house, with an early Tudor façade and panelled interiors. Now contains a Tourist Information Centre and the Glastonbury Lake Village Museum.

Managed by Glastonbury Tribunal Ltd.

### NON-MEMBERS

**Museum:**

| | |
|---|---|
| Adult | £2.00 |
| Concession | £1.50 |
| Senior | £1.00 |
| Child | £1.50 |

## Glastonbury Tribunal

### OPENING TIMES

| | |
|---|---|
| 1 Apr-30 Sep, Sun-Thu | 10am-5pm |
| Fri-Sat | 10am-5.30pm |
| 1 Oct-20 Mar, Sun-Thu | 10am-4pm |
| Fri-Sat | 10am-4.30pm |
| Closed | 25-26 Dec and 1 Jan |

### HOW TO FIND US

**Direction:** In Glastonbury High St

**Bus:** First 375/6 ⇌ Bristol Temple Meads – Street

**Tel:** 01458 832954

Disabled access (ground floor – 2 steps).

Parking (charged).

MAP Page 265 (4H)
OS Map 141 (ref ST 499389)

## Gloucester, Blackfriars
Gloucestershire

One of the most complete surviving friaries of Dominican 'black friars' in England, later converted into a Tudor house and cloth factory. Notable features include the church and the fine scissor-braced dormitory roof.

### ENTRY

| | |
|---|---|
| Non-Member | £3.50 |
| EH Members and Children | £3.00 |
| Heritage Open Days, 8-9 Sep | Free |

### OPENING TIMES

Access by guided tour only

| | |
|---|---|
| Jul-Aug, Sun | 3pm |
| Heritage Open Days, 8-9 Sep | 12.30pm & 3pm |

### HOW TO FIND US

**Direction:** In Blackfriars Lane, off Ladybellegate St, off Southgate St, Gloucester

**Train:** Gloucester ½ mile

**Bus:** From surrounding areas

Parking (adjacent. Charge applies, not managed by EH).

MAP Page 265 (2J)
OS Map 179 (ref SO 830186)

## Gloucester, Greyfriars
Gloucestershire

Substantial remains of an early Tudor friary church of Franciscan 'grey friars'.

### OPENING TIMES

Any reasonable time

### HOW TO FIND US

**Direction:** On Greyfriars Walk

**Train:** Gloucester ½ mile

**Bus:** From surrounding areas

MAP Page 265 (2J)
OS Map 179 (ref SO 832184)

## Great Witcombe Roman Villa
Gloucestershire

The remains of a large and luxurious villa built c. AD 250, with a bathhouse complex and possibly the shrine of a water spirit.

### OPENING TIMES

**Exterior:** Reasonable daylight hours

### HOW TO FIND US

**Direction:** Located 5 miles SE of Gloucester off A46; ½ mile S of reservoir in Witcombe Park; 400 metres (440 yards) from Cotswold Way National Trail

**Train:** Gloucester 6 miles

**Bus:** Stagecoach in Gloucester 10 from ⇌ Gloucester, to within 1½ miles of site

Parking (no access for coaches. No parking permitted in the lane to or beyond the car park).

MAP Page 265 (2J)
OS Map 179 (ref SO 899142)

## Greyfriars, Gloucester:
see Gloucester, Greyfriars – See above

## Grimspound
Devon

The best known of many Dartmoor prehistoric settlements, Grimspound dates from the late Bronze Age. The remains of 24 stone houses survive within a massive boundary wall.

Managed by Dartmoor National Park Authority.

### OPENING TIMES

Any reasonable time

### HOW TO FIND US

**Direction:** 6 miles SW of Moretonhampstead, off B3212

**Bus:** Stagecoach in Devon 82 ⇌ Exeter St David's – Plymouth, to within 2 miles of the site

MAP Page 264 (5E)
OS Map 28 (ref SX 701809)

## Hailes Abbey
Gloucestershire – GL54 5PB

The Cistercian abbey of Hailes was founded in 1246 by Richard of Cornwall, in thanksgiving for deliverance from shipwreck, and dissolved on Christmas Eve 1539. Though never housing large numbers of monks, it had

## Hailes Abbey

extensive and elaborate buildings, financed by pilgrims visiting its renowned relic, 'the Holy Blood of Hailes' – allegedly a phial of Christ's own blood. Sculptures, stonework and other site finds are displayed in the museum. An audio tour helps you to learn even more about the site. The adjacent parish church has medieval wall-paintings. Plant sales are available throughout the season.

**www.english-heritage.org.uk/hailes**



Owned by The National Trust, managed and maintained by English Heritage.

### NON-MEMBERS

| | |
|---|---|
| Adult | £3.40 |
| Concession | £2.60 |
| Child | £1.70 |

National Trust members admitted free, but charge for audio tours (£1) and special events

### OPENING TIMES

| | |
|---|---|
| 1 Apr-30 Jun, daily | 10am-5pm |
| 1 Jul-31 Aug, daily | 10am-6pm |
| 1-30 Sep, daily | 10am-5pm |
| 1-31 Oct, daily | 10am-4pm |
| Closed | 1 Nov-20 Mar |

### HOW TO FIND US

**Direction:** 2 miles NE of Winchcombe off B4632. On the Cotswold Way National Trail

**Train:** Cheltenham 10 miles

**Bus:** Castleways from Cheltenham, to within 1½ miles of site

**Tel:** 01242 602398

OVP

Audio tours (also for visually impaired).

Disabled access (ramp to museum, disabled toilet).

MAP Page 265 (1J)
OS Map 45 (ref SP 050300)

## Halliggye Fogou
Cornwall

Roofed and walled in stone, this complex of passages is the largest and best-preserved of several mysterious underground tunnels associated with Cornish Iron Age settlements. The purpose of such 'fogous' – a Cornish-language word meaning 'cave' – is unknown. Refuges, storage chambers or ritual shrines have all been suggested.

Free entry to the fogou. Entry to the rest of the Trelowarren Estate is charged.

Managed by the Trelowarren Estate.

### OPENING TIMES

Reasonable daylight hours Apr-Oct, but completely blocked Nov-Mar, inclusive. May close early Oct

### HOW TO FIND US

**Direction:** 5 miles SE of Helston off B3293. E of Garras on Trelowarren Estate

**Train:** Penryn 10 miles

**Bus:** Truronian T2/3 from Truro

Parking (free to members).

Visitors are advised to bring a torch.

MAP Page 264 (7B)
OS Map 103 (ref SW 713239)

## Hatfield Earthworks
Wiltshire

The earthworks of a Neolithic henge and monumental mound, by a loop in the River Avon.

### OPENING TIMES

Any reasonable time

### HOW TO FIND US

**Direction:** 5½ miles SE of Devizes, off A342; NE of village of Marden

**Train:** Pewsey 5 miles

MAP Page 265 (3J)
OS Map 130 (ref SU 092583)

## Hound Tor Deserted Medieval Village
Devon

The remains of four 13th-century stone farmsteads, on land originally farmed in the Bronze Age. This isolated Dartmoor hamlet was probably abandoned in the early 15th century.

Managed by the Dartmoor National Park Authority.

### OPENING TIMES

Any reasonable time

### HOW TO FIND US

**Direction:** 1½ miles S of Manaton, ½ mile from the Ashburton road

Parking (½ mile walk across moor to monument).

MAP Page 264 (5E)
OS Map 28 (ref SX 746788)

## Hurlers Stone Circles
Cornwall

Three fine late Neolithic or early Bronze Age stone circles arranged in a line, a grouping unique in England. Probably the best examples of ceremonial circles in the south west, they are traditionally the remains of men petrified for playing 'hurling' on a Sunday.

Managed by the Cornwall Heritage Trust.

### OPENING TIMES

Any reasonable time

### HOW TO FIND US

**Direction:** Located ½ mile NW of Minions, off B3254

**Train:** Liskeard 7 miles

MAP Page 264 (6D)
OS Map 109 (ref SX 258714)

## Jordan Hill Roman Temple
Dorset

The foundations of a 4th-century Romano-Celtic temple.

### OPENING TIMES
Any reasonable time

### HOW TO FIND US
**Direction:** Located 2 miles NE of Weymouth, off A353

**Train:** Upwey or Weymouth, both 2 miles

**Bus:** First 4/A, 31, 500/3, from Weymouth

MAP Page 265 (5H)
OS Map 15 (ref SY 699+821)

## King Doniert's Stone
Cornwall

Two richly carved pieces of a 9th-century 'Celtic' cross, with an inscription commemorating Dumgarth, British King of Dumnonia, who drowned in c. AD 875.

Managed by the Cornwall Heritage Trust.

### OPENING TIMES
Any reasonable time

### HOW TO FIND US
**Direction:** 1 mile NW of St Cleer, off B3254

**Train:** Liskeard 7 miles

**Bus:** Western Greyhound 573 Callington-Looe (passing Liskeard) to within ½ mile

P

Parking (in lay-by).

MAP Page 264 (6D)
OS Map 109 (ref SX 236688)

**Don't forget your membership card**

when you visit any of the properties listed in this handbook.

## Kingston Russell Stone Circle
Dorset

A late Neolithic or early Bronze Age circle of 18 fallen stones, on a hilltop overlooking Abbotsbury and the sea.

### OPENING TIMES
Any reasonable time

### HOW TO FIND US
**Direction:** Located 2 miles N of Abbotsbury; 1 mile along a footpath off minor roads, not signposted, 1¾ miles. No off-road to Hardy Monument

**Train:** Dorchester South or West, both 8 miles

Limited parking on road verge at access to farm. Access to Stone Circle on foot only via public footpaths, off minor roads. 1¾ mile. No off-road vehicle access.

MAP Page 265 (5H)
OS Map 15 (ref SY 578878)

## Kingswood Abbey Gatehouse
Gloucestershire

This 16th-century gatehouse, one of the latest monastic buildings in England, displays a richly sculpted mullioned window. It is the sole survivor of this Cistercian abbey.

### OPENING TIMES
**Exterior:** open any reasonable time

**Interior:** key available from 3 Wotton Road, Abbey St 10am-3.30pm weekdays only

### HOW TO FIND US
**Direction:** In Kingswood, off B4060; 1 mile SW of Wotton-under-Edge

**Train:** Yate 8 miles

**Bus:** First 309 Bristol – Dursley

Public toilets near to monument.

MAP Page 265 (2H)
OS Map 167 (ref ST 747920)

## Kirkham House, Paignton
Devon

This late medieval stone house, afterwards split into three cottages, was restored in the 1960s. Furnished with modern furniture, illustrating traditional craftsmanship and the original use of the rooms.

Guided tours of medieval Paignton available on open days (first at 2.15pm, thereafter on request).

Managed in association with the Paignton Preservation & Local History Society.

### OPENING TIMES
6 Apr, 9 Apr, 7 May, 28 May, 27 Aug and every Sun in Jul-Aug 2pm-5pm

Heritage Open Days, 8-9 Sep 11am-4pm

### HOW TO FIND US
**Direction:** Located in Kirkham St, off Cecil Rd, Paignton

**Train:** Paignton ½ mile

**Bus:** From surrounding areas

MAP Page 265 (6F)
OS Map 20/110 (ref SX 885610)

## Knowlton Church and Earthworks
Dorset

The siting of this ruined medieval church at the centre of a Neolithic ritual henge earthwork symbolises the transition from pagan to Christian worship.

### OPENING TIMES
Any reasonable time

### HOW TO FIND US
**Direction:** SW of Cranborne on B3078

MAP Page 265 (4J)
OS Map 118 (ref SU 024103)

## Launceston Castle
Cornwall – PL15 7DR

Set on a large natural mound, Launceston Castle dominates the surrounding landscape. Begun soon after the Norman Conquest, its focus is an unusual keep consisting of a 13th-century round tower built by Richard of Cornwall, inside an earlier circular shell-keep. Within, the large central chamber is now reached via a dark corridor.

The castle long remained a prison and George Fox, founder of the Quakers, suffered harsh confinement here in 1656. A display traces 1,000 years of history, with finds from site excavations.

### NON-MEMBERS

| | |
|---|---|
| Adult | £2.40 |
| Concession | £1.80 |
| Child | £1.20 |

### OPENING TIMES

| | |
|---|---|
| 1 Apr-30 Jun, daily | 10am-5pm |
| 1 Jul-31 Aug, daily | 10am-6pm |
| 1-30 Sep, daily | 10am-5pm |
| 1-31 Oct, daily | 10am-4pm |
| Closed | 1 Nov-20 Mar |

### HOW TO FIND US

**Direction:** In Launceston

**Bus:** First X8, 76 Plymouth – Bude

**Tel:** 01566 772365

Disabled access (outer bailey, museum and shop).

Toilets (nearest public convenience across the road).

MAP Page 264 (5D)
OS Map 112 (ref SX 331846)

## Ludgershall Castle and Cross
Wiltshire

The ruins and earthworks of a royal castle dating mainly from the 12th and 13th centuries, frequently used as a hunting lodge. The remains of the medieval cross stand in the centre of the village.

### OPENING TIMES

Any reasonable time

### HOW TO FIND US

**Direction:** Located on the N side of Ludgershall, off A342

**Train:** Andover 7 miles

**Bus:** Stagecoach in Hampshire/Wilts & Dorset 7-9 Andover – Salisbury

Disabled access (part of site only and village cross).

Parking (limited).

MAP Page 265 (3K)
OS Map 131 (ref SU 264512)

## Lydford Castle and Saxon Town
Devon

Beautifully sited on the fringe of Dartmoor, Lydford boasts three defensive features. Near the centre is a 13th-century tower keep on a mound, later a prison notorious for harsh punishments – 'the most annoyous, contagious and detestable place within this realm.' To the south is an earlier Norman earthwork castle: to the north, Saxon town defences.

### OPENING TIMES

Any reasonable time

### HOW TO FIND US

Direction: In Lydford off A386; 8½ miles S of Okehampton

Bus: First 86 Plymouth – Barnstaple (passes Plymouth)

MAP Page 264 (5E)
OS Map 28 (ref SX 509848)

## Maiden Castle
Dorset

Among the largest and most complex of Iron Age hillforts in Europe, Maiden Castle's huge multiple ramparts enclose an area equivalent to 50 football pitches, protecting several hundred residents. Excavations in the 1930s and 1980s revealed the site's 4,000-year history, reaching its apogee at a time of inter-tribal rivalry in the 2nd century BC. They also produced evidence of an extensive late Iron Age cemetery. Many of the burials had suffered horrific injuries in attacks or skirmishes, perhaps at the time of the Roman invasion.

### OPENING TIMES

Any reasonable time

### HOW TO FIND US

**Direction:** 2 miles S of Dorchester, off A354, N of bypass

**Train:** Dorchester South or West, both 2 miles

MAP Page 265 (5H)
OS Map 15 (ref SY 669884)

## Meare Fish House
Somerset

The only surviving monastic fishery building in England, this housed the Abbot of Glastonbury's water bailiff and provided facilities for fish-salting and drying.

### OPENING TIMES

Any reasonable time. Key available from Manor House farm

### HOW TO FIND US

**Direction:** In Meare village, on B3151

**Bus:** First 668 Cheddar – Street

MAP Page 265 (4G)
OS Map 141 (ref ST 458417)

## Merrivale Prehistoric Settlement
Devon

The remains of a Bronze Age settlement, side by side with a 'ritual landscape' of sacred sites – three stone rows, a stone circle, standing stones and burial cairns – probably constructed over a long period between c. 2500 BC and 1000 BC.

Managed by Dartmoor National Park Authority.

### OPENING TIMES
Any reasonable time

### HOW TO FIND US
**Direction:** 1 mile E of Merrivale

**Train:** Gunnislake 10 miles

**Bus:** DAC 98 Yelverton – Tavistock (with connections from Plymouth)

MAP Page 264 (6E)
OS Map 28 (ref SX 554748)

## Muchelney Abbey
Somerset – TA10 0DG

Muchelney, the atmospheric and once-remote 'great island' amid the Somerset Levels, has many rewards for visitors. Beside the clearly laid out foundations of the wealthy medieval Benedictine abbey (and its Anglo-Saxon predecessor) stands a complete early Tudor house in miniature. Originally the abbots' lodgings, this charming building includes a magnificent great chamber with ornate fireplace, carved settle and stained glass; two rooms with time-faded walls painted to

Muchelney Abbey

resemble cloth hangings; and a pair of kitchens with fine timber roof. Parts of the richly decorated cloister walk and refectory are incorporated, and nearby is the thatched two-storey monks' lavatory, unique in Britain.

Exhibitions illustrate monastic life with a fascinating collection of site finds, including decorated tiles and stonework. Much improved facilities for disabled visitors include a touch-screen tour of less accessible areas.

Plant sales are available throughout the season.

www.english-heritage.org.uk/muchelney

The fine adjacent parish church and the medieval Priest's House are not managed by English Heritage.

### NON-MEMBERS
| | |
|---|---|
| Adult | £3.20 |
| Concession | £2.40 |
| Child | £1.60 |

### OPENING TIMES
| | |
|---|---|
| 1 Apr-30 Jun, daily | 10am-5pm |
| 1 Jul-31 Aug, daily | 10am-6pm |
| 1-30 Sep, daily | 10am-5pm |
| 1-31 Oct, daily | 10am-4pm |
| Closed | 1 Nov-20 Mar |

### HOW TO FIND US
**Direction:** In Muchelney, 2 miles S of Langport via Huish Episcopi

**Bus:** First 54 Taunton – Yeovil to within 1 mile of site

**Tel:** 01458 250664

E P OVP

Dogs on leads (in grounds only).

Disabled access (grounds and most of ground floor, adapted toilet).

MAP Page 265 (4G)
OS Map 129 (ref ST 429249)

## Netheravon Dovecote
Wiltshire

A charming 18th-century brick dovecote, still with most of its 700 or more nesting boxes.

### OPENING TIMES
Exterior viewing only

### HOW TO FIND US
**Direction:** In Netheravon, 4½ miles N of Amesbury on A345

**Train:** Pewsey 9 miles, Grateley 11 miles

**Bus:** Wilts & Dorset 5/6 Salisbury – Swindon (passes close to Salisbury and Swindon)

MAP Page 265 (3J)
OS Map 130 (ref SU 147484)

## The Nine Stones
Dorset

Now in a wooded glade, this small prehistoric circle of nine standing stones was constructed around 4,000 years ago. Winterbourne Poor Lot Barrows are nearby.

### OPENING TIMES
Any reasonable time

### HOW TO FIND US
**Direction:** 1½ miles SW of Winterbourne Abbas, on A35

**Train:** Weymouth 4½ miles

**Bus:** First 31 Weymouth – Axminster (passing Dorchester South)

P

Parking (in small lay-by opposite, next to barn).

Warning: Very busy main road, cross with care!

MAP Page 265 (5H)
OS Map 15/117 (ref SY 611904)

## Notgrove Long Barrow
Gloucestershire

A grassed-over Neolithic long barrow containing stone-lined burial chambers, on the crest of a high Cotswold ridge.

Managed by Gloucestershire County Council.

### OPENING TIMES
Any reasonable time

### HOW TO FIND US
**Direction:** Located 1½ miles NW of Notgrove, on A436

**Bus:** Pulham's Moreton-in-Marsh – Cheltenham (passes close to Moreton-in-Marsh)

MAP Page 265 (1J)
OS Map 45 (ref SP 096212)

## Nunney Castle
Somerset

The striking and picturesque moated castle of Nunney was built in the 1370s by Sir John de la Mere, who had seemingly served in the French wars. Certainly it was designed in the latest French style, resembling a miniature version of the famous Paris Bastille.

Nunney Castle

Held for the King during the Civil War, it was quickly reduced by Parliamentarian cannon in 1645: but not until Christmas Day 1910 did the gun-damaged portion of the wall collapse.

### OPENING TIMES
Any reasonable time

### HOW TO FIND US
**Direction:** Located in Nunney, 3½ miles SW of Frome, off A361 (no coach access)

**Train:** Frome 3½ miles

**Bus:** First 16½ Frome – Wells

Disabled access (exterior only).

MAP Page 265 (3H)
OS Map 142 (ref ST 737457)

## Nympsfield Long Barrow
Gloucestershire

A large Neolithic burial mound with spectacular vistas over the Severn Valley. Its internal burial chambers are uncovered for viewing.

Managed by Gloucestershire County Council.

### OPENING TIMES
Any reasonable time

### HOW TO FIND US
**Direction:** Located 1 mile NW of Nympsfield on B4066

**Train:** Stroud 5 miles

MAP Page 265 (2H)
OS Map 167/168 (ref SO 794013)

## Odda's Chapel
Gloucestershire

One of the most complete surviving Saxon churches in England, this chapel was built in 1056 by Earl Odda, and rediscovered in 1865 subsumed into a farmhouse. Nearby is the equally famous Saxon parish church.

Managed by Deerhurst Parish Council.

### OPENING TIMES

| | |
|---|---|
| 1 Apr-31 Oct, daily | 10am-6pm |
| 1 Nov-20 Mar, daily | 10am-4pm |
| Closed | 24-26 Dec and 1 Jan |

### HOW TO FIND US
**Direction:** Located in Deerhurst off B4213, at Abbots Court; SW of parish church

**Train:** Cheltenham 8 miles

**Bus:** Swanbrook 351 Gloucester-Upton-upon-Severn (passing close to Gloucester)

Parking (not EH, charges applies).

MAP Page 265 (1J)
OS Map 179 (ref SO 869298)

## Offa's Dyke
Gloucestershire

A three-mile section of the great earthwork boundary dyke built along the Anglo-Welsh border by Offa, King of Mercia, probably during the 780s. This especially impressive wooded stretch includes the

### Offa's Dyke

Devil's Pulpit, with fine views of Tintern Abbey.

**OPENING TIMES**

Any reasonable time

**HOW TO FIND US**

**Direction:** Located 3 miles NE of Chepstow, off B4228. Via Forest Enterprise Tidenham car park, 1 mile walk (waymarked) down to The Devil's Pulpit on Offa's Dyke (access is suitable only for those wearing proper walking shoes and is not suitable for the very young, old or infirm)

**Train:** Chepstow 7 miles

**Bus:** Stagecoach in South Wales; Welcome 69 Chepstow – Monmouth, to within ½ mile

MAP Page 265 (2H)
OS Map 14/167
(ref SO 546011-ST 549975)

## Okehampton Castle

Devon – EX20 1JA

The remains of the largest castle in Devon, in an outstandingly picturesque setting on a wooded spur above the rushing River Okement. Begun soon after the Norman Conquest as a motte and bailey castle with a stone keep, it was converted into a sumptuous residence in the 14th century by Hugh Courtenay, Earl of Devon, much of whose work survives. After the last Courtenay owner fell foul of Henry VIII in 1538, it declined

### Okehampton Castle

into an allegedly haunted ruin. Riverside picnic area and woodland walks nearby.

**NON-MEMBERS**

| | |
|---|---|
| Adult | £3.00 |
| Concession | £2.30 |
| Child | £1.50 |

**OPENING TIMES**

| | |
|---|---|
| 1 Apr-30 Jun, daily | 10am-5pm |
| 1 Jul-31 Aug, daily | 10am-6pm |
| 1-30 Sep, daily | 10am-5pm |
| Closed | 1 Nov-20 Mar |

**HOW TO FIND US**

**Direction:** Located 1 mile SW of Okehampton town centre (signposted)

**Train:** Okehampton (summer Sundays only) ½ mile

**Bus:** First X9 Exeter – Bude; Stagecoach in Devon X30, First 6 Plymouth – Barnstaple

**Tel:** 01837 52844

P OVP

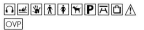

Audio tours (also available for the visually impaired and those with learning difficulties).

MAP Page 264 (5E)
OS Map 28/113 (ref SX 583942)

## Old Sarum

See feature – Page 104

## Old Wardour Castle

See feature – Page 105

## Over Bridge

Gloucestershire

A single-arch stone bridge spanning the River Severn, built in 1825-30 by the great engineer Thomas Telford.

**OPENING TIMES**

Any reasonable time

**HOW TO FIND US**

**Direction:** 1 mile NW of Gloucester, at junction of A40 (Ross) and A417 (Ledbury)

**Train:** Gloucester 2 miles

**Bus:** From Gloucester

P

Parking (in lay-by).

MAP Page 265 (1H)
OS Map 179 (ref SO 816196)

## Pendennis Castle

See feature – Page 108

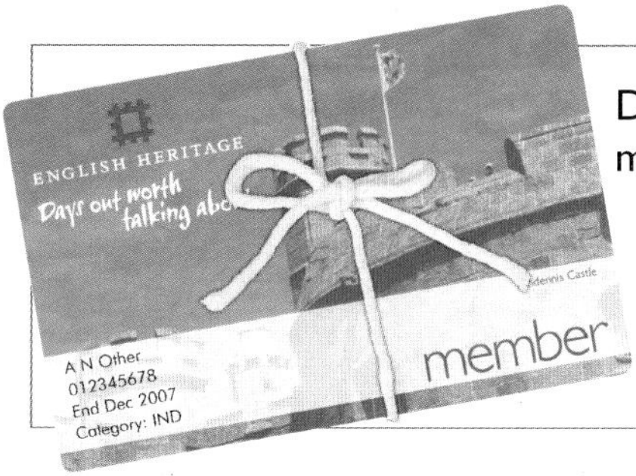


**Don't forget your membership card**

when you visit any of the properties listed in this handbook.

# Old Sarum Wiltshire – SP1 3SD

Photo: Skyscan Balloon Photography

The great earthwork of Old Sarum stands near Salisbury on the edge of Wiltshire's chalk plains. Its mighty ramparts were raised in about 500 BC by Iron Age peoples, and later occupied by the Romans, the Saxons and, most importantly, the Normans.

William the Conqueror paid off his army here in 1070, and in 1086 summoned all the great landowners of England here to swear an oath of loyalty. A Norman castle was built on the inner mound and joined soon afterwards by a royal palace. By the middle of the 12th century a new town occupied much of the great earthwork, complete with a noble new Norman cathedral, the mother church of a huge diocese.

But Norman Sarum was not destined to thrive. Soldiers and priests quarelled, and life on the almost waterless hilltop became intolerable. The solution was a move downhill to the new settlement now known as Salisbury, where a new cathedral was founded in 1220. Thereafter Old Sarum went into steep decline. Its cathedral was demolished and its castle was eventually abandoned. But the largely uninhabited site continued to 'elect' two MPs, becoming the most notorious of the 'Rotten Boroughs' swept away by the 1832 Reform Act.

Today, the remains of the prehistoric fortress and of the Norman palace, castle and cathedral evoke memories of thousands of years of history which are interpreted by graphic panels throughout the site.

Contact the site for details of special events.

**www.english-heritage.org.uk/oldsarum**

## NON-MEMBERS

| | |
|---|---|
| Adult | £2.90 |
| Concession | £2.20 |
| Child | £1.50 |

## OPENING TIMES

| | |
|---|---|
| 1 Apr-30 Jun, daily | 10am-5pm |
| 1 Jul-31 Aug, daily | 9am-6pm |
| 1-30 Sep, daily | 10am-5pm |
| 1-31 Oct, daily | 10am-4pm |
| 1 Nov-29 Feb, daily | 11am-3pm |
| 1-20 Mar, daily | 10am-4pm |
| Closed | 24-26 Dec and 1 Jan |

## HOW TO FIND US

**Direction:** 2 miles N of Salisbury, off A345

**Train:** Salisbury 2 miles

**Bus:** Wilts & Dorset/Stagecoach in Hampshire 3, 5-9 from Salisbury

**Tel:** 01722 335398

**Local Tourist Information**
Salisbury: 01722 334956

OVP

Disabled access (outer bailey and grounds only, disabled toilet).

MAP Page 265 (4J)
OS Map 130 (ref SU 138327)

# Old Wardour Castle Wiltshire – SP3 6RR

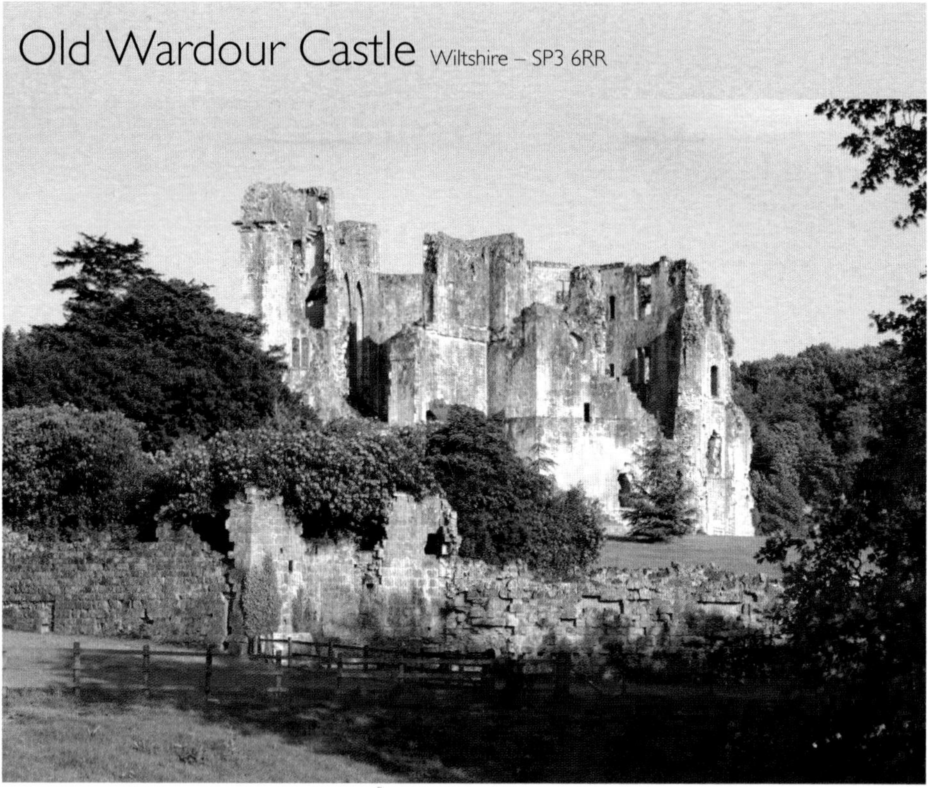

Beautifully sited beside a lake, Old Wardour Castle was built in the late 14th century by John Lord Lovel as a lightly fortified but showy and luxurious residence. A hexagonal tower house ranged round a central courtyard, its form is very unusual in England.

After decorative updating in 1570, the castle was besieged in turn by both sides during the Civil War, and badly damaged. During the 18th century it was incorporated as a romantic ruin into the landscaped grounds of New Wardour House, which was built by Lord Arundell (not managed by English Heritage, no public access). The castle's setting in a Registered Landscape indicates the significance of this hidden jewel.

An audio tour brings the castle's long history to life.

Part of the film *Robin Hood, Prince of Thieves*, was filmed here.

Please contact the site for details of special events.

**www.english-heritage.org.uk/oldwardour**

Licensed for civil wedding ceremonies.

## NON-MEMBERS

| | |
|---|---|
| Adult | £3.40 |
| Concession | £2.60 |
| Child | £1.70 |

## OPENING TIMES

| | |
|---|---|
| 1 Apr-30 Jun, daily | 10am-5pm |
| 1 Jul-31 Aug, daily | 10am-6pm |
| 1-30 Sep, daily | 10am-5pm |
| 1-31 Oct, daily | 10am-4pm |
| 1 Nov-20 Mar, Sat-Sun | 10am-4pm |
| Closed | 24-26 Dec & 1 Jan |

## HOW TO FIND US

**Direction:** Located off A30 2 miles SW of Tisbury. Also accessible from A350 (narrow rural roads)

**Train:** Tisbury 2½ miles

**Bus:** Wilts & Dorset 26 Salisbury – Shaftesbury (passes Tisbury)

**Tel:** 01747 870487

P OVP

Disabled access (grounds and ground floor only), disabled toilet.

**MAP Page 265 (4J)**
**OS Map 118 (ref ST 939263)**

## Penhallam Manor
Cornwall

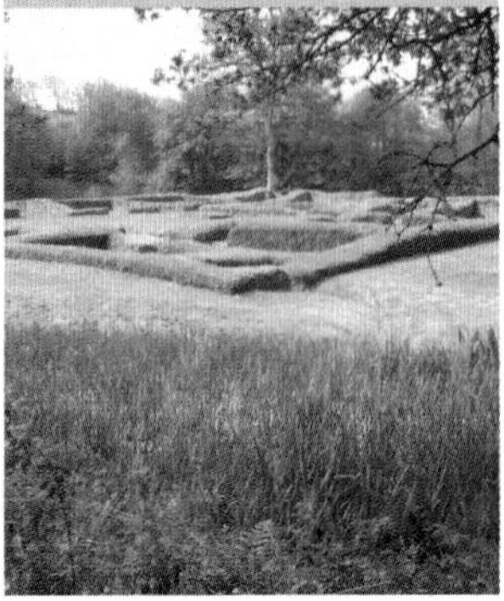

The low and grass-covered but complete ground-plan of a moated 13th-century manor house, in a delightful woodland setting.

### OPENING TIMES
Any reasonable time

### HOW TO FIND US
**Direction:** Signposted from Week St Mary, off a minor road off A39 from Treskinnick Cross (10 minutes' walk from the car park on the forest track)

Parking (limited).

MAP Page 264 (5D)
OS Map 111 (ref SX 224974)

## Portland Castle
See feature – Page 110

## Restormel Castle
Cornwall – PL22 0EE

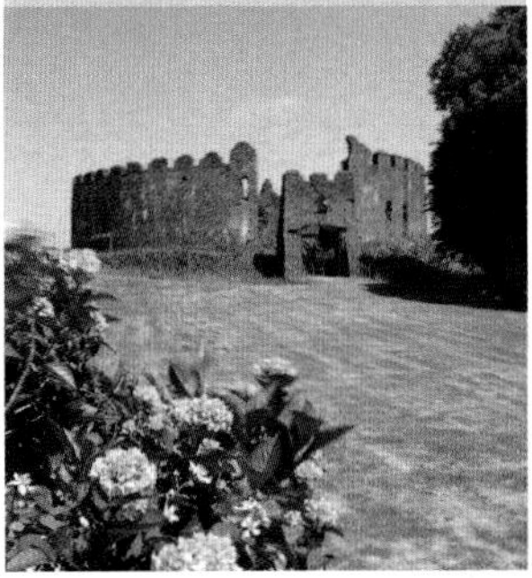

The great 13th-century circular shell-keep of Restormel still encloses the principal rooms of the castle in remarkably good condition. It stands on an earlier Norman mound surrounded by a deep dry ditch, atop a high spur beside the River Fowey. Twice visited by the Black Prince, it finally saw action during the Civil War in 1644. It commands fantastic views and is a favourite picnic spot.

### NON-MEMBERS

| | |
|---|---|
| Adult | £2.40 |
| Concession | £1.80 |
| Child | £1.20 |

### OPENING TIMES

| | |
|---|---|
| 1 Apr-30 Jun, daily | 10am-5pm |
| 1 Jul-31 Aug, daily | 10am-6pm |
| 1-30 Sep, daily | 10am-5pm |
| 1-31 Oct, daily | 10am-4pm |
| Closed | 1 Nov-20 Mar |

### HOW TO FIND US
**Direction:** Located 1½ miles N of Lostwithiel, off A390

**Train:** Lostwithiel 1½ miles

**Tel:** 01208 872687

OVP

Access (via a stock grazing area so appropriate footwear must be worn. There are three steps on the entrance path, so disabled visitors may want to call the site in advance to arrange alternative access).

MAP Page 264 (6C)
OS Map 107 (ref SX 104614)

## Royal Citadel, Plymouth
Devon

A dramatic 17th-century fortress built to defend the coastline from the Dutch, and keep watch on a recently rebellious town. Still in use by the military today. Viewing is only by tours led by Blue Badge Guides – please contact plymouthukbbg@hotmail.com prior to visiting.

## Royal Citadel, Plymouth

### ENTRY

| | |
|---|---|
| Non-member | £3.50 |
| EH members and children | £3.00 |

### OPENING TIMES
By guided tour only, May-Sep:
Tue & Thu only 2.30pm

### HOW TO FIND US
**Direction:** At E end of Plymouth Hoe

**Train:** Plymouth 1 mile

**Bus:** From surrounding areas

MAP Page 264 (6E)
OS Map 20/108 (ref SX 480538)

## St Breock Downs Monolith
Cornwall

Originally 5 metres (16 feet) high and weighing some 16.75 tonnes, this is Cornwall's largest and heaviest prehistoric monolith. It stands on the summit of the St Breock Downs, offering wonderful views.

Managed by the Cornwall Heritage Trust.

### OPENING TIMES
Any reasonable time

### HOW TO FIND US
**Direction:** Located on St Breock Downs; 3½ miles SW of Wadebridge off unclassified road to Rosenannon

**Train:** Roche 5½ miles

MAP Page 264 (6C)
OS Map 106 (ref SW 968683)

## St Briavels Castle
Gloucestershire

The fine twin-towered gatehouse of this castle, built by Edward I in 1292, once defended a crossbow bolt factory that used local Forest of Dean iron. Once a prison, it is now a youth hostel in marvellous walking country.

## St Briavels Castle

### OPENING TIMES

**Exterior:**
Any reasonable time

**Bailey**
1 Apr-30 Sep, daily 1pm-4pm

### HOW TO FIND US

**Direction:** In St Briavels; 7 miles NE of Chepstow off B4228

**Train:** Chepstow 8 miles

**Tel:** 01594 530272

MAP Page 265 (2H)
OS Map 14 (ref SO 559046)

## St Catherine's Castle
Cornwall

One of a pair of small artillery forts built by Henry VIII in the 1530s to defend Fowey Harbour, consisting of two storeys with gun ports at ground level.

### OPENING TIMES

Any reasonable time

### HOW TO FIND US

**Direction:** 1½ miles SW of Fowey, along a woodland footpath off A3082

**Train:** Par 4 miles

**Bus:** First 25/B St Austell-Fowey to within ½ mile

P

Parking (Ready Money Cove Car Park, Fowey ¾ mile walk).

MAP Page 264 (6C)
OS Map 107 (ref SX 119509)

## St Catherine's Chapel, Abbotsbury:
see Abbotsbury, St Catherine's Chapel – Page 91

## St Mary's Church, Kempley
Gloucestershire

A delightful Norman church, displaying one of the most outstandingly complete and well-preserved sets of medieval wall-paintings in England, dating from the 12th and 14th centuries.

Managed by the Friends of Kempley Church.

### OPENING TIMES

1 Mar-31 Oct, daily 10am-6pm

Telephone for appointment in winter

### HOW TO FIND US

**Direction:** 1 mile N of Kempley off B4024; 6 miles NE of Ross-on-Wye

**Train:** Ledbury 8 miles

**Tel:** 01531 660214

MAP Page 265 (1H)
OS Map 189 (ref SO 670313)

## St Mawes Castle
Cornwall – TR2 3AA

The best preserved and most elaborately decorated of Henry VIII's coastal fortresses, St Mawes was built to counter invasion threats from France and Spain. Its counterpart was Pendennis, on the other side of the Fal estuary (see p.108).

The clover-leaf shaped fort fell easily to landward attack by Parliamentarian forces in 1646, and was not properly refortified until the late 19th and early 20th centuries. Other coastal forts built by Henry VIII include Portland, Deal and Walmer Castles.

- Available for corporate and private hire.
- Licensed for civil wedding ceremonies.
- Holiday cottage available to let.

### NON-MEMBERS

| | |
|---|---|
| Adult | £3.90 |
| Concession | £2.90 |
| Child | £2.00 |

### OPENING TIMES

| | |
|---|---|
| 1 Apr-30 Jun, Sun-Fri | 10am-5pm* |
| 1 Jul-31 Aug, Sun-Fri | 10am-6pm* |
| 1-30 Sep, Sun-Fri | 10am-5pm* |
| 1-31 Oct, daily | 10am-4pm |
| 1 Nov-20 Mar, Fri-Mon | 10am-4pm |

*Closed Sat. Property may close at 4pm on Fridays and Sundays for private events

Closed 24-26 Dec & 1 Jan

Castle closed between 1-2pm in winter

### HOW TO FIND US

**Direction:** In St Mawes on A3078

**Train:** Penmere, 4 miles via Prince of Wales Pier and ferry

**Bus:** First 50 Truro – St Mawes to within ½ mile

**Tel:** 01326 270526

P OVP

Dogs on leads (grounds only).

MAP Page 264 (7C)
OS Map 105 (ref SW 841328)

# Pendennis Castle Cornwall – TR11 4LP

Constructed between 1540 and 1545, Pendennis and its sister St Mawes Castle form the Cornish end of the chain of coastal castles built by Henry VIII to counter a threat from France and Spain. Thereafter Pendennis was frequently adapted to face new enemies over 400 years, right through until World War II.

In 1598, during Elizabeth I's reign, a new type of defensive rampart was added around the original fort. The castle was strengthened again prior to the Civil War and played host to the future Charles II in 1646, before he sailed to the Isles of Scilly. It then withstood five months of siege, before becoming the penultimate Royalist garrison on the British mainland to surrender.

Pendennis continued to play a vital role in Cornwall's defences throughout the late 19th and early 20th centuries, and saw significant action during World War II. Evidence of its fascinating history is on show throughout the site. The Noonday Gun is fired every day during July and August, and the Guardhouse has been returned to its World War I appearance. You can also visit the underground magazines, including the World War II Half Moon Battery (by guided tour only), as well as the original 16th-century keep with its recreated Tudor gun deck.

The refurbished 1901 Royal Artillery Barracks houses an interactive exhibition, tracing the history of the castle, its people, and its links with Falmouth and the trade routes of the British Empire. A key feature is a hands-on scale model of the castle: with the aid of special effects, children will also now be able to step into the shoes of a soldier on kit parade.

The education suite, with two large child-friendly education rooms and a wet room for creative workshops, can accommodate up to 120 children.

The hospitality area is not only a fully-equipped conference centre but also an exceptional wedding venue, with the Fal Estuary as a stunning backdrop.

**www.english-heritage.org.uk/pendenniscastle**

Available for corporate and private hire.

Licensed for civil wedding ceremonies.

Holiday cottage available to let.

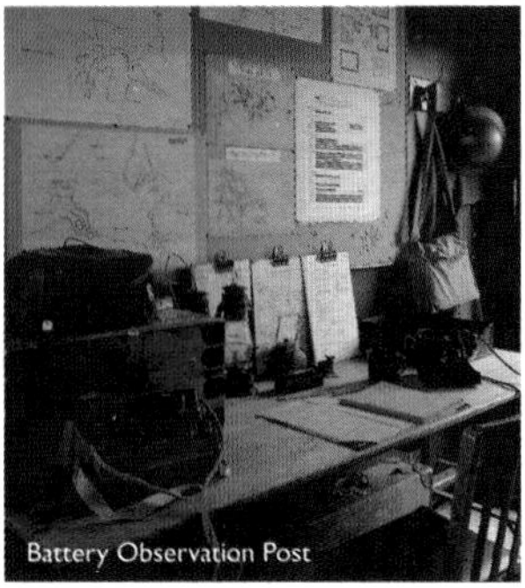

Battery Observation Post

## NON-MEMBERS

| | |
|---|---|
| Adult | £5.40 |
| Concession | £4.10 |
| Child | £2.70 |
| Family | £13.50 |

## OPENING TIMES

| | |
|---|---|
| 1 Apr-30 Jun, daily | 10am-5pm* |
| 1 Jul-31 Aug, daily | 10am-6pm* |
| 1-30 Sep, daily | 10am-5pm* |
| 1-31 Oct, daily | 10am-4pm |
| 1 Nov-20 Mar, daily | 10am-4pm |

Certain buildings by guided tour only. Please call for details

| | |
|---|---|
| Closed | 24-26 Dec and 1 Jan |

*Closes at 4pm on Saturdays. The keep also closes for 1 hour at lunch on Saturdays if an event is booked

## HOW TO FIND US

**Direction:** On Pendennis Headland, 1 mile SE of Falmouth

**Train:** Falmouth Docks ½ mile

**Bus:** First 400 from Falmouth, Jun-Aug only

**Tel:** 01326 316594

**Local Tourist Information:** 01326 312300

OVP

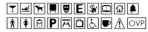

Disabled access (wheelchair access to the grounds, there are steep steps or drops in places). There is full wheelchair access to the Barracks, and a virtual tour of the whole site.

Tearooms (Closed 22 Dec to 6 Jan).

MAP Page 264 (7C)
OS Map 103/105 (ref SW 824318)

# Portland Castle Dorset – DT5 1AZ

The history of this fortress, which overlooks Portland harbour, is diverse and fascinating. Built by Henry VIII to defend the anchorage against possible French and Spanish invasion, its squat appearance is typical of the artillery forts built in the early 1540s.

Unusually for a fortress of this period, the castle has seen much interior alteration, though the exterior remains largely unchanged. It first witnessed serious fighting during the Civil War, when it was seized by both Parliamentarians and Royalists.

It became a Seaplane Station during World War I, and was in the forefront of the D-Day preparations which helped to end World War II.

The Governor's Garden, designed by Christopher Bradley-Hole as part of the Contemporary Heritage Garden series, contains an impressive circular amphitheatre made from local Portland stone, with two-level seating for about 200 people. This perfectly sheltered spot is a great place to relax and enjoy the dramatic sea and harbour views.

There are audio tours and a Touch Tour for the visually impaired. You can even come face-to-face with Henry VIII in the Great Hall.

**www.english-heritage.org.uk/portland**

Enjoy a refreshing sea journey to Portland Castle from Weymouth aboard *My Girl*, a World War II veteran boat. 10% discount for EH members – valid April to October 2007. Tel 01305 785000 or visit **www.whitemotorboat.freeuk.com**

Available for corporate and private hire.

Licensed for civil wedding ceremonies.

## NON-MEMBERS

| | |
|---|---|
| Adult | £3.80 |
| Concession | £2.90 |
| Child | £1.90 |

## OPENING TIMES

| | |
|---|---|
| 1 Apr-30 Jun, daily | 10am-5pm |
| 1 Jul-31 Aug, daily | 10am-6pm |
| 1-30 Sep, daily | 10am-5pm |
| 1-31 Oct, daily | 10am-4pm |
| Closed | 1 Nov-20 Mar |

## HOW TO FIND US

**Direction:** Overlooking Portland Harbour in Castletown, Isle of Portland

**Train:** Weymouth 4½ miles

**Bus:** First 1, 501 from Weymouth (passing close to Weymouth)

**Ferry:** From Weymouth Harbour, Good Fri-end Sep (weather permitting). Call the castle for details.

**Tel:** 01305 820539

P OVP

Disabled access, disabled toilet (Captain's House, ground floor of the castle and Governor's Garden). Captain's House Tearooms (table service and outdoor servery).

MAP Page 265 (6H)
OS Map 15 (ref SY 685744)

## The Sanctuary
Wiltshire

Begun in about 3000 BC, the Sanctuary became a complex of timber post rings and stone circles. Its components are now indicated by concrete slabs. A place of great ritual significance, it was later linked to Avebury by West Kennet Avenue.

Managed by The National Trust.

Part of the Avebury World Heritage Site.

### OPENING TIMES

Any reasonable time

Usual facilities may not be available around the Summer Solstice 20-22 June. Please check before you visit

### HOW TO FIND US

**Train:** Pewsey 9 miles, Bedwyn 12 miles

**Bus:** Wilts and Dorset 5/6 Salisbury – Swindon (passes close to ≠ Swindon)

Parking (in lay-by).

MAP Page 265 (3J)
OS Map 157 (ref SU 118680)

Sherborne Old Castle
Dorset – DT9 3SA

## Sherborne Old Castle

Built by Bishop Roger of Salisbury in the 12th century as a strongly defended palace, Sherborne Old Castle became a powerful Royalist base during the Civil War. Described as 'malicious and mischievous' by Cromwell, it fell in 1645 after a fierce eleven-day siege. Sherborne 'New' Castle is nearby (see p.123).

www.english-heritage.org.uk/sherborne

### NON-MEMBERS

| | |
|---|---|
| Adult | £2.40 |
| Concession | £1.80 |
| Child | £1.20 |

Joint ticket for Sherborne Castle grounds £5.50. Members' discounts: see page 123

### OPENING TIMES

| | |
|---|---|
| 1 Apr-30 Jun, daily | 10am-5pm |
| 1 July-31 Aug, daily | 10am-6pm |
| 1-30 Sep, daily | 10am-5pm |
| 1-31 Oct, daily | 10am-4pm |
| Closed | 1 Nov-20 Mar |

### HOW TO FIND US

**Direction:** Located ½ mile E of Sherborne, off B3145

**Train:** Sherborne ¾ mile

**Tel:** 01935 812730

OVP

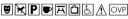

MAP Page 265 (4H)
OS Map 129 (ref ST 648168)

Silbury Hill
Wiltshire

## Silbury Hill

The largest man-made mound in Europe, huge and mysterious Silbury Hill is comparable in height and volume to the roughly contemporary Egyptian pyramids.

Probably completed by about 2350 BC and part of the Avebury 'sacred landscape', it apparently contains no burial or shrine, and was clearly important in itself, but its purpose and significance remain enigmatic.

Vital and extensive conservation work will be undertaken during 2007. There is no access to the hill itself.

Part of the Avebury World Heritage Site.

www.english-heritage.org.uk/silbury

### OPENING TIMES

Viewing area during reasonable daylight hours. Strictly no access to the hill itself

Usual facilities may not be available around the Summer Solstice 20-22 June. Please check before you visit

### HOW TO FIND US

**Direction:** 1 mile W of West Kennet on A4

**Train:** Pewsey 9 miles, Swindon 13 miles

**Bus:** Stagecoach in Swindon/First 49 Swindon – Trowbridge; Wilts & Dorset 5/6 Salisbury – Swindon (all pass within ¾ mile and pass close to ≠ Swindon)

Disabled access (viewing area).

MAP Page 265 (3J)
OS Map 157 (ref SU 100685)

# Stonehenge Wiltshire – SP4 7DE

The great and ancient stone circle of Stonehenge is one of the wonders of the world. What visitors see today are the substantial remnants of the last in a sequence of such monuments erected between c. 3000 BC and 1600 BC. Each monument was a circular structure, aligned with the rising of the sun at the solstice.

There has always been intense debate over quite what purpose Stonehenge served. Certainly it was the focal point in a landscape filled with prehistoric ceremonial structures. It also represented an enormous investment of labour and time. A huge effort and great organisation was needed to carry the stones tens – and sometimes hundreds – of miles by land and water, and then to shape and raise them. Only a sophisticated society could have mustered so large a workforce, and the design and construction skills necessary to produce Stonehenge and its surrounding monuments.

Stonehenge's orientation in relation to the rising and setting sun has always been one of its most remarkable features. Whether this was because its builders came from a sun-worshipping culture or because – as some scholars have asserted – the circle and its banks were part of a huge astronomical calendar, remains a mystery.

What cannot be denied is the ingenuity of the builders of Stonehenge. With only very basic tools at their disposal, they shaped the stones and formed the mortises and tenons that linked uprights to lintels.

Using antlers and bones, they dug the pits to hold the stones and made the banks and ditches that enclosed them.

There are direct links with the people who built Stonehenge through their tools, artefacts, pottery and even the contents of their graves. Some of these are displayed in the museums at Salisbury and Devizes.

The first monument in the Stonehenge landscape consisted of a circular bank and ditch with a ring of 56 wooden posts, the pits for which are now known as Aubrey Holes. Later monuments all used and reused the great stones we see today, many of which were brought from some distance away. The final phase comprised the construction of an outer circle of huge standing stones – super-hard sarsens, from the Marlborough Downs. These were topped by lintels, forming a ring. Inside this stood a horseshoe of five still-larger constructions, known as trilithons: pairs of uprights with a lintel across each. All the stones were connected using mortise-and-tenon joints. Smaller bluestones, from the Preseli Mountains in South Wales, were arranged in a ring and a horseshoe, within the great circle and horseshoe of sarsen stones. In an earlier phase, these bluestones had been erected in a different arrangement.

Burial mounds, possibly containing the graves of ruling families, are also integral to the landscape. Neolithic long barrows and the various types of circular barrows which came later are still visible. So too are other earthworks and monuments. Some remain enigmatic, such as the long oval earthwork to the north, the Cursus – once thought to be a chariot racecourse. You can visit the Cursus and other parts of the Stonehenge landscape. Woodhenge, two miles to the north east, was a wooden oval-post structure, also aligned with the Solstice sunrise. It is believed to be contemporary with the first phase of Stonehenge.

A World Heritage Site, Stonehenge and all its surroundings remain powerful witnesses to the once great civilisations of the Stone and Bronze Ages, between 5,000 and 3,000 years ago.

Stonehenge is surrounded by 1,500 acres of land owned by The National Trust, with excellent walks.

www.english-heritage.org.uk/stonehenge

Stone Circle access outside normal opening hours by advance booking only. Book during weekday office hours.

## NON-MEMBERS

| | |
|---|---|
| Adult | £6.30 |
| Concession | £4.70 |
| Child | £3.20 |
| Family | £15.80 |

National Trust members admitted free

## OPENING TIMES

| | |
|---|---|
| 16 Mar-31 May, daily | 9.30am-6pm |
| 1 Jun-31 Aug, daily | 9am-7pm |
| 1 Sep-15 Oct, daily | 9.30am-6pm |
| 16 Oct-15 Mar, daily | 9.30am-4pm |
| 26 Dec & 1 Jan | 10am-4pm |
| Closed | 24-25 Dec |

Opening times from 20 to 22 June may be subject to change due to Summer Solstice. Please check with Customer Services before your visit

Recommended last admission time no later than 30 minutes before the advertised closing time. Stonehenge will close promptly 20 minutes after the advertised closing time

When weather conditions are bad, access may be restricted and visitors may not be able to use the walkway around the stone circle

## HOW TO FIND US

**Direction:** 2 miles W of Amesbury on junction of A303 and A344/A360

**Train:** Salisbury 9½ miles

**Bus:** Wilts & Dorset 3 from Salisbury

**Tel:** 0870 333 1181 (Customer Services)

**Local Tourist Information** Amesbury: 01980 622833; and Salisbury: 01722 334956

**Stone Circle Access Line:** 01722 343834, advance booking only

OVP

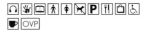

Audio tours (complimentary – available in nine languages and hearing loop: subject to availability).

Catering, hot and cold refreshments available throughout the year.

Guidebooks (also available in French, German, Spanish and Japanese; large print and braille guides in English only).

No dogs allowed (except guide and hearing dogs).

Parking (free for members. Seasonal charge for non-members, refundable on entry).

MAP Page 265 (4J)
OS Map 130 (ref SU 122422)

## Sir Bevil Grenville's Monument
Bath & NE Somerset

Erected to commemorate the heroism of a Royalist commander and his Cornish pikemen at the Battle of Lansdown, 1643.

### OPENING TIMES
Any reasonable time

### HOW TO FIND US
**Direction:** Located 4 miles NW of Bath on the N edge of Lansdown Hill, near the road to Wick

**Train:** Bath Spa 4½ miles

**Bus:** Ebley 620 Bath Spa – Tetbury

P

Parking (in lay-by).

MAP Page 265 (3H)
OS Map 155 (ref ST 722703)

## Stanton Drew Circles and Cove
Bath & NE Somerset

Though the third largest collection of prehistoric standing stones in England, the three circles and three-stone 'cove' of Stanton Drew are surprisingly little-known. Recent surveys have revealed that they were only part of a much more elaborate ritual site.

## Stanton Drew Circles and Cove

### OPENING TIMES
Cove: any reasonable time. Two main stone circles; access at the discretion of the landowner, who may levy a charge

### HOW TO FIND US
**Direction:** Cove: located in the garden of the Druid's Arms public house. Circles: located E of Stanton Drew village

**Train:** Bristol Temple Meads 7 miles

**Bus:** Chew Valley Explorer 672 Bristol Temple Meads – Cheddar

MAP Page 265 (3H)
OS Map 154/155
(cove ref ST 597631,
circles ref ST 601633)

## Stonehenge
See feature – Page 112

## Stoney Littleton Long Barrow
Bath & NE Somerset

One of the finest accessible examples of a Neolithic chambered tomb, with its multiple burial chambers open to view.

### OPENING TIMES
Any reasonable daylight hours

### HOW TO FIND US
**Direction:** 1 mile S of Wellow off A367

**Train:** Bath Spa 6 miles

P

Parking (limited).

Note: visitors are advised to bring a torch, and that there may be mud on approach and interior floor.

MAP Page 265 (3H)
OS Map 142 (ref ST 735572)

## Temple Church
Bristol

The 'leaning tower' and walls of this large late medieval church survived bombing during World War II. The graveyard is now a public garden.

## Temple Church

### OPENING TIMES
Exterior only: any reasonable time

### HOW TO FIND US
**Direction:** Located in Temple St, off Victoria St

**Train:** Bristol Temple Meads ¼ mile

**Bus:** From surrounding areas

MAP Page 265 (3H)
OS Map 154/155 (ref ST 593727)

## Tintagel Castle
See feature – Page 118

## Totnes Castle
Devon – TQ9 5NU

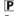

Photo: Peter Anderson

A classic Norman motte and bailey castle, founded soon after the Conquest to overawe the Saxon town. A later stone shell-keep crowns its steep mound, giving sweeping views across the town rooftops to the River Dart.

Keep accessible only via steep steps.

### NON-MEMBERS

| | |
|---|---|
| Adult | £2.40 |
| Concession | £1.80 |
| Child | £1.20 |

Totnes Castle

## OPENING TIMES

| | |
|---|---|
| 1 Apr-30 Jun, daily | 10am-5pm |
| 1 Jul-31 Aug, daily | 10am-6pm |
| 1-30 Sep, daily | 10am-5pm |
| 1-31 Oct, daily | 10am-4pm |
| Closed | 1 Nov-20 Mar |

## HOW TO FIND US

**Direction:** In centre of Totnes, at Castle Street, off Station Road opposite railway station. From town centre, turn north off High Street.

**Train:** Totnes ¼ mile

**Tel:** 01803 864406

OVP

Parking (charged, 64 metres (70 yards); cars only, narrow approach roads).

MAP Page 264 (6E)
OS Map 20/110 (ref SX 800605)

# Tregiffian Burial Chamber
Cornwall

A Neolithic or early Bronze Age chambered tomb with an entrance passage, walled and roofed with stone slabs, leading into the central chamber.

Managed by the Cornwall Heritage Trust.

## OPENING TIMES

Any reasonable time

## HOW TO FIND US

**Direction:** Located 2 miles SE of St Buryan, on B3315

**Train:** Penzance 5½ miles

MAP Page 264 (7B)
OS Map 102 (ref SW 431244)

# Trethevy Quoit
Cornwall

This well-preserved and impressive Neolithic 'dolmen' burial chamber stands 2.7 metres (8.9 ft) high. There are five standing stones, surmounted by a huge capstone.

Managed by Cornwall Heritage Trust.

## OPENING TIMES

Any reasonable time

## HOW TO FIND US

**Direction:** 1 mile NE of St Cleer, near Darite; off B3254

**Train:** Liskeard 3½ miles

**Bus:** Western Greyhound 573 Callington – Looe (passes ⇌ Liskeard) within ½ mile

MAP Page 264 (6D)
OS Map 109 (ref SX 259688)

# Uley Long Barrow (Hetty Pegler's Tump)
Gloucestershire

A partly reconstructed Neolithic chambered mound, 37 metres (120 ft) long, atmospherically sited overlooking the Severn Valley. 'Hetty Pegler' was its 17th-century landowner.

Managed by Gloucestershire County Council.

## OPENING TIMES

Any reasonable time

## HOW TO FIND US

**Direction:** Located 3½ miles NE of Dursley, on B4066

**Train:** Stroud 6 miles

**Bus:** Stagecoach in the Cotswolds 20 Stroud – Uley (passes close to ⇌ Stroud), then 1 mile

MAP Page 265 (2H)
OS Map 167/168 (ref SO 790000)

# Upper Plym Valley
Devon

Some 300 Bronze Age and medieval sites, covering 15½ square kilometres (6 square miles) of Dartmoor landscape.

## OPENING TIMES

Any reasonable time

## HOW TO FIND US

**Direction:** 4 miles E of Yelverton

MAP Page 264 (6E)
OS Map 20/28 (ref SX 580660)

# West Kennet Avenue
Wiltshire

An 'avenue', originally of around 100 pairs of prehistoric standing stones, raised to form a winding 1½ mile ritual link between the pre-existing monuments of Avebury and The Sanctuary.

Part of the Avebury World Heritage Site.

Owned and managed by The National Trust.

## OPENING TIMES

Any reasonable time

Usual facilities may not be available around the Summer Solstice 20-22 Jun. Please check before you visit

## HOW TO FIND US

**Direction:** Runs alongside B4003

**Train:** Pewsey 9 miles, Swindon 12 miles

**Bus:** Stagecoach in Swindon/First 49 Swindon – Trowbridge; Wilts and Dorset 5/6 Salisbury – Swindon (all pass close to ⇌ Swindon)

Disabled access (on roadway).

MAP Page 265 (3J)
OS Map 157 (ref SU 105695)

## West Kennet Long Barrow
Wiltshire

One of the largest, most impressive and most accessible Neolithic chambered tombs in Britain. Built in around 3400 BC, and used by a whole community for at least a thousand years.

**Part of the Avebury World Heritage Site.**

Managed by The National Trust.

### OPENING TIMES
Any reasonable time

Usual facilities may not be available around the Summer Solstice 20-22 Jun. Please check before you visit

### HOW TO FIND US
**Direction:** ¾ mile SW of West Kennet, along footpath off A4

**Train:** Pewsey 9 miles, Swindon 13 miles

**Bus:** Stagecoach in Swindon/First 49 Swindon – Trowbridge; Wilts and Dorset 5/6 Salisbury – Swindon (all pass close to Swindon)

Parking (in lay-by).

**MAP Page 265 (3J)**
**OS Map 157 (ref SU 105677)**

## Windmill Hill
Wiltshire

The classic Neolithic 'causewayed enclosure', with three concentric but intermittent ditches. Large quantities of animal bones found here indicate feasting, animal

Windmill Hill

trading or rituals here, or perhaps all three.

**Part of the Avebury World Heritage Site.**

Owned and managed by The National Trust.

### OPENING TIMES
Any reasonable time

### HOW TO FIND US
**Direction:** 1¼ mile NW of Avebury

**Train:** Swindon 11 miles

**Bus:** Stagecoach in Swindon/First 49 Swindon – Trowbridge; Wilts and Dorset 5/6 Salisbury – Swindon (all pass close to Swindon)

**MAP Page 265 (3J)**
**OS Map 157 (ref SU 087714)**

## Windmill Tump Long Barrow, Rodmarton
Gloucestershire

A Neolithic chambered tomb with an enigmatic 'false entrance'.

Managed by Gloucestershire County Council.

### OPENING TIMES
Any reasonable time

### HOW TO FIND US
**Direction:** 1 mile SW of Rodmarton

**Train:** Kemble 5 miles

**Bus:** Stagecoach in the Cotswolds 881 from Kemble

**MAP Page 265 (2J)**
**OS Map 168 (ref ST 933973)**

## Winterbourne Poor Lot Barrows
Dorset

A 'cemetery' of 44 Bronze Age burial mounds of varying types and sizes, straddling the A35 main road.

### OPENING TIMES
Any reasonable time

Winterbourne Poor Lot Barrows

### HOW TO FIND US
**Direction:** 2 miles W of Winterbourne Abbas, S of junction of A35 with a minor road to Compton Valence. Access via Wellbottom Lodge – 180 metres (200 yards) E along A35 from junction

**Train:** Dorchester West or South, both 7 miles

**Bus:** First 31 Weymouth – Axminster (passes Dorchester South)

No adjacent parking.

Warning: cross road with care.

**MAP Page 265 (5H)**
**OS Map 15/117 (ref SY 590907)**

## Woodhenge
Wiltshire

Neolithic monument, dating from about 2300 BC, with concrete markers replacing six concentric rings of timber posts, once possibly supporting a ring-shaped building.

**Part of the Stonehenge World Heritage Site.**

### OPENING TIMES
Any reasonable time

Usual facilities may not be available around the Summer Solstice 20-22 Jun. Please check before you visit

### HOW TO FIND US
**Direction:** 1½ miles N of Amesbury, off A345, just S of Durrington

**Train:** Salisbury 9 miles

**Bus:** Wilts & Dorset 5/6 Salisbury – Swindon (passes close to Salisbury and Swindon); 16 from Amesbury

**MAP Page 265 (4J)**
**OS Map 130 (ref SU 151434)**

## Yarn Market, Dunster:
see Dunster, Yarn Market – Page 94

# Tintagel Castle Cornwall – PL34 0HE

With its spectacular location on one of Britain's most dramatic coastlines, Tintagel is an awe-inspiring and romantic spot, a place of legends.

Joined to the mainland by a narrow neck of land, Tintagel Island faces the full force of the Atlantic. On the mainland itself, the gaunt remains of the medieval castle represent only one phase in a long history of occupation. Even before Richard Earl of Cornwall built his castle, Tintagel was already associated with the conception of King Arthur. This connection was later renewed by Alfred, Lord Tennyson, in his *Idylls of the King*.

After a period as a Roman settlement and military outpost, Tintagel is thought to have been a trading settlement of Celtic kings during the 5th and 6th centuries. Legend has it that one of these was King Mark, whose nephew Tristan fell in love with Yseult (or Isolde). Their doomed romance is part of Tintagel's story.

The remains of the 13th-century castle are breathtaking. Steep stone steps, stout walls and rugged windswept cliff edges encircle the Great Hall, where Richard Earl of Cornwall once feasted.

There are many unanswered questions and legends surrounding Tintagel. The castle has an amazing capacity to surprise us, even after years of investigation.

In June 1998, excavations were undertaken under the direction of Professor Chris Morris of the University of Glasgow, on a relatively sheltered and small site on the eastern side of the island, first excavated in the 1930s. Pottery from the 5th and 6th centuries was found, as well as some fine glass fragments believed to be from 6th or 7th-century Málaga in Spain. Even more remarkable was a 1,500-year-old piece of slate on which remained two Latin inscriptions. The second inscription reads: 'Artognou, father of a descendant of Coll, has had [this] made.' Who exactly Artognou was continues to be a subject for lively speculation.

'Searching for King Arthur', a short audio visual tour through the ages, introduces visitors to the castle, its legends and history.

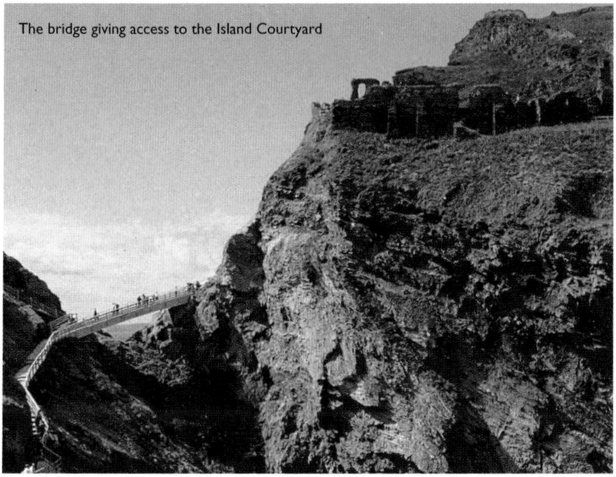
The bridge giving access to the Island Courtyard

During the summer you can also enjoy special introductory talks. The site offers a newly refurbished shop and visitor facilities.

Access to the castle is difficult for disabled visitors (via over 100 steep steps). There is a Land Rover service from the village which can take visitors to the exhibition and shop (Apr-Oct only). Contact the site for service information.

**www.english-heritage.org.uk/tintagelcastle**

### NON-MEMBERS

| | |
|---|---|
| Adult | £4.50 |
| Concession | £3.40 |
| Child | £2.30 |

### OPENING TIMES

| | |
|---|---|
| 1 Apr-30 Sep, daily | 10am-6pm |
| 1-31 Oct, daily | 10am-5pm |
| 1 Nov-20 Mar, daily | 10am-4pm |
| Closed | 24-26 Dec and 1 Jan |

### HOW TO FIND US

**Direction:** On Tintagel Head, 600 metres (660 yards) along uneven track from Tintagel; no vehicles except Land Rover Service

**Bus:** Western Greyhound 524 Bude – Wadebridge, 594 Bude – Truro (with connections on 555 at Wadebridge to ⇌ Bodmin Parkway)

**Tel:** 01840 770328

**Local Tourist Information:** Tintagel Visitors' Centre: 01840 779084; Camelford (summer only): 01840 212954 Padstow: 01841 533449

OVP

Disabled access (limited via Land Rover service to castle Apr-Oct, extra charge).

Parking (600 metres (660 yards) in the village) – not part of English Heritage.

MAP Page 264 (5C)
OS Map 111 (ref SX 049891)

# The Heritage of Scilly Isles of Scilly

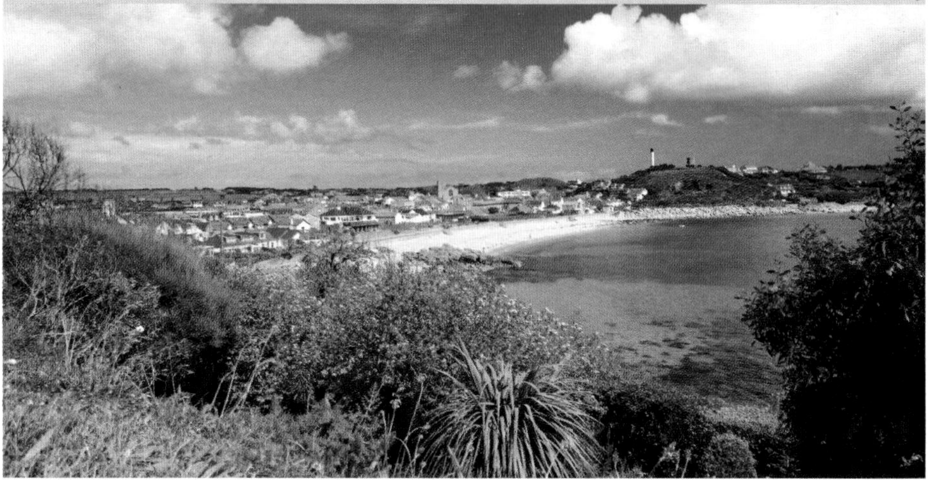

The stunningly beautiful Isles of Scilly hold vast arrays of archaeological riches both above and below sea level. English Heritage recognises the importance of promoting this unique cultural landscape, and provides expert advice and significant funding to regeneration and conservation projects throughout the Isles.

This compact archipelago of about 100 islands lies around 28 miles to the south-west of Land's End. None of them is any bigger than three miles across and only five are inhabited. Despite their landmass of only 16 square kilometres (6.18 square miles), these islands contain a remarkable number of historic sites. These range from traditional farmhouses and dwellings to ritual burial monuments, cist grave cemeteries and Romano-Celtic shrines. Early settlements provide evidence of a distinctive Scillonian culture which thrived in the island group 2,000 years ago. More recently, defensive monuments constructed during the Civil War and World War II stand as testament to the strategic importance of the islands. The Gulf Stream keeps the climate warm, enabling exotic plants and wildlife to thrive.

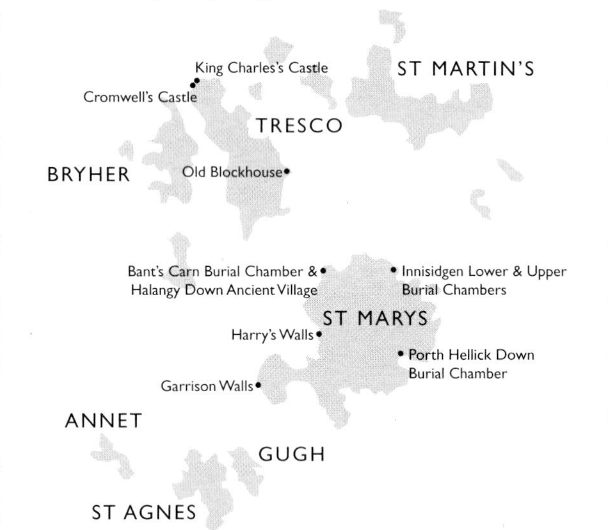


### OPENING TIMES

All EH properties on the Scillies are open at any reasonable time

### HOW TO FIND US

**Direction:** See individual property entries (opposite) for access details

**Tel:** 0117 9750700 (Regional office)

## Bant's Carn Burial Chamber and Halangy Down Ancient Village
St Mary's, Isles of Scilly

In a wonderfully scenic location, on a hill above the site of the ancient Iron Age village, stands this Bronze Age burial mound with entrance passage and inner chamber.

**OPENING TIMES**

Any reasonable time

**HOW TO FIND US**

**Direction:** 1 mile N of Hugh Town

MAP Page 264 (5B)
OS Map 101 (ref SV 910123)

## Cromwell's Castle
Tresco, Isles of Scilly

Standing on a rocky promontory guarding the lovely anchorage between Bryher and Tresco, this round tower is one of the few surviving Cromwellian fortifications in Britain, built after the conquest of the Royalist Scillies in 1651.

**OPENING TIMES**

Any reasonable time

**HOW TO FIND US**

**Direction:** On the shoreline, approach with care, ¾ mile NW of New Grimsby

MAP Page 264 (4A)
OS Map 101 (ref SV 882159)

## Garrison Walls
St Mary's, Isles of Scilly

You can enjoy a two-hour walk alongside the ramparts of these defensive walls and earthworks, dating from the 16th to 18th centuries.

Garrison Walls

**OPENING TIMES**

Any reasonable time

**HOW TO FIND US**

**Direction:** Around the headland W of Hugh Town

MAP Page 264 (5A)
OS Map 101 (ref SV 898104)

## Harry's Walls
St Mary's, Isles of Scilly

An unfinished artillery fort, built above St Mary's Pool harbour in 1551.

**OPENING TIMES**

Any reasonable time

**HOW TO FIND US**

**Direction:** ¼ mile NE of Hugh Town

P

MAP Page 264 (5B)
OS Map 101 (ref SV 909109)

## Innisidgen Lower and Upper Burial Chambers
St Mary's, Isles of Scilly

Two Bronze Age communal burial cairns of particularly Scillonian type, with fine views. The upper cairn is the best preserved in the islands.

**OPENING TIMES**

Any reasonable time

**HOW TO FIND US**

**Direction:** 1¾ miles E of Hugh Town

P

MAP Page 264 (5B)
OS Map 101 (ref SV 922127)

## King Charles's Castle
Tresco, Isles of Scilly

The ruins of a mid 16th-century coastal artillery fort, later garrisoned – hence the name –

King Charles's Castle

by Civil War Royalists. Reached from New Grimsby by footpath.

**OPENING TIMES**

Any reasonable time

**HOW TO FIND US**

**Direction:** Located ¾ mile NW of New Grimsby. Coastal location, approach with care

MAP Page 264 (4A)
OS Map 101 (ref SV 882161)

## Old Blockhouse
Tresco, Isles of Scilly

Substantial remains of a small 16th-century gun tower protecting Old Grimsby harbour, vigorously defended during the Civil War.

**OPENING TIMES**

Any reasonable time

**HOW TO FIND US**

**Direction:** Located on Blockhouse Point, at the S end of Old Grimsby harbour

MAP Page 264 (4A)
OS Map 101 (ref SV 897155)

## Porth Hellick Down Burial Chamber
St Mary's, Isles of Scilly

A large and imposing Scillonian Bronze Age entrance grave, with kerb, inner passage and burial chamber all clearly visible.

**OPENING TIMES**

Any reasonable time

**HOW TO FIND US**

**Direction:** 1¾ miles NE of Hugh Town

MAP Page 264 (5B)
OS Map 101 (ref SV 928108)

# Other historic attractions

Discounted entry to our members (discounts may not apply on event days)

## The Arthurian Centre
Cornwall – PL32 9TT

Walk through newly exposed archaeology to 'King Arthur's Stone' and Camlann battlefield. Lots to see and learn for all ages, including a 'Grail Trail' and unique exhibition. The site of King Arthur's last battle with Mordred. 10 mins from Tintagel Castle.

### ENTRY

| | |
|---|---|
| Adult | £3.00 |
| Concession/Child | £2.00 |
| Family | £8.50 |

20% discount for EH members

### OPENING TIMES

| | |
|---|---|
| Easter-31 Oct, daily | 10am-5pm |

**Directions:** On B3314 at Slaughterbridge, Camelford

**Tel:** 01840 213947

www.arthur-online.co.uk

MAP Page 264 (5C)
OS Map 109/111 (ref SX 109857)

## Coldharbour Mill Museum
Devon – EX15 3EE

This 200-year-old woollen mill still produces knitting yarns and woven tartans, and tells the story of the once flourishing West Country woollen industry. It houses a restored waterwheel, steam-powered mill engines and a 1910 Lancashire boiler, which are still operated on special steam-up days.

Coldharbour Mill Museum

Owned and managed by the Coldharbour Mill Trust.

### NON-MEMBERS

| | |
|---|---|
| **Special event days** | |
| Adult | £6.25 |
| Concession | £5.75 |
| Child | £2.95 |
| Family | £17.00 |
| **Site only** | |
| Adult | £1.50 |
| Children | Free |

EH members, and up to 6 children within their family group, get free entry. Discount does not extend to EH Corporate Partners or Cadw and Historic Scotland members. For tour times and special events details please call 01884 840960

### OPENING TIMES

| | |
|---|---|
| Mar-Oct, daily | 10.30am-5pm |
| Nov-Feb | 11am-4pm |

For 2007 Site, Shop & Restaurant only are open daily but no factory tours available. However, Guided Group Tours can be arranged and there will be Guided Factory Tours run on our Special Events Weekends. Telephone: 01884 840960 for dates and details

**Direction:** Located just off B3440 as it enters Uffculme from Willand. 2 miles south-east of J27 on M5

**Train:** Tiverton Parkway 2 miles

**Bus:** Stagecoach in Devon 1/B Exeter – Tiverton (passes ⇌ Tiverton Parkway); First 92/A Taunton – Exeter/Tiverton

**Tel:** 01884 840960

www.coldharbourmill.org.uk

Disabled access (partial). Dogs on leads (grounds only).

MAP Page 265 (5F)
OS Map 128 (ref ST 062122)

## Lulworth Castle
Dorset – BH20 5QS

A 17th-century hunting lodge set in extensive parkland. Following a fire in 1929, the exterior has been restored to its former glory: the walls, interior and displays revealing past secrets. Stunning views across the World Heritage Coast.

Owned and managed by the Lulworth Estate.

### ENTRY

Please call or check website for details

25% discount for EH members

### OPENING TIMES

| | |
|---|---|
| 25 Mar-28 Sep, Sun-Fri | 10.30am-6pm |
| 30 Sep-21 Mar, Sun-Fri | 10.30am-4pm |

Last admission 1 hour before closing

Closed 24-25 Dec and 6-19 Jan 2008 and Saturdays throughout the year except Easter weekend and 11 Aug

**Direction:** Located in E Lulworth off B3070; 3 miles NE of Lulworth Cove

**Train:** Wool 4 miles

**Bus:** Nordcat 103 ⇌ Wool-Dorchester

**Tel:** 0845 450 1054

www.lulworth.com

MAP Page 265 (5J)
OS Map 15 (ref SY 853822)

## Sherborne Castle
Dorset – DT9 5NR

Original house built by Sir Walter Raleigh in 1594. Splendid decorative interiors and collections. 'Capability' Brown lake and landscaped lakeside gardens. Home of the Digby family since 1617.

### ENTRY

£2.50 entry to grounds for EH members, except on special event days

Additional charge for castle interior. Children free

Discount does not extend to EH Corporate Partners

### OPENING TIMES

1 Apr-31 Oct, Sat, Sun, Tue, Wed, Thu & Bank Hol Mons 11am-last admission 4.30pm (Castle interior opens 2pm on Sat)

**Directions:** E of Sherborne, off A30

**Tel:** 01935 812072/813182

www.sherbornecastle.com

MAP Page 265 (4H)
OS Map 129 (ref ST 649164)

## Woodchester Mansion
Gloucestershire – GL10 3TS

Woodchester Mansion was abandoned by its builders before it was completed, and has been virtually untouched by time since the mid-1870s. A wonderful opportunity to explore a neo-Gothic building 'frozen' in mid-assembly.

### ENTRY

| | |
|---|---|
| EH members | £5.00 |

Discount does not extend to EH Corporate Partners

### OPENING TIMES

Apr-Oct, 1st Sat of every month, and every Sun. Every weekend Jul-Aug.

**Directions:** B4066, 5 miles south of Stroud

**Tel:** 01453 861541

www.woodchestermansion.org.uk

MAP Page 265 (2H)
OS Map 179/168/167
(ref SO 809014)

Stonehenge – see page 112

Framlingham Castle – see page 134

# East of England

'...they must be bold fellows indeed who will venture in the biggest ship the world has heard of to pass such a battery'

Daniel Defoe, describing Tilbury Fort,
in *A Tour Through the Whole Island of Great Britain*', 1724

# Properties See individual listings for details

### Bedfordshire
Bushmead Priory
De Grey Mausoleum
Houghton House
Wrest Park

### Cambridgeshire
Denny Abbey and the Farmland Museum
Duxford Chapel
Isleham Priory Church
Longthorpe Tower

### Essex
Audley End House and Gardens
Hadleigh Castle
Hill Hall
Lexden Earthworks and Bluebottle Grove
Mistley Towers
Prior's Hall Barn
St Botolph's Priory
St John's Abbey Gate
Tilbury Fort
Waltham Abbey Gatehouse and Bridge

### Hertfordshire
Berkhamsted Castle
Old Gorhambury House
Roman Wall of St Albans

### Norfolk
Baconsthorpe Castle
Berney Arms Windmill
Binham Priory
Binham Market Cross
Blakeney Guildhall
Burgh Castle
Caister Roman Site
Castle Acre: Bailey Gate Castle Acre Castle and Castle Acre Priory
Castle Rising Castle
Church of the Holy Sepulchre
Cow Tower in Norwich
Creake Abbey
Great Yarmouth Row Houses & Greyfriars' Cloisters
Grime's Graves
North Elmham Chapel
St Olave's Priory
Thetford Priory
Thetford Warren Lodge
Weeting Castle

### Suffolk
Bury St Edmunds Abbey
Framlingham Castle
Landguard Fort
Leiston Abbey
Lindsey/St James's Chapel
Moulton Packhorse Bridge
Orford Castle
Saxtead Green Post Mill

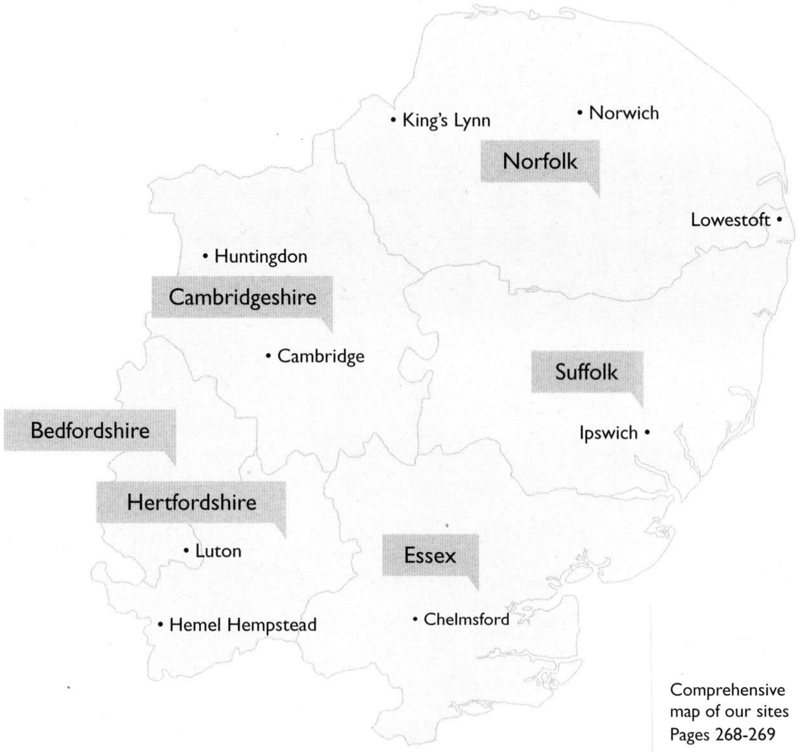


Comprehensive map of our sites Pages 268-269

Above: (top left) Framlingham Castle, (top centre) Lexden Earthworks and Bluebottle Grove, (top right) Bury St Edmunds Abbey, (bottom left) Audley End House and Gardens, (bottom centre) Saxtead Green Post Mill, (bottom right) Orford Castle.



# Ports and Forts

The East of England region begins on the edge of Greater London, extending northwards through Hertfordshire, Bedfordshire and Cambridgeshire, and through Essex, Suffolk and Norfolk to the sea which forms by far its longest boundary. Much of it now a playground for bathers, naturalists and yachtsmen, East Anglia's sea-coast (and its many deep-penetrating estuaries) were long the source both of its greatest prosperity and its greatest dangers.

In Roman times, this North Sea coast was particularly vulnerable to sea-borne Germanic invaders – including the Angles who later gave the area its name. **Burgh Castle** and **Caister Roman Site** belonged to the 'Saxon Shore' system of forts built against them, together watching over the then navigable but now silted-up Waveney estuary. Coastline changes have indeed made many once-prosperous East Anglian ports redundant: **Blakeney Guildhall** is one of the few reminders of this pretty village's late-medieval prosperity as the third most important port in Norfolk. With sad appropriateness, one of its last uses was as a temporary mortuary for shipwrecked sailors during World War I.

The unique polygonal 12th-century keep of **Orford Castle**, with its intriguingly well-preserved interior chambers and passages, also presides over a now silted-up port, developed by Henry II to help defend the coast against invaders called in by rebel barons – like the Bigods of impressive **Framlingham Castle**.

Once famous for the 'prodigious catches' of its herring fishermen, and later for the 'great purity and bracing quality of its air … a powerful yet wholesome stimulant to the human frame', Great Yarmouth enjoyed a much longer period of prosperity: aspects of its history, from the 17th century to the disastrous World War II bombing raids, are imaginatively brought to life in **Great Yarmouth Row Houses**. Further south, **Landguard Fort**, near the now thriving freighter port of Felixstowe, defended the estuaries of the Stour and Orwell and repulsed a Dutch landing force in 1667 – the last opposed invasion of England.

The most powerful and best-preserved of all the region's maritime defences, **Tilbury Fort**, owes its impressive appearance to this Dutch invasion scare. Guarding the vital Thames approach to London, and already renowned for its associations with Queen Elizabeth's 'Armada Speech', it was totally rebuilt in the 1670s, and remains the most complete surviving 17th-century artillery fortress in Britain.

# Audley End House and Gardens Essex – CB11 4JF

Sir Thomas Audley was given the lands of Walden Abbey by Henry VIII, and adapted the abbey buildings as his mansion. His grandson Thomas, first Earl of Suffolk, rebuilt this mansion between 1603 and 1614. The new Audley End was truly palatial in scale, but Suffolk fell from power after 1618.

Charles II bought the house in 1668, using it as a base for attending Newmarket races. By the 1680s, Sir Christopher Wren was warning of the need for major repairs. The cost of these caused William III to return Audley End to the Suffolk family. When the Suffolk line died out in 1745, it was bought by the Countess of Portsmouth for her nephew and heir, Sir John Griffin Whitwell. Following his inheritance, he became known as Sir John Griffin Griffin – also the fourth Baron Howard de Walden and first Baron Braybrooke. He made changes to the house, adding a suite of neo-Classical rooms designed by Robert Adam and a Gothic chapel. Meanwhile, 'Capability' Brown had been employed to remodel the grounds.

Today, the house's interior is largely the result of ownership by the third Baron Braybrooke, who inherited it in 1825. He installed his extensive picture collection and filled the rooms with furnishings. The fourth Baron Braybrooke's natural history collection also remains an appealing feature of the house.

After nearly 30 years in store, a rare set of English tapestries by the Soho weaver Paul Saunders has been conserved and displayed in the Tapestry Room. Depicting figures in a landscape with ruined buildings, they were originally supplied to Audley End in 1767. Following paint research, the room has also been redecorated in the warm stone colour used when the tapestries were first installed there.

## The Gardens

Much has been done recently to restore the park and the fine Victorian gardens to their former glory. An artificial lake, created with water from the River Cam, runs through delightful 18th-century parkland. The Classical Temple of Concorde, built in 1790 in honour of George III, and the restored 19th-century formal parterre garden dominate the views from the back of the house.

Visitors can see Robert Adam's ornamental garden buildings, and the Elysian Garden cascade. The thriving organic walled Victorian kitchen garden – with its box-edged paths, trained fruit and 52 m (170 feet) long vine house, still as it was in its Victorian heyday – is a memorable part of any visit. Also worth visiting are the historic kitchen and dry laundry.

**Please note:** In some rooms, light levels are reduced to preserve vulnerable textiles and other collections. No photography or stiletto heels allowed in the house. Please call the site for special events information.

**www.english-heritage.org.uk/audleyend**

- Available for corporate and private hire.
- Licensed for civil wedding ceremonies.
- Holiday cottage available to let.

## NON-MEMBERS

| House & Gardens | |
|---|---|
| Adult | £9.20 |
| Concession | £6.90 |
| Child | £4.60 |
| Family | £23.00 |
| **Gardens Only** | |
| Adult | £5.00 |
| Concession | £3.80 |
| Child | £2.50 |
| Family | £12.50 |

## OPENING TIMES

**House:**

| | |
|---|---|
| 1-31 Mar, Sat | 10am-4pm* |
| Sun | 10am-4pm* |
| 1 Apr-30 Jun, Wed-Sun<br>11am-5pm (closes 3pm Sat)<br>Guided Historical Tours | |
| 1 Jul-31 Aug, Wed-Sun<br>11am-5pm (closes 3pm Sat) | |
| 1-30 Sep, Wed-Sun (closes 3pm Sat)<br>Guided Historical Tours | 11am-5pm |
| 1-31 Oct, Sat | 10am-3pm* |
| Sun | 10am-4pm* |
| 1-20 Mar, Sat | 10am-4pm* |
| Sun | 10am-4pm* |

Last admission 1 hour before closing

**Gardens:**

| | |
|---|---|
| 1-31 Mar Sat-Sun | 10am-5pm |
| 1 Apr-30 Sep, Wed-Sun & Bank Hols | 10am-6pm |
| 1-31 Oct, Sat-Sun | 10am-5pm |
| 1-20 Mar, Sat-Sun | 10am-5pm |

* Behind the scenes tours

At certain times of the year, access to the house is by 'Behind The Scenes Tours' and 'Guided Historical Tours' only. In Mar and Oct, tours will be 'Behind The Scenes Tours' only. Some rooms will not be open to the public throughout the season. Please call for details

## HOW TO FIND US

**Direction:** 1 mile W of Saffron Walden on B1383 (M11 exit 8 or 10)

**Train:** Audley End 1¼ miles. Note: Footpath is beside busy main road

**Bus:** Hedingham/Four Counties 59, Stansted Transit 301 from Audley End stopping in Saffron Walden

**Tel:** 01799 522399 (info line)

**Disabled access:** Tel 01799 522842

**Local Tourist Information**
Saffron Walden: 01799 510444
Cambridge: 01223 464732

OVP

**MAP Page 269 (5F)**
**OS Map 195 (ref TL 525382)**

## Baconsthorpe Castle
Norfolk

The extensive ruins of a late medieval and Tudor fortified manor house, its knapped flint walls reflected in the lake enlarged from its original moat. Baconsthorpe is the work of several generations of the locally powerful (but somewhat disreputable) Heydon family. Sir John Heydon probably built the strong inner gatehouse and curtain wall, equipped for artillery, during the Wars of the Roses. In more peaceful times a descendant converted part of the house into a textile factory, and in c. 1560 Sir Christopher Heydon added the turreted outer gateway, inhabited until 1920.

### OPENING TIMES
Any reasonable time

### HOW TO FIND US
**Direction:** ¾ mile N of village of Baconsthorpe off unclassified road, 3 miles E of Holt

**Train:** Sheringham 4½ miles

MAP Page 269 (1H)
OS Map 252 (ref TG 121382)

## Berkhamsted Castle
Hertfordshire

The substantial remains of a strong and important motte and bailey castle dating from the 11th to 13th centuries, with surrounding walls, ditches and earthworks.

### OPENING TIMES

| | |
|---|---|
| Summer, daily | 10am 6pm |
| Winter, daily | 10am-4pm |
| Closed | 25 Dec and 1 Jan |

### HOW TO FIND US
Direction: Near Berkhamsted

Bus: From surrounding areas

Train: Berkhamsted, adjacent

MAP Page 268 (6D)
OS Map 181 (ref SP 995082)

## Berney Arms Windmill
Norfolk

One of Norfolk's best and largest extant marsh mills, built to grind a constituent of cement and in use until 1951, finally pumping water to drain surrounding marshland.

### OPENING TIMES
Closed for conservation
For further details please telephone: 01799 522842

## Berney Arms Windmill

### HOW TO FIND US
**Direction:** 3½ miles NE of Reedham on the N bank of River Yare. Accessible by hired boat, or by footpath from Halvergate (3½ miles). ¼ mile walk from train

**Train:** Berney Arms ¼ mile

MAP Page 269 (3K)
OS Map 40 (ref TG 465049)

## Binham Priory
Norfolk

The most complete and impressive monastic ruins, in Norfolk, of a Benedictine priory with a well-documented history. The nave, with its splendid 13th-century west front and great bricked-up window, is now the parish church, displaying a screen with medieval saints overpainted with Protestant texts.

Managed by Binham Parochial Church Council.

### OPENING TIMES
Any reasonable time

### HOW TO FIND US
**Direction:** ¼ mile NW of village of Binham-on-Wells on road off B1388

**Bus:** Sanders 45 Norwich-Fakenham

**Tel:** 01328 830362

MAP Page 269 (1H)
OS Map 251 (ref TF 982399)

## Binham Market Cross
Norfolk

The tall shaft of a 15th-century cross, on the site of an annual fair held from the 1100s until the 1950s.

Managed by Binham Parochial Church Council.

### OPENING TIMES
Any reasonable time

### HOW TO FIND US
**Direction:** Located on the Binham village green adjacent to the Priory

**Bus:** Sanders 45 Norwich-Fakenham

**MAP Page 269 (1H)**
**OS Map 251 (ref TF 984396)**

## Blakeney Guildhall
Norfolk

The remains of the house of a prosperous Blakeney merchant, with a fine 15th-century brick-vaulted undercroft. Later the guildhall of Blakeney's guild of fish merchants.

Managed by Blakeney Parish Council.

### OPENING TIMES
Any reasonable time

### HOW TO FIND US
**Direction:** In Blakeney off A149

**Train:** Sheringham 9 miles

**Bus:** Norfolk Green 36 Sheringham – Hunstanton

**Tel:** 0845 300 6116

**MAP Page 269 (1H)**
**OS Map 251 (ref TG 028441)**

## Burgh Castle
Norfolk

The imposing stone walls, with added towers for catapults, of a Roman 3rd-century Saxon Shore fort. Panoramic views over Breydon Water, into which the fourth wall long since collapsed.

## Burgh Castle

Managed by Norfolk Archaeological Trust.

### OPENING TIMES
Any reasonable time

### HOW TO FIND US
**Direction:** At far W end of Breydon Water on unclassified road, 3 miles W of Great Yarmouth

**Train:** Great Yarmouth 5 miles

**Bus:** First 6/7 from Great Yarmouth

**MAP Page 269 (3K)**
**OS Map 40 (ref TG 475047)**

## Bury St Edmunds Abbey
Suffolk

The extensive ruins of the wealthiest and most powerful Benedictine monastery in England, shrine of St Edmund. They include the noble 14th-century Great Gate, the Norman Tower, and the ground plan and altered west front of the immense church.

Managed by St Edmundsbury Borough Council.

### OPENING TIMES
Any reasonable time

### HOW TO FIND US
**Direction:** E end of town centre

**Train:** Bury St Edmunds 1 mile

**Bus:** From surrounding areas

**Tel:** 01284 764667

**MAP Page 269 (4G)**
**OS Map 211 (ref TL 857642)**

## Bushmead Priory
Bedfordshire – MK44 2LD

A rare survival of the complete refectory of an Augustinian priory, with fine timber roof and notable 14th-century wall paintings.

### NON-MEMBERS

| | |
|---|---|
| Adult | £5.00 |
| Concession | £3.80 |
| Child | £2.50 |

### OPENING TIMES
1 May-31 Aug. Pre-booked guided tours only

**Tel:** 01799 522842

### HOW TO FIND US
**Direction:** Located off B660, 2 miles S of Bolnhurst

**Train:** St Neots 6 miles

**MAP Page 268 (4E)**
**OS Map 225 (ref TL 115607)**

## Caister Roman Site
Norfolk

The partial remains of a Roman Saxon Shore fort, operating in partnership with Burgh Castle, including wall and ditch sections and building foundations.

Managed by Great Yarmouth Borough Council.

### OPENING TIMES
Any reasonable time

### HOW TO FIND US
**Direction:** Near Caister-on-Sea, 3 miles N of Great Yarmouth

**Train:** Great Yarmouth 3 miles

**Bus:** First Bus 1, 3, 8 from Great Yarmouth

**MAP Page 269 (2K)**
**OS Map 40 (ref TG 517123)**

## Castle Acre Priory, Castle and Bailey Gate
Norfolk

The delightful village of Castle Acre boasts an extraordinary wealth of history.

Situated on the Peddar's Way, a major trade and pilgrim route to Thetford, Bromholm Priory and Walsingham, it is a very rare and complete survival of a Norman planned settlement, including a castle, town, parish church and associated monastery. All this is the work of a great Norman baronial family, the Warennes, mainly during the 11th and 12th centuries.

First came the castle, founded soon after the Conquest by the first William de Warenne, initially as a stone 'country house'. During the first half of the 12th century, however, more disturbed conditions prompted its progressive conversion into a strong keep, further defended by stone walls and an immense system of ditched earthworks. Still impressively visible, these are perhaps the finest village earthworks in England.

Meanwhile, the 'planned town' deliberately established outside the castle was also protected by ditched earthwork defences with stone gates. The north or Bailey Gate of c. 1200 still survives, with the main road into the village still running between its towers.

Visitors to Castle Acre can likewise trace the ancient street layout of this now peaceful village, lined with attractive flint or brick houses, before exploring both the great castle earthworks and the extensive priory remains.

### Castle Acre Castle and Bailey Gate
Norfolk

#### OPENING TIMES
Any reasonable time

#### HOW TO FIND US
**Direction:** Located at the E end of Castle Acre, 5 miles N of Swaffham

(Castle only)

MAP Page 269 (2G)
OS Map 236/238 (ref TF 819152)

### Castle Acre Priory
See feature opposite

## Castle Rising Castle
Norfolk – PE31 6AH

One of the largest, best-preserved and most lavishly decorated keeps in England, surrounded by 20 acres of mighty earthworks. Begun in 1138 by William d'Albini for his new wife, the widow of Henry I, in the 14th century it became the luxurious exile-place of Queen Isabella, widow (and alleged murderess) of Edward II.

Owned and managed by Lord Howard of Rising.

#### NON-MEMBERS

| | |
|---|---|
| Adult | £3.85 |
| Concession | £3.10 |
| Child | £2.20 |
| Family | £11.50 |

#### OPENING TIMES

| | |
|---|---|
| 1 Apr-1 Nov, daily | 10am-6pm |
| Closes at dusk if earlier in Oct | |
| 2 Nov-31 Mar, Wed-Sun | 10am-4pm |
| Closed | 24-26 Dec |

#### HOW TO FIND US
**Direction:** Located 4 miles NE of King's Lynn off A149

**Train:** King's Lynn 4½ miles

**Bus:** First 410/1 King's Lynn-Hunstanton

**Tel:** 01553 631330

Audio tours (charged).

Disabled access (exterior, only toilets).

Dogs on leads (restricted areas).

MAP Page 269 (2G)
OS Map 250 (ref TF 666246)

# Castle Acre Priory Norfolk – PE32 2XD

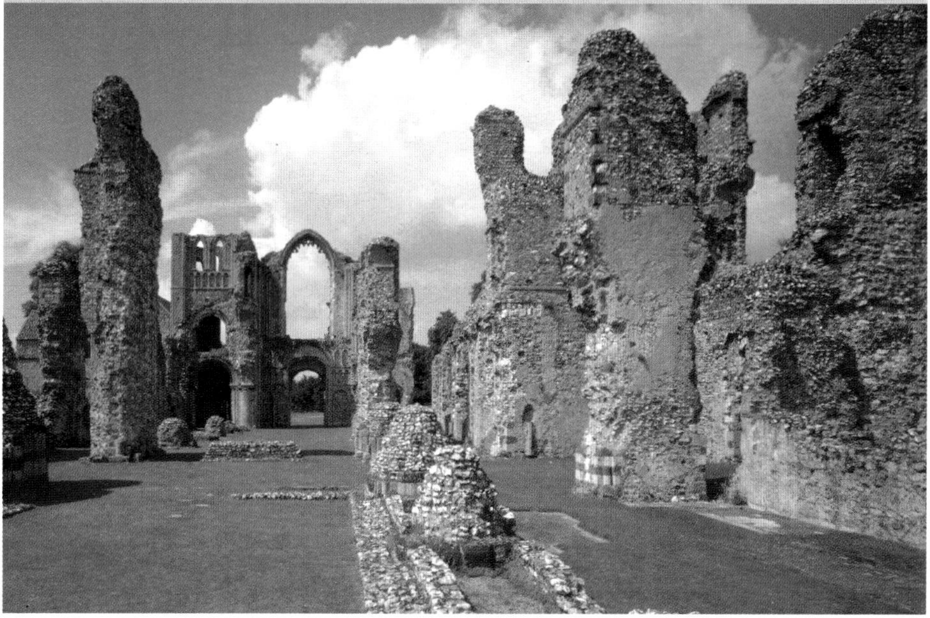

One of the largest and best-preserved monastic sites in England, the foundation of Castle Acre Priory in about 1090 sprang directly from a visit by William de Warenne II and his wife Gundrada to the great French monastery of Cluny. So impressed were they by its beauty and holiness that they vowed to introduce the Cluniac order of monks to England.

The Cluniac love of decoration is everywhere reflected in the extensive ruins of Castle Acre Priory, whose great 12th-century church directly imitated that of Cluny itself. Its beautiful west end, standing almost to its full height, displays tiered ranks of intersecting round arches: it forms an attractive group with the late medieval porch, part timber-framed and part flint-chequered, and the extremely well-preserved prior's lodging. A mansion in itself, this includes a first-floor chapel retaining traces of wall-paintings, and a private chamber with two fine oriel windows.

There is much more to see at the priory, including the substantial remains of many of the buildings round the cloister. The recreated herb garden next to the visitor centre grows herbs which the monks would have used for medicinal, culinary and decorative purposes.

**NEW FOR 2007** Exhibition, including a new display of artefacts, model and computer fly-through of the Prior's lodging. Audio tour, including a recording of a 15th-century chant from a song book from Castle Acre.

## NON-MEMBERS

| | |
|---|---|
| Adult | £4.70 |
| Concession | £3.50 |
| Child | £2.40 |
| Family | £11.80 |

## OPENING TIMES

| | |
|---|---|
| 1 Apr-30 Sep, daily | 10am-6pm |
| 1 Oct-20 Mar, Thu-Mon | 10am-4pm |
| Closed | 24-26 Dec and 1 Jan |

## HOW TO FIND US

**Direction:** ¼ mile W of village of Castle Acre, 5 miles N of Swaffham

**Tel:** 01760 755394

E P OVP

Disabled access (ground floor and grounds only).

MAP Page 269 (2G)
OS Map 236/238 (ref TF 814148)

# Framlingham Castle Suffolk – IP13 9BP

Framlingham is a magnificent example of a late 12th-century castle. Built by Roger Bigod, Earl of Norfolk, the castle, together with Framlingham Mere, was designed both as a stronghold and as a symbol of power and status – as befitted one of the most influential people at the court of Henry II. Architecturally, the castle is notable for its curtain wall and mural towers, an early example of this design.

The castle fulfilled a number of roles. It was at the centre of the struggle between the Bigod barons and the Crown, and Mary Tudor mustered her supporters here in 1553, before being crowned Queen. At the end of the 16th century it was a prison; later still a poorhouse and school were built in the grounds. Today the imposing stone walls and crenellated towers with their ornate Tudor chimneys dominate, while the grassy earthworks around the castle are subdued reminders of busier times. To the west, the Mere provides a stunning setting.

While visiting, why not take a walk around the magnificent Framlingham Mere and the castle's outer courts and moats? Or perhaps negotiate the impressive wall-walk and take in the beautiful views of the surrounding countryside, or enjoy one of Framlingham's many pubs or tearooms.

**Please note:** Entry also includes access to the Lanman Trust's Museum of local history.

**www.english-heritage.org.uk/framlinghamcastle**

## NON-MEMBERS

| | |
|---|---|
| Adult | £4.70 |
| Concession | £3.50 |
| Child | £2.40 |
| Family | £11.80 |

## OPENING TIMES

| | |
|---|---|
| 1 Apr-30 Sep, daily | 10am-6pm |
| 1 Oct-20 Mar, Thu-Mon | 10am-4pm |
| Closed | 24-26 Dec and 1 Jan |

The property may close early if an event is booked, please ring in advance for details

## HOW TO FIND US

**Direction:** In Framlingham on B1116

**Train:** Wickham Market 6½ miles; Saxmundham 7 miles

**Bus:** First 63, Gemini/Goldline 164 from ≠ Ipswich (passes ≠ Woodbridge); Beeston 118/9 from Ipswich

**Tel:** 01728 724189

**Local Tourist Information**
Woodbridge: 01394 382240

E P OVP

Disabled access (grounds and ground floor only). No disabled toilet on site.

MAP Page 269 (4J)
OS Map 212 (ref TM 287637)

## Church of the Holy Sepulchre, Thetford, Norfolk:

see Thetford, Church of the Holy Sepulchre – Page 143

## Colchester, St Botolph's Priory
Essex

The 12th-century nave of the first Augustinian priory church in England, with an impressive west front.

Managed by Colchester Borough Council.

### OPENING TIMES
Any reasonable time

### HOW TO FIND US
**Direction:** Nr Colchester Town station

**Train:** Colchester Town, adjacent

**Bus:** From surrounding areas

**Tel:** 01206 282931

MAP Page 269 (5H)
OS Map 184 (ref TL 999249)

## Colchester, St John's Abbey Gate
Essex

This elaborate pinnacled 15th-century gatehouse, in East Anglian flushwork, is the sole survivor of the Benedictine abbey of St John. It was stormed by Parliamentarian soldiers during the Civil War siege of 1648.

Managed by Colchester Borough Council.

### OPENING TIMES
Any reasonable time

### HOW TO FIND US
**Direction:** S side of central Colchester

**Train:** Colchester Town ¼ mile

**Bus:** From surrounding areas

**Tel:** 01206 282931

MAP Page 269 (5H)
OS Map 184 (ref TL 998248)

## Cow Tower, Norwich
Norfolk

One of the earliest purpose-built artillery blockhouses in England, this brick tower was built in c. 1398-9 to command a strategic point in Norwich's city defences.

Managed by Norwich City Council.

### OPENING TIMES
Any reasonable time

### HOW TO FIND US
**Direction:** In Norwich, near cathedral (approx. 1 mile walk)

**Bus:** From surrounding areas

**Train:** Norwich ½ mile

**Tel:** 01603 213434

MAP Page 269 (2J)
OS Map 40/237 (ref TG 240092)

## Creake Abbey
Norfolk

The ruined church of an Augustinian abbey, reduced in size after fire and plague.

### OPENING TIMES
Any reasonable time

### HOW TO FIND US
**Direction:** N of North Creake off B1355

MAP Page 269 (1H)
OS Map 251 (ref TF 856395)

### Keep in touch!

Check *Heritage Today* for news and information on forthcoming events and exclusive members' offers.

## De Grey Mausoleum, Flitton
Bedfordshire

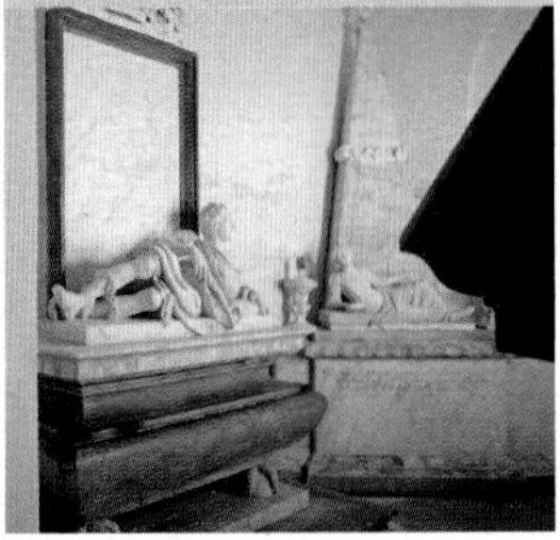

Among the largest sepulchral chapels attached to any English church, this cruciform mausoleum houses a remarkable sequence of 17 sculpted and effigied monuments, spanning nearly three centuries (1615-1899), to the De Grey family of Wrest Park.

### OPENING TIMES

Weekends only. Contact the keykeeper in advance: Mrs Stimson, 3 Highfield Road, Flitton (01525 860094)

### HOW TO FIND US

**Direction:** Through Flitton, attached to the church, on an unclassified road 1½ miles W of A6 at Silsoe

**Train:** Flitwick 2 miles

MAP Page 268 (5E)
OS Map 193 (ref TL 059359)

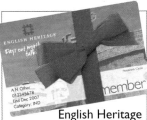

## Denny Abbey and the Farmland Museum
Cambridgeshire – CB25 9PQ

Denny Abbey has a unique and fascinating history. Founded in 1159 as a Benedictine monastery, it then became a retirement home for elderly Knights Templars. After the Templars' suppression for alleged heresy in 1308, it next passed to the Countess of Pembroke, who converted part into a house and established in the rest a convent of 'Poor Clare' Franciscan nuns. This in turn was dissolved by Henry VIII in 1539, whereafter the buildings became a farm until the 1960s, with the nuns' great refectory as its barn. Among its tenants was Thomas Hobson, the horse-hirer whose refusal to allow customers to select their mounts gave rise to the expression 'Hobson's choice'.

All these changes are still traceable in the building: they are now interpreted for visitors by new graphic panels illustrated by local artist Anne Biggs, together with a time-line tracing the site's history from 4000 BC, a new viewing platform and displays of site-finds. New family-friendly activities include imaginative hands-on interactives about medieval tiles, stained glass and arches.

## Denny Abbey and the Farmland Museum

Denny's later farming story is continued by 'Walnut Tree Cottage', furnished as a labourer's home of the 1940s. The site's Farmland Museum also features a fenman's hut, blacksmith's and wheelwright's workshops, a village shop display and many other aspects of Cambridgeshire rural life.

**Please note:** There is a charge of £2.40 for EH members and OVP holders for entry to the museum.

Managed by the Farmland Museum Trust.

### OPENING TIMES

| | |
|---|---|
| 1 Apr-31 Oct, daily | 12pm-5pm |

### NON-MEMBERS

| | |
|---|---|
| **Museum and Abbey** | |
| Adult | £4.00 |
| Concession | £3.00 |
| Child | £1.70 |
| Children under 5 | Free |
| Family | £10.00 |
| **Museum charge** | |
| EH Members and OVP | £2.40 |

### HOW TO FIND US

**Direction:** Located 6 miles N of Cambridge on A10

**Train:** Waterbeach 3 miles

**Bus:** Stagecoach in Cambridge 9, X9 Cambridge-Ely

**Tel:** 01223 860489/860988

OVP

Disabled access (museum and abbey ground floor only).

Dogs on leads (restricted areas only).

Tearooms/restaurant (weekends only).

MAP Page 269 (4F)
OS Map 226 (ref TL 492685)

## Duxford Chapel
Cambridgeshire

A modest but complete and attractive 14th-century chantry chapel, perhaps originally a hospital.

Managed by South Cambridgeshire District Council.

### OPENING TIMES

Any reasonable time

### HOW TO FIND US

**Direction:** Adjacent to Whittlesford station off A505

**Train:** Whittlesford, adjacent

MAP Page 269 (4F)
OS Map 226 (ref TL 485473)

## Framlingham Castle
See feature – Page 134

## Great Yarmouth Row Houses and Greyfriars' Cloisters
Norfolk – NR30 2RG

Living space was very much at a premium in early 17th-century Great Yarmouth, then among the most prosperous fishing ports in England. Hence the inhabitants crowded into the town's distinctive 'Rows', a network of narrow alleyways linking Yarmouth's three main thoroughfares. Many 'Row houses' were damaged by World War II bombing or demolished during post-War clearances, but two surviving properties in the care of English Heritage show what these characteristic dwellings looked like at various stages in their history.

Both Row 111 and the Old Merchant's House were originally built in the early 17th century as wealthy merchants' residences, but later sub-divided into tenements. The Old Merchant's House, which has spectacular Jacobean plaster ceilings in two of its rooms, is presented as it was in about 1870, when the Atkins and Rope families of fishermen – represented by models of family members at work or rest – shared the property. Adjacent Row 111 house is shown as it was in about 1942 (just before it received a direct hit from an incendiary bomb), likewise with figures of the three families which then occupied parts of it. Both houses also display a wonderful collection of fixtures and fittings – including painted panels, elaborate wall-ties and door-knockers – rescued from other now-demolished Row dwellings, a treasure trove for lovers of period decoration.

Nearby stands Greyfriars Cloister, the remains of a 13th-century friary of Franciscan 'grey friars', later swallowed up by Row development and converted into a number of dwellings large and small. Traces of their interior features can still be seen on the brick-built walls of parts of the cloister and church, laid bare by wartime bombing. Early 14th-century wall-paintings were discovered here in the 1960s. (Enquire at Row 111 for arrangements to view the paintings.)

### NON-MEMBERS

| | |
|---|---|
| Adult | £3.50 |
| Concession | £2.60 |
| Child | £1.80 |

### OPENING TIMES

1 Apr-30 Sep, daily 12pm-5pm

Free guided tour of Greyfriars' Cloisters at 10.30am on the first Wed of every month. Please call site for details

### HOW TO FIND US

**Direction:** Great Yarmouth, follow signs for Historic Quay. The houses are directly behind the Norfolk Nelson Museum on the Historic South Quay

**Train:** Great Yarmouth ½ mile

**Bus:** From surrounding areas

**Tel:** 01493 857900

OVP

MAP Page 269 (2K)
OS Map 40 (Houses ref TG 525072, Cloisters ref TG 524073)

## Grime's Graves
See feature – Page 138

# Grime's Graves – prehistoric flint mine Norfolk – IP26 5DE

Grime's Graves is the only Neolithic flint mine open to visitors in Britain. A grassy lunar landscape of over 400 shafts, pits, quarries and spoil dumps, they were first named Grim's Graves – meaning the pagan god Grim's quarries, or 'the Devil's holes' – by the Anglo-Saxons. It was not until one of them was excavated in 1870 that they were found to be flint mines dug over 5,000 years ago, during the later Neolithic and early Bronze Ages.

What the prehistoric miners sought here was the fine quality jet-black flint 'floorstone', which occurs some nine metres below surface level. This was prized as an easily 'knapped' material for axes and other tools – and much later elsewhere for well-sparking flintlock muskets. Digging with red-deer antler picks, they sank shafts from which radiated gallery-tunnels, following the seams of flint. Today visitors can descend 9 metres (30 ft) by ladder into one excavated shaft, an unforgettable experience.

The small exhibition area illustrates the history of this fascinating site.

Set amid the distinctive Breckland heath landscape, Grime's Graves is also a Site of Special Scientific Interest, the home of a wide variety of plants and fauna.

## NON-MEMBERS

| | |
|---|---|
| Adult | £2.90 |
| Concession | £2.20 |
| Child | £1.50 |
| Family | £7.30 |

**No entry to the mines for children under 5 years of age**

## OPENING TIMES

| | |
|---|---|
| 1-31 March, Thu-Mon | 10am-5pm |
| 1 Apr-30 Sep, daily | 10am-6pm |
| 1-31 Oct, Thu-Mon | 10am-5pm |

## HOW TO FIND US

**Direction:** Located 7 miles NW of Thetford off A134

**Train:** Brandon 3½ miles

**Bus:** Burton's 200 Thetford – Newmarket, alight Santon Downham; then 2 miles

**Tel:** 01842 810656

P OVP

Disabled access (exhibition area only; access track rough).

Dogs on leads (restricted areas).

Visitors intending to descend the shaft should wear flat shoes.

MAP Page 269 (3G)
OS Map 229 (ref TL 817899)

## Hadleigh Castle
Essex

The romantic ruins of a once-royal castle overlooking the Essex marshes. Hadleigh was begun in about 1230 by Hubert de Burgh, but extensively refortified as a strong royal residence in 1360-70 by Edward III. The barbican and the two striking eastern drum towers – one seemingly used by Georgian revenue men looking out for smugglers – are his work. Recent archaeological research has also discovered evidence of Roman activity here.

### OPENING TIMES
Any reasonable time

### HOW TO FIND US
**Direction:** ¾ mile S of A13 at Hadleigh

**Train:** Leigh-on-Sea 1½ miles by footpath

**Bus:** First and Arriva Southend services from surrounding areas to within ½ mile

Disabled access (hilly).

MAP Page 269 (7G)
OS Map 175 (ref TL 485473)

## Hill Hall
Essex – CM6 7QQ

This fine Elizabethan mansion features some of the earliest external Renaissance architectural detail in the country, and two rare and outstanding sets of 16th-century wall paintings of mythical and Biblical subjects. Hill Hall has now been divided into private houses, but parts remain open to the public by prior arrangement.

## Hill Hall

### NON-MEMBERS

| | |
|---|---|
| Adult | £5.00 |
| Concession | £3.80 |
| Child | £2.50 |

### OPENING TIMES
1 Apr-30 Sep. Pre-booked guided tours on Wed only

Tel: 01799 522842

### HOW TO FIND US
**Direction:** 3 miles SE of Epping. Entrance ½ mile N of Theydon Mount

**Underground:** Epping 2½ miles

MAP Page 269 (6F)
OS Map 174 (ref TQ 489995)

## Houghton House
Bedfordshire

The shell of a 17th-century mansion with magnificent views, reputedly the inspiration for the 'House Beautiful' in John Bunyan's *Pilgrim's Progress*. Built around 1615 for Mary, Dowager Countess of Pembroke, in a mixture of Jacobean and Classical styles: the ground floors of two Italianate loggias survive, possibly the work of Inigo Jones.

## Houghton House

### OPENING TIMES
Any reasonable time

### HOW TO FIND US
**Direction:** 1 mile NE of Ampthill off A421, 8 miles S of Bedford

**Train:** Flitwick or Stewartby, both 3 miles

**Bus:** Stagecoach in Northants 142, Red Rose 223 Bedford – ⇌ Flitwick

MAP Page 268 (5E)
OS Map 193 (ref TL 039395)

## Isleham Priory Church
Cambridgeshire

The best example in England of a small Norman Benedictine priory church, surviving in a surprisingly unaltered state despite later conversion into a barn.

### OPENING TIMES
Any reasonable time.
Contact the keykeeper,
Mrs R Burton, 18 Festival Road,
Isleham – 5 mins walk

### HOW TO FIND US
**Direction:** Located in centre of Isleham, 16 miles NE of Cambridge on B1104

**Train:** Newmarket 8½ miles, Ely 9 miles

MAP Page 269 (4G)
OS Map 226 (ref TL 642743)

## Landguard Fort
Suffolk – IP11 3TX

The site of the last opposed invasion of England in 1667 and the first land battle of the Royal Marines. The current fort was built in the 18th century, and modified in the 19th century with substantial additional 19th/20th-century outside batteries.

Guided tours and audio tours of the fort are supplemented by a DVD presentation of the site's history, and by guided tours of the outside batteries.

The nearby submarine mining building houses Felixstowe Museum's Collections of local interest.

Managed by Landguard Fort Trust.

### NON-MEMBERS

| | |
|---|---|
| Adult | £3.00 |
| Concession | £2.50 |
| Child | £1.00 |

Free entry for children under 5 and wheelchair users

### OPENING TIMES

| | |
|---|---|
| 1 Apr-31 May, daily | 10am-5pm |
| 1 Jun-30 Sep, daily | 10am-6pm |
| 1-31 Oct, daily | 10am-5pm |

Last admission 1 hour before closing

Tel 07749 695523 to book battery and group tours

### HOW TO FIND US

**Direction:** 1 mile S of Felixstowe town centre – follow signs to Landguard Point

**Train:** Felixstowe 2½ miles

**Bus:** First 75-7 Ipswich-Felixstowe Dock to within ¾ mile of site

MAP Page 269 (5J)
OS Map 197 (ref TM 284319)

## Leiston Abbey
Suffolk

One of Suffolk's most impressive monastic ruins, of a 14th-century abbey of Premonstratensian 'white canons', with a 16th-century brick gatehouse.

Managed by Pro Corda Music School.

### OPENING TIMES

Any reasonable time

### HOW TO FIND US

**Direction:** N of Leiston off B1069

**Bus:** First 64, Gemini/Goldline 164, Anglian/Goldline 165 Ipswich-Aldeburgh (pass close Saxmundham)

**Train:** Saxmundham 5 miles

MAP Page 269 (4K)
OS Map 212 (ref TM 445642)

## Lexden Earthworks and Bluebottle Grove
Essex

## Lexden Earthworks and Bluebottle Grove

The banks and ditches of a series of late Iron Age defences protecting the western side of Camulodunum – pre-Roman Colchester. There are also many pre-Roman graves hereabouts, including Lexden Tumulus, allegedly the burial place of the British chieftain Cunobelinus.

Managed by Colchester Borough Council.

### OPENING TIMES

Any reasonable time

### HOW TO FIND US

**Direction:** 2 miles W of Colchester off A604. Lexden Earthworks are on Lexden Straight Rd. To visit Bluebottle Grove from Lexden, turn left into Heath Rd, left into Church Lane, right into Beech Hill and follow the brown-and-white tourist signs to the site

**Train:** Colchester or Colchester Town, both 2½ miles

**Bus:** Network Colchester 5 from Colchester

**Tel:** 01206 282931

MAP Page 269 (5H) OS Map 184 (Lexden Earthworks ref TL 965246 Bluebottle Grove ref TL 975245)

## Lindsey/St James's Chapel
Suffolk

A pretty thatched 13th-century chapel with lancet windows.

### OPENING TIMES

| | |
|---|---|
| All year: daily | 10am-4pm |

### HOW TO FIND US

**Direction:** Located on an unclassified road ½ mile E of Rose Green and 8 miles E of Sudbury

**Train:** Sudbury 8 miles

Disabled access (single step).

MAP Page 269 (5H)
OS Map 196 (ref TM 445642)

## Longthorpe Tower
Cambridgeshire – PE1 1HA

Longthorpe displays one of the most complete and important sets of 14th-century domestic wall paintings in northern Europe. This varied 'spiritual encyclopaedia' of worldly and religious subjects includes the Wheel of Life, the Nativity and King David.

### NON-MEMBERS

| | |
|---|---|
| Adult | £5.00 |
| Concession | £3.80 |
| Child | £2.50 |

### OPENING TIMES

1 May-31 Aug, Pre-booked guided tours only

Tel: 01799 522842

### HOW TO FIND US

**Direction:** Located 2 miles W of Peterborough on A47

**Train:** Peterborough 1½ miles

**Bus:** Stagecoach in Peterborough Citi 2, Kime 9 from city centre (passing ≠ Peterborough)

**Tel:** 01799 522842

Parking (not at site).

MAP Page 268 (3E)
OS Map 227/235 (ref TL 162984)

Don't forget to check our website for updated news and information **www.english-heritage.org.uk**

## Mistley Towers
Essex

Two porticoed Classical towers, which stood at each end of a grandiose but highly unconventional Georgian church, designed by Robert Adam in 1776.

Managed by Mistley Thorn Residents' Association.

### OPENING TIMES

Key available from Mistley Quay Workshops: 01206 393884

### HOW TO FIND US

**Direction:** Located on B1352, 1½ miles E of A137 at Lawford, 9 miles E of Colchester

**Train:** Mistley ¼ mile

**Bus:** First 103/4 Colchester-Harwich

Disabled access (exterior only).

Dogs on leads (restricted areas).

MAP Page 269 (5H)
OS Map 184/197 (ref TM 116320)

## Moulton Packhorse Bridge
Suffolk

A pretty four-arched 15th-century bridge, spanning the River Kennett on the old route from Cambridge to Bury St Edmunds.

### OPENING TIMES

Any reasonable time

### HOW TO FIND US

**Direction:** In Moulton off B1085, 4 miles E of Newmarket

## Moulton Packhorse Bridge

**Train:** Kennett 2 miles

P

MAP Page 269 (4G)
OS Map 210/226 (ref TL 698645)

## North Elmham Chapel
Norfolk

A place with an unusual story, told by new graphic panels. The small Norman chapel here stood on the site of an earlier timber church, probably the Saxon cathedral of East Anglia. In the 14th century it was converted into a fortified manor house by Henry Despenser, the unpopular Bishop of Norwich who brutally suppressed the Peasants' Revolt of 1381.

Managed by North Elmham Parish Council.

### OPENING TIMES

Any reasonable time

### HOW TO FIND US

**Direction:** Located 6 miles N of East Dereham on B1110

MAP Page 269 (2H)
OS Map 238 (ref TF 988216)

## Old Gorhambury House
Hertfordshire

The remains of a once immense mansion built in 1563-8 by Sir Nicholas Bacon, Queen Elizabeth's Lord Keeper, and twice visited by the Queen. Its extravagantly showy two-storey porch survives, with parts of the hall, chapel and clock-tower.

### OPENING TIMES

All year (except 1 Jun), any reasonable time

## Old Gorhambury House

### HOW TO FIND US

**Direction:** On foot by permissive 2 mile path: any reasonable time. By car (1 May-30 Sep, Thurs pm only), drive to Gorhambury Mansion and walk across the gardens

**Train:** St Albans Abbey 3 miles, St Albans 3½ miles

**Bus:** Arriva 300/1 St Albans-Hemel Hempstead to start of drive

**MAP Page 268 (6E)**
**OS Map 182 (ref TL 110076)**

## Orford Castle
Suffolk – IP12 2ND

The unique polygonal tower-keep of Orford Castle stands beside the pretty town and former port which Henry II also developed here in the 1160s. His aim was to counterbalance the power of turbulent East Anglian barons like Hugh Bigod of Framlingham, and to guard the coast against foreign mercenaries called to their aid.

An 18-sided drum with three square turrets, and a forebuilding reinforcing its entrance, the keep was built to a highly innovative design. The progress of its construction between 1165 and 1173 is extensively recorded in royal documents. Both exterior and interior survive almost intact, allowing visitors to explore the basement with its vital well, and the lower and upper halls – the latter the principal room of the castle. Round these polygonal rooms is a maze of passages, leading to the chapel, kitchen and other chambers in the turrets. From the roof there are magnificent views seaward to Orford Ness.

Recent archaeological work has provided a clearer understanding of how the castle worked, and a new painting by Frank Gardiner shows how the keep and its vanished outer defences looked in their heyday. The upper hall now houses a display by the Orford Museum Trust, including local finds of Roman brooches, medieval seals and coins and some of the borough regalia. Graphic panels display maps, documents, pictures and photographs, illustrating Orford's history down to the 20th century.

### NON-MEMBERS

| | |
|---|---|
| Adult | £4.70 |
| Concession | £3.50 |
| Child | £2.40 |
| Family | £11.80 |

### OPENING TIMES

| | |
|---|---|
| 1 Apr-30 Sep, daily | 10am-6pm |
| 1 Oct-20 Mar, Thu-Mon | 10am-4pm |
| Closed | 24-26 Dec and 1 Jan |

### HOW TO FIND US

**Direction:** In Orford on B1084, 20 miles NE of Ipswich

**Train:** Wickham Market 8 miles

**Bus:** Country Travel 160 Woodbridge-Orford (passes Melton)

**Tel:** 01394 450472

OVP

**MAP Page 269 (4J)**
**OS Map 212 (ref TL 110076)**

## Prior's Hall Barn, Widdington
Essex

One of the finest surviving medieval barns in eastern England, tree-ring dated to the mid-15th century, with a breathtaking aisled interior and crown post roof, the product of some 400 oaks.

### OPENING TIMES

| | |
|---|---|
| 1 Apr-30 Sep, Sat-Sun | 10am-6pm |

### HOW TO FIND US

**Direction:** In Widdington, on unclassified road 2 miles SE of Newport, off B1383

**Train:** Newport 2 miles

**Bus:** Stansted Transit 301 Bishops Stortford-Saffron Walden

**MAP Page 269 (5F)**
**OS Map 195 (ref TL 537318)**

## Roman Wall, St Albans
Hertfordshire

A section of the two-mile long wall built between AD 265 and 270 to defend the Roman city of Verulamium: including the foundations of towers and the London Gate.

### OPENING TIMES

Any reasonable time

### HOW TO FIND US

**Direction:** Located on the S side of St Albans, ½ mile from the centre, off the A4147

**Train:** St Albans Abbey ½ mile, St Albans 1¼ miles

**Bus:** From surrounding areas

**MAP Page 268 (6E)**
**OS Map 182 (ref TL 137066)**

## Saxtead Green Post Mill
Suffolk – IP13 9QQ

This corn mill, whose whole body revolves on its base, was one of many built in Suffolk from the late 13th century. Though milling ceased in 1947, it is still in working order. Climb the wooden stairs to the various floors, which are full of fascinating mill machinery.

### NON-MEMBERS

| | |
|---|---|
| Adult | £2.90 |
| Concession | £2.20 |
| Child | £1.50 |

### OPENING TIMES

| | |
|---|---|
| 1 Apr-29 Sep, Fri-Sat & Bank Hols | 12pm-5pm |

### HOW TO FIND US

**Direction:** 2½ miles NW of Framlingham on A1120

**Train:** Wickham Market 9 miles

**Bus:** Country Travel 160, 182 Woodbridge – Orford (passes close to Woodbridge)

**Tel:** 01728 685789

OVP

**MAP Page 269 (4J)**
**OS Map 212 (ref TM 253644)**

## St Botolph's Priory
Essex: see Colchester, St Botolph's Priory – Page 135

## St John's Abbey Gate
Essex: see Colchester, St John's Abbey Gate – Page 135

## St Olave's Priory
Norfolk

The wonderfully complete 14th-century brick-vaulted refectory undercroft – later a cottage occupied until 1902 – of a small Augustinian priory.

### OPENING TIMES
Any reasonable time

## St Olave's Priory

### HOW TO FIND US

**Direction:** Located 5½ miles SW of the town of Great Yarmouth on A143

**Train:** Haddiscoe 1¼ miles

Dogs on leads (restricted areas only).

**MAP Page 269 (3K)**
**OS Map 40 (ref TM 459996)**

## Thetford, Church of the Holy Sepulchre
Norfolk

The only surviving remains in England of a priory of Canons of the Holy Sepulchre, who aided pilgrims to Christ's tomb: the ruined nave of their 14th-century church, later used as a barn. Thetford Priory is within walking distance.

### OPENING TIMES
Any reasonable time

### HOW TO FIND US

**Direction:** Located on the W side of Thetford off B1107

**Bus:** From surrounding areas

**Train:** Thetford ¾ mile

**MAP Page 269 (3H)**
**OS Map 229 (ref TL 865831)**

## Thetford Priory
Norfolk

The extensive remains of one of the most important East Anglian monasteries, the Cluniac Priory of Our Lady of Thetford. Founded in the early 12th century, it owed much of its prosperity to a miraculous appearance of the Virgin Mary, whose statue here was discovered to conceal relics of saints, and became a magnet for pilgrims. Two of the greatest men in early Tudor England,

## Thetford Priory

Thomas Howard, victor of Flodden, and Henry Fitzroy, illegitimate son of Henry VIII, were buried near her shrine.

Survivals include the lower walls of the church and cloister, along with the impressive shell of the priors' lodging and, reached by a pathway from the main site, an almost complete 14th-century gatehouse. The Church of the Holy Sepulchre is within walking distance.

### OPENING TIMES
Any reasonable time

### HOW TO FIND US

**Direction:** Located on the W side of Thetford, near the station

**Train:** Thetford ¼ mile

**Bus:** From surrounding areas

**MAP Page 269 (3G)**
**OS Map 229 (ref TL 866834)**

## Thetford Warren Lodge
Norfolk

Probably built c.1400 by the Prior of Thetford, this defensible lodge protected gamekeepers and hunting parties against armed poachers. Much later used by the local 'warreners' who harvested rabbits here.

### OPENING TIMES
Any reasonable time

### HOW TO FIND US

**Direction:** Located 2 miles W of Thetford off B1107

**Train:** Thetford 2½ miles

**Bus:** Burton's 200 Thetford – Newmarket (passes close Thetford)

**MAP Page 269 (3G)**
**OS Map 229 (ref TL 839841)**

# Wrest Park Bedfordshire – MK45 4HS

This is one of the most magnificent gardens in England, yet one of the least well known. Unlike 'Capability' Brown's natural landscape styling, favoured during the late 18th century, Wrest Park's formal gardens provide a fascinating history of gardening styles, laid out over 150 years and inspired by the great gardens of Versailles in France.

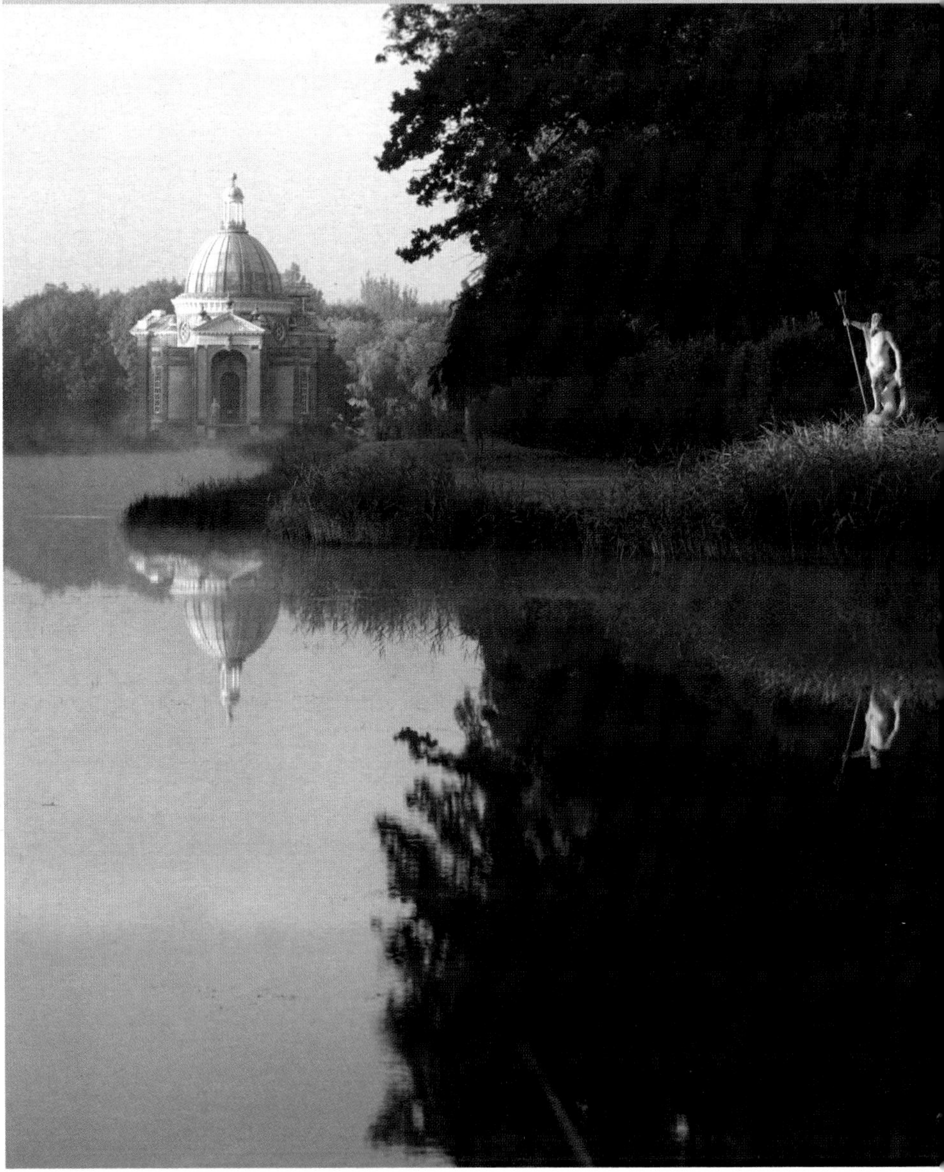

The Orangery

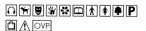

Wrest Park was the home of the De Grey family – whose serried monuments fill the nearby De Grey Mausoleum – from the 13th century until 1917. The gardens are celebrated for their rare survival of a formal early 18th-century layout of wooded walks and canals, centred on the architectural highlight of the pavilion designed by Thomas Archer in 1710. Subsequent generations added garden buildings such as the Bath House and the Chinese Pavilion, valuing the special atmosphere of the established garden even when more fashionable landscapers would have swept it away.

The old manor house was demolished when the present house was completed by 1834. This was designed by Thomas, Earl de Grey, an enthusiast for 18th-century French architecture. It is set further north than the site of the old house, and new formal gardens were laid out between the mansion and the woodland garden. The Orangery, Italian garden and Parterre with magnificent lead statues date from the 19th century.

Don't miss our English Heritage St George's Day event here, the largest in the country.

**Please note:** public access to the house is limited at present.

**NEW FOR 2007**

Earl de Grey, aristocrat and architect, broke with over 500 years of family tradition when he built the sumptuous new house at Wrest Park. But his ancestor the Duke of Kent would have approved of his care of the exceptional early 18th-century garden, lovingly maintained and enhanced by every later generation. A new display introduces the three personalities who made Wrest what it is today: the Duke and his gardens, his granddaughter Jemima's inheritance and the architect Earl's expansion.

www.english-heritage.org.uk/wrestpark

## NON-MEMBERS

| | |
|---|---|
| Adult | £4.70 |
| Concession | £3.50 |
| Child | £2.40 |
| Family | £11.80 |

## OPENING TIMES

| | |
|---|---|
| 1 Apr-30 Jun, Sat-Sun & Bank Hols | 10am-6pm |
| 1 Jul-31 Aug, Thu-Mon | 10am-6pm |
| 1-30 Sep, Sat-Sun | 10am-6pm |
| 1-31 Oct, Sat-Sun | 10am-5pm |

## HOW TO FIND US

**Direction:** ¾ mile E of Silsoe off A6, 10 miles S of Bedford

**Train:** Flitwick 4 miles

**Bus:** Stagecoach in Northants X1 Bedford – Luton

**Tel:** 01525 860152

OVP

Buggies available for disabled visitors.

**MAP Page 268 (5E)**
**OS Map 193 (ref TL 091355)**

### Tilbury Fort
Essex – RM18 7NR

The artillery fort at Tilbury on the Thames estuary protected London's seaward approach from the 16th century through to World War II. Henry VIII built the first fort here, and Queen Elizabeth famously rallied her army nearby to face the threat of the Armada. The present fort was begun in 1672 under Charles II: it is much the best example of its type in England, with its complete circuit of moats and bastioned outworks still substantially surviving. The fort mounted powerful artillery to command the river, as well as landward defences. Later, two magazines were constructed to store vast quantities of gun-powder. In one of these a new exhibition traces the role of the fort in the defence of London. Perhaps because of its strength, Tilbury Fort has never been involved in the kind of action for which it was designed. The worst bloodshed within the fort occurred in 1776, when a fight following a Kent-Essex cricket match left a cricketer and the fort's sergeant dead.

Visitors can now enter one of Tilbury's 19th-century magazines through dark and atmospheric passages in the north-east bastion. For those

### Tilbury Fort

with an interest in military history there are new displays of guns and gunpowder barrels, and information on advances in military engineering.

The recently revised audio tour includes Elizabeth I's Armada speech, and a description of life at the fort by Nathan Makepiece, the fort's Master Gunner.

The recently installed interpretation scheme in the north-east bastion magazine passages, and an interactive oral history programme, provide every visitor with a fascinating new insight into Tilbury.

*Sharpe*, the TV historical drama set during the Napoleonic Wars.

#### NON-MEMBERS

| | |
|---|---|
| Adult | £3.50 |
| Concession | £2.60 |
| Child | £1.80 |
| Family | £8.80 |

#### OPENING TIMES

| | |
|---|---|
| 1 Apr-31 Oct, daily | 10am-5pm |
| 1 Nov-20 Mar, Thu-Mon | 10am-4pm |
| Closed | 24-26 Dec and 1 Jan |

#### HOW TO FIND US

**Direction:** Located ½ mile E of Tilbury off A126. Close to the Port of Tilbury

**Train:** Tilbury Town 1½ miles

**Bus:** Rail shuttle Tilbury – Tilbury Ferry, then ¼ mile

**Ferry:** Gravesend-Tilbury Ferry, then ¼ mile

**Tel:** 01375 858489

OVP

Disabled access (exterior, magazines and fort square).

Dogs on leads (restricted areas).

**MAP Page 269 (7G)**
**OS Map 162/163 (ref TQ 651753)**

### Waltham Abbey Gatehouse and Bridge
Essex

A fine 14th-century gatehouse, bridge and other remains of the abbey refounded by Harold, last Saxon King of England.

Managed by Lee Valley Park.

#### OPENING TIMES

Any reasonable time

#### HOW TO FIND US

**Direction:** In Waltham Abbey off A112

**Train:** Waltham Cross 1¼ miles

**Bus:** Frequent services by different operators from Waltham Cross

**Tel:** 01992 702200

Sensory trail guide.

**MAP Page 269 (6F) OS Map 174 (Gatehouse ref TL 381007, Harold's Bridge ref TL 382009)**

### Weeting Castle
Norfolk

The ruins of a substantial early medieval moated manor house, built in local flint.

#### OPENING TIMES

Any reasonable time

#### HOW TO FIND US

**Direction:** Located 2 miles N of Brandon off B1106

**Train:** Brandon 1¼ miles

**MAP Page 269 (3G)**
**OS Map 229 (ref TL 778891)**

### Wrest Park
See feature – Page 144

# Other historic attractions

Discounted entry to our members (discounts may not apply on event days)

## Felixstowe Museum
Suffolk – IP11 7JG

Display rooms looking at local social and military history, including a new exhibition in 2007 focusing on the 25th anniversary of the Falkands War.

| ENTRY | |
|---|---|
| Adult | £1.00 |
| Child | £0.50 |
| 20% discount for EH members | |
| Discount does not extend to EH Corporate Partners | |

| OPENING TIMES | |
|---|---|
| 1 Apr-3 Jun, Sun & Bank Hols | 1pm-5.30pm |
| 6 Jun-26 Sep, Wed, Sun & Bank Hols | 1pm-5.30pm |
| 30 Sep-28 Oct, Sun & Bank Hols | 1pm-5.30pm |
| Other times by appointment only | |

**Direction:** Located 1 mile S of Felixstowe, near the docks

**Tel:** 01394 674355

MAP Page 269 (5J)
OS Map 197/184 (ref TM 283320)

### Don't forget your membership card

when you visit any of the properties listed in this handbook.

## Flag Fen Bronze Age Centre
Cambridgeshire – PE6 7QU

Britain's Bronze Age centre, including preserved timbers of a 3,000 year old fen causeway, recreated Bronze Age village and museum of excavated finds. Extensive shop, café and events programme.

| ENTRY |
|---|
| Admission fees apply. Please call for details |
| 20% discount for EH members |
| Discount does not extend to EH Corporate Partners |

| OPENING TIMES | |
|---|---|
| **Summer** Tue-Sun and Bank Hols | 10am-5pm (last entry 4pm) |
| **Winter** Tue-Sun | 10am-4pm (last entry 3pm) |
| Closed | Nov-Feb |

**Direction:** Located 5 miles north of Whittlesey, 3 miles east of Peterborough City Centre

**Tel:** 01733 313414

www.flagfen.com

MAP Page 268 (3E)
OS Map 235/227 (ref TL 225989)

## Time and Tide Museum
Norfolk – NR30 3BX

Come and find out about Great Yarmouth's fascinating history, including its rich maritime and fishing heritage. Wander down a typical 1913 'Row'; experience the heady atmosphere of a 1950s fishwharf; take the wheel of a steam drifter and hear gripping tales of wreck and rescue. Located in a Victorian herring curing works, there is something for all the family, with lively hands-on displays and free audio guides.

| ENTRY | |
|---|---|
| Adult | £6.00 |
| Adult in family group | £5.10 |
| Concession | £5.10 |
| Child | £4.20 |
| 25% discount on all ticket categories for EH Members | |

| OPENING TIMES | |
|---|---|
| 2 Apr-28 Oct, Mon-Sun | 10am-5pm |
| 29 Oct-1 Apr, Mon-Fri<br>Sat & Sun | 10am-4pm<br>12pm-4pm |
| Closed | 21-26 Dec and 31 Dec-1 Jan |

**Tel:** 01493 743930

www.museums.norfolk.gov.uk

MAP Page 269 (2K)
OS Map 235/227 (ref TL 225989)

Bolsover Castle – see page 154

# East Midlands

'my wyked and malysyous wife'

George Talbot, Earl of Shrewsbury,
describing Bess of Hardwick

# Properties See individual listings for details

**Derbyshire**
Arbor Low Stone Circle and Gib Hill Barrow
Bolsover Castle
Bolsover Cundy House
Hardwick Old Hall
Hob Hurst's House
Nine Ladies Stone Circle
Peveril Castle
Sutton Scarsdale Hall
Wingfield Manor

**Leicestershire**
Ashby de la Zouch Castle
Jewry Wall
Kirby Muxloe Castle

**Lincolnshire**
Bolingbroke Castle
Gainsborough Old Hall
Lincoln Medieval Bishops' Palace
Sibsey Trader Windmill
Tattershall College

**Northamptonshire**
Chichele College
Eleanor Cross Geddington
Kirby Hall
Rushton Triangular Lodge

**Nottinghamshire**
Mattersey Priory
Rufford Abbey

**Rutland**
Lyddington Bede House

Comprehensive map of our sites Pages 270-271

Above: (top left to right) Rushton Triangular Lodge, Ashby de la Zouch Castle, Sibsey Trader Windmill, (bottom) Kirby Hall and (right) Bolsover Castle.



# Dominant Mansions, Dominant Personalities

Travellers north along the M1 are treated to a panorama of great mansions crowning the flanking hills: first **Hardwick Old Hall** beside its 'New Hall' companion; then the intriguing shell of **Sutton Scarsdale Hall**; and next, most impressive of all, the dramatic white-stone battlements and terraces of **Bolsover Castle**. These are only a few of the attractions of English Heritage's East Midlands region, which stretches from the Derbyshire Peak District to the Lincolnshire Fens, and from the Nottinghamshire Trent Plain to the rolling limestone hills of Leicestershire, Rutland and Northamptonshire.

The region's dominant great houses recall the many notable personalities who founded and lived in them: St Hugh of Lincoln, who began **Lincoln Medieval Bishops' Palace** on its cathedral crowned hilltop; unlucky Lord Hastings, who rebuilt **Ashby de la Zouch Castle** and left **Kirby Muxloe Castle** unfinished when Richard III took his head; or Queen Elizabeth I's favourite Sir Christopher Hatton, of noble, part-ruined **Kirby Hall**.

Most dominant of all these personalities, however, is Bess of Hardwick, the daughter of an obscure Derbyshire squire who via four advantageous marriages and much social manoeuvring became one of the richest and most powerful women in Elizabethan England. Not content with building **Hardwick Old Hall** on the site of her modest family home, even before it was finished she immediately began the still more ambitious **New Hall** ('more glass than wall') beside it. By then she had acrimoniously parted from her last and richest husband, George, Earl of Shrewsbury, the reluctant gaoler of Mary Queen of Scots at **Rufford Abbey** and several of his many other properties – where, according to a malicious rumour spread by Bess, he had conducted an illicit affair with the Scots queen, Bess's former friend and now hated enemy. Through an earlier marriage, Bess was also the mother of Charles Cavendish, who began **Bolsover Castle**, and grandmother of William, Duke of Newcastle, who continued and wonderfully embellished it. Himself a larger than life personality, devoted to masques, dancing and horse-breeding centred on Bolsover's vast stables, Newcastle abandoned his chivalric dream-castle after his Civil War defeat at Marston Moor, choosing exile rather than 'endure the laughter of the Court'. In 1660 he returned to repair and complete it: now English Heritage is busy conserving and restoring Bolsover, a mansion outstanding even in this region of great mansions.

## Arbor Low Stone Circle and Gib Hill Barrow
Derbyshire

The region's most important prehistoric site, Arbor Low is a Neolithic henge monument atmospherically set amid high moorland. Within an earthen bank and ditch, a circle of some 50 white limestone slabs, all now fallen, surrounds a central stone 'cove' – a feature found only in major sacred sites. Nearby is enigmatic Gib Hill, a large burial mound.

**Please note:** The farmer who owns right of way to the property may levy a charge for entry.

Managed by Peak District National Park Authority.

### OPENING TIMES

| | |
|---|---|
| Daily, in summer | 10am-6pm |
| Daily, rest of year | 10am-4pm |
| Closed | 24-26 Dec and 1 Jan |

### HOW TO FIND US

**Direction:** ½ mile W of A515, 2 miles S of Monyash

**Train:** Buxton 10 miles

**Bus:** TM Travel 181 from Sheffield, 202 from Alfreton, Hulleys 171 from Chesterfield, all to Parsley Hay, then 1 mile

**Tel:** 01629 816200

MAP Page 270 (2E)
OS Map 24 (ref SK 160636)

## Ashby de la Zouch Castle
See feature opposite

## Bolingbroke Castle
Lincolnshire

The remains of a 13th-century hexagonal castle, birthplace in 1366 of the future King Henry IV, with adjacent earthworks. Besieged and taken by Cromwell's Parliamentarians in 1643.

Managed by Heritage Lincolnshire.

### OPENING TIMES

Any reasonable time

### HOW TO FIND US

**Direction:** In Old Bolingbroke, 16 miles N of Boston off A16

**Train:** Thorpe Culvert 10 miles

**Tel:** 01529 461499

MAP Page 271 (2J)
OS Map 273 (ref TF 349650)

## Bolsover Castle
See feature – page 154

## Bolsover Cundy House
Derbyshire

This charming cottage-like 17th-century conduit house once supplied water to Bolsover Castle. Recently restored, including its vaulted stone-slab roof.



Managed by Bolsover Civic Society.

### OPENING TIMES

Any reasonable time

### HOW TO FIND US

**Direction:** Off M1 at junction 29, follow signs for Bolsover Castle. At junction of Craggs Rd and Houghton Rd, Bolsover, 6 miles E of Chesterfield on A362

**Train:** Chesterfield 6 miles

**Bus:** Stagecoach in Chesterfield service 81-3, Chesterfield-Bolsover

**Tel:** 01246 822844 (Bolsover Castle)

MAP Page 271 (2F)
OS Map 269 (ref SK 470707)

## Chichele College
Northamptonshire

The gatehouse, chapel and other remains of a communal residence for priests serving the parish church, founded by locally-born Archbishop Chichele before 1425. Regularly used to display works of art.

For full details, visit www.east northamptonshire.gov.uk

Managed by Cultural Community Partnerships.

### OPENING TIMES

Quadrangle – any reasonable time. For the chapel, contact the keykeeper, Mrs D Holyoak, 12 Lancaster St, Higham Ferrers. Or telephone 01933 314157

### HOW TO FIND US

**Direction:** In Higham Ferrers

**Train:** Wellingborough 5 miles

**Bus:** Stagecoach in Northants X46, 46 from Wellingborough

**Tel:** 01933 655401

Dogs on leads (restricted areas only).

MAP Page 271 (6G)
OS Map 224 (ref SP 960687)

# Ashby de la Zouch Castle Leicestershire – LE65 1BR





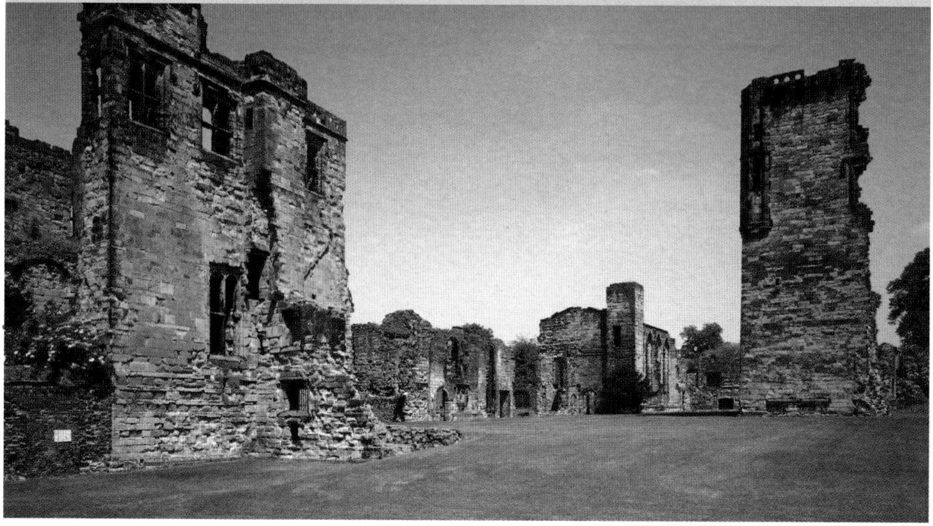

Ashby Castle forms the backdrop to the famous jousting scenes in Sir Walter Scott's classic novel of 1819, *Ivanhoe*. Now a ruin, the castle began as a manor house in the 12th century. It only achieved castle status in the 15th century, by which time the hall and buttery had been enlarged, with a solar to the east and a large integral kitchen added to the west.

Between 1474 and his execution by Richard III in 1483, Edward IV's Chamberlain Lord Hastings added the chapel and the impressive keep-like Hastings Tower – a castle within a castle. Visitors can now climb the 24 metre (78 feet) tower, which offers fine views. Later the castle hosted many royal visitors, including Henry VII, Mary Queen of Scots, James I and Charles I.

A Royalist stronghold during the Civil War, the castle finally fell to Parliament in 1646, and was then made unusable. An underground passage from the kitchen to the tower, probably created during this war, can still be explored today. In 2006 archaeologists investigated the mysterious castle garden, famous for its elaborately shaped sunken features.

**www.english-heritage.org.uk/ashbydelazouchcastle**

## NON-MEMBERS

| | |
|---|---|
| Adult | £3.50 |
| Concession | £2.60 |
| Child | £1.80 |
| Family | £8.80 |

## OPENING TIMES

| | |
|---|---|
| 1 Apr-30 Jun, Thu-Mon | 10am-5pm |
| 1 Jul-31 Aug, daily | 10am-6pm |
| 1 Sep-31 Oct, Thu-Mon | 10am-5pm |
| 1 Nov-20 Mar, Thu-Mon | 10am-4pm |
| Closed | 24-26 Dec and 1 Jan |

## HOW TO FIND US

**Direction:** In Ashby de la Zouch, 12 miles S of Derby on A511. Restricted parking on site, please park in town car park

**Train:** Burton on Trent 9 miles

**Bus:** Arriva 9, 25/7 Burton on Trent-Ashby de la Zouch; Arriva 118, 218 Leicester-Ashby de la Zouch

**Local Tourist Information:** 01530 411767

**Tel:** 01530 413343

P OVP

Disabled access (grounds only).

Parking (restricted on site, please park in town car park – charge applies).

MAP Page 270 (4E)
OS Map 245 (ref SK 361166)

# Bolsover Castle Derbyshire – S44 6PR

'By an unlikely miracle,' wrote the architectural historian Mark Girouard, 'the keep at Bolsover has survived into this century as an almost untouched expression in stone of the lost world of Elizabethan chivalry and romance.'

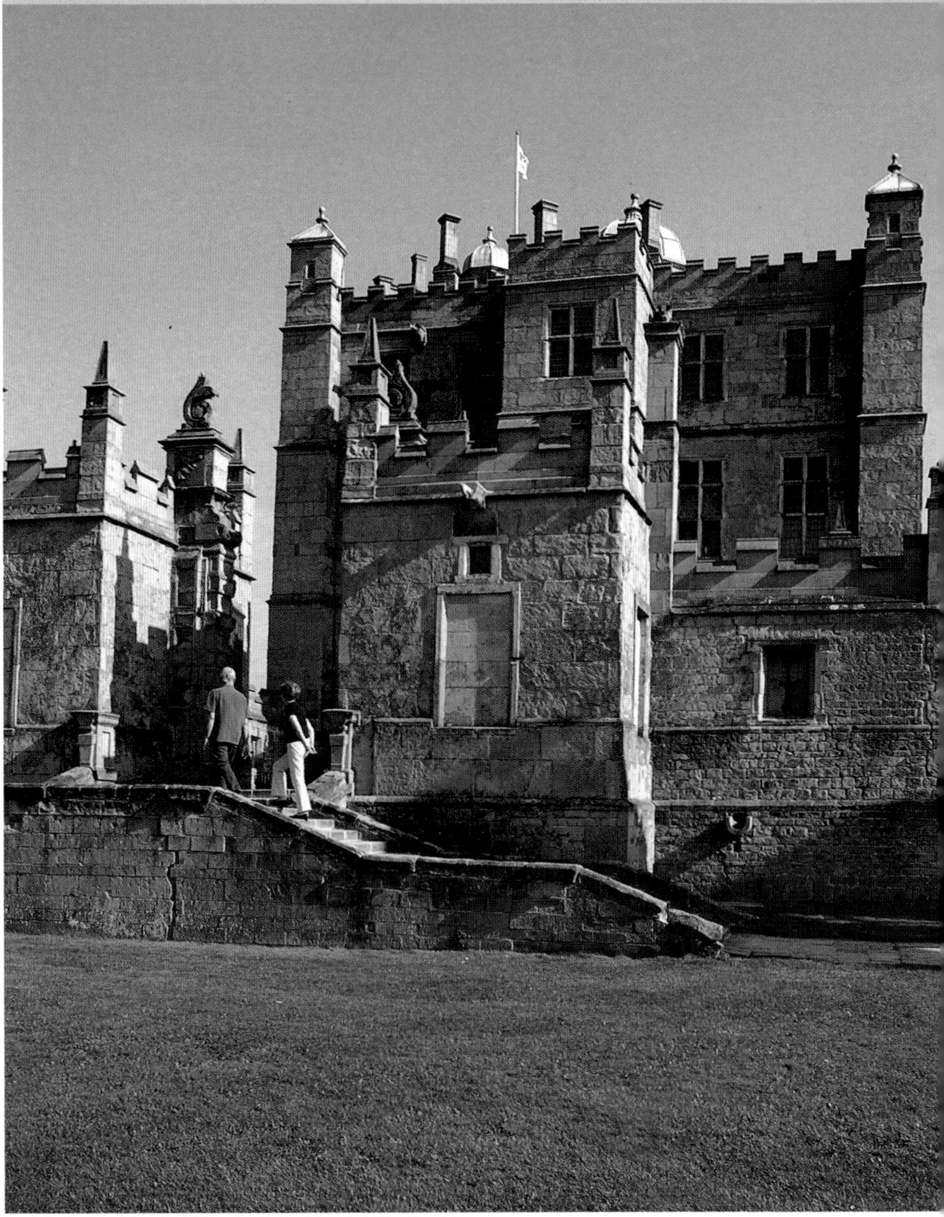

Dominating the countryside from its hilltop, Bolsover occupies the site of a medieval castle built by the Peverel family shortly after the Norman Conquest. Sir Charles Cavendish bought the old castle in 1612 and began work on his 'Little Castle' project. Despite its embattled appearance, his creation was not designed for defence, but for elegant living.

Sir Charles intended the house as a retreat from the world to an imaginary golden age of chivalry and pleasure. His son William, later Duke of Newcastle, inherited the Little Castle in 1616 and set about its completion, assisted by the architect John Smythson. An extraordinary survival, the exquisitely carved fireplaces and recently conserved murals and painted panelling of its interiors take the visitor on an allegorical journey from earthly concerns to heavenly (and erotic) delights.

William also added the vast and stately rooms of the Terrace Range, now a dramatic roofless shell. To show off his achievement, in 1634 he invited the Stuart court to 'Love's Welcome to Bolsover', a masque specially written by Ben Jonson for performance in the Fountain Garden. Finally he constructed the cavernous Riding House with its magnificent roof, perhaps the finest surviving indoor riding school in Britain: here he indulged his passion for training 'great horses'. There is also a Discovery Centre in the Stables, with audio-visual displays.

The castle battlements and the Venus Garden are in the process of being restored, and the fountain, with 23 new statues, plays again for the first time in centuries. A series of 'Caesar paintings' depicting Roman emperors and empresses has also recently returned to Bolsover. These were commissioned by William Cavendish and copied from originals by the great Venetian artist Titian – which have since been destroyed – making the Bolsover versions uniquely important.

Bolsover Castle regularly hosts living history events, open-air concerts and evening plays. It also offers an interactive audio tour. There is reasonable disabled access to the main buildings and good access to the grounds: the Little Castle is not accessible to wheelchairs.

The 2006 adaptation of *Jane Eyre* by the BBC.

**www.english-heritage.org.uk/bolsovercastle**

Available for corporate and private hire.

Licensed for civil wedding ceremonies.

Above: The Star Chamber

## NON-MEMBERS

| | |
|---|---|
| Adult | £6.80 |
| Concession | £5.10 |
| Child | £3.40 |
| Family | £17.00 |

## OPENING TIMES

| | |
|---|---|
| 1-30 Apr, Thu-Mon | 10am-5pm* |
| 1 May-30 Sep, daily | 10am-6pm* |
| 1-31 Oct, Thu-Mon | 10am-5pm* |
| *Closes at 4pm on Saturday | |
| 1 Nov-20 Mar, Thu-Mon | 10am-4pm |
| Closed | 24-26 Dec and 1 Jan |

Part of the castle may close for 1 hour if an event is booked. Please call to check

## HOW TO FIND US

**Direction:** In Bolsover, 6 miles E of Chesterfield on A632. Off M1 at junction 29 (signposted)

**Train:** Chesterfield 6 miles

**Bus:** Stagecoach in Chesterfield 81-3 Chesterfield-Bolsover

**Tel:** 01246 822844

**Local Tourist Information** (Chesterfield): 01246 345777

P OVP

Parking (in Castle car park off main gate, also coach drop-off point).

MAP Page 271 (2F)
OS Map 269 (ref SK 470707)

The Terrace Range

## Eleanor Cross, Geddington
Northamptonshire

In 1290 Eleanor of Castile, the beloved wife of Edward I and mother of his 14 children, died at Harby in Nottinghamshire. The places where her body rested on the journey south to its tomb in Westminster Abbey were marked by stone crosses. The stately triangular Geddington cross, with its canopied statues surmounted by a slender hexagonal pinnacle, is the best-preserved of only three intact survivors. Other crosses stand at Hardingstone near Northampton, and Waltham Cross, Hertfordshire.

### OPENING TIMES
Any reasonable time

### HOW TO FIND US
**Direction:** Located in the village of Geddington, off A43 between Kettering and Corby

**Train:** Kettering 4 miles

**Bus:** Stagecoach in Northants 8 Kettering-Corby

MAP Page 271 (5G)
OS Map 207/223 (ref SP 894830)

## Gainsborough Old Hall
Lincolnshire – DN21 2NB

A little-known gem, Gainsborough Old Hall is among the best-preserved medieval manor houses in England. Partly brick and partly timber-framed, and mainly later 15th century with Elizabethan additions; it has a kitchen with an enormous fireplace, a noble great hall, and an imposing lodgings tower.

Managed by Lincolnshire County Council.

### NON-MEMBERS

| | |
|---|---|
| Adult | £3.80 |
| Concession | £2.60 |
| Child | £2.60 |
| Family | £10.00 |

**Small charge to special events for EH members. Discount for groups of 30 or more**

### OPENING TIMES

| | |
|---|---|
| 1 Apr-31 Oct, Mon-Sat | 10am-5pm |
| Sun | 1pm-4.30pm |
| 1 Nov-20 Mar, Mon-Sat | 10am-5pm |
| Closed | 24-26, 31 Dec and 1 Jan |

### HOW TO FIND US
**Direction:** In Gainsborough, opposite the library

**Train:** Gainsborough Central ½ mile, Gainsborough Lea Road 1 mile

**Bus:** From surrounding areas

**Tel:** 01427 612669

Disabled access (most of ground floor).

MAP Page 271 (1G)
OS Map 280 (ref SK 813900)

## Hardwick Old Hall
Derbyshire – S44 5QJ

The remodelled family home of Bess of Hardwick, one of the richest and most remarkable women of Elizabethan England, stands beside the New Hall she raised later in the 1590s. Though the Old Hall is now roofless, visitors can still ascend four floors to view surviving decorative plasterwork, as well as the kitchen and service rooms.

A recently installed exhibition in the West Lodge describes Bess's adventures in architecture, and how she transformed her birthplace from a medieval manor house into a luxurious Elizabethan mansion. A new audio tour tells Bess's story.

Managed by English Heritage and owned by The National Trust.

### NON-MEMBERS

| | |
|---|---|
| Adult | £3.90 |
| Concession | £2.90 |
| Child | £2.00 |
| Family | £9.80 |

**National Trust members admitted free, but small charge at EH events. Tickets for the New Hall (The National Trust) and joint tickets for both properties available at extra cost**

### OPENING TIMES

| | |
|---|---|
| 17 Mar-30 Sep, Wed, Thu, Sat, Sun | 10am-6pm |

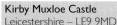

## Hardwick Old Hall

| | |
|---|---|
| 1-31 Oct,<br>Wed, Thu, Sat, Sun | 10am-5pm |
| Closed | 1 Nov-20 Mar |

### HOW TO FIND US

**Direction:** 9½ miles SE of Chesterfield, off A6175, from J29 of M1

**Train:** Chesterfield 8 miles

**Bus:** Stagecoach in Chesterfield 'Pronto' Chesterfield-Nottingham, alight Glapwell 'Young Vanish', 1½ miles

**Tel:** 01246 850431

P OVP

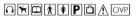

MAP Page 271 (2F)
OS Map 269 (ref SK 462637)

## Hob Hurst's House
Derbyshire

A square prehistoric burial mound with an earthwork ditch and outer bank. Named after a local goblin.

Managed by the Peak District National Park Authority.

### OPENING TIMES

Any reasonable time

### HOW TO FIND US

**Direction:** From unclassified road off B5057, 9 miles W of Chesterfield

**Train:** Chesterfield 9 miles

**Bus:** Hulleys 170, TM Travel 66/7 from Chesterfield to within 2 miles

**Tel:** 01629 816200

MAP Page 270 (2E)
OS Map 24 (ref SK 287692)

## Jewry Wall
Leicestershire

A length of Roman bath-house wall over 9 metres (30 feet) high, near a museum displaying the archaeology of Leicester and its region.

### OPENING TIMES

| | |
|---|---|
| Daily, summer | 10am-6pm |
| Daily, rest of year | 10am-4pm |
| **Museum**<br>Open Sat only | 11am-4.30pm |
| Closed | 24-26 Dec and 1 Jan |

### HOW TO FIND US

**Direction:** In St Nicholas St, W of Church of St Nicholas

**Train:** Leicester ¾ mile

**Bus:** From surrounding areas

**Tel:** 01162 254971 (Jewry Wall Museum)

P

Parking (by museum, within St Nicholas Circle).

MAP Page 271 (4F)
OS Map 233 (ref SK 582045)

## Kirby Hall
See feature – Page 158

## Kirby Muxloe Castle
Leicestershire – LE9 9MD

The picturesque remains – including the fine gatehouse and a complete corner tower – of a moated, brick-built fortified mansion begun in 1480 by Lord Hastings, but left unfinished after his execution by Richard III in 1483. Recently re-opened after extensive conservation work by English Heritage.

### NON-MEMBERS

| | |
|---|---|
| Adult | £2.90 |
| Concession | £2.20 |
| Child | £1.50 |

### OPENING TIMES

| | |
|---|---|
| 1 Jul-31 Aug,<br>Sat & Sun | 10am-5pm |

### HOW TO FIND US

**Direction:** 4 miles W of Leicester off B5380; close to M1 junction 21A, northbound exit only

**Train:** Leicester 5 miles

**Bus:** Arriva 63, 152-4 from Leicester

**Tel:** 01162 386886

P OVP

MAP Page 271 (4F)
OS Map 233 (ref SK 524046)

## Lincoln Medieval Bishops' Palace
See feature – Page 159

# Kirby Hall Northamptonshire – NN17 3EN

Kirby Hall is one of England's greatest Elizabethan and 17th-century houses. Begun by Sir Humphrey Stafford in about 1570, it was purchased six years later by Sir Christopher Hatton, one of Queen Elizabeth's 'comely young men' and later her Lord Chancellor, who hoped in vain to receive the Queen here during one of her annual 'progresses' around the country.

Although this vast mansion is partly roofless, most of its walls survive to their full impressive height: so does the stupendous three-tier inner porch, begun following French pattern books and later further embellished in the Classical style by the sculptor Nicholas Stone. Kirby Hall's exceptionally rich decoration, indeed, proclaims that its successive owners were always in the forefront of new ideas about architecture and design. The Great Hall and state rooms also remain intact, and have been refitted and redecorated to authentic 17th- and 18th-century specifications.

Sir Christopher Hatton the Fourth added the great gardens (described as 'ye finest garden in England') in the late 17th century. They are now partly restored and laid out in an elaborate 'cutwork' design. The gardens and ground floor of the building are both easily accessible by wheelchair.

Jane Austen's *Mansfield Park* (1999) and *Tristram Shandy: A Cock and Bull Story* (2005).

**www.english-heritage.org.uk/kirbyhall**

Owned by the Earl of Winchilsea and managed by English Heritage.

## NON-MEMBERS

| | |
|---|---|
| Adult | £4.70 |
| Concession | £3.50 |
| Child | £2.40 |
| Family | £11.80 |

## OPENING TIMES

| | |
|---|---|
| 1 Apr-30 Jun, Thu-Mon | 10am-5pm |
| 1 Jul-31 Aug, daily | 10am-6pm |
| 1 Sep-31 Oct, Thu-Mon | 10am-5pm |
| 1 Nov-20 Mar, Thu-Mon | 11am-3pm |
| Closed | 24-26 Dec and 1 Jan |

## HOW TO FIND US

**Direction:** On an unclassified road off A43, 4 miles NE of Corby

**Train:** Kettering 9 miles

**Tel:** 01536 203230

P OVP

Disabled access (grounds, gardens and ground floor only).

Dogs on leads (restricted areas).

**MAP Page 271 (5G)**
**OS Map 224 (ref SP 926927)**

# Lincoln Medieval Bishops' Palace Lincolnshire – LN2 1PU



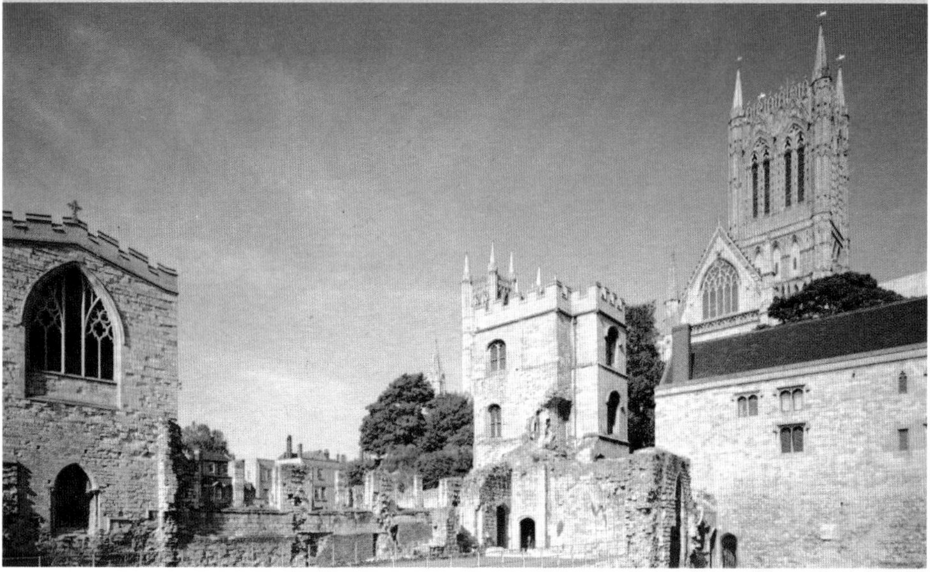

Standing almost in the shadow of Lincoln cathedral, with sweeping views over the ancient city and the countryside beyond, the medieval bishops' palace was once among the most important buildings in the country. The administrative centre of the largest diocese in medieval England, stretching from the Humber to the Thames, its architecture reflected the enormous power and wealth of the bishops as princes of the church.

The vineyard

Begun in the late 12th century, the palace's most impressive feature is the undercrofted West Hall, initiated by Bishop St Hugh and completed in the 1230s. The chapel range and entrance tower were built by Bishop William Alnwick, who modernised the palace in the 1430s. Having hosted visits from Henry VIII and James I, the palace was sacked by Royalist troops during the Civil War.

Built on hillside terraces, the palace also boasts one of the most northerly working vineyards in Europe, and a Contemporary Heritage Garden. Designed by Mark Anthony Walker, its form was inspired by the cathedral's medieval vaulting and the curves of the vines, with trees shaped to echo spires. Award-winning audio tour.

www.english-heritage.org.uk/lincolnbishops

## NON-MEMBERS

| | |
|---|---|
| Adult | £3.90 |
| Concession | £2.90 |
| Child | £2.00 |
| Family | £9.80 |

## OPENING TIMES

| | |
|---|---|
| 1 Apr-30 Jun, daily | 10am-5pm |
| 1 Jul-31 Aug, daily | 10am-6pm |
| 1 Sep-31 Oct, daily | 10am-5pm |
| 1 Nov-20 Mar, Thu-Mon | 10am-4pm |
| Closed | 24-26 Dec and 1 Jan |

## HOW TO FIND US

**Direction:** On the downhill side of Lincoln Cathedral. From the Cathedral Precinct gatehouse, follow the wall on the right and go through a doorway in the wall half way along

**Train:** Lincoln 1 mile

**Bus:** From surrounding areas

**Tel:** 01522 527468

OVP

Parking (limited disabled parking on site).

MAP Page 271 (2H)

OS Map 272 (ref SK 978717)

## Lyddington Bede House
Rutland – LE15 9LZ

Set beside the church of a picturesque ironstone village, Lyddington Bede House originated as the late medieval wing of a palace belonging to the Bishops of Lincoln. By 1600 it had passed to Sir Thomas Cecil, son of Queen Elizabeth's chief minister, who converted it into an almshouse for twelve poor 'bedesmen' over 30 years old and two women (over 45), all free of lunacy, leprosy or the French pox. Visitors can wander through the bedesmen's rooms, with their tiny windows and fireplaces, and view the former bishops' Great Chamber with its beautifully carved ceiling cornice.

There is a small herb garden.

### NON-MEMBERS

| | |
|---|---|
| Adult | £3.30 |
| Concession | £2.50 |
| Child | £1.70 |
| Family | £8.30 |

### OPENING TIMES

| | |
|---|---|
| 1 Apr-31 Oct, Thu-Mon | 10am-5pm |

### HOW TO FIND US

**Direction:** In Lyddington, 6 miles N of Corby; 1 mile E of A6003, next to the church

**Bus:** Rutland Flyer 1 Corby-Oakham (passes close to ⇌ Oakham)

**Tel:** 01572 822438

OVP

Disabled access (ground floor only).

MAP Page 271 (5G)
OS Map 234 (ref SP 876970)

## Mattersey Priory
Nottinghamshire

The remains, mainly the 13th-century refectory and kitchen, of a small monastery for just six Gilbertine canons – the only wholly English monastic order.

### OPENING TIMES

Any reasonable time

### HOW TO FIND US

**Direction:** ¾ mile down rough drive, 1 mile E of Mattersey off B6045

**Train:** Retford 7 miles

MAP Page 271 (1G)
OS Map 280 (ref SK 703896)

## Nine Ladies Stone Circle
Derbyshire

A small early Bronze Age stone circle of (actually) ten stones, traditionally women petrified for dancing on Sunday. Part of a complex of prehistoric circles and standing stones on Stanton Moor.

Managed by Peak District National Park Authority.

### OPENING TIMES

Any reasonable time

### HOW TO FIND US

**Direction:** From an unclassified road off A6, 5 miles SE of Bakewell

**Train:** Matlock 4½ miles

**Bus:** Hulleys 170 Matlock-Bakewell to within 1 mile

**Tel:** 01629 816200

MAP Page 270 (2E)
OS Map 24 (ref SK 249635)

## Peveril Castle
See feature opposite

## Rufford Abbey
Nottinghamshire

The best-preserved remains of a Cistercian abbey west cloister range in England, dating mainly from c. 1170. Incorporated into part of a 17th-century and later mansion, set in Rufford Country Park.

### OPENING TIMES

| | |
|---|---|
| Open all year from | 10am-5pm |
| Jan-Feb | 10am-4pm |
| Closed | 25 Dec |

For full details of opening times, please call

### HOW TO FIND US

**Direction:** 2 miles S of Ollerton off A614

**Train:** Mansfield 8 miles

**Bus:** Stagecoach in Bassetlaw 33 Nottingham-Worksop; Heanor/Nottingham-Clumber

**Tel:** 01623 822944

Occasional charge for members on event days.

Parking (charge applies – not managed by EH).

Shop – craft centre.

MAP Page 271 (2F)
OS Map 270 (ref SK 646648)

# Peveril Castle Derbyshire – S33 8WQ

Perched high above the pretty village of Castleton, the castle offers breathtaking views of the Peak District. Founded soon after the Norman Conquest of 1066 by William Peverel, one of King William's most trusted knights, it played an important role in guarding the Peak Forest area.

When 'Castle Peak' (as it was known in the Middle Ages) passed into the hands of Henry II, he made a number of additions. Most notable is the great square keep, with its round-headed windows, built in 1176. Thirteenth-century developments included the great hall, and though by 1400 the fortress had ceased to be of strategic importance, its impregnability guaranteed its continued use as a prison.

Following extensive conservation work on the keep, a walk-way has been erected at first floor level, enabling visitors to enter two chambers previously inaccessible: a medieval garderobe, and a small room with beautiful views of the surrounding countryside.

A new visitor centre now assures an even warmer welcome. New displays tell the story of Peveril as the focal point of the Royal Forest of the Peak, a hunting preserve for monarchs since the 11th century. There is also improved access, with a lift from the new gift shop to the first floor interpretation room, castle model and toilet facilities.

**www.english-heritage.org.uk/peverilcastle**

## NON-MEMBERS

| | |
|---|---|
| Adult | £3.50 |
| Concession | £2.60 |
| Child | £1.80 |
| Family | £8.80 |

## OPENING TIMES

| | |
|---|---|
| 1-30 Apr, daily | 10am-5pm |
| 1 May-31 Aug, daily | 10am-6pm |
| 1 Sep-31 Oct, daily | 10am-5pm |
| 1 Nov-20 Mar, Thu-Mon | 10am-4pm |
| Closed | 24-26 Dec and 1 Jan |

## HOW TO FIND US

**Direction:** Via the market place in Castleton; 15 miles W of Sheffield on A6187

**Train:** Hope 2½ miles

**Bus:** First/Stagecoach in Chesterfield 272-4 ⇌ Sheffield-Castleton, then 1 mile

**Tel:** 01433 620613

OVP

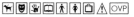

Parking (in town).

**MAP Page 270 (2E)**
**OS Map 1 (ref SK 149826)**

## Rushton Triangular Lodge
Northamptonshire – NN14 1RP

This delightful triangular building was designed by Sir Thomas Tresham (father of one of the Gunpowder Plotters) and constructed between 1593 and 1597. It is a testament to Tresham's Roman Catholicism: the number three, symbolising the Holy Trinity, is apparent everywhere. There are three floors, trefoil windows and three triangular gables on each side. On the entrance front is the inscription 'Tres Testimonium Dant' ('there are three that give witness'), a Biblical quotation from St John's Gospel referring to the Trinity. It is also a pun on Tresham's name; his wife called him 'Good Tres' in her letters.

### NON-MEMBERS

| | |
|---|---|
| Adult | £2.50 |
| Concession | £1.90 |
| Child | £1.30 |

### OPENING TIMES

| | |
|---|---|
| 1 Apr-31 Oct, Thu-Mon | 11am-4pm |

### HOW TO FIND US

**Direction:** 1 mile W of Rushton, on unclassified road; 3 miles from Desborough on A6

### Rushton Triangular Lodge

**Train:** Kettering 5 miles

**Bus:** Stagecoach in Northants 19 Kettering-Market Harborough, alight Desborough, then 2 miles

**Tel:** 01536 710761

OVP

Dogs on leads (restricted areas only).

Parking (nearby lay-by).

MAP Page 271 (5G)
OS Map 224 (ref SP 830831)

## Sibsey Trader Windmill
Lincolnshire – PE22 0SY

Built in 1877, this restored six-storey mill with complete gear, sails and fantail still works today. The award-winning tearoom sells produce made from the mill's organic, stone-ground flour.

Managed by Ian Ansell.
Tel: 07718 320449.

### NON-MEMBERS

| | |
|---|---|
| Adult | £2.00 |
| Concession | £1.50 |
| Child | £1.00 |

### Sibsey Trader Windmill

### OPENING TIMES

| | |
|---|---|
| 1 Mar-30 Apr, Sat, & Bank Hols | 10am-6pm |
| Sun | 11am-6pm |
| 1 May-30 Sep, Sat & Bank Hols | 10am-6pm |
| Sun and Tue | 11am-6pm |
| 1-31 Oct, Sat & Bank Hols | 10am-6pm |
| Sun | 11am-6pm |
| 1 Nov-29 Feb Sat (Mill only) | 11am-5pm |
| Closed | 25 Dec-1 Jan |
| 1-20 Mar, Sat & Bank Hols | 10am-6pm |
| Sun | 11am-6pm |

### HOW TO FIND US

**Direction:** ½ mile W of Sibsey off A16, 5 miles N of Boston

**Train:** Boston 5 miles

**Bus:** Various services and operators from Boston to Sibsey, then ½ mile

**Tel:** 01205 750036/460647

OVP

Disabled access (exterior only).

MAP Page 271 (3J)
OS Map 261 (ref TF 345510)

## Sutton Scarsdale Hall
Derbyshire

The imposing shell of a grandiose Georgian mansion built in 1724-29, with an immensely columned exterior. Roofless since 1919, when its interiors were dismantled and some exported to America: but there is still much to discover within, including traces of sumptuous plaster-work. Set amid contemporary garden remains, including ha ha ditch and parish church.

## Sutton Scarsdale Hall

### OPENING TIMES

| | |
|---|---|
| Summer, daily | 10am-6pm |
| Rest of year, daily | 10am-4pm |
| Closed | 24-26 Dec and 1 Jan |

### HOW TO FIND US

**Direction:** Between Chesterfield and Bolsover, 1½ miles S of Arkwright Town

**Train:** Chesterfield 5 miles

**Bus:** Hallmark 48 from Chesterfield

MAP Page 271 (2F)
OS Map 269 (ref SK 442689)

## Tattershall College
Lincolnshire

Remains of a grammar school for church choristers, founded in the mid-15th century by Ralph, Lord Cromwell, the builder of nearby Tattershall Castle (National Trust) and of English Heritage's Wingfield Manor.

The college is managed by Heritage Lincolnshire.

### OPENING TIMES

Any reasonable time

### HOW TO FIND US

**Direction:** In Tattershall, 14 miles NE of Sleaford on A153

**Train:** Ruskington (U) 10 miles

**Bus:** Brylaine 5 Lincoln-Boston (passing close ⇌ Lincoln and Boston)

**Tel:** 01529 461499

MAP Page 271 (2H)
OS Map 261 (ref TF 213578)

## Wingfield Manor
Derbyshire – DE55 7NH

The vast and immensely impressive ruins of a palatial medieval manor house arranged round a pair of courtyards, with a huge undercrofted Great Hall and a defensible High Tower 22 metres (72 feet) tall. This monument to late medieval 'conspicuous consumption' was built in the 1440s for the wealthy Ralph, Lord Cromwell, Treasurer of England. Later the home of Bess of Hardwick's husband, the Earl of Shrewsbury, who imprisoned Mary Queen of Scots here in 1569, 1584 and 1585.

Visitors must pre-book a 45-minute minimum guided tour (free education visits included). Tours available on Saturdays throughout April, and Saturday and Sunday afternoons May-September. To book a tour please call 01246 857436 or 01246 856456 (Mon-Fri, 9am-5pm).

## Wingfield Manor

TV's *Peak Practice* and Zeffirelli's film *Jane Eyre*.

### NON-MEMBERS

| | |
|---|---|
| Adult | £3.50 |
| Concession | £2.60 |
| Child | £1.80 |

### OPENING TIMES

Entry by pre-booked guided tour on first Sat of the month Apr–Sep only

Please call 01246 856456/857436 during office hours to book

### HOW TO FIND US

**Direction:** 17 miles N of Derby; 11 miles S of Chesterfield on B5035; ½ mile S of South Wingfield. From M1 junction 28, W on A38, A615 (Matlock Road) at Alfreton, 1½ miles and turn onto B5035

**Train:** Alfreton 4 miles

**Bus:** Stagecoach in Chesterfield/ Doyles 140 Matlock-Alfreton

**Tel:** 01773 832060

Parking (none on site).

Orientation guide available.

MAP Page 270 (3E)
OS Map 269 (Ref SK 374548)

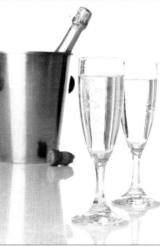

# Other historic attractions

Discounted entry to our members (discounts may not apply on event days)

## Althorp
Northamptonshire – NN7 4HQ

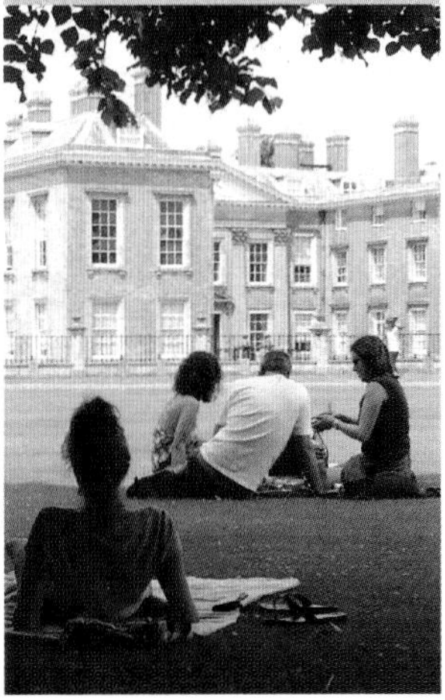

Visitors are invited to view the house, grounds and exhibition 'Diana – A Celebration', as well as the island in the Round Oval where Diana, Princess of Wales is laid to rest.

### ENTRY

EH members get free entry to the upstairs of the house. Please call for admission prices

### OPENING TIMES

Please call for details of opening times

**Direction:** Althorp is located 7 miles North-West of Northampton off the A428. From the North leave M1 at Junction 18, From the South leave M1 at Junction 16, From West leave A14 at Junction 1(west bound only)

**Tel:** 01604 770107

www.althorp.com

MAP Page 271 (6F)
OS Map 223 (ref SP 682651)

## Ashby Museum
Leicestershire – LE65 1HU

Ashby Museum works closely with the county Museum Service and other independent museums, sharing expertise and artefacts. The new 'Castle Gallery', to be opened in 2007, will contain prints and paintings of Ashby de la Zouch Castle and a model to show how the castle may have looked in its heyday.

### ENTRY

Free to EH members

### OPENING TIMES

8 Apr-30 Sep Mon- Fri 11am-4pm (closed 1-2pm) Sat 10am-4pm

Closed Sun

### HOW TO FIND US

**Direction:** The Museum is situated in North Street in Ashby de la Zouch, and is housed in the same building as the town's Library and Tourist Information Centre

**Tel:** 01530 560090

www.ashbydelazouchmuseum.org.uk.

MAP Page 270 (4E)
OS Map 245 (ref SK 358169)

## Burghley House
Lincolnshire – PE9 3JY

### Burghley House

Burghley was built and mostly designed by William Cecil, Lord High Treasurer to Queen Elizabeth I, between 1555 and 1587, and is still lived in by his descendants. The main part of the house has 35 major rooms on the ground and first floors, as well as more than 80 lesser rooms. Surrounded by historic parkland laid out by Capability Brown.

### ENTRY

**House, Brewhouse interpretation centre, Sculpture Garden & Garden of Surprises**

| | |
|---|---|
| Adult | £10.40 |
| Child (5-15 years) | £5.00 |
| Concession | £9.00 |
| Family (2+2) | £25.00 |

**Sculpture Garden & Garden of Surprises only**

| | |
|---|---|
| Adult | £6.00 |
| Child (over 5 years) | £3.00 |

20% discount to EH members

### OPENING TIMES

**House**
31 Mar-28 Oct
daily (except Fri) 11am-5pm
(last admission 4.30pm)

**Sculpture Garden**
Open all year

**Directions:** 1 mile from Stamford, 20 minutes north of Peterborough on A1

**Tel:** 01780 752451

www.burghley.co.uk

MAP Page 271 (4H)
OS Map 234 (ref TF 049061)

## 78 Derngate, Northampton
Northamptonshire – NN1 1UH

A house re-designed by Charles Rennie Mackintosh for model-manufacturer W.J. Bassett-Lowke. Carefully restored to its 1917 appearance in 2003, it is among Mackintosh's last architectural works, and is the only Mackintosh house open in England. Supporting exhibitions explore the Mackintosh designs and celebrate the life and work of Bassett-Lowke.

Managed by the 78 Derngate Northampton Trust.

### NON-MEMBERS

| | |
|---|---|
| Adult | £5.50 |
| Concession, inc. child | £4.50 |
| Family | £14.00 |
| School parties (per head) | £3.00 |

EH members and up to 6 children within their family group get free entry. Discount does not extend to EH Corporate Partners or members of Cadw and Historic Scotland

### OPENING TIMES

28 Mar-30 Nov, Wed-Sun and Bank Hols 10.30am-5pm

Last admission 3.30pm

Visits must be booked, please call 01604 603407

**Direction:** In Northampton, close to Derngate theatre

**Train:** Northampton ¾ miles

**Bus:** From surrounding areas

MAP Page 271 (6G)
OS Map 223 (ref SP 759603)

## Kelmarsh Hall
Northampton – NN6 9LT

Kelmarsh Hall, built in 1732 to a James Gibbs design, is surrounded by its traditional working estate, grazed parkland and beautiful gardens attributable to Nancy Lancaster, Norah Lindsay and Geoffrey Jellicoe.

### ENTRY

Admission charge applies. Please call for details. One EH member free with one paying visitor

### OPENING TIMES

Please call or check our website for details

**Direction:** Junction 2 of A14 on A508 between Northampton and Market Harborough

**Tel:** 01604 686543

www.kelmarsh.com

MAP Page 271 (5G)
OS Map 223 (ref SP 736796)

## Moira Furnace
Leicestershire – DE12 6AT

An early 19th-century blast furnace which tells the story of the iron-making process: short boat trips available.

### ENTRY

| | |
|---|---|
| Adult | £3.50 |
| Concession | £2.50 |
| Child (3-12 yrs) | £1.50 |
| Family (2+3) | £9.00 |

50% discount for EH Members

Discount does not extend to EH Corporate Partners

## Moira Furnace

### OPENING TIMES

| | |
|---|---|
| 1 Apr-30 Sep, Tue-Sun | 10am-5pm |
| 1 Oct-31 Mar, Wed-Sun | 11am-4pm |

**Direction:** Moira Furnace is 2 miles away from Ashby de la Zouch and 2 miles away from Swadlincote

**Tel:** 01283 224667/07976 637858

www.nwleicestershire.gov.uk

MAP Page 270 (4E)
OS Map 245 (ref SK 314151)

## Papplewick Pumping Station
Nottinghamshire – NG15 9AJ

Britain's finest working Victorian water pumping station, with ornate engine house, cooling pond, landscaped grounds, original twin steam engines and six boilers, woodland play area and miniature railway.

### ENTRY

| | |
|---|---|
| Adult | £4.80 |
| Concession | £3.80 |
| Child | £2.80 |
| Family (2+2) | £13.50 |

25% off all ticket categories for EH members

Discount does not extend to EH Corporate Partners

### OPENING TIMES

Please call for details

### HOW TO FIND US

**Direction:** Off the A60 near Ravenshead, midway between Mansfield and Nottingham

**Tel:** 0115 963 2938

www.papplewick pumpingstation.co.uk

MAP Page 271 (3F)
OS Map 270 (ref SK 583521)

Fireplace in Leicester's Gatehouse, Kenilworth Castle – see page 176

# West Midlands

'Live here, good Queen, live here;
you are amongst your friends.
Their comfort comes when you approach,
and when you part it ends.'

George Gascoigne, *Queen Elizabeth's Farewell to Kenilworth*, 1575

# Properties See individual listings for details

**Herefordshire**
Arthur's Stone
Edvin Loach Old Church
Goodrich Castle
Longtown Castle
Mortimer's Cross Water Mill
Rotherwas Chapel
Wigmore Castle

**Shropshire**
Acton Burnell Castle
Boscobel House and the Royal Oak
Buildwas Abbey
Cantlop Bridge
Clun Castle
Haughmond Abbey
Iron Bridge
Langley Chapel
Lilleshall Abbey
Mitchell's Fold Stone Circle
Moreton Corbet Castle
Old Oswestry Hill Fort
Stokesay Castle
Wenlock Priory
White Ladies Priory
Wroxeter Roman City

**Staffordshire**
Croxden Abbey
Wall Roman Site

**West Midlands**
Halesowen Abbey

**Warwickshire**
Kenilworth Castle

**Worcestershire**
Leigh Court Barn
Witley Court and Gardens

Comprehensive map of our sites Page 270

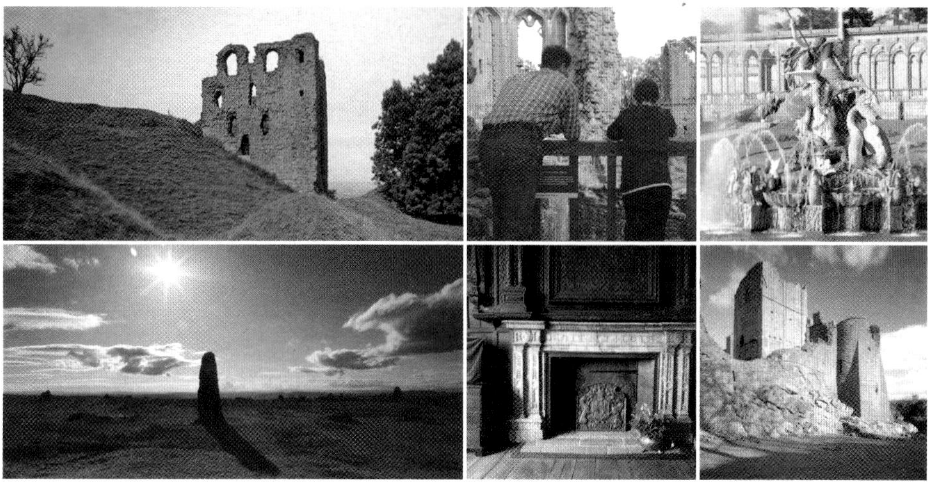

Above: (top left to right) Clun Castle, Kenilworth Castle, Witley Court and Gardens and (bottom left to right) Mitchell's Fold Stone Circle, Kenilworth Castle and Goodrich Castle.



# Elizabethan Splendour, Medieval Abbeys

Stretching from the Welsh Border hills in Shropshire and Herefordshire to the 'Shakespeare county' of Warwickshire, the West Midlands includes some of the finest countryside in England, and some of English Heritage's most impressive sites. In one of these, **Kenilworth Castle**, visitors can now enjoy the fruits of a major investment project, making this vast fortress-palace complex more accessible at many levels.

Kenilworth's history – now interpreted in an interactive exhibition in the great timbered barn – spans over nine centuries. But its most famous associations are with Queen Elizabeth I and Robert Dudley, Earl of Leicester: her favourite, would-be husband and (some believed) actual lover. Their relationship is celebrated in a sumptuous display – featuring portraits, tapestries and even a pair of Elizabeth I's boots – on the top floor of the Gatehouse he built to welcome her. Accessible for the first time in decades, this Gatehouse also preserves a huge and elaborate fireplace and other survivors of Leicester's original interior furnishings. Other chambers are set as they appeared during the 1930s, when the building was last inhabited and visitors were shown round it for a shilling a head. After careful archaeological excavation, the private garden Leicester laid out for the Queen's visit is also being recreated. This will be work in progress during 2007.

Elsewhere in the region, the West Wing at **Witley Court** will be opened, allowing access to parts of the building which have been inaccessible to the public for years.

The West Midlands also contains many other delights, for example Shropshire's collection of evocative monastic ruins, visitable by the determined in a a single day's tour. Each has its own distinctive character and features. **Buildwas Abbey** displays an unusually unaltered 12th-century monastic church with massive round pillars, and an even rarer and recently re-opened crypt chapel. Outstandingly picturesque **Wenlock Priory** has magnificent carving in its chapter house, and a tiered monastic washing fountain in its topiaried grounds. **Haughmond Abbey**'s chapter house, with its early Tudor timber roof, is bedecked with splendid medieval statuary. Remote **Lilleshall Abbey** is worth seeking out for the gallery-level view over its church, reached via a dark wall stairway; while little **White Ladies Priory**, an uncommon survivor of a nunnery church near **Boscobel House**, was briefly the hiding place of the fugitive Charles II.

## Acton Burnell Castle
Shropshire

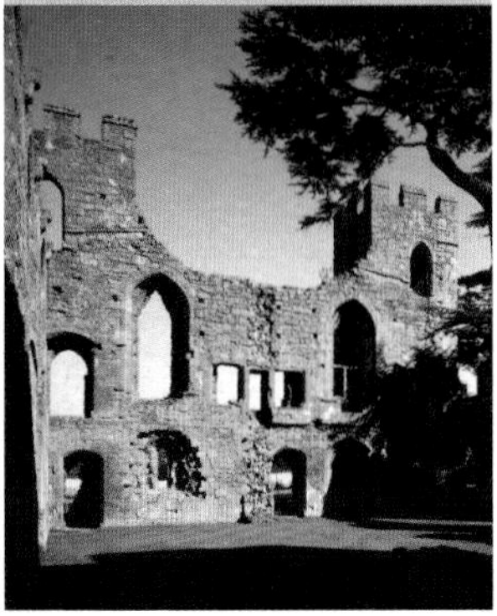

The red sandstone shell of a semi-fortified tower house, built in 1284-93 by Bishop Burnell, Edward I's Lord Chancellor. Parliaments were twice held here, in 1283 and 1285.

### OPENING TIMES
Any reasonable time

### HOW TO FIND US
**Direction:** Located in Acton Burnell, signposted from A49, 8 miles S of Shrewsbury

**Train:** Shrewsbury or Church Stretton, both 8 miles.

MAP Page 270 (4B)
OS Map 241 (ref SJ 534019)

## Arthur's Stone
Herefordshire

## Arthur's Stone

An atmospheric Neolithic 'cromlech' burial chamber made of great stone slabs, in the hills above Herefordshire's Golden Valley.

### OPENING TIMES
Any reasonable time

### HOW TO FIND US
**Direction:** 7 miles E of Hay-on-Wye off B4348 near Dorstone

**Bus:** Stagecoach in South Wales 39, Yeomans Canyon 40 Hereford – Brecon to within ¾ mile

MAP Page 270 (7B)
OS Map 13/201 (ref SO 319431)

## Boscobel House and The Royal Oak
See feature opposite

## Buildwas Abbey
Shropshire – TF8 7BW

Impressive ruins of a Cistercian abbey, including its unusually unaltered 12th-century church, beautiful vaulted and tile-floored chapter house, and recently re-opened crypt chapel. In a wooded Severn-side setting, not far from the Iron Bridge and Wenlock Priory.

www.english-heritage.org.uk/buildwas

### NON-MEMBERS

| | |
|---|---|
| Adult | £2.90 |
| Concession | £2.20 |
| Child | £1.50 |

## Buildwas Abbey

### OPENING TIMES
1 Apr-30 Sep, Wed-Sun & Bank Hol Mons 10am-5pm

### HOW TO FIND US
**Direction:** On S bank of River Severn on A4169, 2 miles W of Ironbridge

**Train:** Telford Central 6 miles

**Bus:** Arriva 96 Telford-Shrewsbury (passes close to Telford Central)

**Tel:** 01952 433274

OVP

Disabled access is limited.

Plant sales.

Nature trail [not managed by EH] including site of abbey fishponds.

MAP Page 270 (4C)
OS Map 242 (ref SJ 643043)

## Cantlop Bridge
Shropshire

A single-span, cast-iron road bridge over the Cound Brook. Designed by the great engineer Thomas Telford, who was instrumental in shaping industrial Shropshire and the West Midlands.

### OPENING TIMES
Any reasonable time

### HOW TO FIND US
**Direction:** ¾ mile SW of Berrington on an unclassified road off A458

**Train:** Shrewsbury 5 miles

MAP Page 270 (4B)
OS Map 241 (ref SJ 517062)

# Boscobel House and the Royal Oak

Staffordshire – ST19 9AR

Boscobel House was built in about 1632, when John Gifford of Whiteladies converted a timber-framed farmhouse into a hunting lodge. The Gifford family were Roman Catholics, at a time when the religion suffered persecution. Tradition holds that the true purpose of Boscobel was to serve as a secret place for the shelter of Catholics in times of need.

The house was, however, destined for greater fame. Following the execution of King Charles I in 1649, his eldest son made a brave though misguided attempt to regain the throne. In 1651 his hopes were crushed at Worcester in the final conflict of the Civil War. Young Charles was forced to flee for his life.

Initially the future King Charles II set out to cross the River Severn into Wales, but found his way blocked by Cromwell's patrols. He sought refuge instead at Boscobel, hiding first in a tree that is now known as the Royal Oak and then spending the night in a priest-hole in the house's attic. He then travelled on in disguise via other safe houses before escaping to France.

Boscobel later became a much visited place, although it remained a working farm. Visitors can also see the dairy, farmyard, smithy, gardens, and a descendant of the Royal Oak. Tearoom available. House Tours by guide only.

www.english-heritage.org.uk/boscobelhouse

## NON-MEMBERS

| | |
|---|---|
| Adult | £4.90 |
| Concession | £3.70 |
| Child | £2.50 |
| Family | £12.30 |

## NON-MEMBERS

**Grounds only**

| | |
|---|---|
| Adult | £2.40 |
| Concession | £1.80 |
| Child | £1.20 |

## OPENING TIMES

| | |
|---|---|
| 1 Apr-31 Oct, Wed-Sun & Bank Hol Mons | 10am-5pm |

Last entry 1 hour before closing

## HOW TO FIND US

**Direction:** On minor road from A41 to A5, 8 miles NW of Wolverhampton. 5 mins drive from M54 J3

**Train:** Cosford 3 miles

**Tel:** 01902 850244

E P OVP

Parking (coaches welcome).

MAP Page 270 (4C)
OS Map 242 (ref SJ 838082)

## Clun Castle
Shropshire

The dramatic riverside ruins and extensive earthworks of a Welsh Border castle, its tall 13th-century keep unusually set on the side of its mound.

### OPENING TIMES
Any reasonable time

### HOW TO FIND US
**Direction:** In Clun, off A488, 18 miles W of Ludlow

**Train:** Hopton Heath 6½ miles; Knighton 6½ miles

Guidebooks available from Stokesay Castle.

MAP Page 270 (5B)
OS Map 201 (ref SO 299809)

## Croxden Abbey
Staffordshire

## Croxden Abbey

The impressive remains of an abbey of Cistercian 'white monks', including towering fragments of its 13th-century church, infirmary and 14th-century abbot's lodging.

### OPENING TIMES
| | |
|---|---|
| All year round | 10am-5pm |

### HOW TO FIND US
**Direction:** 5 miles NW of Uttoxeter off A522

**Train:** Uttoxeter 6 miles

MAP Page 270 (3D)
OS Map 259 (ref SK 066397)

## Edvin Loach Old Church
Herefordshire

The ruins of an 11th-century and later church built within the earthworks of a Norman motte and bailey castle, with a Victorian church nearby.

### OPENING TIMES
Any reasonable time

### HOW TO FIND US
**Direction:** Located 4 miles N of Bromyard on an unclassified road off B4203

MAP Page 270 (6C)
OS Map 202 (ref SO 663584)

## Goodrich Castle
See feature – Page 174

## Halesowen Abbey
West Midlands – B62 8RJ

Contact Regional Office on 0121 625 6820 for details.

## Haughmond Abbey
Shropshire – SY4 4RW

The extensive remains of an Augustinian abbey, including its abbots' quarters, refectory and cloister. The substantially surviving chapter house has a frontage richly bedecked with 12th- and 14th-century carving and statuary, and a fine timber roof of c. 1500. New pictorial interpretation boards guide the visitor, and an introductory exhibition displays archaeological finds. Picnic area and light refreshments available.

www.english-heritage.org.uk/haughmond

### NON-MEMBERS
| | |
|---|---|
| Adult | £2.90 |
| Concession | £2.20 |
| Child | £1.50 |

## Haughmond Abbey

### OPENING TIMES

| | |
|---|---|
| 1 Apr-30 Sep, Wed-Sun & Bank Hol Mons | 10am-5pm |

### HOW TO FIND US

**Direction:** Located 3 miles NE of Shrewsbury off B5062

**Train:** Shrewsbury 3½ miles

**Bus:** Arriva 519 Shrewsbury – Newport

**Tel:** 01743 709661

OVP

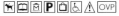

Disabled access (not easy).

New guidebook.

MAP Page 270 (4B)
OS Map 241 (ref SJ 542152)

## Iron Bridge
See feature – Page 175

## Kenilworth Castle
See feature – Page 176

## Langley Chapel
Shropshire

A small chapel tranquilly set all alone in charming countryside. Its atmospheric interior contains a perfect set of 17th-century timber furnishings, including a musicians' pew.

### OPENING TIMES

| | |
|---|---|
| 1 Mar-31 Oct, daily | 10am-5pm |
| 1 Nov-29 Feb, daily | 10am-4pm |

### HOW TO FIND US

**Direction:** 1½ miles S of Acton Burnell, on an unclassified road off A49; 9½ miles S of Shrewsbury

Langley Chapel

**Train:** Shrewsbury 7½ miles

MAP Page 270 (5B)
OS Map 241 (ref SO 663584)

## Leigh Court Barn
Worcestershire

An outstanding display of English medieval carpentry, this mighty timber-framed barn is the largest cruck structure in Britain. Built for Pershore Abbey in 1344, it is 46 metres (150 feet) long, with 18 cruck blades each made from a single oak tree.

### OPENING TIMES

| | |
|---|---|
| 1 Apr-30 Sep, Thu-Sun and Bank Hol Mons | 10am-5pm |

### HOW TO FIND US

**Direction:** 5 miles W of Worcester on an unclassified road off A4103

**Train:** Worcester Foregate Street 5 miles

**Bus:** First 417 from Worcester to within 1 mile

Parking Charge – £1.00

MAP Page 270 (6C)
OS Map 204 (ref SO 783535)

## Lilleshall Abbey
Shropshire

Extensive ruins of an Augustinian abbey, later a Civil War stronghold, in a deeply rural setting. Much of the church survives, unusually viewable from gallery level, along with the lavishly sculpted processional door and other cloister buildings.

### OPENING TIMES

| | |
|---|---|
| 1 Apr-30 Sep, daily | 10am-5pm |
| Closed | 1 Oct-20 Mar |

### HOW TO FIND US

**Direction:** On an unclassified road off A518, 4 miles N of Oakengates

**Train:** Oakengates 4½ miles

**Bus:** Arriva 481 Telford – Stafford (passes close to Telford Central and Stafford) to within 1 mile

**Tel:** 0121 625 6820 (Regional office)

New guidebook from Haughmond Abbey, or upon order.

MAP Page 270 (4C)
OS Map 242 (ref SJ 738142)

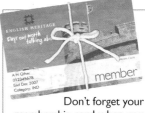

# Goodrich Castle Herefordshire – HR9 6HY

Goodrich stands majestically on a wooded hill commanding the passage of the River Wye into the picturesque valley of Symonds Yat. The castle was begun in the late 11th century, by the English thegn Godric who gave it his name. A generation later the splendidly preserved square keep which still forms its core was added, probably in the time of Richard 'Strongbow' de Clare, Earl of Pembroke and Lord of Goodrich 1148-76.

Under King John, Goodrich was granted along with the earldom of Pembroke to the famous William Marshal, a great castle-builder who may have initiated work on the inner ward. Each of the Marshal's four sons inherited the fortress in turn, the last dying childless at Goodrich in 1245.

Thereafter the fortress and earldom passed to Henry III's half-brother, William de Valence, who rebuilt its defences and living quarters in the most up-to-date style.

Goodrich still boasts one of the most complete sets of medieval domestic buildings surviving in any English castle. William's widow Countess Joan frequently stayed here with an entourage of up to 200, entertaining her relations and friends in the most lavish style.

During the Civil War, Goodrich was held successively by both sides. Sir Henry Lingen's Royalists eventually surrendered in 1646 under threats of undermining and a deadly Parliamentarian mortar. The famous 'Roaring Meg', the only surviving Civil War mortar, has returned to the castle after over 350 years.

**www.english-heritage.org.uk/goodrichcastle**

**NEW FOR 2007** From Spring 2007, a new café, shop and visitor facilities will be available.

## NON-MEMBERS

| | |
|---|---|
| Adult | £4.90 |
| Concession | £3.70 |
| Child | £2.50 |
| Family | £12.30 |

## OPENING TIMES

| | |
|---|---|
| 1 Apr-31 May, daily | 10am-5pm |
| 1 Jun-31 Aug, daily | 10am-6pm |
| 1 Sep-31 Oct, daily | 10am-5pm |
| 1 Nov-29 Feb, Wed-Sun | 10am-4pm |
| 1-20 Mar, daily | 10am-5pm |
| Closed | 24-26 Dec and 1 Jan |

## HOW TO FIND US

**Direction:** 5 miles S of Ross-on-Wye off A40

**Bus:** Stagecoach in Wye & Dean 34 Monmouth Ross-on-Wye (with connection from Gloucester) to within ½ mile

**Tel:** 01600 890538

OVP

Parking charge £1 (400 metres from castle).

Disabled access (limited, please call for details).

MAP Page 270 (7C)
OS Map 14 (ref SO 577200)

# Iron Bridge Shropshire

he world's first iron bridge was rected over the River Severn ere in 1779. Designed by the hrewsbury architect Thomas ritchard, it was cast by local onmaster Abraham Darby III in is nearby Coalbrookdale oundry, using 378 tons of iron. ecent research shows that nost parts were individually nade to fit, adapting traditional voodworking joints. Perhaps Britain's best-known industrial monument, the bridge gave its name to the spectacular wooded gorge which became the cradle of the Industrial Revolution. Ironbridge Gorge is now a World Heritage Site.

The Iron Bridge is the perfect place to begin a tour of the Gorge's many museums, and the many other English Heritage sites nearby, including Buildwas Abbey, Wenlock Priory and Wroxeter Roman City.

## OPENING TIMES

**Any reasonable time**

## HOW TO FIND US

**Direction:** Adjacent to A4169

**Bus:** From Telford (all services pass close to ⇌ Telford Central and Wellington Telford West)

**MAP Page 270 (4C)**
**OS Map 242 (ref SJ 672034)**

# Kenilworth Castle Warwickshire – CV8 1NE

Among the largest and most impressive historic sites in England, Kenilworth Castle is a vast complex of ruined fortifications and palatial apartments spanning over five centuries. With English Heritage's re-opening of Leicester's Gatehouse and two new exhibitions charting the castle's history, there is now more than ever to see here.

Kenilworth's many and varied buildings and architectural styles reflect its long connection with successive English monarchs and their favourites. Its founder was Geoffrey de Clinton, Henry I's treasurer, who began the massive Norman keep at the core of the castle in the 1120s. Judged too strong for a subject, Kenilworth thereafter became a royal fortress. King John greatly strengthened it between 1210 and 1215, enlarging the surrounding watery 'mere' which effectively made it an island stronghold. Thus it could withstand an epic siege in 1266, when rebellious barons held out against Henry III's siege engines for six months, succumbing only to starvation.

During the 1390s, John of Gaunt, Duke of Lancaster, rebuilt the splendid great hall and state-rooms of Kenilworth's inner court. His grandson Henry V created in its grounds the moated summer-house called the Pleasaunce: here too, according to tradition, he received the insulting French 'gift' of tennis-balls which sparked off the Agincourt campaign. Henry VIII added more grand apartments: but it was his daughter Queen Elizabeth's favourite, Robert Dudley, Earl of Leicester, who left the greatest impression on Kenilworth, and gave it its greatest fame.

Granted Kenilworth in 1563, Leicester lavished fortunes on converting it into a palace fit to receive Queen Elizabeth and her court. It was here that her 19-day 'great entertainment' took place in 1575. Not content with adapting the existing buildings, he added the towering mansion-sized 'Leicester's Building' – complete with a purpose-built 'dancing chamber' – specifically for her use: as well as a noble new entrance to his quasi-royal palace, 'Leicester's Gatehouse'.

Fireplace in Leicester's Gatehouse

Though largely unscathed during the Civil War, Kenilworth was afterwards rendered indefensible and gradually fell into dilapidation. Made famous by Walter Scott's romantic novel, *Kenilworth* (1821), it was eventually saved for the nation in 1938.

2006 saw the part-completion of a multi-million pound investment project at Kenilworth Castle, including two major new exhibitions, excavations to the Elizabethan gardens and the restoration of Leicester's Gatehouse which up until now had been closed to the public for decades. The gatehouse is now fully restored and open : chambers on the lower floors have been dressed and furnished as they might have appeared when the gatehouse was last inhabited in the 1930s, and the top floor houses the **Queen and Castle: Robert Dudley's Kenilworth** exhibition. Featuring items both from museums and private collections, the exhibition tells the story of Elizabeth I's relationship with Robert Dudley, Earl of Leicester. The Elizabethan garden project continues into 2007.

**www.english-heritage.org.uk/kenilworth**

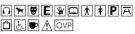

Available for corporate and private hire.

## NON-MEMBERS

| | |
|---|---|
| Adult | £6.00 |
| Concession | £4.50 |
| Child | £3.00 |
| Family | £15.00 |

## OPENING TIMES

| | |
|---|---|
| 1 Apr-31 May, daily | 10am-5pm |
| 1 Jun-31 Aug, daily | 10am-6pm |
| 1 Sep-31 Oct, daily | 10am-5pm |
| 1 Nov-29 Feb, daily | 10am-4pm |
| 1-20 Mar, daily | 10am-5pm |

Note: the Gatehouse may close early on Saturdays for private events

| | |
|---|---|
| Closed | 24-26 Dec and 1 Jan |

## HOW TO FIND US

**Direction:** In Kenilworth off A46. Clearly signposted from the town centre, off B4103

**Train:** Warwick or Coventry 5 miles

**Bus:** Stagecoach in Warwickshire X1 Coventry – Stratford-upon-Avon calls at Castle; otherwise X17, Travel West Midlands 12 Coventry – Leamington Spa to within a few minutes walk. All pass close to Coventry & Leamington Spa

**Tel:** 01926 864152

**Local Tourist Information**
Kenilworth: 01926 748900

OVP

Audio tours (also in French and German).

Tearoom (Open Easter-Oct daily, Tel: 01926 864376).

New ticket office and shop.

Car parking charges to be introduced during 2007. Call site for details.

MAP Page 270 (5E)
OS Map 221 (ref SP 278723)

## Longtown Castle
Herefordshire

A powerful thick-walled round keep of c.1200, characteristic of the Welsh Borders, on a large earthen mound within a stone-walled bailey. Set in the beautiful Olchon valley, with magnificent views of the Black Mountains.

### OPENING TIMES
Any reasonable time

### HOW TO FIND US
**Direction:** Located 4 miles WSW of Abbey Dore, off B4347

**MAP Page 270 (7B)**
**OS Map 13 (ref SO 321291)**

## Mitchell's Fold Stone Circle
Shropshire

Mitchell's Fold Stone Circle

A Bronze Age stone circle, the focus of many legends, set in dramatic moorland on Stapeley Hill. It once consisted of some 30 stones, 15 of which are still visible.

### OPENING TIMES
Any reasonable time

### HOW TO FIND US
**Direction:** 16 miles SW of Shrewsbury

**Train:** Welshpool 10 miles

**Bus:** Minsterley/Arriva 553 Shrewsbury – Bishop's Castle (passes close to Shrewsbury) to within 1 mile

**Tel:** 01939 232771

**MAP Page 270 (5B)**
**OS Map 216 (ref SO 304984)**

## Moreton Corbet Castle
Shropshire

The ruins of the medieval castle and Tudor manor house of the Corbets are dominated by the theatrical shell of an ambitious Elizabethan mansion wing in Italianate style, which was devastated during the Civil War. Fine Corbet monuments fill the adjacent church.

Moreton Corbet Castle

### OPENING TIMES
Any reasonable time

### HOW TO FIND US
**Direction:** In Moreton Corbet off B5063 (a turning off A49), 7 miles NE of Shrewsbury

**Train:** Yorton 4 miles

**Bus:** Arriva 64 Shrewsbury – Hanley (passes close to Shrewsbury and Stoke-on-Trent) to within 1 mile

Guidebooks from Buildwas and Haughmond Abbeys.

**MAP Page 270 (4C)**
**OS Map 241 (ref SJ 561231)**

## Mortimer's Cross Water Mill
Herefordshire – HR6 9PE

A rare one-man-operated 18th-century water mill in part working order. Nearby there are attractive gardens and woodland walks, a stone weir and the significant Aymestrey Limestone Quarry. Special day and evening guided tours for groups are available by arrangement with the owner. Please call for details.

Managed by Mr C Partington.

### Mortimer's Cross Water Mill

**NON-MEMBERS**

| | |
|---|---|
| Adult | £4.00 |
| Concession | £3.50 |
| Child | £2.50 |

**OPENING TIMES**

1 Apr-30 Sep, Sun & Bank Hol Mons 10am-4pm

Other times by arrangement

Access to the mill is by guided tour only 11am, 1pm & 3pm

**HOW TO FIND US**

**Direction:** Located 7 miles NW of Leominster on B4362

**Train:** Leominster 7½ miles

**Tel:** 01568 708820

Disabled access (exterior and ground floor only).

Warning (there are steep river banks and sluice channels which are hazardous at all times).

MAP Page 270 (6B)
OS Map 203 (ref SO 426637)

## Old Oswestry Hill Fort
Shropshire

The most hugely impressive Iron Age hillfort on the Welsh Borders, covering 40 acres, with formidable multiple ramparts.

### Old Oswestry Hill Fort

**OPENING TIMES**

Any reasonable time

**HOW TO FIND US**

**Direction:** 1 mile N of Oswestry, off an unclassified road off A483

**Train:** Gobowen 2 miles

**Bus:** Arriva 2, 53, 63 from Gobowen

MAP Page 270 (3B)
OS Map 240 (ref SJ 295310)

## Rotherwas Chapel
Herefordshire

### Rotherwas Chapel

The family chapel of the Roman Catholic Bodenham family. The originally simple medieval building has a fine Elizabethan timber roof, a rebuilt 18th-century tower, and striking Victorian interior decoration and furnishings by the Pugins.

**OPENING TIMES**

Any reasonable time. Keykeeper located at nearby filling station

**HOW TO FIND US**

**Direction:** 1½ miles SE of Hereford on B4399, left into Chapel Road

**Train:** Hereford 3½ miles

**Bus:** First 78 from Hereford

Disabled access (kissing gate).

MAP Page 270 (7B)
OS Map 189 (ref SO 536383)

## Stokesay Castle
See feature – Page 180

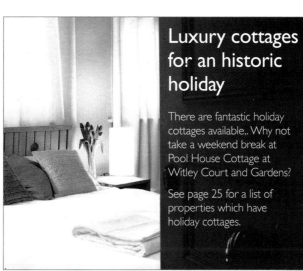

# Stokesay Castle Shropshire – SY7 9AH

Stokesay Castle is the finest and best preserved 13th-century fortified manor house in England. It offers visitors a unique glimpse into a distant age, when strength and elegance were combined.

The panelled Solar Chamber

Take the audio tour

Set amid peaceful countryside near the Welsh border, Stokesay Castle forms an outstandingly picturesque group with its timber-framed gatehouse and the parish church.

Lawrence of Ludlow, who made his fortune as a wool merchant and set up as a country gentleman, acquired the manor in 1281. Extensive recent tree-ring dating confirms that he had completed virtually the whole of the still-surviving buildings by 1291, the date of his 'licence to crenellate' from Edward I.

The dating also revealed that Stokesay's magnificent open-hearthed great hall, with its fine cruck-built timber roof, shuttered gable windows and precipitous staircase, has scarcely been altered since it was built. The north tower displays an original medieval tiled floor and remains of wall painting, while the south tower with fine views from its roof contains a panelled solar chamber added in the 17th century. Its dominating feature is a fireplace with richly carved overmantel, still bearing clear traces of gold, pink, red, green and white painting.

Across the courtyard stands the truly delightful gatehouse, an elaborate example of the regional style of lavishly showy timber-framing, with charming carvings of Adam and Eve. This was built in 1640, a few years before Stokesay's only known military encounter, when it surrendered without fighting during the Civil War.

An audio tour will help you to imagine Stokesay as the centre of medieval life. Its grounds include cottage-style gardens, a tearoom open from April to October, and a gift shop.

**www.english-heritage.org.uk/stokesaycastle**

## NON-MEMBERS

| | |
|---|---|
| Adult | £4.90 |
| Concession | £3.70 |
| Child | £2.50 |
| Family | £12.30 |

## OPENING TIMES

| | |
|---|---|
| 1-30 Apr, Wed-Sun & Bank Hol Mons | 10am-5pm |
| 1 May-30 Jun, daily | 10am-5pm |
| 1 Jul-31 Aug, daily | 10am-6pm |
| 1 Sep-31 Oct, Wed-Sun | 10am-5pm |
| 1 Nov-29 Feb, Thu-Sun | 10am-4pm |
| 1-20 Mar, Wed-Sun & Bank Hol Mons | 10am-5pm |
| Closed | 24-26 Dec & 1 Jan |

## HOW TO FIND US

**Direction:** 7 miles NW of Ludlow off A49

**Train:** Craven Arms 1 mile

**Bus:** Whittle 435 Shrewsbury – Ludlow

**Tel:** 01588 672544

**Local Tourist Information**
Ludlow: 01584 875053

P OVP

Disabled access (call site for details).

Entrance to the courtyard is through an historic gate. Unsuitable for motorised scooters and unassisted wheelchair users.

Tearoom (Seasonal: 1 Apr-31 Oct).

MAP Page 270 (5B)
OS Map 217 (ref SO 436817)

## Wall Roman Site (Letocetum)
Staffordshire – WS14 0AW

Wall was an important staging post on Watling Street, the Roman military road to North Wales. It provided overnight accommodation for travelling Roman officials and imperial messengers. The foundations of an inn and bathhouse can be seen, and many of the excavated finds are displayed in the on-site museum*.

Managed by English Heritage and owned by The National Trust.

### OPENING TIMES

Any reasonable time

*Museum by appointment only, please call for details

### HOW TO FIND US

**Direction:** Off A5 at Wall, near Lichfield

**Train:** Shenstone 1½ miles

**Tel:** Regional Head Office – 0121 625 6820

MAP Page 270 (4D)
OS Map 244 (ref SK 098066)

## Wenlock Priory
Shropshire – TF13 6HS

Picturesque ruins of a large priory of Cluniac monks, whose love of decoration is reflected in the glorious carving of its 12th-century chapter house and rare 'lavabo' – a tiered washing fountain in a topiary-bedecked cloister garden.

Parts of the great church also stand, against the backdrop of the full-height infirmary wing. Set on the fringe of beautiful Much Wenlock, not far from Buildwas Abbey and the Iron Bridge.

### NON-MEMBERS

| | |
|---|---|
| Adult | £3.40 |
| Concession | £2.60 |
| Child | £1.70 |

### OPENING TIMES

| | |
|---|---|
| 1-30 Apr, Wed-Sun & Bank Hol Mons | 10am-5pm |
| 1 May-31 Aug, daily | 10am-5pm |
| 1 Sep-31 Oct, Wed-Sun | 10am-5pm |
| 1 Nov-29 Feb, Thu-Sun | 10am-4pm |
| 1-20 Mar, Wed-Sun & Bank Hol Mons | 10am-5pm |
| Closed | 24-26 Dec and 1 Jan |

### HOW TO FIND US

**Direction:** In Much Wenlock

**Train:** Telford Central 9 miles

**Bus:** Shropshire Bus 436/7 Shrewsbury – Bridgnorth (passes close to Shrewsbury)

**Tel:** 01952 727466

Plant sales.

MAP Page 270 (5C)
OS Map 242 (ref SJ 625001)

## White Ladies Priory
Shropshire

Ruins of the late 12th-century church of a small nunnery of 'white ladies' or Augustinian canonesses. Charles II hid nearby in 1651, before moving to Boscobel House.

### OPENING TIMES

| | |
|---|---|
| 1 Apr-31 Oct, daily | 10am-5pm |
| Closed | 1 Nov-20 Mar |

### HOW TO FIND US

**Direction:** Located 1 mile SW of Boscobel House off an unclassified road between A41 and A5; 8 miles NW of Wolverhampton

**Train:** Cosford 2½ miles

Information sheets available from Boscobel House.

MAP Page 270 (4C)
OS Map 242 (ref SJ 826076)

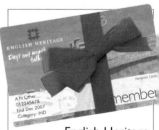

## Wigmore Castle
Herefordshire

Once the stronghold of the turbulent Mortimer family, Wigmore Castle was abandoned by the 17th century. Now it is among the most remarkable ruins in England, largely buried up to first floor level by earth and fallen masonry. Yet many of its fortifications survive to full height, including parts of the keep on its towering mound.

### OPENING TIMES
Any reasonable time

### HOW TO FIND US
**Direction:** Located 8 miles W of Ludlow on A4110. Accessible via footpath ¾ mile from the village on Mortimer Way

**Train:** Bucknell 6 miles, Ludlow 10 miles

Toilets (including disabled) at the Village Hall and also the Compasses Hotel by arrangement. Tel: 01568 770705.

There are steep steps to the summit, which are hazardous in icy conditions. Children must stay under close control and should not climb the walls or banks. Strong footwear is recommended. There is no staff presence.

MAP Page 270 (6B)
OS Map 203 (ref SO 408693)

Stokesay Castle – see page 180

# Witley Court and Gardens Worcestershire – WR6 6JT

A hundred years ago, Witley Court was one of England's great country houses, hosting many extravagant parties. Today it is a spectacular ruin, the result of a disastrous fire in 1937.

The Perseus and Andromeda Fountain

The vast and rambling remains of the palatial 19th-century mansion are surrounded by magnificent landscaped gardens – the 'Monster Work' of William Nesfield – which still contain huge stone fountains. The largest, representing Perseus and Andromeda, which has been restored, was described as making the 'noise of an express train' when fired.

Before 1846, when William Humble Ward (later first Earl of Dudley) inherited Witley Court, the land surrounding the house was laid out in the English landscape style of the mid-18th century. As part of Ward's transformation of the estate, he called in the leading landscape designer of the time, William Andrews Nesfield, whose skills in designing intricate and elegant parterres were complemented by his great ability as an artist and engineer.

Nesfield started work in 1854, creating the south parterre with its great Perseus and Andromeda fountain. His scheme involved elegantly designed plantings of clipped evergreens and shrubs, with parterres enclosed by more clipped evergreens. The central avenue of planting from the house led to the fountains terminating at the south parterre. The east parterre garden with its Flora Fountain was designed in the Parterre de Broderie style, meaning that it was intended to have the appearance of embroidery, with box-edged shapes filled with coloured gravel and flowers.

Following the disastrous fire in 1937 the Witley Estate, including its gardens, fell into long decline. English Heritage has now restored the south garden.

The Woodland Walks in the North Park pass many different species of tree and shrub, acquired from all over the world to create a showpiece. A new garden in 'the Wilderness' is part of the Contemporary Heritage Garden project. This provides yet more opportunities for walking within Witley Court's grounds. Attached to Witley Court is Great Witley Church, which has an amazing Italianate Baroque interior (not managed by English Heritage). The church also has a tearoom close by, and Witley Court has a superb gift shop. The Perseus and Andromeda fountain is back in working order, with even the original high cascades operating. The fountain will be firing between April and October. (Weekdays: 12pm, 2pm and 4pm. Weekends: on the hour every hour from 11am to 4pm.)

Site graphics include information on recent conservation work and there is a new audio tour including information on local flora, wildlife and birdcalls.

A new terrain guide is available on the website.

**www.english-heritage.org.uk/witleycourt**

**NEW FOR 2007** Restoration work to the West Wing has now made several rooms accessible for the first time to the public. In addition, funding from the Wolfson Foundation has assisted English Heritage with major restoration works within the East Parterre garden, enabling us to repair steps and balustrades, and to develop the formal gardens based on the original Nesfield designs.

Holiday cottage available to let.

## NON-MEMBERS

| | |
|---|---|
| Adult | £5.40 |
| Concession | £4.10 |
| Child | £2.70 |
| Family | £13.50 |

## OPENING TIMES

| | |
|---|---|
| 1 Apr-31 May, daily | 10am-5pm |
| 1 Jun-31 Aug, daily | 10am-6pm |
| 1 Sep-31 Oct, daily | 10am-5pm |
| 1 Nov-29 Feb, Wed-Sun | 10am-4pm |
| 1-20 Mar, Wed-Sun | 10am-5pm |
| Closed | 24-26 Dec and 1 Jan |

## HOW TO FIND US

**Direction:** 10 miles NW of Worcester on A443

**Train:** Worcester Foregate St 9½ miles

**Bus:** Yarranton 758 Worcester – Tenbury Wells (passes close to Worcester Foregate St)

**Tel:** 01299 896636

**Local Tourist Information**
Worcester: 01905 726311

OVP

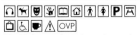

Disabled access (exterior and grounds only).

Tearooms open daily, Apr-Sep and Sat and Sun, Oct (not managed by EH).

New audio tour and a new terrain guide is available on the website.

MAP Page 270 (6C)
OS Map 204 (ref SO 769649)

# Wroxeter Roman City Shropshire – SY5 6PH

Wroxeter (or 'Viroconium' ) was the fourth largest city in Roman Britain. It began as a legionary fortress and later developed into a thriving civilian city, populated by retired soldiers and traders. Though much still remains below ground, today the most impressive features are the 2nd-century municipal baths, and the remains of the huge wall dividing them from the exercise hall in the heart of the city.

The site museum and audio tour reveal how Wroxeter worked in its heyday, and the health and beauty practices of its 5,000 citizens. Dramatic archaeological discoveries provide a glimpse of the last years of the Roman city, and its possible conversion into the headquarters of a 5th-century British or Irish warlord.

www.english-heritage.org.uk/wroxeter

## NON-MEMBERS

| | |
|---|---|
| Adult | £4.10 |
| Concession | £3.10 |
| Child | £2.10 |
| Family | £10.30 |

## OPENING TIMES

| | |
|---|---|
| 1 Apr-31 Oct, daily | 10am-5pm |
| 1 Nov-29 Feb, Wed-Sun | 10am-4pm |
| 1 Mar-20 Mar, daily | 10am-5pm |
| Closed | 24-26 Dec & 1 Jan |

## HOW TO FIND US

**Direction:** Located at Wroxeter, 5 miles E of Shrewsbury on B4380

**Train:** Shrewsbury 5½ miles; Wellington Telford West 6 miles

**Bus:** Arriva 96 Telford – Shrewsbury (passes close to Telford Central)

**Tel:** 01743 761330

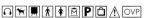

MAP Page 270 (4B)
OS Map 241 (ref SJ 565087)

# Other historic attractions

Discounted entry to our members (discounts may not apply on event days)



**Stoneleigh Abbey**
Warwickshire – CV8 2LF

Established in 1154, Stoneleigh Abbey has more than 800 years of history: Jane Austen lived here and used descriptions of its grand interiors in her novels; Queen Victoria and Prince Albert stayed in 1858; and Prince Charles visited in 2003. Medieval Gatehouse; Great West Wing; magnificent State Rooms; Gothic Revival Riding School; 690-acre parkland, riverside gardens, Repton's Red Book, tearoom.

## ENTRY

**West Wing and Stables**

| | |
|---|---|
| Adult | £6.50 |
| Senior Citizens | £5.00 |
| One child free with each Adult ticket | |
| Additional Child | £3.00 |

**Grounds only**

| | |
|---|---|
| Per person | £3.00 |

10% discount to EH members
All prices are subject to change and are correct at time of going to print

## OPENING TIMES

Good Friday-31 Oct
Tue, Wed, Thu, Sun and Bank Hols

| | |
|---|---|
| Guided Tours | 11am, 1pm, 3pm |
| Grounds open | 10am-5pm |

**Direction:** B4115 off the A452/A46, just a short journey from Kenilworth Castle

**Tel:** 01926 858535

www.stoneleighabbey.org

MAP Page 270 (5E)
OS Map 221 (ref SP 318712)



The Barn, Kenilworth Castle – see page 176

Rievaulx Abbey – see page 204

# Yorkshire

'You can always tell a Yorkshireman: but you can't tell him much'

Proverb

# Properties

See individual listings for details

**East Riding of Yorkshire**
Burton Agnes Manor House
Howden Minster
Skipsea Castle

**North Lincolnshire**
Gainsthorpe Medieval Village
St Peter's Church
Thornton Abbey and Gatehouse

**North Yorkshire**
Aldborough Roman Site
Byland Abbey
Clifford's Tower
Easby Abbey
Fountains Abbey
Helmsley Castle
Kirkham Priory
Marmion Tower
Middleham Castle
Mount Grace Priory
Pickering Castle
Piercebridge Roman Bridge
Richmond Castle
Rievaulx Abbey
St Mary's Church
Scarborough Castle
Spofforth Castle
Stanwick Iron Age Fortifications
Steeton Hall Gateway
Wharram Percy Deserted Medieval Village
Wheeldale Roman Road
Whitby Abbey
York Cold War Bunker

**South Yorkshire**
Brodsworth Hall and Gardens
Conisbrough Castle
Monk Bretton Priory
Roche Abbey



Comprehensive map of our sites Page 273

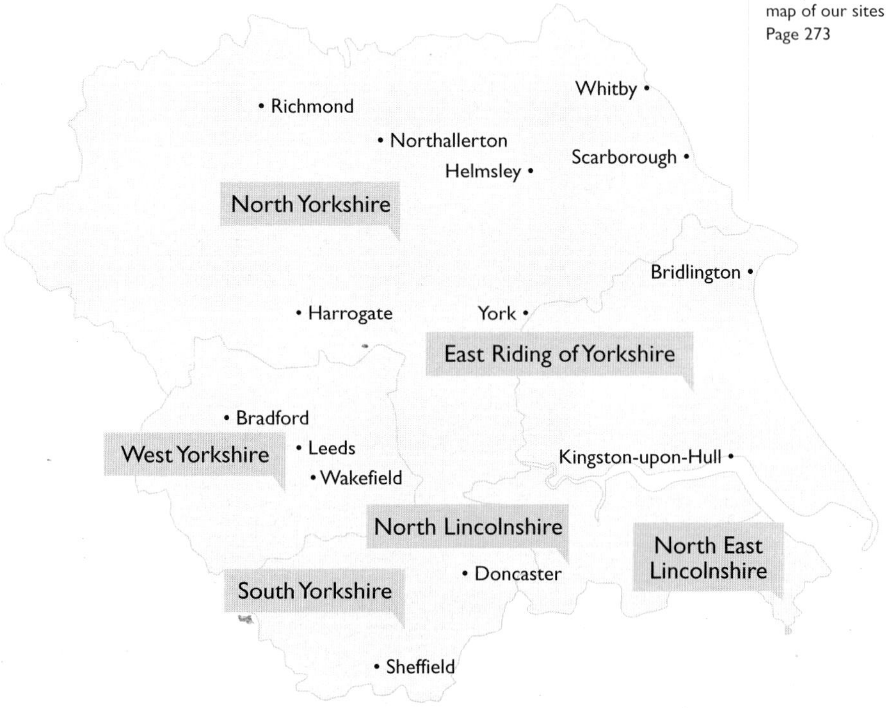

Above: (top left to right) Kirkham Priory, Brodsworth Hall, (bottom left to right) Brodsworth Hall, Whitby Abbey and (right) Conisbrough Castle.



# Historic Regions, New Developments

Although perhaps more often used by Yorkshiremen's neighbours than by Yorkshiremen themselves, this wry proverb serves to emphasise the renowned independent-mindedness of England's biggest county. It includes an immensely varied range of landscapes, from the western Pennine Dales and the north-eastern Moors, via the broad Plain of York, to the East Riding's chalk Wolds and coast and the flat lands on both sides of the Humber – for North Lincolnshire is also included in this English Heritage region. This variety is matched by a wide range of English Heritage sites, the best-known being perhaps the area's unrivalled and impressive monastic remains: these include **Rievaulx Abbey**, which celebrates the 875th anniversary of its foundation this year, and iconic **Whitby Abbey** on its historic headland, extensively researched and interpreted in a spectacular attendant display.

At another of the region's monasteries, **Thornton Abbey and Gatehouse**, the spectacular brick gatehouse will be open to visitors fully for the first time from summer 2007, with a new exhibition tracing the abbey's medieval and equally fascinating post-Dissolution history. A 17th-century mansion unwisely built within the precinct suddenly 'fell quite down to the bare ground without any visible cause': and later Thornton was the focus of huge Victorian Temperance Society rallies. Not far away, much older **St Peter's Church, Barton-on-Humber**, begun in c.970 and the very first building in England to be identified as 'Anglo-Saxon', also has something new to offer from summer 2007, following major restoration work. Long studied by archaeologists, the remains of at least 2,800 burials around it have produced invaluable evidence of the lives, diet and diseases of past congregations: these revelations are now displayed in a new exhibition.

There is more to see, too, at one of the region's favourite attractions, **Brodsworth Hall**, in whose lovely gardens the rose dell and fountain have recently been restored. In 2007 a new temporary exhibition – 'Work and Play: Life on the Yorkshire Estate' – vividly reveals how the country house estate shaped the lives of both the family and the workers of Victorian Brodsworth. The story is told through original photographs, new and archival evidence and oral history.

York, ancient capital and always the focus of the region, displays near its centre **Clifford's Tower**, core of its once-mighty castle: in its suburbs, however, is also one of English Heritage's lesser-known but most unusual 'attractions', the blood-chilling **York Cold War Bunker**.

# Brodsworth Hall and Gardens South Yorkshire – DN5 7XJ

Brodsworth Hall was built in the 1860s in the Italianate style also favoured for Queen Victoria's Osborne House, though furnished on a more comfortable and domestic scale. Much of its original scheme survives today, making it one of England's most unaltered Victorian country houses. The gardens, a collection of 'grand gardens in miniature', have been restored to their Victorian splendour, reflecting the desires and aspirations of Victorian country gentry.

Ground Floor Hall

Brodsworth's creator was Charles Thellusson, whose family devoted themselves to yachting and horse-racing, among other sporting pursuits. Alongside the abandoned tennis raquet of so many families, is the impressive billiards room, the immaculate croquet lawn, in addition to proud displays of sporting success including the magnificent silver Goodwood Cup, won by a family racehorse in 1835.

The house was occupied in unbroken succession for 150 years by members of the Thellusson family and their accumulated impedimenta, a factor which lends it special charm.The last resident, the indomitable Sylvia Grant-Dalton, fought a losing battle against subsidence and leaking roofs for 56 years. Following her death in 1988, English Heritage made the bold but highly successful decision to conserve the interiors 'as found' rather than replacing or restoring them, recounting the tale of how a once opulent Victorian house grew comfortably old and inviting to all.

Exhibitions offering an insight into life at Brodsworth include 'Serving the House', 'Family Life', 'The Gardens', and 'Work and Play'.

### For garden lovers

The family gardens, a series of 'grand gardens in miniature', have been substantially restored since English Heritage took over management of the property in 1990: they are now a fine example of 1860s 'gardening book' design. Restoration work continues, revealing new features and opening up vistas last enjoyed before World War I. The original focus of the formal garden, the three-tiered Italian marble 'Dolphin Fountain', has recently been conserved, and now flows again for the first time in living memory.

The flower garden displays a fine selection of period bedding plants, and the romantic views from the restored summer-house take in both the formal gardens and the pleasure grounds. Of special interest are the restored woodland garden, the statue walks and the fern dell, planted with unusual specimens. There is also a new collection of species roses near the rose garden in the newly developed Rose Dell. The gardens at Brodsworth Hall are a delight in any season, but here are our suggested dates for enjoying the best of the collections. Please bear in mind that exact display times are subject to seasonal variation.

**Feb/Mar**
180,000 snowdrops and 36 varieties of daffodil.

**Apr**
At least 5,000 tulips form the backbone of the spring bedding design.

**May**
Laburnum Arch in flower.

**May/June**
Rose display and over 100 historic varieties of geranium at their peak.

**July**
Summer bedding around the fountain; 250 varieties of ferns at their best.

**Sep-Oct**
Ornamental trees display their autumn colours.

**Oct**
The magnificently restored gardens are illuminated to become a place of wonder and enchantment.

**Nov-Jan**
Over 400 yew trees and many laurels provide shelter for a bracing winter walk.

**All summer**
Sunday in summer – enjoy the gardens in the company of some of the best of South Yorkshire's muscial brass bands.

### Mobility around the site

Visitors please note that prams and back carriers for babies are not allowed in the fragile interiors of the hall. Staff can however provide small padded pushchairs and slings for visitors' use. For visitors with mobility needs, the leg-weary or families with young children, a new six-seater electric buggy now operates a shuttle service from the public car parks. The smooth paths and benches throughout the gardens enable visitors to rest and enjoy the atmosphere, although some steps and steep slopes limit access to parts of the garden. The hall is accessed by ramps and has seats along the route for visitors to use, many handrails and a lift to enable visitors to enjoy the first floor.

### For families

There are special activities throughout the Hall and Gardens to help keep children interested along the way.

**On Sunday afternoons from 24 June to 16 September** enjoy the best of South Yorkshire's Brass Bands in the gardens – a perfect way to spend the summer. Band concerts from 3pm onwards.

From 19 to 28 October, visit **The Enchanted Garden:** a sublime night-time experience from 6.30pm-8.30pm. The magnificent gardens are illuminated to become a place of wonder and enchantment. The shop will be open and refreshments available on these special evening openings. Please note there is no access to the Hall itself. Tickets available in advance or on the night.

NEW FOR 2007

**Work & Play: Life on the Yorkshire Estate**
A wealth of stories about the family and workers of Victorian Brodsworth vividly reveal how the country house estate shaped both people's lives and the English landscape. Told through original photographs, new and archival evidence, oral history and special events.

The Summerhouse

www.english-heritage.org.uk/brodsworthhall

### NON-MEMBERS

| | |
|---|---|
| **House and gardens** | |
| Adult | £6.60 |
| Concession | £5.00 |
| Child | £3.30 |
| **Gardens only** | |
| Adult | £4.60 |
| Concession | £3.50 |
| Child | £2.30 |

### OPENING TIMES

| | |
|---|---|
| **House** | |
| 1 Apr-30 Sep, Tue-Sun and Bank Hols | 1pm-5pm |
| 1-31 Oct, Sat-Sun | 12pm-4pm |
| **Gardens and tearoom** | |
| 1 Apr-31 Oct, daily | 10am-5.30pm |
| **Gardens, tearoom, shop and servants' wing** | |
| 1 Nov-20 Mar, Sat-Sun | 10am-4pm |
| Closed | 24-26 Dec and 1 Jan |

Last admission is ½ hour before closing

### HOW TO FIND US

**Direction:** In Brodsworth, 5 miles NW of Doncaster off A635 Barnsley Road; from junction 37 of A1(M)

**Train:** South Elmsall 4 miles; Moorthorpe 4½ miles; Doncaster 5½ miles

**Bus:** Stagecoach in Yorkshire 211 Doncaster – Barnsley (passing close ⇌ Doncaster and passing ⇌ South Elmsall & Moorthorpe). Alight at Pickburn, Five Lanes End, then ½ mile walk

**Local Tourist Information**
Doncaster: 01302 734309

**Tel:** 01302 724969 (info-line)

OVP

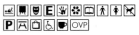

No cameras (house).

MAP Page 273 (5G)
OS Map 279 (ref SE 506070)

## Aldborough Roman Site
N. Yorkshire – YO51 9EP

Among the northernmost urban centres in the Roman Empire, Aldborough was the 'capital' of the Romanised Brigantes, the largest tribe in Britain. One corner of the defences is laid out amid a Victorian arboretum, and two mosaic pavements can be viewed in their original positions. The site museum has an outstanding collection of Roman finds, a handling collection of Roman objects, and other 'hands-on' aids for children and families.

### NON-MEMBERS

| | |
|---|---|
| Adult | £3.00 |
| Concession | £2.30 |
| Child | £1.50 |

### OPENING TIMES

| | |
|---|---|
| 1 Apr-30 Jun, Sat-Sun | 11am-5pm |
| 1 Jul-31 Aug, Thu-Mon | 10am-5pm |
| 1-30 Sep, Sat-Sun | 11am-5pm |

### HOW TO FIND US

**Direction:** Located in Aldborough, ¾ mile SE of Boroughbridge on a minor road off B6265; within 1 mile of junction of A1 and A6055

**Bus:** Arriva/Harrogate Coach Travel 142 ≋ York-Ripon

**Tel:** 01423 322768

OVP

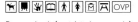

Dogs on leads (restricted areas only).

MAP Page 273 (3G)
OS Map 299 (ref SE 405662)

## Brodsworth Hall and Gardens
See feature – Page 192

## Burton Agnes Manor House
East Riding of Yorkshire

A medieval manor house interior, with a rare and well-preserved Norman undercroft and a 15th-century roof, all encased in brick during the 17th and 18th centuries.

### OPENING TIMES

| | |
|---|---|
| 1 Apr-31 Oct, daily | 11am-5pm |

The nearby Burton Agnes Hall and Gardens are privately owned and are not managed by English Heritage

### HOW TO FIND US

**Direction:** In Burton Agnes village, 5 miles SW of Bridlington on A166

**Train:** Nafferton 5 miles

**Bus:** E Yorkshire 744 York – Bridlington

MAP Page 273 (3J)
OS Map 295 (ref TA 102632)

## Byland Abbey
N. Yorkshire – YO61 4BD

Byland was one of the great Yorkshire Cistercian abbeys, housing at its zenith well over 200 monks and lay brothers. Much of its huge cathedral-sized church survives, including the whole north side and the greater part of the 13th-century west front. The mixture of rounded Romanesque and pointed Gothic arches shows how architectural styles changed, and reveals that Byland was one of the earliest Gothic buildings in the north.

Byland Abbey

Its great circular rose window, now surviving only in part, was probably the model for the rose window of York Minster.

The museum displays colourful interpretation panels together with archaeological finds from the site, giving insight into monastic life.

Rievaulx Abbey and Helmsley Castle are within reasonable travelling distance.

### NON-MEMBERS

| | |
|---|---|
| Adult | £3.50 |
| Concession | £2.60 |
| Child | £1.80 |

### OPENING TIMES

| | |
|---|---|
| 1 Apr-31 Jul, Thu-Mon | 11am-6pm |
| 1-31 Aug, daily | 11am-6pm |
| 1-30 Sep, Thu-Mon | 11am-6pm |

**The Abbey Inn**
A gastro-pub overlooking Byland Abbey, the Abbey Inn was originally built within the monastic precinct on the site of medieval buildings and used as a farmhouse. It was converted to a pub in the 20th century and now offers high quality English food, using the best of local ingredients.
www.bylandabbeyinn.co.uk

### HOW TO FIND US

**Direction:** 2 miles S of A170, between Thirsk and Helmsley; near Coxwold village

**Train:** Thirsk 10 miles

**Bus:** Stephensons 31/X, Moorsbus M15 York-Helmsley

**Tel:** 01347 868614 (Byland Abbey)
01347 868204 (Abbey Inn)

OVP

Parking at Abbey Inn.

Toilets at Abbey Inn.

MAP Page 273 (2G)
OS Map 26/299 (ref SE 549789)

## Clifford's Tower, York
N. Yorkshire – YO1 9SA

In 1068-9, William the Conqueror built two motte and bailey castles in York, to strengthen his military hold on the north. Clifford's Tower, an unusual four-lobed keep built in the 13th century atop the mound of William's larger fortress, is now the principal surviving stonework remnant of York's medieval castle. The sweeping views of the city from the tower still show why it played such an important part in controlling northern England.

On summer weekends a costumed interpreter brings to life key events in the history of York and the Tower.

### NON-MEMBERS

| | |
|---|---|
| Adult | £3.00 |
| Concession | £2.30 |
| Child | £1.50 |
| Family | £7.50 |

### OPENING TIMES

| | |
|---|---|
| 1 Apr-30 Sep, daily | 10am-6pm |
| 1-31 Oct, daily | 10am-5pm |
| 1 Nov-20 Mar, daily | 10am-4pm |
| Closed | 24-26 Dec and 1 Jan |

### HOW TO FIND US

**Direction:** Tower St, York

**Train:** York 1 mile

**Bus:** From surrounding areas

**Tel:** 01904 646940

**Local Tourist Information**
York: 01904 621756

OVP

Parking (local charge).

MAP Page 273 (3G)
OS Map 290 (ref SE 605515)

## Conisbrough Castle
S. Yorkshire – DN12 3BU

The white, cylindrical keep of this 12th-century castle is a spectacular structure. Built of magnesian limestone, it is the only example of its kind in England. Restored, with two new floors and a roof, it is a fine example of medieval architecture, and was one of the inspirations for Sir Walter Scott's classic novel, *Ivanhoe*.

### NON-MEMBERS

| | |
|---|---|
| Adult | £4.00 |
| Concession | £3.00 |
| Child | £2.00 |
| Family | £10.00 |

### OPENING TIMES

| | |
|---|---|
| 1 Apr-30 Sep, daily (last admission 4.20pm) | 10am-5pm |
| 1 Oct-20 Mar, Thu-Mon (last admission 3.20pm) | 10am-4pm |
| Closed | 24-26 Dec and 1 Jan |

### HOW TO FIND US

**Direction:** Located NE of Conisbrough town centre off A630; 4½ miles SW of Doncaster

**Train:** Conisbrough ½ mile

**Bus:** From surrounding areas

**Tel:** 01709 863329

## Conisbrough Castle

Dogs on leads (restricted areas only).

Parking (visitors with disabilities, please call the site to reserve a space).

MAP Page 273 (5G)
OS Map 279 (ref SK 515989)

## Easby Abbey
N. Yorkshire

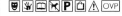

The substantial remains of an abbey of Premonstratensian 'white canons', most notably its lavish roof-height refectory of c. 1300 and other monastic buildings. Within the precinct is the still-active parish church, displaying fine 13th-century wall-paintings. In a beautiful setting by the River Swale, Easby can be reached via a pleasant walk from Richmond Castle.

### OPENING TIMES

| | |
|---|---|
| 1 Apr-30 Sep, daily | 10am-6pm |
| 1-31 Oct, daily | 10am-5pm |
| 1 Nov-20 Mar, daily | 10am-4pm |
| Closed | 24-26 Dec and 1 Jan |

### HOW TO FIND US

**Direction:** 1 mile SE of Richmond, off B6271

**Bus:** Arriva X26/7, 27/8 Darlington-Richmond (pass close Darlington) then 1½ miles

Guidebooks (from Richmond Castle).

MAP Page 273 (2F)
OS Map 304 (ref NZ 185003)

## Gainsthorpe Medieval Village
Lincolnshire

A deserted medieval village, one of the best-preserved examples in England, clearly visible as a complex of grassy humps and bumps. According to legend demolished as a den of thieves, the real reason for its abandonment remains uncertain.

### OPENING TIMES
Any reasonable time

### HOW TO FIND US
**Direction:** Located on minor road W of A15; S of Hibaldstow; 5 miles SW of Brigg

**Train:** Kirton Lindsey 3 miles

MAP Page 273 (5J)
OS Map 281 (ref SE 954011)

## Helmsley Castle
See feature – Page 198

## Howden Minster
East Riding of Yorkshire

The elaborately decorated ruins of a 14th-century chancel and chapter house (viewable only from the outside), attached to the still operational cathedral-like minster church.

### OPENING TIMES
Any reasonable time

| | |
|---|---|
| Closed | 24-26 Dec and 1 Jan |

### HOW TO FIND US
**Direction:** In Howden; 23 miles W of Kingston Upon Hull, 25 miles SE of York, near the junction of A63 and A614

**Train:** Howden 1½ miles

**Bus:** East Yorkshire 155/6 Goole-Hull

P

Parking (street parking nearby).

MAP Page 273 (4H)
OS Map 291 (ref SE 748283)

## Kirkham Priory
N. Yorkshire – YO60 7JS

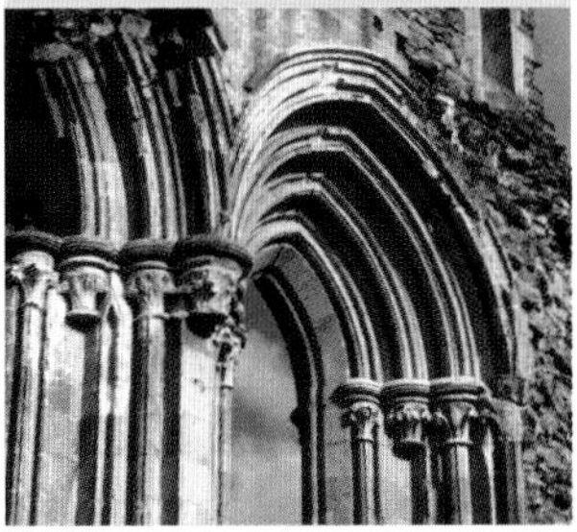

The riverside ruins of an Augustinian priory, picturesquely set in the beautiful Derwent valley near the Yorkshire Wolds. Features include a gatehouse bedecked with the heraldry of the Roos family of Helmsley Castle, and a handsome set of monastic washbasins. On-site interpretation includes the story of Winston Churchill's secret visit, and Kirkham's role in preparations for D-Day during World War II.

### NON-MEMBERS

| | |
|---|---|
| Adult | £3.00 |
| Concession | £2.30 |
| Child | £1.50 |

### OPENING TIMES

| | |
|---|---|
| 1 Apr-30 May, Thu-Mon | 10am-5pm |
| 1 Jun-31 Aug, daily | 10am-5pm |
| 1-30 Sep, Thu-Mon | 10am-5pm |
| 1-31 Oct, Sat-Sun | 10am-4pm |

### HOW TO FIND US
**Direction:** 5 miles SW of Malton, on a minor road off A64

**Train:** Malton 6 miles

**Bus:** Yorkshire Coastliner 840/2/3/5 Leeds – Malton/ Scarborough/Whitby (pass to within ¾ mile

**Tel:** 01653 618768

P OVP

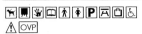

MAP Page 273 (3H)
OS Map 300 (ref SE 736658)

## Marmion Tower
N. Yorkshire

The fine 15th-century gatehouse of a vanished riverside manor house, with a beautiful oriel window. The monuments of the manor's Marmion family owners grace the adjacent church.

### OPENING TIMES

| | |
|---|---|
| 1 Apr-30 Sep, daily | 10am-6pm |
| 1-31 Oct, daily | 10am-5pm |
| 1 Nov-20 Mar, daily | 10am-4pm |
| Closed | 24-26 Dec and 1 Jan |

### HOW TO FIND US
**Direction:** On A6108 in West Tanfield

**Train:** Thirsk 10 miles

MAP Page 273 (3F)
OS Map 298 (ref SE 268787)

# Helmsley Castle North Yorkshire – YO62 5AB

Surrounded by spectacular banks and ditches, the great medieval castle's impressive ruins stand beside the attractive market town of Helmsley. The fortress was probably begun after 1120 by Walter Espec – 'Walter the Woodpecker'. Renowned for piety as well as soldiering, this Norman baron of 'gigantic stature' also founded nearby Rievaulx Abbey and Kirkham Priory, both English Heritage properties.

Most of Helmsley's surviving stonework defences were raised during the late 12th and 13th centuries, by the crusader Robert de Roos and his descendants. They include a pair of immensely strong 'barbican' entrances and the high, keep-like east tower, unusually D-shaped in plan, which still dominates the town.

But Helmsley is not only a medieval fortress. During the Elizabethan period the Manners family remodelled the castle's chamber block into a luxurious mansion, whose fine plasterwork and panelling still partly survive. The castle's first and last military trial came during the Civil War. Held for King Charles, it endured a three month siege before being starved into submission in November 1644 by Parliamentarians under Sir Thomas Fairfax, who was seriously wounded in the fighting. Fairfax then dismantled the defences but spared the mansion, subsequently the home of his daughter and her husband, the profligate Duke of Buckingham.

Demoted to a romantic backdrop when later owners moved to nearby Duncombe Park, Helmsley Castle has recently undergone a thorough makeover by English Heritage, making it more accessible to a wide range of visitors. This includes a brand-new visitor centre also providing tourist information, an audio tour, and an imaginative hands-on exhibition in the mansion range. Displaying a fascinating array of finds from Civil War cannon balls to early tableware, this exhibition explores the social and domestic as well as the military aspects of the fortress. New facilities for disabled visitors include full ground-level ramping, a virtual tour of less accessible areas, and a tactile model with braille text. Enhanced learning resources include family-friendly books and activities.

Find out about other sites and accommodation in the area from the Tourist Information Centre, which is located in the visitor centre.

Rievaulx and Byland Abbeys are both nearby: Rievaulx can be reached on foot via the Cleveland Way (approx. 3½ miles/1½ hours each way, strong footwear required).

**www.english-heritage.org.uk/helmsleycastle**

The South Barbican and outer ditch

Visitor Centre

Exhibition in the West Range

## NON-MEMBERS

| | |
|---|---|
| Adult | £4.00 |
| Concession | £3.00 |
| Child | £2.00 |
| Family | £10.00 |

## OPENING TIMES

| | |
|---|---|
| 1 Apr-30 Sep, daily | 10am-6pm |
| 1-31 Oct, daily | 10am-5pm |
| 1 Nov-29 Feb, Thu-Mon | 10am-4pm |
| 1-20 Mar, daily | 10am-5pm |
| Closed | 24-26 Dec and 1 Jan |

## HOW TO FIND US

**Direction:** Near the town centre

**Bus:** Scarborough & District 128 from Scarborough

**Tourist Information Centre**
Tel: 01439 770173

**Tel:** 01439 770442

Parking (large car park adjacent to castle; charge payable).

Toilets (in car park and town centre).

MAP Page 273 (2G)
OS Map 26 (ref SE 611836)

## Middleham Castle
N. Yorkshire – DL8 4RJ

The childhood and favourite home of Richard III, Middleham Castle was a fortress of the mighty Neville family, Earls of Westmoreland and of Warwick. Around the massive 12th-century central keep, they progressively constructed three ranges of luxurious chambers and lodgings, turning the castle into a fortified palace by the mid-15th century. Though roofless, many of these buildings survive, making Middleham a fascinating castle to explore. Here Richard spent part of his youth, in the guardianship of 'Warwick the Kingmaker'.

An exhibition about notable personalities from the castle's past includes a replica of the beautiful Middleham Jewel, a 15th-century pendant decorated with a large sapphire found near the castle. Family-friendly books and activities.

### NON-MEMBERS

| | |
|---|---|
| Adult | £3.50 |
| Concession | £2.60 |
| Child | £1.80 |

### OPENING TIMES

| | |
|---|---|
| 1 Apr-30 Sep, daily | 10am-6pm |
| 1 Oct-20 Mar, Sat-Wed | 10am-4pm |
| Closed | 24-26 Dec and 1 Jan |

### HOW TO FIND US

**Direction:** Located at Middleham; 2 miles S of Leyburn on A6108

**Bus:** Dales & District 159 Ripon-Richmond

### Middleham Castle

**Tel:** 01969 623899

**Local Tourist Information**
Leyburn: 01969 623069

OVP

**Disabled access (except keep).**

MAP Page 273 (2F)
OS Map 30 (ref SE 127876)

## Monk Bretton Priory
S. Yorkshire

The substantial ruins of a Cluniac monastery, with an unusually well-marked ground plan, an almost complete west range and a 15th-century gatehouse.

### NON-MEMBERS

Charge may apply on event days

### OPENING TIMES

| | |
|---|---|
| 1 Apr-30 Sep, daily | 10am-6pm |
| 1-31 Oct, daily | 10am-5pm |
| 1 Nov-20 Mar, daily (managed by a keykeeper) | 10am-4pm |
| Closed | 24-26 Dec and 1 Jan |

### HOW TO FIND US

**Direction:** Located 1 mile E of Barnsley town centre, off A633

**Train:** Barnsley 2½ miles

**Bus:** From surrounding areas

MAP Page 273 (5G)
OS Map 278 (ref SE 373065)

## Mount Grace Priory
N. Yorkshire – DL6 3JG

Set amid woodland below the escarpment of the North York Moors and the Cleveland Way National Trail, Mount Grace is a monastic ruin of an unusual kind. It is the best-preserved of the ten British 'charterhouses', whose Carthusian monks lived as hermits in cottage-like cells. A reconstructed and furnished monk's cell and a recently revamped herb plot offer a glimpse into the lives of the medieval residents. The site hosts art exhibitions throughout the year, and the gardens are a haven for wildlife, including the famous 'Priory Stoats'. There is a children's story box, and special children's trails during school holidays.

Owned by The National Trust, maintained and managed by EH.

Holiday cottage available to let.

### NON-MEMBERS

| | |
|---|---|
| Adult | £4.00 |
| Concession | £3.00 |
| Child | £2.00 |
| Family | £10.00 |

**National Trust members admitted free, except on special event days**

### OPENING TIMES

| | |
|---|---|
| 1 Apr-30 Sep, Thu-Mon | 10am-6pm |
| 1 Oct-20 Mar, Thu-Sun | 10am-4pm |
| Closed | 24-26 Dec and 1 Jan |

### HOW TO FIND US

**Direction:** 12 miles N of Thirsk; 6 miles NE of Northallerton, on A19

### Mount Grace Priory

**Train:** Northallerton 6 miles

**Bus:** Arriva North East 80, 89 from Northallerton – Stokesley, alight Priory Road End, then ½ mile

**Tel:** 01609 883494

**Local Tourist Information**
Thirsk: 01845 522755

P OVP

MAP Page 273 (2G)
OS Map 26 (ref SE 449985)

## Pickering Castle
N. Yorkshire – YO18 7AX

Pickering Castle is set in an attractive moors-edge market town. It is a classic and well-preserved example of an early earthwork castle refortified in stone during the 13th and 14th centuries, centred upon a shell-keep crowning an impressive motte. There is an exhibition in the chapel, and family-friendly books and activities.

### NON-MEMBERS

| | |
|---|---|
| Adult | £3.00 |
| Concession | £2.30 |
| Child | £1.50 |
| Family | £7.50 |

### OPENING TIMES

| | |
|---|---|
| 1 Apr-30 Sep, daily | 10am-6pm |
| 1-31 Oct, Thu-Mon | 10am-5pm |

### HOW TO FIND US

**Direction:** In Pickering; 15 miles SW of Scarborough

### Pickering Castle

**Train:** Malton 9 miles; Pickering (N York Moors Rly) ¼ mile

**Bus:** Yorkshire Coastliner 840/2 from Malton; Scarborough & District 128 from Scarborough

**Tel:** 01751 474989

E P OVP

Disabled access (except motte).

MAP Page 273 (2H)
OS Map 27 (ref SE 99845)

## Piercebridge Roman Bridge
N. Yorkshire

Stonework foundations, now marooned in a field, of a bridge which once led to Piercebridge Roman Fort.

### OPENING TIMES

Any reasonable time

### HOW TO FIND US

**Direction:** At Piercebridge; 4 miles W of Darlington, on B6275

**Train:** Darlington 5 miles

**Bus:** Arriva 75/6 Darlington – Barnard Castle (passes close to Darlington)

MAP Page 273 (1F)
OS Map 304 (ref NZ 214155)

## Richmond Castle
N. Yorkshire – DL10 4QW

Breathtakingly sited on a rocky promontory above the River Swale, the great castle of Richmond is among the oldest Norman stone fortresses in Britain, begun in the decades after the Conquest. The towering keep, over 30 metres (100 feet) high and remarkably complete within, was added during the reign of Henry II in the 1170s: its roof provides splendid views over the clustered houses of the pretty market town. Traditionally King Arthur lies sleeping in a cavern beneath the castle: more certainly, conscientious objectors were imprisoned in the keep during World War I. Their story is told in an interactive display exploring Richmond's nine centuries of development, and woven into the contemporary Cockpit Garden. Created to reflect the castle's history and architecture, this tranquil haven of topiary, grasses and herbaceous borders has superb vistas over the River Swale. Family-friendly books and activities and plant sales.

### NON-MEMBERS

| | |
|---|---|
| Adult | £4.00 |
| Concession | £3.00 |
| Child | £2.00 |

### OPENING TIMES

| | |
|---|---|
| 1 Apr-30 Sep, daily | 10am-6pm |
| 1 Oct-20 Mar, Thu-Mon | 10am-4pm |
| Closed | 24-26 Dec and 1 Jan |

### HOW TO FIND US

**Direction:** In Richmond

**Bus:** Arriva X26/7, 27/8 Darlington – Richmond (passes close to Darlington)

**Tel:** 01748 822493

E OVP

MAP Page 273 (2F)
OS Map 304 (ref NZ 172007)

## Rievaulx Abbey
See feature – Page 204

## Roche Abbey
S. Yorkshire – S66 8NW

Beautifully set in a valley landscaped by 'Capability' Brown in the 18th century, the most striking feature of this Cistercian abbey is the eastern end of its church, built in the new Gothic style c. 1170. It has one of the most complete ground plans of any English Cistercian monastery, laid out as excavated foundations. The story of the pillaging of Roche, recorded by the son of an eye-witness, is among the most vivid documents of the Dissolution of the Monasteries.

### NON-MEMBERS

| | |
|---|---|
| Adult | £3.00 |
| Concession | £2.30 |
| Child | £1.50 |

### OPENING TIMES

| | |
|---|---|
| 1 Apr-30 Sept, Thu-Mon | 10am-4pm |

### HOW TO FIND US

**Direction:** 1½ miles S of Maltby, off A634

**Train:** Conisbrough 7 miles

**Bus:** First 1, 2, 10, Powell 122 Rotherham-Maltby, then 1½ miles

**Tel:** 01709 812739

OVP

MAP Page 273 (6G)
OS Map 279 (ref SK 544898)

## St Mary's Church, Studley Royal
N. Yorkshire

This magnificent High Victorian Anglican church was designed in the 1870s by the flamboyant architect William Burges, and

St Mary's Church, Studley Royal

has been called his 'ecclesiastical masterpiece'. The extravagantly decorated interior displays coloured marble, stained glass, a splendid organ, and painted and gilded figures in all their original glory.

EH property managed by The National Trust as part of the Fountains Abbey and Studley Royal Estate (see p. 210).

### OPENING TIMES

| | |
|---|---|
| 1 Apr-30 Sep, daily | 1pm-5pm |

### HOW TO FIND US

**Direction:** Located 2½ miles W of Ripon, off B6265; in the grounds of the Studley Royal Estate

**Bus:** 'Ripon Roweller' 139 from Ripon (with connections from Harrogate on Harrogate & District 36); also Arriva 802 Leeds, Suns, May-Sep only

**Tel:** 01765 608888

Parking (at visitor centre).

MAP Page 273 (3F)
OS Map 298/299 (ref SE 275693)

## St Peter's Church, Barton-upon-Humber
Lincolnshire – DN18 5EX

With a history spanning over a millennium, St Peter's is one of the most studied churches in England. It features a remarkably complete Anglo-Saxon tower and baptistry, dating mainly from c. 970, and a large medieval nave and chancel displaying a range of architectural styles. The church is an archaeological treasure-trove, yielding unprecedented insights into medieval disease and diet, plus medical and burial practices from the analysis of 2,800 burials over a period of nine centuries.

### NON-MEMBERS

| | |
|---|---|
| Adult | £4.00 |
| Concession | £3.00 |
| Child | £2.00 |

St Peter's Church

NEW FOR 2007

Following major restoration work, 2007 will see the opening of a new interactive exhibition offering greater understanding of this important church and the archaeological revelations it has produced, including reconstructions of individual lives from the past.

### OPENING TIMES

| | |
|---|---|
| 26 May-30 Sep, daily | 10am-5pm |
| 1 Oct-20 Mar, Sat-Mon | 10am-4pm |
| Closed | 24-26 Dec and 1 Jan |
| Charge may apply on event days | |

### HOW TO FIND US

**Direction:** In Barton-upon-Humber

**Train:** Barton-upon-Humber ½ mile

**Bus:** Stagecoach in Lincolnshire/ E Yorks 350 Hull-Scunthorpe

**Tel:** 01652 632516

OVP

MAP Page 273 (5J)
OS Map 281 (ref TA 035219)

## Scarborough Castle
See feature opposite

## Skipsea Castle
East Riding of Yorkshire

An impressive Norman motte and bailey castle, dating from before 1086 and among the first raised in Yorkshire, with the earthworks of an attendant fortified 'borough'.

### OPENING TIMES

Any reasonable time

### HOW TO FIND US

**Direction:** Located 8 miles S of Bridlington; W of Skipsea village

**Train:** Bridlington 9 miles

Dogs on leads (restricted areas only).

Waterproof footwear recommended.

MAP Page 273 (3J)
OS Map 295 (ref TA 162551)

# Scarborough Castle North Yorkshire – YO11 1HY

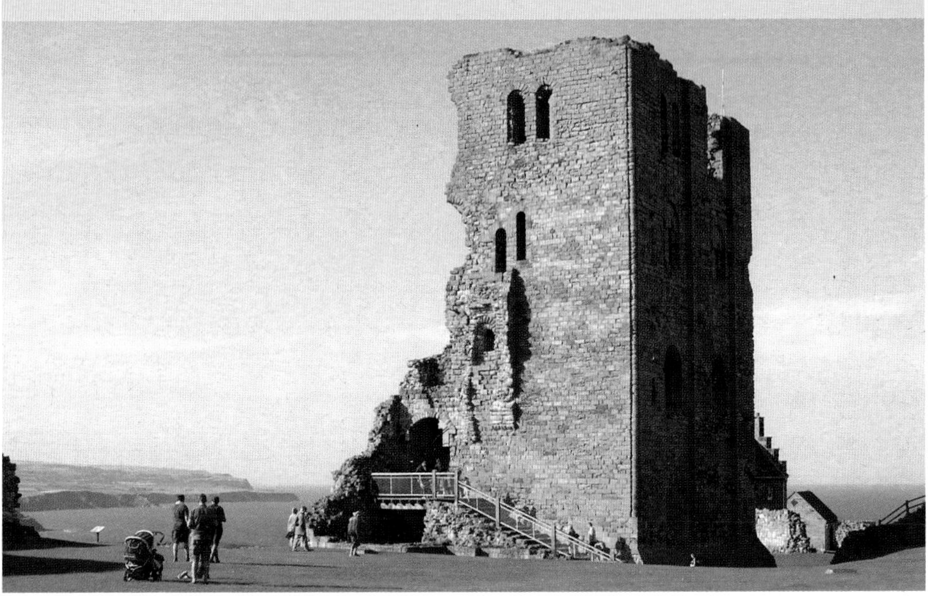

Scarborough Castle defends a prominent headland between two bays, with sheer drops to the sea and only a narrow landward approach. Specially constructed viewing platforms on the battlements offer panoramic views. Long before the castle was built, this natural fortress was favoured by prehistoric settlers – a splendid Bronze Age sword, perhaps deposited here as a sacrifice to the gods, is on display – and later housed a defended Roman signal station.

Henry II's towering 12th-century keep, dominating the approach, is the centrepiece of fortifications developed over later centuries in response to repeated sieges – notably by rebel barons in 1312, and twice during the Civil War. Though again strengthened with barracks and gun-batteries against Jacobite threats in 1745, the castle failed to defend the harbour against the American sea-raider John Paul Jones in 1779, and was itself damaged by German naval bombardment in 1914. During World War II it played the more covert role of hosting a secret listening post.

The site's 3,000-year history is explored in interactive displays in the restored Master Gunner's House, accompanied by artefacts from each period of Scarborough's past. Less mobile visitors can enjoy a ground-floor touch-screen virtual tour of the displays, as well as virtual views reproducing those from the raised platforms.

Timelined graphic panels around the castle focus on characters from the past, and there are free activity sheets, an audio tour and an investigative story box to help younger visitors visualise and understand the history of the castle.

www.english-heritage.org.uk/scarboroughcastle

### NON-MEMBERS

| | |
|---|---|
| Adult | £4.00 |
| Concession | £3.00 |
| Child | £2.00 |
| Family | £10.00 |

### OPENING TIMES

| | |
|---|---|
| 1 Apr-30 Sep, daily | 10am-6pm |
| 1-31 Oct, Thu-Mon | 10am-5pm |
| 1 Nov-20 Mar, Thu-Mon | 10am-4pm |
| Closed | 24-26 Dec and 1 Jan |

### HOW TO FIND US

**Direction:** Castle Road, E of the town centre

**Train:** Scarborough 1 mile

**Bus:** From surrounding areas

**Tel:** 01723 372451

OVP

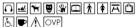

Parking (pre-booked parking only for disabled visitors, otherwise located in town centre).

MAP Page 273 (2J)
OS Map 301 (ref TA 050892)

# Rievaulx Abbey North Yorkshire – YO62 5LB

'Everywhere peace, everywhere serenity, and a marvellous freedom from the tumult of the world.' Written over eight centuries ago by the monastery's third abbot St Aelred, these words could describe Rievaulx today. Set in a beautiful and tranquil valley, it is among the most atmospheric and complete of all the ruined abbeys of the north.

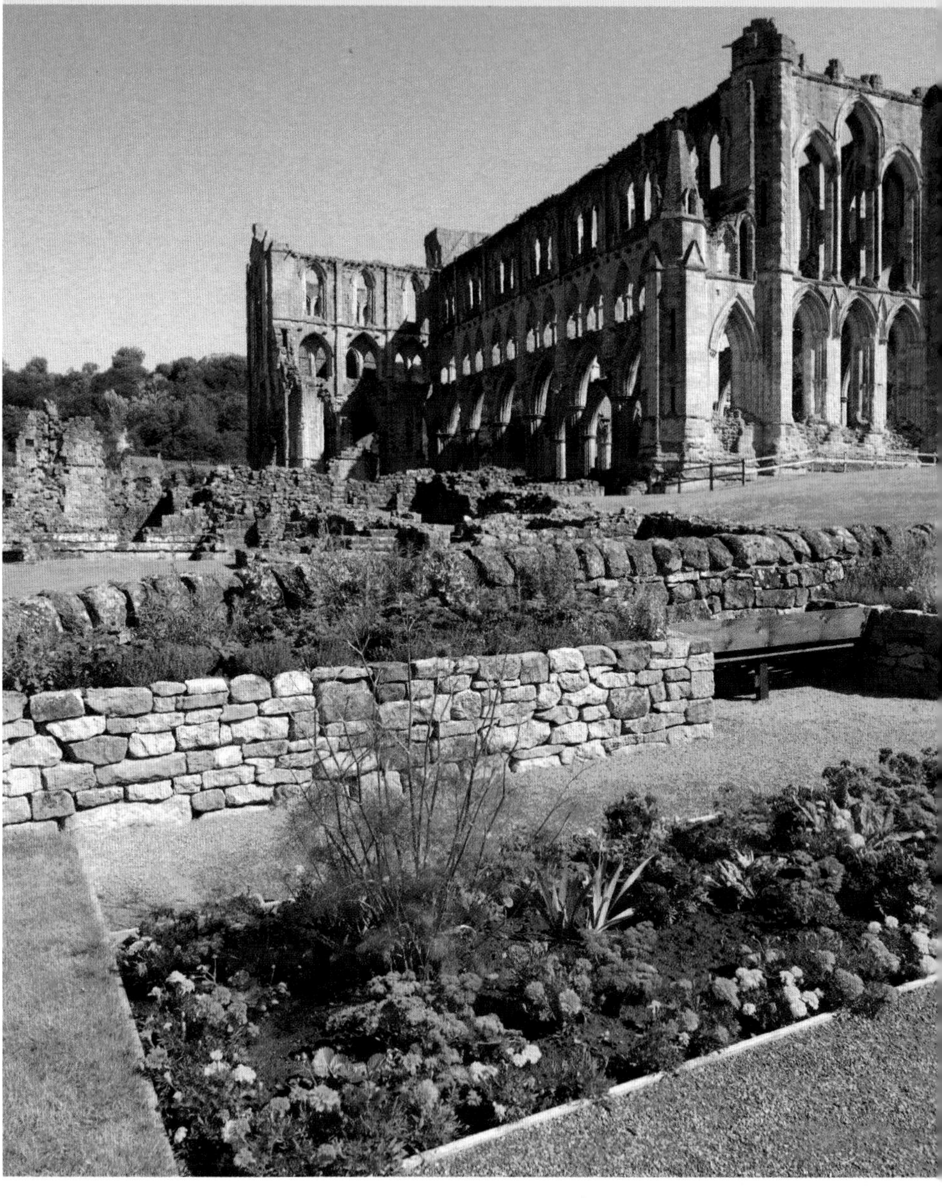

Words are not the only link to Rievaulx's medieval monks. Over the past few years, the site has become something of an archaeological treasure, with unexpected discoveries shedding new light on the lives of the monks, and the extensive renewal and rebuilding of their abbey church in the Early English Gothic style. Archaeologists continue to study the landscape around Rievaulx, revealing the remarkable extent of the abbey's influence and industry. Their discoveries are showcased at the the site's annual archaeology day in July, and within the on-site museum.

The abbey was founded by St Bernard of Clairvaux, as part of the missionary effort to reform Christianity in western Europe. Just 12 Clairvaux monks came to Rievaulx in 1132. From these modest beginnings grew one of the wealthiest monasteries of medieval England and the first northern Cistercian monastery. Rievaulx also enjoyed the protection of Walter Espec of nearby Helmsley Castle, who provided much of the abbey's land. The monks of neighbouring Byland Abbey disputed land ownership with Rievaulx, which led to engineering works to divert the course of the River Rye, the boundary between their properties. You can still see traces of the old river and the channels dug by the monks.

A steady flow of monks came to Rievaulx, attracted by the prestige of Abbot Aelred, author and preacher, who was regarded then and later as a wise and saintly man. Following his death in 1167, the monks of Rievaulx sought canonisation for their former leader, and in the 1220s they rebuilt the east part of their church in a much more elaborate style to house his tomb. Most of this 13th-century 'presbytery' still stands to virtually its full impressive height, a reminder of Rievaulx's original splendour.

Rievaulx was still a vibrant community when Henry VIII dissolved it in 1538. Its new owner, Thomas Manners, first Earl of Rutland, swiftly instigated the systematic destruction of the buildings. However, the substantial remains still constitute one of the most eloquent of all monastic sites, free 'from the tumult of the world'. School children from the local area have helped in creating a Sensory garden full of scented and flavoured herbs, amid tile motifs based on medieval designs.

Don't miss the exciting indoor exhibition, 'The Work of God and Man', which explores the agricultural, industrial, spiritual and commercial aspects of Rievaulx's history, employing a variety of lively and interactive displays. There are family-friendly books and activities, and special children's trails during school holidays.

Byland Abbey and Helmsley Castle are both within reasonable travelling distance: Helmsley Castle can be reached on foot via the Cleveland Way National Trail. Approx. 3½ miles (1½ hours) each way. Strong footwear required.

Holiday cottage available to let.

**www.english-heritage.org.uk/rievaulxabbey**

## NON-MEMBERS

| | |
|---|---|
| Adult | £4.50 |
| Concession | £3.40 |
| Child | £2.30 |

## OPENING TIMES

| | |
|---|---|
| 1 Apr-30 Sep, daily | 10am-6pm |
| 1-31 Oct, Thu-Mon | 10am-5pm |
| 1 Nov-20 Mar, Thu-Mon | 10am-4pm |
| Closed | 24-26 Dec and 1 Jan |

## HOW TO FIND US

**Direction:** In Rievaulx; 2¼ miles N of Helmsley, on minor road off B1257

**Bus:** Hutchinson 198, Moorsbus M8 from Helmsley (connections on Scarborough & District 128 from Scarborough) Tue & Thu & Sat all year, Mon-Sat June-Sep, Sundays Apr-Oct

**Tel:** 01439 798228

**Local Tourist Information**
Helmsley: 01439 770173

E P OVP

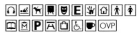

**Audio tours (also available for the visually impaired, those with learning difficulties and in French and German).**

**MAP Page 273 (2G)**
**OS Map 26 (ref SE 577850)**

## Spofforth Castle
N. Yorkshire

The ruined hall and chamber of a fortified manor house of the powerful Percy family, dating mainly from the 14th and 15th-centuries. Its undercroft is cut into a rocky outcrop.

Managed by Spofforth-with-Stockeld Parish Council.

### OPENING TIMES

| | |
|---|---|
| 1 Apr-30 Sep, daily | 10am-6pm |
| 1 Oct-20 Mar, daily (managed by a keykeeper) | 10am-4pm |
| Closed | 24-26 Dec and 1 Jan |

### HOW TO FIND US

**Direction:** 3½ miles SE of Harrogate; off A661 at Spofforth

**Train:** Pannal 4 miles

**Bus:** Harrogate & District 770/1 Harrogate-Leeds

Dogs on leads (restricted areas only).

MAP Page 273 (4G)
OS Map 289 (ref SE 360511)

English Heritage membership makes a lovely gift.

## Stanwick Iron Age Fortifications
N. Yorkshire

An excavated section, part cut into rock, of the ramparts of the huge Iron Age trading and power-centre of the Brigantes, the most important tribe in pre-Roman northern Britain. Some 4 miles (6½ kilometres) long, the defences enclosed an area of 766 acres (310 hectares). Following Roman conquest, the Brigantian centre moved to Aldborough Roman Site (see p.195).

### OPENING TIMES

Any reasonable time

### HOW TO FIND US

**Direction:** Located on a minor road off A6274, at Forcett Village

**Train:** Darlington 10 miles

Dogs on leads (restricted areas only).

MAP Page 273 (1F)
OS Map 304 (ref NZ 179124)

## Steeton Hall Gateway
N. Yorkshire

A fine example of a small, well-preserved manorial gatehouse dating from the 14th century.

### OPENING TIMES

| | |
|---|---|
| Daily (exterior only) | 10am-5pm |

### HOW TO FIND US

**Direction:** Located 4 miles NE of Castleford, on a minor road off A162 at South Milford

**Train:** South Milford 1 mile

Dogs on leads (restricted areas only).

MAP Page 273 (4G)
OS Map 290 (ref SE 484314)

## Thornton Abbey & Gatehouse
North Lincolnshire

The enormous and ornate fortified gatehouse of Thornton Abbey is among the finest surviving in Britain. An early example of brick building, it proclaimed the prosperity of one of the wealthiest English Augustinian monasteries. Built in the nervous years following the Peasants' Revolt of 1381, it may also have protected the abbey's treasures, as well as providing lodgings for the abbot and his guests. Within the grounds stand the remains of the monastic buildings, notably the elegantly decorated octagonal chapter house of 1282-1308.

**NEW FOR 2007** From July 2007 the magnificent gatehouse will be open daily, including a new exhibition offering greater insight into the abbey's history from its foundation to the present day, and new features revealed following restoration work.

### NON-MEMBERS

| | |
|---|---|
| Adult | £4.00 |
| Concession | £3.00 |
| Child | £2.00 |

### OPENING TIMES

| | |
|---|---|
| 30 Jun-30 Sep, daily | 10am-5pm |
| 1 Oct-20 Mar, Fri-Sun | 10am-4pm |
| Closed | 24-26 Dec and 1 Jan |

### Thornton Abbey & Gatehouse

**HOW TO FIND US**

**Direction:** 18 miles NE of Scunthorpe, on a road N of A160; 7 miles SE of the Humber Bridge, on a road E of A1077

**Train:** Thornton Abbey ¼ mile

[dogs] [P] [picnic] [disabled] [OVP]

Disabled access (except gatehouse interior and part of chapter ruins).

Dogs on leads (restricted areas only).

MAP Page 273 (5J)
OS Map 284 (ref TA 118189)

### Wharram Percy Deserted Medieval Village
N. Yorkshire

The most famous and intensively studied of Britain's 3,000 or so deserted medieval villages, Wharram Percy occupies a remote but attractive site in a beautiful Wolds valley. Above the substantial ruins of the church and a recreated fishpond, the outlines of many lost houses are traceable on a grassy plateau. First settled in prehistoric times, Wharram flourished as a village between the 12th and 14th centuries, before final abandonment in c. 1500. Graphic interpretation panels tell its story, and recreate the original appearance of the buildings.

**OPENING TIMES**

Any reasonable time

**HOW TO FIND US**

**Direction:** 6 miles SE of Malton, on minor road from B1248; ½ mile S of Wharram-le-Street. Park in car park, then ¾ mile walk via uneven



track, steep in places. Site also accessible on foot via Wolds Way ramblers' path. Sturdy and waterproof footwear required. Parts of site slope steeply, and farm livestock likely to be present on site and access path.

**Train:** Malton 8 miles

[dogs] [guidebook] [P] [picnic] [warning]

MAP Page 273 (3H)
OS Map 300 (ref SE 859644)

### Wheeldale Roman Road
N. Yorkshire

A mile-long stretch of enigmatic ancient road – probably Roman but possibly later or earlier – amid wild and beautiful moorland, still with its hard core and drainage ditches.

Managed by North York Moors National Park.

**OPENING TIMES**

Any reasonable time

**HOW TO FIND US**

**Direction:** S of Goathland; W of A169; 7 miles S of Whitby

**Train:** Goathland (N York Moors Rly) 4 miles

[dogs] [warning]

MAP Page 273 (2H)
OS Map 27 (ref SE 806977)

### York Cold War Bunker
N. Yorkshire – YO24 4HT

English Heritage's most modern, most unusual and perhaps most spine-chilling site, 'No.20 Group Royal Observer Corps HQ' is the semi-subterranean bunker which would have monitored nuclear explosions and fallout in the Yorkshire region. In service between 1961 and 1991, the Bunker's control rooms display 'colour-psychology décor' together with original monitoring and communications equipment. Decontamination rooms with air filters and special sewage ejectors were intended to seal off the 60 strong workforce from the devastated outside world. A guided tour by EH staff enhanced by a striking 10-minute film and interpretation with the aid of original Corps members, tells the story of the Cold War's 'Mutually Assured Destruction.'

**NON-MEMBERS**

| | |
|---|---|
| Adult | £5.00 |
| Concession | £4.00 |
| Child | £3.00 |

**OPENING TIMES**

| | |
|---|---|
| 1 Apr-31 Oct, Weekends & Bank Hols Tours every ½ hour No need to book | 10am-4pm |
| Weekdays appointment only | |
| 1 Nov-20 Mar, 1st and 3rd weekend in month Tours every ½ hour No need to book | 10am-4pm |

**HOW TO FIND US**

**Direction:** Off Acomb Road, approx. 1 mile from York city centre

[toilets] [shop] [no dogs] [OVP]

MAP Page 273 (3G)
OS Map 290 (ref SE 580515)

# Whitby Abbey North Yorkshire – YO22 4JT

Perched high on a cliff, the haunting remains of this once magnificent abbey stand proudly above the picturesque seaside town of Whitby.

The first abbey was founded in 657 by the formidable St Hilda, a princess of the Northumbrian royal house, whose Saxon name Hild means 'battle'. Recent archaeological research undertaken by English Heritage suggests that it was once a bustling settlement, as well as the burial place of the Northumbrian royal family, the setting of an epoch-making international meeting between Celtic and Roman clerics, and the home of saints such as the poet Caedmon.

The Anglo-Saxon monastery was destroyed during a Viking invasion in 867, but one of William the Conqueror's knights refounded it in the late 1070s. By 1220, his Norman church proved inadequate for the many pilgrims, and the building of the present church began. After its dissolution by Henry VIII in 1538, the abbey did not suffer as much destruction as many other monasteries, as it was (and still is) used by shipping as a navigation marker. The site then passed to the Cholmley family, who built a mansion largely out of materials plundered from the monastery.

An imaginative visitor centre now sits within the walls of the Cholmley family mansion, part of a major interpretation and access project encompassing the whole of the 'headland', hailed as one of the most important archaeological sites in England. One of the aims of the project has been to enhance and protect the natural beauty and historic character of this headland. English Heritage's research excavations have added to our understanding of Whitby's complex history, including the discovery of a rare 17th-century 'hard garden', inspired by Cholmley's visits to France and Spain and now restored. Continuing research may yield further insights into this multi-layered site.

The visitor centre houses archaeological material excavated at Whitby, as well as computer-generated images revealing how the headland has changed over time. Rich finds from the Anglo-Saxon and medieval periods are also exhibited, together with objects relating to the Cholmley family. Spectacular audio-visual displays recreate the medieval abbey and the 17th-century house, its interiors and gardens. Visitors can also gain an insight into the people who have lived in Whitby, from St Hilda to Bram Stoker, author of Dracula.

**Please note:** from the Whitby harbour area, the abbey can only be directly reached on foot via the 199 'abbey steps' (or Caedmon's Trod): alternatively a well-signposted road leads from the town outskirts to the cliff top abbey.

**www.english-heritage.org.uk/whitbyabbey**

## NON-MEMBERS

| | |
|---|---|
| Adult | £4.20 |
| Concession | £3.20 |
| Child | £2.10 |
| Family | £10.50 |

## OPENING TIMES

| | |
|---|---|
| 1 Apr-30 Sep, daily | 10am-6pm |
| 1-31 Oct, daily | 10am-5pm |
| 1 Nov-20 Mar, Thu-Mon | 10am-4pm |
| Closed | 24-26 Dec and 1 Jan |

## HOW TO FIND US

**Direction:** On cliff top, E of Whitby

**Train:** Whitby ½ mile

**Bus:** From surrounding areas

**Tel:** 01947 603568

**Local Tourist Information**
Whitby: 01947 602674

OVP

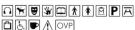

Disabled access (south entrance parking, charged).

Dogs on leads (restricted areas only).

Parking (charge payable).

Tearoom (managed by Youth Hostel Association).

MAP Page 273 (1J)
OS Map 27 (ref NZ 903112)

# Other historic attractions

Discounted entry to our members (discounts may not apply on event days)

## Castle Howard
N. Yorkshire – YO60 7DA

Magnificent 18th-century house with extensive collections and breathtaking grounds. Outdoor tours, exhibitions, events, adventure playground and boat trips. Cafés, farm shop and plant centre.

Managed by The Castle Howard Estate.

### ENTRY FOR EH MEMBERS

| | |
|---|---|
| Adult | £8.50 |
| Concession | £8.00 |
| Child | £5.50 |

Discounted entry with house and garden ticket only

### OPENING TIMES

| | |
|---|---|
| 1 Mar-4 Nov, daily | from 10am |

Please call for times

**Tel:** 01653 648333

www.castlehoward.co.uk

MAP Page 273 (3H)
OS Map 300 (ref SE 716701)

## DIG, York
N. Yorkshire – YO1 8NN

Experience the ultimate archaeological adventure – a simulated excavation. Find real artefacts and study what they tell us about Roman, Viking, medieval and Victorian history.

### ENTRY

| | |
|---|---|
| Adult | £5.50 |
| Concession | £5.00 |
| Child | £5.00 |
| Family (x4) | £16.00 |
| Family (x5) | £19.60 |

10% discount for EH members

### OPENING TIMES

| | |
|---|---|
| Daily | 10am-5pm |

Closed 24-26 Dec

DIG, York

**Tel:** 01904 543403

www.digyork.co.uk

MAP Page 273 (3H)
OS Map 290 (ref SE 606520)

## Duncombe Park, Helmsley
N. Yorkshire – YO62 5EB

The recently restored home of Lord and Lady Feversham is surrounded by over 300 acres of stunning grounds and parkland.

Managed by Duncombe Park Estate Ltd.

### ENTRY

| | |
|---|---|
| Adult | £7.25 |
| Concession | £5.50 |
| Child | £3.25 |
| Family | £15.00 |

Entry to house and gardens for EH members £3.00, except on event days

Discount does not extend to EH Corporate Partners

### OPENING TIMES

6 May-28 Oct, Sun-Thu by guided tour only: 12.30pm, 1.30pm, 2.30pm and 3.30pm

**Tel:** 01439 772625

www.duncombepark.com

MAP Page 273 (2G)
OS Map 26 (ref SE 604830)

## Fountains Abbey
Ripon, N. Yorkshire – HG4 3DY

Fountains Abbey

Fountains Abbey has been described as the 'crown and glory of all that monasticism has left us in England'. There are 800 years of history to be explored in the 320-hectare (790-acre) estate, a World Heritage Site combining architecture and landscape of outstanding historical and aesthetic importance. The ruins of the Cistercian abbey, which was founded in 1132, are the largest such remains in Europe: they provide a dramatic focal point for the landscape garden, which was laid out during the first half of the 18th century by William and John Aislabie.

Fountains Mill, one of Europe's oldest surviving mills, once supplied the monks of Fountains Abbey with flour for baking. It has now been in continuous use for more than 800 years. Today, visitors can see the working water wheel turning as it has for centuries, and explore the life and times of the mill through displays and ancient artefacts.

Other features within the estate include St Mary's Church (owned by English Heritage), a masterpiece of Victorian Gothic design (see p. 202), and the Elizabethan mansion, Fountains Hall, built partly with stone from the abbey. St Mary's Church also provides a focus for the medieval deer park.

## Fountains Abbey

Fountains Abbey and Studley Royal is owned and managed by The National Trust. English Heritage works in partnership with The National Trust to protect this World Heritage Site.

### NON-MEMBERS

| Fountains Abbey & Water Garden | |
|---|---|
| Adult | £7.50 |
| Child | £4.00 |
| Family | £20.00 |

EH and NT members admitted free

**Deer Park** free of charge

Parking £3.00 at Deer Park
Free at Visitor Centre

### OPENING TIMES

| Abbey and Water Garden: | |
|---|---|
| Mar-Oct, daily | 10am-5pm |
| Nov-Feb, daily | 10am-4pm* |
| *Closed Fridays | Nov-Jan |

**Deer Park:**
Daily during daylight hours

| | |
|---|---|
| Closed | 24-25 Dec |

Guided tours available – please call for details

### HOW TO FIND US

**Direction:** 4 miles W of Ripon, off B6265

**Public Transport:** Traveline 0870 6082608. Bus services in operation to Ripon and Fountains Abbey from Leeds, York, Yorkshire Dales and Harrogate. 'Ripon Roweller' runs from Ripon to Fountains Abbey daily except Sundays. Call 01423 526655

**Tel:** 01765 608888

www.fountainsabbey.org.uk

Disabled access (not suitable for three-wheel battery cars).

MAP Page 273 (3F)
OS Map 298/299 (ref SE 275683)

## JORVIK Viking Centre, York
N. Yorkshire – YO1 9WT

Explore Viking history on the very site where archaeologists discovered remains of Viking York. Discover what life was like 1,000 years ago, and journey through a reconstruction of Viking streets.

### ENTRY

| | |
|---|---|
| Adult | £7.75 |
| Concession | £6.60 |
| Child | £5.50 |
| Family (2+2) | £21.95 |
| Family (2+3) | £26.50 |

Prices subject to change, please check website. 15% discount for EH members

### OPENING TIMES

Daily except 24-26 Dec

**Tel:** 01904 543403

www.jorvik-viking-centre.com

MAP Page 273 (4G)
OS Map 290 (ref SE 604516)

## Merchant Adventurers' Hall, York
N. Yorkshire – YO1 9XD

The finest surviving medieval guild hall in Britain, built 1357-1361 and largely unaltered. A visit includes an audio tour. The Hall and its collections are fully accessible from Fossgate.

Managed by The Company of Merchant Adventurers of the City of York.

### ENTRY

| | |
|---|---|
| Adult | £2.50 |
| Concession | £2.00 |
| Child (7-17 years) | £1.00 |
| Under 7 | Free |
| Family (2 adults + 2 or more children) | £6.00 |

50% discount for EH members

Discount does not extend to EH Corporate Members

## Merchant Adventurers' Hall, York

### OPENING TIMES

| | |
|---|---|
| Oct-Mar, Mon-Sat | 9am-3.30pm |
| Apr-Sep, Mon-Thu | 9am-5pm |
| Apr-Sep, Fri & Sat | 9am-3.30pm |
| Apr-Sep, Sun | 12pm-4pm |
| Closed | Christmas and New Year |
| Closed | Jan-Feb 2008 |

Please call for details

**Tel:** 01904 654818

www.theyorkcompany.co.uk

MAP Page 273 (3H)
OS Map 290 (ref SE 605517)



## York Minster
York – YO1 7HH

Enjoy the peaceful atmosphere of the largest Gothic cathedral in Northern Europe, a place of worship for over 1,000 years, and a treasure house of stained glass.

### ENTRY

Prices subject to change

| Minster Only | |
|---|---|
| Adult | £5.50 |
| Concession | £4.50 |
| **Combined Minster and Undercroft** | |
| Adult | £7.50 |
| Concession/student | £5.50 |
| Child | £2.00 |

Free access to Undercroft for EH members on purchase of a Minster ticket (not valid with any other offer)

### OPENING TIMES

| | |
|---|---|
| Mon-Sat (last entry 5pm) | 9.30am-6.30pm |
| Sunday (last entry 3.45pm) | 12.30pm-6.00pm |

**Tel:** 01904 557216

www.yorkminster.org

MAP Page 273 (4H)
OS Map 290 (ref SE 603522)

Castlerigg Stone Circle, Cumbria – see page 217

# North West

'Now Sark runs to the Solway sands
And Tweed runs to the ocean
To mark where England's province stands
Such a parcel of rogues in a nation'

From *Such a Parcel of Rogues in a Nation*,
by Robert Burns (1759-1796)

# Properties See individual listings for details

**Cheshire**
Beeston Castle
Chester Castle: Agricola Tower and Castle Walls
Chester Roman Amphitheatre
Sandbach Crosses

**Cumbria**
Ambleside Roman Fort
Bow Bridge
Brough Castle
Brougham Castle
Carlisle Castle
Castlerigg Stone Circle
Clifton Hall
Countess Pillar
Furness Abbey
Hadrian's Wall (see p228)
Hardknott Roman Fort
King Arthur's Round Table
Lanercost Priory
Mayburgh Henge
Penrith Castle
Piel Castle
Ravenglass Roman Bath House
Shap Abbey
Stott Park Bobbin Mill
Wetheral Priory Gatehouse

**Lancashire**
Goodshaw Chapel
Sawley Abbey
Warton Old Rectory
Whalley Abbey Gatehouse

Comprehensive map of our sites Pages 272 and 274

Above: (left top) Piel Castle, (left bottom) Castlerigg Stone Circle, (centre left) Countess Pillar, (centre right top and bottom) Brough Castle, Whalley Abbey Gatehouse, and (right) Carlisle Castle.



# A Parcel of Rogues?

English Heritage's North West region extends from the boundary of Wales near Chester, via Lancashire, the Lake District and Cumbria, to the Scottish Border north of Carlisle. 2007 sees two anniversaries which focus attention on this much fought-over northern border.

The first is the death on 7 July 1307, at Burgh-by-Sands near Carlisle, of King Edward I of England, as he was about to embark on yet another of his many campaigns in Scotland. The tough and heroic 'Hammer of the Scots' in some English eyes, but a brutal overbearing tyrant from a Scots or Welsh viewpoint, Edward had recently spent six months struggling against grave illness at **Lanercost Priory**. Treatment there with medicines including amber, gold and pearls had allowed the 68 year-old king to continue his progress: but could not stem the dysentery which eventually killed him.

Among the most beautiful and atmospheric of all English Heritage's monastic sites, Lanercost had already endured major Scottish raids before Edward's death: afterwards the priory was again twice badly damaged by Scottish invaders. The old king's death in fact initiated a particularly disastrous period for the English north-west, with only the successful defence of **Carlisle Castle** in 1315 relieving a disastrous tale of castles, towns and abbeys sacked by resurgent Scots invaders. Carlisle would remain a vital bastion of the border for several more centuries, before becoming in 1746 the very last English fortress ever to suffer a siege, during the final outburst of Anglo-Scottish warfare.

This last outbreak arose in some measure from the second 2007 anniversary – that of the Act of Union of 1707 between England and Scotland. Though supported by many Scots politicians – the 'parcel of rogues in a nation' of Robert Burns' song – the Act was resented by other Scots as making their nation a mere English province. It was thus a readier recruiting ground for the Jacobite risings of 1715 and 1745-6. On the retreat northwards which ended at Culloden, 'Bonnie Prince Charlie' ( 'the Young Pretender' to his English opponents) left a hapless Jacobite garrison at Carlisle, to resist in vain the Hanoverian army of the Duke of Cumberland – 'Sweet William' to the English, but 'Stinking Billy' or 'The Butcher' to the Scots. Then as now, just who the rogues or heroes of Anglo-Scottish warfare really were remains a matter of national opinion.

## Ambleside Roman Fort
Cumbria

The well-marked remains of a 2nd-century fort with large granaries, probably built under Hadrian to guard the Roman road from Brougham to Ravenglass and act as a supply base.

Managed by The National Trust.

### OPENING TIMES

Any reasonable time

### HOW TO FIND US

**Direction:** 182 metres W of Waterhead car park, Ambleside

**Train:** Windermere 5 miles

**Bus:** Stagecoach in Cumbria 555/6, 599 from Windermere

MAP Page 274 (6D)
OS Map 7 (ref NY 372034)



## Beeston Castle
Cheshire – CW6 9TX

Standing majestically on a sheer rocky crag, Beeston has perhaps the most stunning views of any castle in England. Excavations indicate that a Bronze Age settlement and Iron Age hillfort occupied the site long before the castle was begun in 1225. For centuries an impregnable royal fortress, it finally fell to Parliamentarian forces in the Civil War.

## Beeston Castle

The 'Castle of the Rock' exhibition outlines the 4,000 year history of this strategic site. There are family-friendly books and activities.

### NON-MEMBERS

| | |
|---|---|
| Adult | £4.00 |
| Concession | £3.00 |
| Child | £2.00 |
| Family | £10.00 |

### OPENING TIMES

| | |
|---|---|
| 1 Apr-30 Sep, daily | 10am-6pm |
| 1 Oct-20 Mar, Thu-Mon | 10am-4pm |
| Closed | 24-26 Dec and 1 Jan |

### HOW TO FIND US

**Direction:** Located 11 miles SE of Chester, on minor road off A49

**Train:** Chester 10 miles

**Tel:** 01829 260464

**Local Tourist Information**
Chester: 01244 402111

Please note: Steep climb (no disabled access to the top of the hill).

New guidebook.

MAP Page 272 (7D)
OS Map 257 (ref SJ 537593)

## Bow Bridge
Cumbria

This narrow 15th-century stone bridge across Mill Beck carried an old pack-horse route to nearby Furness Abbey (see p.220).

### OPENING TIMES

Any reasonable time

### HOW TO FIND US

**Direction:** Located ½ mile N of Barrow-in-Furness, on minor road off A590; near Furness Abbey

**Train:** Barrow-in-Furness 1½ miles

**Bus:** Stagecoach in Cumbria 6/A Barrow-in Furness – Ulverston to within ¾ mile

## Bow Bridge

MAP Page 274 (7D)
OS Map 6 (ref SD 224715)

## Brough Castle
Cumbria

Commanding a magnificent view of the Pennines, medieval Brough Castle stands within the earthworks of a Roman fort guarding the strategic Stainmore routeway. The impressive tower-keep dates from c. 1200, replacing an earlier stronghold destroyed by William the Lion of Scotland in 1174. Like so many other castles hereabouts, Brough was restored in the 17th century by Lady Anne Clifford: traces of her interior fittings and kitchen gardens can still be seen.

### OPENING TIMES

Any reasonable time

### HOW TO FIND US

**Direction:** 8 miles SE of Appleby S of A66

**Train:** Kirkby Stephen 6 miles

**Bus:** Grand Prix 563 Penrith – Brough (passing Penrith)

MAP Page 275 (6F)
OS Map 19 (ref NY 791141)

## Brougham Castle
Cumbria – CA10 2AA

Picturesque Brougham Castle was begun in the early 13th century by Robert de Vieuxpont, near the site of a Roman fort guarding the crossing of the River Eamont. His great keep largely survives, reinforced by an impressive double gatehouse and other 14th-century additions made by the powerful Clifford family, Wardens of the Marches. The castle thus became a formidable barrier to Scots invaders.

Though both James I and Charles I stayed here, Brougham was in poor condition by the time of the Civil War. It was thereafter restored as a residence by the indomitable Lady Anne Clifford (see also Brough Castle and the Countess Pillar): she often visited with her travelling 'court', and died here in 1676.

Today, the site features an introductory exhibition, including carved stones from the nearby Roman fort. The site has good wheelchair access to entry point, toilet, shop and small introductory exhibition. There is a wheelchair route to the castle ruins, which enables visitors to make a circuit of the site and read the interpretation panels. The keep is not accessible to wheelchairs.

### Brougham Castle

#### NON-MEMBERS

| | |
|---|---|
| Adult | £3.00 |
| Concession | £2.30 |
| Child | £1.50 |
| Family | £7.50 |

#### OPENING TIMES

| | |
|---|---|
| 1 Apr-30 Sep, daily | 10am-5pm |

#### HOW TO FIND US

**Direction:** 1½ miles SE of Penrith, off A66.

**Train:** Penrith 2 miles

**Local Tourist information**
Penrith: 01768 867466;
Rheged: 01768 860034

**Tel:** 01768 862488

OVP

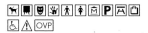

MAP Page 274 (5E)
OS Map 5 (ref NY 537290)

## Carlisle Castle
See feature – Page 218

## Castlerigg Stone Circle
Cumbria

Castlerigg is perhaps the most atmospheric and dramatically sited of all British stone circles, with panoramic views and the mountains of Helvellyn and High Seat as a backdrop. It is also among the earliest British

### Castlerigg Stone Circle

circles, raised in about 3000 BC during the Neolithic period.

Managed by The National Trust.

#### OPENING TIMES

Any reasonable time

#### HOW TO FIND US

**Direction:** 1½ miles E of Keswick

**Train:** Penrith 16 miles

**Bus:** Stagecoach in Cumbria X4/5 from Penrith to within 1 mile

MAP Page 274 (5D)
OS Map 4 (ref NY291236)

## Chester Castle: Agricola Tower and Castle Walls
Cheshire

The original gateway to Chester Castle, this 12th-century tower houses a chapel with exceptionally fine wall-paintings of c. 1220, rediscovered in the 1980s. An access stair to the castle's wall-walk is nearby.

Managed by Chester City Council.

#### OPENING TIMES

Walls open any reasonable time

| | |
|---|---|
| Cell block open: | |
| 1 Apr-30 Sep, daily | 10am-5pm |
| 1 Oct-20 Mar, daily | 10am-4pm |
| Closed | 24-26 Dec and 1 Jan |

#### HOW TO FIND US

**Direction:** Access via Assizes Court car park on Grosvenor St

**Train:** Chester 1 mile

**Bus:** From surrounding areas

Disabled access (parts only).

MAP Page 272 (7C)
OS Map 266 (ref SJ 405657)

# Carlisle Castle Cumbria – CA3 8UR

Impressive and forbidding, Carlisle Castle is a formidable fortress, amply repaying exploration of its absorbing 900-year history.

Solar in de Ireby's Tower Photo: Andrew Tryner

Long commanding the especially turbulent western end of the Anglo-Scottish border, Carlisle has witnessed many conflicts and sieges. The earliest castle (on the site of a sequence of Roman forts dating from the 1st to 4th centuries AD) was of earth and timber, raised by King William Rufus in c. 1092. During the following century it was refortified in stone, possibly by Henry I. The 12th-century stone keep is the oldest surviving structure in the castle, which was frequently updated as befitted a stronghold always in the front line of Anglo-Scottish warfare. In 1315 it triumphantly saw off a determined Scots attack. The rounded 'shot-deflecting' battlements of the keep were added when Henry VIII adapted the castle for artillery in c. 1540.

Elaborate carvings in a small cell, by captives held here by the future Richard III in 1480, vividly demonstrate that Carlisle Castle was also a prison. Mary Queen of Scots was confined here after her flight from Scotland in 1568: but in 1596 the Border reiver Kinmont Willie Armstrong managed a daring night escape, to the fury of his captors.

Carlisle played its part in the English Civil War. Besieged for eight months by Parliament's Scots allies, its Royalist garrison surrendered in 1645 only after eating rats and even their dogs. A century later in 1746, the castle became the last English fortress ever to suffer a siege, when Bonnie Prince Charlie's Jacobite garrison vainly attempted to hold off the Duke of Cumberland's Hanoverian army. The fortress became their prison: many died here, and others left only for hanging or transportation.

Housed in the keep is a model of the city in 1745, and an exhibition on Bonnie Prince Charlie and the Jacobite rising of that year; visitors can also see the legendary 'licking stones', which parched Jacobite prisoners desperately licked for moisture in order to stay alive. Admission also includes entry to the King's Own Royal Border Regiment Museum. Another feature of the site is the Carlisle Roman Dig, a fully accessible exhibition displaying the finds from recent excavations.

**www.english-heritage.org.uk/carlislecastle**

## NON-MEMBERS

| | |
|---|---|
| Adult | £4.20 |
| Concession | £3.20 |
| Child | £2.10 |

## OPENING TIMES

| | |
|---|---|
| 1 Apr-30 Sep, daily | 9.30am-5pm |
| 1 Oct-20 Mar, daily | 10am-4pm |
| Closed | 24-26 Dec and 1 Jan |

## HOW TO FIND US

**Direction:** In Carlisle city centre

**Train:** Carlisle ½ mile

**Bus:** From surrounding areas

**Tel:** 01228 591922

**Local Tourist Information:** 01228 625600

E OVP

Disabled access (except interiors).

Dogs on leads (restricted areas only).

Guided tours (available at peak times at a small extra charge; groups please pre-book).

Parking (disabled only, but signposted city centre car parks nearby).

**MAP Page 274 (4D)**

**OS Map 315 (ref NY 396562)**

## Chester Roman Amphitheatre
Cheshire

The largest Roman amphitheatre in Britain, used for entertainment and military training by the 20th Legion, based at the fortress of 'Deva' (Chester). Excavations by English Heritage and Chester City Council in 2004-5 revealed two successive stone-built amphitheatres with wooden seating. The first included access to the upper tiers of seats via stairs on the rear wall, as at Pompeii, and had a small shrine next to its north entrance. The second provided seat access via vaulted stairways. The two buildings differed both from each other and from all other British amphitheatres, underlining the importance of Roman Chester.

Managed by Chester City Council.

### OPENING TIMES
Any reasonable time

### HOW TO FIND US
**Direction:** On Vicars Lane, beyond Newgate, Chester

**Train:** Chester ¾ mile

**Bus:** From surrounding areas

Disabled access (no access to amphitheatre floor).

MAP Page 272 (7C)
OS Map 266 (ref SJ 408662)

## Clifton Hall
Cumbria

This 15th-century tower, sole survivor of the manor house of the Wybergh family, was plundered by Jacobites in 1745 before the Battle of Clifton Moor, the last battle fought on English soil.

### Clifton Hall

### OPENING TIMES
Any reasonable time

Closed 24-26 Dec and 1 Jan

### HOW TO FIND US
**Direction:** Next to Clifton Hall Farm; 2 miles S of Penrith, on A6

**Train:** Penrith 2½ miles

MAP Page 274 (5E)
OS Map 5 (ref NY 530271)

## Countess Pillar, Brougham
Cumbria

A monument erected in 1656 by Lady Anne Clifford of nearby Brougham Castle, to commemorate her final parting here from her mother. On the low stone beside it, money was given to the poor each anniversary of their parting.

### OPENING TIMES
Any reasonable time

### HOW TO FIND US
**Direction:** ¼ mile E of Brougham

**Train:** Penrith 2½ miles

**Warning:** site on a very busy main road.

MAP Page 274 (5E)
OS Map 5 (ref NY 546289)

## Furness Abbey
Cumbria – LA13 0PJ

The impressive remains of an abbey founded by Stephen, later King of England, including much of the east end and west tower of the church, the ornately decorated chapter house and the cloister buildings. Originally of the Savigniac order, it passed to the Cistercians in 1147, and despite damage by Scottish raiders became (after Fountains Abbey) the second most prosperous Cistercian abbey in all England. Set in the 'vale of nightshade', the romantic ruins were celebrated by Wordsworth in his Prelude of 1805.

An exhibition on the history of the abbey, with a display of elaborately carved stones, can be seen in the visitor centre. (See also Bow Bridge, p. 216)

### NON-MEMBERS

| | |
|---|---|
| Adult | £3.50 |
| Concession | £2.60 |
| Child | £1.80 |

### OPENING TIMES

| | |
|---|---|
| 1 Apr-30 Sep, daily | 10am-5pm |
| 1-31 Oct, Thu-Mon | 10am-4pm |
| 1 Nov-20 Mar, Thu-Sun | 10am-4pm |
| Closed | 24-26 Dec and 1 Jan |

## Furness Abbey

### HOW TO FIND US

**Direction:** Located 1½ miles N of Barrow-in-Furness, off A590

**Train:** Barrow-in-Furness 2 miles

**Bus:** Stagecoach in Cumbria 6/A Barrow-in-Furness – Ulverston, to within ¾ mile

**Tel:** 01229 823420

OVP

Dogs on leads (restricted areas only).

MAP Page 274 (7D)
OS Map 6 (ref SD 218717)

## Goodshaw Chapel
Lancashire

English Heritage's only Nonconformist place of worship, this atmospheric Baptist chapel displays a complete set of box-pews, galleries and pulpit dating from c. 1742 to 1809. A festival of hymns and sermons is held every first Sunday in July.

### OPENING TIMES

Please call the keykeeper for details. Tel: 01706 227333

### HOW TO FIND US

**Direction:** In Crawshawbooth, 2 miles N of Rawtenstall via A682 (in Goodshaw Ave – turning off A682 opp. Jester public house). Chapel approx. 1½ miles from main road

**Train:** Burnley Manchester Road 4½ miles

**Bus:** Burnley & Pendle X43/4 Nelson – Manchester. Both pass Burnley Manchester Road

## Goodshaw Chapel

MAP Page 272 (4E)
OS Map 21 (ref SD 814261)

## Hadrian's Wall
See page 228

## Hardknott Roman Fort
Cumbria

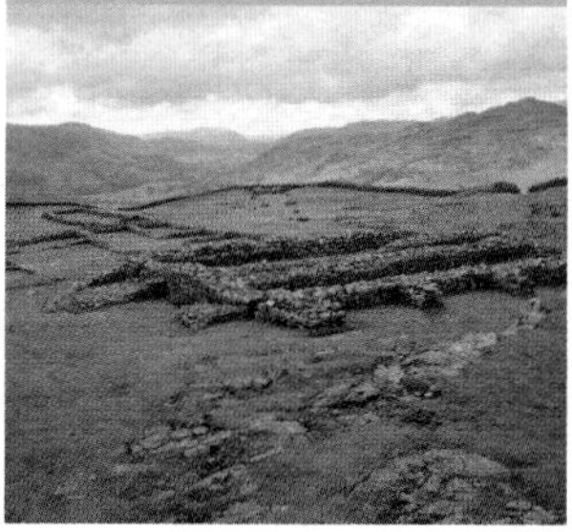

This remote and dramatically-sited fort was founded under Hadrian in the 2nd century. Well-marked remains include the headquarters building, commandant's house and bath-house. The site of the parade-ground survives beside the fort, and the road which Hardknott guarded can be traced for some distance as an earthwork.

Managed by The National Trust.

### OPENING TIMES

Any reasonable time

### HOW TO FIND US

**Direction:** 9 miles NE of Ravenglass; at W end of Hardknott Pass

**Train:** Eskdale (Dalegarth) (Ravenglass & Eskdale Rly) 3 miles

Warning (access may be hazardous during the winter months).

MAP Page 274 (6C)
OS Map 6 (ref NY 218015)

## King Arthur's Round Table
Cumbria

A Neolithic earthwork 'henge', dating from c. 2000 BC, but much later believed to be King Arthur's jousting arena. Mayburgh Henge is adjacent.

### OPENING TIMES

Any reasonable time

### HOW TO FIND US

**Direction:** Located at Eamont Bridge, 1 mile S of Penrith. Mayburgh Henge is nearby

**Train:** Penrith 1½ miles

MAP Page 274 (5E)
OS Map 5 (ref NY 523284)

## Lanercost Priory
Cumbria – CA8 2HQ

Standing close to Hadrian's Wall, the Augustinian priory of Lanercost was much involved in the Anglo-Scottish wars. During his last campaign in 1306-7 the mortally sick Edward I rested here for six months, before dying at Burgh-by-Sands as he prepared to enter Scotland. The abbey suffered terribly from Scottish raids, being sacked at least four times. It was finally dissolved by Henry VIII in 1537, but today its beautiful 13th-century church remains remarkably well-preserved, standing to its full height: part is now in use as the parish church. See the unique 16th-century wall-paintings in the Dacre Hall.

### Lanercost Priory

New interpretation now on display.

Parish church not managed by English Heritage.

**NON-MEMBERS**

| | |
|---|---|
| Adult | £3.00 |
| Concession | £2.30 |
| Child | £1.50 |
| Family | £7.50 |

**OPENING TIMES**

| | |
|---|---|
| 1 Apr-30 Sep, daily | 10am-5pm |
| 1-31 Oct, Thu-Mon | 10am-4pm |
| 3 Nov-16 Dec, Sat-Sun | 10am-4pm |
| Closed | 24-25 Dec |



**HOW TO FIND US**

**Direction:** Off a minor road S of Lanercost; 2 miles NE of Brampton

**Train:** Brampton 3 miles

**Bus:** Stagecoach in Cumbria 685 Carlisle-Newcastle-upon-Tyne to within 1½ miles

**Tel:** 01697 73030

OVP

**MAP Page 274 (4E)**
**OS Map 315 (ref NY 556637)**

## Mayburgh Henge
Cumbria

A large and impressive Neolithic henge, much better preserved than neighbouring King Arthur's Round Table. Its banks stand up to 3 metres (10 feet) high, and unusually are constructed of pebbles collected from the nearby river. Near the centre is a single standing stone: old drawings suggest that it was one of a group of four here, four more having been removed from the entranceway.

**OPENING TIMES**

Any reasonable time

### Mayburgh Henge

**HOW TO FIND US**

**Direction:** 1 mile S of Penrith off A6

**Train:** Penrith 1½ miles

**MAP Page 274 (5E)**
**OS Map 5 (ref NY 519284)**

## Penrith Castle
Cumbria

The mainly 15th-century remains of a castle begun by Bishop Strickland of Carlisle and developed by the Nevilles and Richard III. Set in a municipal park opposite the railway station.

**OPENING TIMES**

| | |
|---|---|
| Summer | 7.30am-9pm |
| Winter | 7.30am-4.30pm |

**HOW TO FIND US**

**Direction:** Opposite Penrith railway station

**Train:** Penrith (adjacent)

**MAP Page 274 (5E)**
**OS Map 5 (ref NY 513299)**

## Piel Castle
Cumbria

### Piel Castle

The impressive ruins of a 14th-century castle with a massive keep, inner and outer baileys, and towered curtain walls still standing. It was built by the Abbot of Furness on the south-eastern point of Piel Island, to guard the deep-water harbour of Barrow-in-Furness against pirates and Scots raiders.

**OPENING TIMES**

Any reasonable time
Access by ferry boat not managed by EH

**HOW TO FIND US**

**Direction:** Piel Island, 3¼ miles SE of Barrow-in-Furness

By small boat: from 11am, from Roa Island, summer only; subject to tides and weather. There is a small charge for this service; for details, call John Cleasby on 01229 475770 or 07798 794550

**Train:** Barrow-in-Furness 4 miles

**Bus:** Stagecoach in Cumbria 11 Barrow-in Furness – Ulverston

**MAP Page 274 (7D)**
**OS Map 6 (ref SD 233636)**

## Ravenglass Roman Bath House
Cumbria

The remains of the bath house of Ravenglass Roman fort, established in AD 130, are among the tallest Roman structures surviving in northern Britain: the walls stand almost 4 metres (13 feet) high. The fort at Ravenglass (whose earthworks can be seen near the bath house)

## Ravenglass Roman Bath House

guarded what was probably a useful harbour, and there is evidence that soldiers stationed here served in Hadrian's fleet.

### OPENING TIMES

Any reasonable time

### HOW TO FIND US

**Direction:** ¼ mile E of Ravenglass, off minor road leading to A595

**Train:** Ravenglass (adjacent)

MAP Page 274 (6C)
OS Map 6 (ref SD 088959)

## Sandbach Crosses
Cheshire

The two massive Saxon stone crosses, elaborately carved with animals and Biblical scenes including the Nativity of Christ and the Crucifixion, dominate the cobbled market square of Sandbach. Probably dating from the 9th century, and originally painted as well as carved, they are among the finest surviving examples of Anglo-Saxon high crosses.

### OPENING TIMES

Any reasonable time

### HOW TO FIND US

**Direction:** Market Sq, Sandbach

**Train:** Sandbach 1½ miles

**Bus:** From surrounding areas

MAP Page 272 (7D)
OS Map 268 (ref SJ 759608)

## Sawley Abbey
Lancashire

The remains of a Cistercian abbey founded in 1148, set on the banks of the Ribble against a backdrop of dramatic hills. After its dissolution in 1536, the monks were briefly returned to the abbey during the Pilgrimage of Grace. They remained in possession until the insurrection's collapse and the execution of their abbot.

Managed by the Heritage Trust for the North West.

### OPENING TIMES

| | |
|---|---|
| 1 Apr-30 Sep, daily | 10am-6pm |
| 1 Oct-20 Mar, daily | 10am-4pm |
| Closed | 24-26 Dec and 1 Jan |

### HOW TO FIND US

**Direction:** Located at Sawley; 3½ miles N of Clitheroe, off A59

**Train:** Clitheroe 4 miles

MAP Page 272 (4D)
OS Map 41 (ref SD 777464)

## Shap Abbey
Cumbria

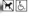

The impressive full-height 15th-century tower and other remains of a remote abbey of Premonstratensian 'white canons'.

### OPENING TIMES

Any reasonable time

### HOW TO FIND US

**Direction:** 1½ miles W of Shap, on the bank of the River Lowther

**Train:** Penrith 10 miles

**Bus:** Stagecoach in Cumbria/ Apollo/K&B 106 Penrith-Kendal to within 1½ miles

Disabled access (limited views from outside the site).

MAP Page 274 (6E)
OS Map 5 (ref NY 548152)

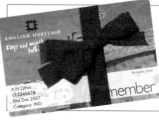

## Stott Park Bobbin Mill
Cumbria – LA12 8AX

This extensive working mill was begun in 1835 to produce the wooden bobbins vital to the Lancashire spinning and weaving industries. Although small compared to other mills, some 250 men and boys (some drafted in from workhouses) worked here in often arduous conditions to produce a quarter of a million bobbins a week. Guided tours are included in the admission charge: the last tour begins ½ hour before closing. Please call for details of steam days.

### NON-MEMBERS

| | |
|---|---|
| Adult | £4.20 |
| Concession | £3.20 |
| Child | £2.10 |
| Family | £10.50 |

### OPENING TIMES

| | |
|---|---|
| 1 Apr-31 Oct, Mon-Fri | 10am-5pm |

### HOW TO FIND US

**Direction:** Located 1½ miles N of Newby Bridge, off A590

**Train:** Grange-over-Sands 8 miles

**Ferry:** Windermere ferry from Ambleside or Bowness to Lakeside, then 1 mile

**Tel:** 01539 531087

### Stott Park Bobbin Mill

**Local Tourist Information**
Hawkshead: 01539 436525

OVP

Disabled access (ground floor only. Specific interpretation for visually impaired visitors).

Parking (lower car park).

MAP Page 274 (6D)
OS Map 7 (ref SD 372881)

## Warton Old Rectory
Lancashire

A rare survival of a large 14th-century stone house with great hall and chambers. It served as a residence and courthouse for the wealthy and powerful rectors of Warton.

Managed by Heritage Trust for the North West.

### OPENING TIMES

| | |
|---|---|
| 1 Apr-30 Sep, daily | 10am-6pm |
| 1 Oct-20 Mar, daily | 10am-4pm |
| Closed | 24-26 Dec and 1 Jan |

### HOW TO FIND US

**Direction:** At Warton; 1 mile N of Carnforth, on minor road off A6

**Train:** Carnforth 1 mile

**Bus:** Stagecoach in Lancashire 55/A from Lancaster (passing close Carnforth)

MAP Page 272 (3D)
OS Map 7 (ref SD 499723)

## Wetheral Priory Gatehouse
Cumbria

The 15th-century gatehouse of a Benedictine priory, where wrongdoers could claim pardon if they enlisted to fight the Scots. It survived because it later served as the vicarage for the parish church.

### OPENING TIMES

| | |
|---|---|
| 1 Apr-30 Sep, daily | 10am-6pm |
| 1 Oct-20 Mar, daily | 10am-4pm |
| Closed | 24-26 Dec and 1 Jan |

### HOW TO FIND US

**Direction:** In Wetheral village; 6 miles E of Carlisle, on B6263

**Train:** Wetheral ½ mile

**Bus:** Stagecoach in Cumbria 74/5 Carlisle-Wetheral

MAP Page 274 (4E)
OS Map 315 (ref NY 468541)

## Whalley Abbey Gatehouse
Lancashire

The 14th-century gatehouse of the nearby Cistercian abbey, the second wealthiest monastery in Lancashire, beside the River Calder. The first floor was probably a chapel.

### OPENING TIMES

Any reasonable time

### HOW TO FIND US

**Direction:** In Whalley; 6 miles NE of Blackburn, on minor road off A59

**Train:** Whalley ¼ mile

**Bus:** Lancashire United 225 Bolton- Clitheroe (passes Blackburn)

MAP Page 272 (4D)
OS Map 287 (ref SD 729362)

# Other historic attractions

Discounted entry to our members (discounts may not apply on event days)

## Holker Hall and Gardens

Cark-in-Cartnel,
Cumbria – LA11 7PL

Holker Hall is a superb Victorian house built on a grand scale, with rich and varied gardens that offer 24 acres of woodland and magnificent formal garden areas.

### ENTRY

**Hall and gardens**

| | |
|---|---|
| Adult | £9.25 |
| Concession | £8.50 |
| Child | £5.00 |
| Family | £25.00 |

25% off regular adult and senior citizen entry to the Hall and Gardens. Offer valid 1 Apr-28 Oct. Not valid during special events

### OPENING TIMES

**Hall and Gardens**

1 Apr-28 Oct
Sun-Fri 12pm-4pm

**Gardens**

1 Apr-28 Oct
Sun-Fri 10.30am-5.30pm

**Direction:** Exit junction 36 from M6. Signposted from A590

**Tel:** 01539 558328

www.holker-hall.co.uk

MAP Page 274 (7D)
OS Map 7 (ref SD 359774)

## Muncaster Castle

Ravenglass,
Cumbria – CA18 1RQ

Historic castle, home to the Pennington family for 800 years. Extensive gardens with glorious views. World owl centre with daily bird show and heron happy hour. Indoor meadowvole maze. Gift shop, café and plant centre. Magical winter evenings.

Managed by Peter and Iona Frost-Pennington.

### ENTRY

**Castle, gardens, owls and maze**

| | |
|---|---|
| Adult | £9.50 |
| Child (5-15) | £6.50 |
| Family | £27.00 |

**Gardens, owls and maze**

| | |
|---|---|
| Adult | £7.00 |
| Child | £5.00 |
| Family | £22.00 |

EH Members get £1.50 off castle ticket, and £1 off garden ticket

Discount does not extend to EH Corporate Partners

### OPENING TIMES

**Gardens, owl centre and maze:**

11 Feb-4 Nov
Daily 10.30am-6pm

**Castle:**

Sun-Fri 12pm-5pm

Please call 01229 717614

**Direction:** Signposted from A595

www.muncaster.co.uk

MAP Page 274 (6C)
OS Map 6 (ref SD 103963)

## Norton Priory Museum and Gardens

Runcorn, Cheshire – WA7 1SX

Discover the ruins of the 12th-century Augustinian Priory, set in 38 acres of beautiful gardens. Giant St Christopher statue, museum galleries and Georgian Walled Garden. Events all year round.

### ENTRY

| | |
|---|---|
| Adult | £4.95 |
| Concession/Child | £3.50 |
| Family | £12.75 |

EH members: 2 adults for the price of 1 full paying adult

Discount does not extend to EH Corporate Partners

### OPENING TIMES

| | |
|---|---|
| Apr-Oct, Mon-Fri | 12pm-5pm |
| Sat-Sun & Bank Hols | 12pm-6pm |
| Nov-Mar, daily | 12pm-4pm |
| Closed | 24-26 Dec and 1 Jan |

**Direction:** Take junction 11 off M56. Well signposted

**Tel:** 01928 569895

www.nortonpriory.org

MAP Page 272 (6D)
OS Map 275/267/276
(ref SJ 548830)

## Pendle Heritage Centre
Barrowford,
Lancashire – BB9 6JQ

The centre features an 18th-century walled garden and exhibitions about the area.

Managed by Heritage Trust for the North West.

### ENTRY

| | |
|---|---|
| Adult | £4.00 |
| Concession | £2.00 |
| Child | £2.00 |
| Family | £9.00 |

50% discount for EH members

### OPENING TIMES

Daily except 25 Dec 10am-5pm

**Direction:** Junction 13 from M65

**Tel:** 01282 661701

www.htnw.co.uk

MAP Page 272 (4E)
OS Map 21/41 (ref SD 862398)

## Ravenglass and Eskdale Railway
Cumbria – CA18 1SW

The railway runs for seven miles from the coastal village of Ravenglass through two valleys to Dalegarth station in Eskdale, nestling at the foot of England's highest mountains. Steam trains operate every day from 17 Mar to 31 Oct 2007, over most winter weekends and during the Christmas holidays (26 Dec-3 Jan). Sites nearby include Ravenglass Roman Fort (see p. 222), and there is also a challenging walk to Hardknott Roman fort (see p.221). Please call 01229 717171 for details before travelling.

Ravenglass and Eskdale Railway

### PRICES

| | |
|---|---|
| Adult return fare (Jan-Dec) | £9.60 |
| Child, aged 5-15 return fare (Jan-Dec) | £4.80 |
| Children under five | FREE |

20% discount for EH members.

### OPENING TIMES

Please call or check website for details

**Tel:** 01229 717171

www.ravenglass-railway.co.uk

MAP Page 272 (2B)

## St George's Hall, Liverpool
Merseyside – L1 1JJ

A superb neo-Classical building, designed by Harvey Lonsdale Elmes as law courts and a venue for concerts. Completed in 1855. The small Concert Hall is an excellent example of early Victorian design, and the highly decorative Great Hall boasts one of the finest concert organs in the UK. Entry by guided tour only.

Owned and managed by Liverpool City Council.

St George's Hall, Liverpool

### NON-MEMBERS

| | |
|---|---|
| Guided Tours (no concessions) | £3.00 |

EH members and up to 6 children within their family group get free entry. Discount does not extend to EH Corporate Partners or members of Cadw and Historic Scotland

### OPENING TIMES

Please call 0151 233 2008

**Direction:** City Centre, adjacent to Lime Street railway station and Queen Street bus station

**Train:** Liverpool Lime Street, adjacent

**Bus:** From surrounding areas

**Tel:** 0151 225 5530

Disabled access (for tours; limited).
Parking (street).

MAP Page 272 (6C)
OS Map 266/275 (ref SJ 349907)

## Salt Museum
Northwich,
Cheshire – CW9 8AB

Discover the people whose lives were shaped by salt and glimpse some of the 14,000 uses of salt.

### ENTRY

| | |
|---|---|
| Adult | £2.50 |
| Concession | £2.00 |
| Child | £1.30 |
| Family (2+2) | £6.00 |

EH members: 1 free entry for every full paying adult (not applicable for group visits)

### OPENING TIMES

| | |
|---|---|
| Tue-Fri | 10am-5pm |
| Sat-Sun | 2pm-5pm |
| Bank holidays and every Monday in August | 10am-5pm |

Salt Museum

**Tel:** 01606 41331

www.saltmuseum.org.uk

MAP Page 272 (6D)
OS Map 267 (ref SJ 658731)

## Smithills Hall
Bolton, Lancashire – BL1 7NP

Grade I-listed manor house, one of the oldest in the north west region.

### ENTRY

| | |
|---|---|
| Adult | £3.00 |
| Concession | £1.75 |

20% discount for EH members

Smithills Hall

### OPENING TIMES

Please call 01204 332377

**Direction:** Signposted from A58

www.boltonmuseums.org.uk

MAP Page 272 (5D)
OS Map 287/276 (ref SD 699119)

## Stretton Watermill
Nr Farndon,
Cheshire – SY14 7RS

Step back in time and visit a working mill in beautiful rural Cheshire. See one of the country's best-preserved demonstration water-powered corn mills.

Stretton Watermill

### ENTRY

| | |
|---|---|
| Adult | £2.00 |
| Child | £0.75 |
| Family (2+2) | £4.75 |

EH members: 1 free entry for every full paying adult

### OPENING TIMES

| | |
|---|---|
| Apr-Sep, Sat & Sun | 1pm-5pm |
| May-Aug, Tue-Sun & Bank Hols | 1pm-5pm |

**Direction:** 10 miles from Chester. Well signposted

**Tel:** 01606 41331

www.strettonwatermill.org.uk

MAP Page 272 (7C)
OS Map 257 (ref SJ 455531)

Detail of prisoners' carving, Carlisle Castle – see page 218

# Hadrian's Wall

'Verily I have seen the tract of it over the high pitches and steep descents of hills, wonderfully rising and falling'

William Camden, *Britannia*, 1607

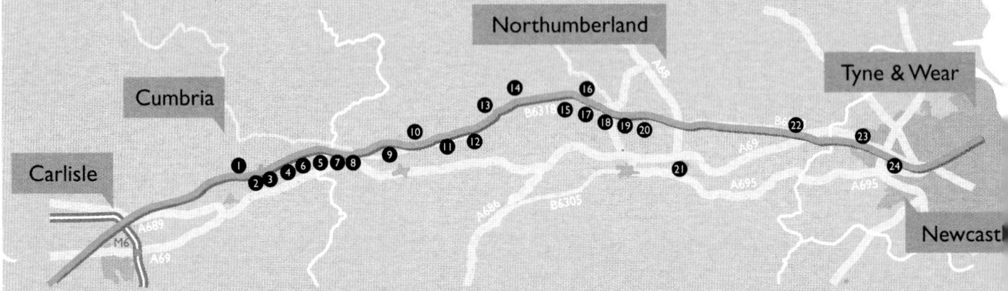


1 Hare Hill
2 Banks East Turret
3 Pike Hill Signal Tower
4 Leahill Turret and Piper Sike Turret
5 Birdoswald Roman Fort
6 Harrow's Scar Milecastle and Wall
7 Willowford Wall, Turrets & Bridge
8 Poltross Burn Milecastle
9 Walltown Crags
10 Cawfields Roman Wall
11 Winshields Wall
12 Vindolanda Fort
13 Housesteads Roman Fort
14 Sewingshields Wall
15 Temple of Mithras
16 Black Carts Turret
17 Chesters Roman Fort
18 Chesters Bridge Abutment
19 Brunton Turret
20 Planetrees Roman Wall
21 Corbridge Roman Town
22 Heddon-on-the-Wall
23 Denton Hall Turret
24 Benwell Roman Temple and Vallum Crossing

www.english-heritage.org.uk/hadrianswall

Above: Hadrian's Wall including (top centre) Chesters Roman Fort, (bottom centre) Cawfields Roman Wall and (right) Birdoswald Roman Fort.



# A Spectacular World Heritage Site

Incomparably the most impressive Roman monument in Britain, Hadrian's Wall was the 'north-west frontier' of the whole Roman Empire. It stretched for some 73 miles from sea to sea, from Wallsend near Newcastle in the east to Bowness-on-Solway in Cumbria in the west. Considerable portions of it still remain to be seen, often amid wild and dramatic countryside.

Begun at the command of the Emperor Hadrian in AD 122, the Wall defined the boundary between the Romanised province of 'Britannia' to the south and the unconquered lands to the north. It remained in service for some two and a half centuries, up until the collapse of Roman rule in Britain in the early 400s.

During this time the Wall underwent several changes, most still traceable in the 24 English Heritage sites along its length. A complex system of defence in depth, its core was the Wall itself, particularly impressive where it traverses rugged country across **Walltown Crags**, **Sewingshields** and **Winshields**.

The eastern half was built in stone, completed to a narrower width than that first conceived, as seen at **Planetrees**. The western part of the Wall was built in turf and replaced in stone some 40 years later.

To the north of the Wall was a defensive ditch, and to the south (as at **Benwell**) ran the vallum ditch and the military way road. At each Roman mile along the Wall stood a milecastle (like **Poltross Burn**), and between each milecastle were two turrets (as at **Willowford**). But the main garrisons of the system – 'auxiliary' cavalry and infantry units originating from all over the Empire – were stationed at the 16 major Wall forts, including **Birdoswald**, **Chesters** and **Housesteads**.

Behind the Wall, serving as a supply-base and 'rest and recreation' centre for these troops, was **Corbridge Roman Town**.

i Help conserve Hadrian's Wall for future generations: please do not walk on the Wall or climb on the forts. This monument is very vulnerable to damage.

# Birdoswald Roman Fort Cumbria – CA8 7DD

Birdoswald stands high above a meander in the River Irthing, in one of the most picturesque settings on Hadrian's Wall. A Roman fort, turret and milecastle can all be seen on this excellent stretch of the Wall.

With probably the best-preserved defences of any Wall fort, this was an important base for some 1,000 Roman soldiers, succeeding an earlier fort of turf and timber. The section of Wall to the east, also of stone replacing turf, is the longest continuous stretch visible today.

Archaeological discoveries over the past 150 years have revealed a great deal about Roman military life at Birdoswald. Three of the four main gateways of the fort have been unearthed, as have the outside walls, two granary buildings, workshops and a unique drill hall.

People continued to live at Birdoswald after the Roman withdrawal. In the 5th century a large timber hall was built over the collapsed Roman granaries, perhaps for a local British chieftain. Later, a medieval tower house was raised here, replaced in the 16th century by a fortified 'bastle' farmhouse designed to protect its inhabitants from the notorious 'Border Reivers'. Later still in more peaceful times, a farmhouse stood there.

The Birdoswald Visitor Centre provides a good introduction to Hadrian's Wall, and tells the intriguing story of Birdoswald and the people who have lived there over the past 2,000 years. There is a cosy tearoom at the site if you need refreshments, and a well-stocked shop for souvenirs.

### Accommodation

If you would like to stay within the walls of the fort, there is a 39 bed residential centre, which can be booked for groups. It provides a great base for exploring this and other sites on the Wall, and is an excellent educational resource.

If you would like to find out more about staying at Birdoswald, please call 01697 747602 for a residential pack.

### NON-MEMBERS

| | |
|---|---|
| Adult | £4.10 |
| Concession | £3.10 |
| Child | £2.10 |

Education charge applies – ring site for details

### OPENING TIMES

| | |
|---|---|
| 1 Apr-30 Sep, daily | 10am-5.30pm (last admission 5pm) |
| 1-31 Oct, daily | 10am-4pm |

### HOW TO FIND US

**Direction:** 2¾ miles west of Greenhead off B6318. Signposted from A69

**Train:** Brampton 8 miles, Haltwhistle 7 miles

**Bus:** Stagecoach in Cumbria AD122 Carlisle – ⇌ Hexham (Jun-Sep plus Suns Apr, May & Oct)

**Tel:** 01697 747602

E OVP

Disabled access (to visitor centre, toilets, shop, tearoom and part of site. Disabled parking on site).

MAP Page 274 (4E)
OS Map 43 (ref NY 615663)

# Chesters Roman Fort Northumberland – NE46 4EU

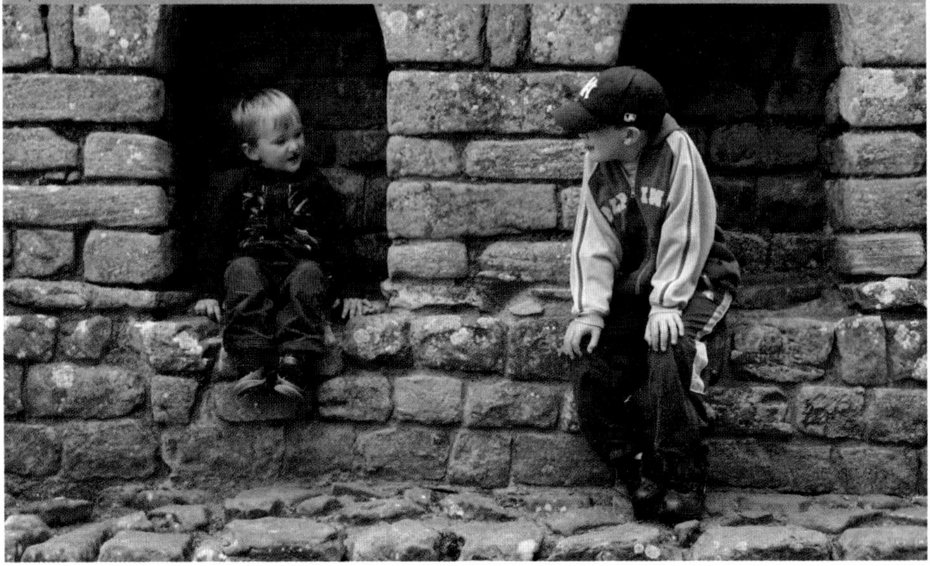



Chesters Fort was built to guard the Roman bridge which carried Hadrian's Wall and the military road over the North River Tyne. It was one of a series of permanent troop bases added during the construction of the Wall.

Occupied for nearly three centuries, its six-acre area housed a cavalry regiment of around 500 men: in the 3rd century its garrison was a unit from Asturias in northern Spain. There is much to see on the ground: all four principal gateways are well preserved, with short lengths of Wall adjoining them. The entire foundations of the headquarters building are visible, with a courtyard, hall, regimental temple and strongroom clearly laid out. The commandant's house is the most luxurious building in the fort.

Down by the river, the changing rooms, steam rooms and bathing areas of the garrison's bath house are extremely well preserved, as is the Roman bridge abutment on the opposite bank of the river.

The on-site museum, housed in a fine Victorian building, displays a collection of Roman finds retrieved by the local antiquarian John Clayton, including important early archaeological discoveries relating to the central section of the Wall.

## NON-MEMBERS

| | |
|---|---|
| Adult | £4.10 |
| Concession | £3.10 |
| Child | £2.10 |

## OPENING TIMES

| | |
|---|---|
| 1 Apr-30 Sep, daily | 9.30am-6pm |
| 1 Oct-20 Mar, daily | 10am-4pm |
| Closed | 24-26 Dec and 1 Jan |

## HOW TO FIND US

**Direction:** ¼ mile W of Chollerford, on B6318

**Train:** Hexham 5½ miles

**Bus:** Stagecoach in Cumbria AD122 Carlise – ⇌ Hexham (Jun-Sep plus Suns Apr, May & Oct); also Tyne Valley/Kimberleys 880/2 from ⇌ Hexham, to within ½ mile

**Tel:** 01434 681379

**Local Tourist Information**
Hexham: 01434 652220

P OVP

Disabled access (companion recommended. Disabled parking and toilets).

Dogs on leads (restricted areas only).

Tearoom (summer only; not managed by EH).

MAP Page 275 (4F)
OS Map 43 (ref NY 912702)

# Housesteads Roman Fort Northumberland – NE47 6NN

Housesteads is the most complete example of a Roman fort in Britain, and one of the most popular sites on the Wall. It stands high on the exposed Whin Sill escarpment, commanding breathtaking views. Like Chesters, it was one of 12 permanent forts added to the new frontier by Hadrian in about AD 124. Known as 'Vercovicium' ('the place of effective fighters' or 'hilly place'), it was garrisoned by a cohort of around 800 infantry (for most of its history Tungrians from Belgium), later reinforced by Germanic cavalry. Entry is through a small museum, displaying a complete model of how Housesteads once appeared. Excavations at the fort have revealed four double-portal gateways, the turreted curtain wall, three visible barrack blocks and of course the famous and well-preserved latrines. At the centre are the most important buildings: the commandant's house, headquarters building and hospital.

The fort lies uphill from the car park (a ten-minute walk).

Owned by The National Trust, in the care of English Heritage.

## NON-MEMBERS

| | |
|---|---|
| Adult | £4.10 |
| Concession | £3.10 |
| Child | £2.10 |

Free entry to NT members

## OPENING TIMES

| | |
|---|---|
| 1 Apr-30 Sep, daily | 10am-6pm |
| 1 Oct-20 Mar, daily | 10am-4pm |
| Closed | 24-26 Dec and 1 Jan |

## HOW TO FIND US

**Direction:** Bardon Mill 4 miles

**Bus:** Stagecoach in Cumbria AD122 Carlise – ≷ Hexham (Jun-Sep plus Suns Apr, May & Oct). Limited winter timetable, please contact Traveline 0870 608 2608

**Tel:** 01434 344363

**Local Tourist Information**
Hexham: 01434 652220

P OVP

Disabled access (companion recommended. Limited access to site. 50 metre walk on steep gradient. Car park at site; enquire at information centre on main road).

Parking (charge payable to National Park).

MAP Page 275 (4F)
OS Map 43 (ref NY 790688)

## Banks East Turret
Cumbria

Imposing and well-preserved turret with adjoining stretches of Hadrian's Wall.

### HOW TO FIND US

**Direction:** On minor road E of Banks village; $3\frac{1}{2}$ miles NE of Brampton

P ♿ ⚠

MAP OS Map 315 (ref NY 575647)

## Benwell Roman Temple
Tyne and Wear

The remains of a small temple to the native god 'Antenociticus', in the 'vicus' (civilian settlement) which stood outside Benwell fort.

### HOW TO FIND US

**Direction:** Temple located immediately S of A69, at Benwell in Broomridge Ave; Vallum Crossing in Denhill Park

**Train:** Newcastle 2 miles

**Bus:** Frequent from centre of Newcastle

MAP OS Map 316 (ref NZ 217647)

## Benwell Vallum Crossing
Tyne and Wear

A stone-built causeway, where the road from the south crossed the Vallum earthwork on its way to Benwell fort.

### HOW TO FIND US

**Direction:** Temple located immediately S of A69, at Benwell in Broomridge Ave; Vallum Crossing in Denhill Park

**Train:** Newcastle 2 miles

**Bus:** Frequent from centre of Newcastle

MAP OS Map 136 (ref NY 884713)

## Birdoswald Roman Fort
See feature – Page 230

## Black Carts Turret
Northumberland

A 460-metre (1,509 feet) length of Hadrian's Wall including one turret.

**Please note:** It is not possible for visitors to park here.

### HOW TO FIND US

**Direction:** 2 miles W of Chollerford on B6318

MAP OS Map 43 (ref NY 884713)

## Brunton Turret
Northumberland

Wall section and a $2\frac{1}{2}$ metre (8.2 feet) high turret, built by men of the Twentieth Legion.

### HOW TO FIND US

**Direction:** $\frac{1}{4}$ mile S of Low Brunton, off A6079

**Train:** Hexham $4\frac{1}{2}$ miles

**Bus:** Stagecoach in Cumbria AD122 Carlise – ⇌ Hexham (Jun-Sep plus Suns Apr, May & Oct); also Tyne Valley/Kimberleys 880/2 from ⇌ Hexham

🐕

MAP OS Map 43 (ref NY 922698)

## Cawfields Roman Wall
Northumberland

A fine stretch of Hadrian's Wall on a steep slope, with turrets and an impressive mile-castle, probably built by the Second Legion.

## Cawfields Roman Wall

### HOW TO FIND US

**Direction:** $1\frac{1}{4}$ miles N of Haltwhistle, off B6318

🚹 🚺 P

MAP OS Map 43 (ref NY 716667)

## Chesters Bridge Abutment
Northumberland

The remains of the bridge which carried Hadrian's Wall across the North Tyne are visible on both banks, but most impressively on the eastern side.

### HOW TO FIND US

**Direction:** $\frac{1}{2}$ mile S of Low Brunton, on A6079

**Train:** Hexham $4\frac{1}{2}$ miles

**Bus:** Stagecoach in Cumbria AD122 Carlise – ⇌ Hexham (Jun-Sep plus Suns Apr, May & Oct); also Tyne Valley/Kimberleys 880/2 from ⇌ Hexham, to within $\frac{1}{2}$ mile

MAP OS Map 43 (ref NY 914701)

## Chesters Roman Fort
See feature – Page 232

## Corbridge Roman Town
Northumberland – NE45 5NT

On the pivotal intersection of Roman Dere Street and Stanegate near the Tyne crossing, Corbridge played a vital role in every Roman campaign in northern Britain. The first forts here were founded c. AD 79-85 during the campaigns into Scotland under Agricola; the third in association with Hadrian's Wall; the last used during the campaigns of Antoninus Pius in the mid-2nd century. Corbridge then became a busy garrison town.

The extensively excavated remains include a fountain house with an aqueduct, a pair of granaries, and walled military compounds containing barracks, temples, houses and a headquarters building with a below-ground strongroom. You can even walk on the original Stanegate Roman road, which predated Hadrian's Wall and passes through the centre of the site.

The museum displays a rich selection of Roman finds, and has extensive schools handling collections of real and replica Roman objects, including armour. An audio tour is provided to guide you around the site.

### NON-MEMBERS

| | |
|---|---|
| Adult | £4.10 |
| Concession | £3.10 |
| Child | £2.10 |

### OPENING TIMES

| | |
|---|---|
| 1 Apr-30 Sep, daily | 10am-5.30 pm (last admission 5pm) |
| 1-31 Oct, daily | 10am-4pm |
| 1 Nov-20 Mar, Sat-Sun | 10am-4pm |
| Closed | 24-26 Dec and 1 Jan |

### HOW TO FIND US

**Direction:** ½ mile NW of Corbridge, on minor road, then signposted

**Train:** Corbridge 1¼ miles

**Bus:** Arriva Northumbria/ Stagecoach in Cumbria 602, 685 Newcastle-upon-Tyne – Hexham, to within ½ mile

**Tel:** 01434 632349

**Local Tourist Information**
01434 652220

OVP

Dogs on leads (restricted areas only).

Disabled access (parking, toilet, audio tour, access to the museum and perimeter of site).

MAP Page 275 (4F)
OS Map 43 (ref NY 982648)

## Denton Hall Turret
Tyne and Wear

The foundations of a turret and a 65-metre (213 feet) length of Wall.

### HOW TO FIND US

**Direction:** 4 miles W of Newcastle upon Tyne city centre, on A69

**Train:** Blaydon 2 miles

**Bus:** Frequent from centre of Newcastle

MAP OS Map 316 (ref NZ 198655)

## Hare Hill
Cumbria

A short length of Wall, still standing 2.7 metres (8.8 feet) high.

### HOW TO FIND US

**Direction:** ¾ mile NE of Lanercost

MAP OS Map 43 (ref NY 564646)

## Harrow's Scar Milecastle and Wall
Cumbria

A mile-long section of the Wall, rebuilt in stone later in Hadrian's reign. It is linked to Birdoswald Roman Fort.

### HOW TO FIND US

**Direction:** ¼ mile E of Birdoswald, on minor road off B6318

P (wheelchair access)

Parking at Birdoswald Roman Fort

MAP OS Map 43 (ref NY 620664)

## Heddon-on-the-Wall
Northumberland

A consolidated stretch of Wall, up to 2 metres (6½ feet) thick in places.

### HOW TO FIND US

**Direction:** Immediately E of Heddon village; S of A69

**Train:** Wylam 3 miles

**Bus:** Go-Northern 684, Arriva Northumbria 685 from Newcastle upon Tyne

MAP OS Map 316 (ref NZ 137669)

## Housesteads Roman Fort
See feature – Page 233

## Leahill Turret and Piper Sike Turret
Cumbria

Turrets west of Birdoswald: Piper Sike has a cooking-hearth.

### HOW TO FIND US

**Direction:** On minor road 2 miles W of Birdoswald Fort

MAP OS Map 43/315 (ref NY 586652)

## Pike Hill Signal Tower
Cumbria

The remains of one of a network of signal towers predating Hadrian's Wall, Pike Hill was later joined to the Wall at an angle of 45 degrees.

### HOW TO FIND US

**Direction:** On minor road E of Banks village

P

MAP OS Map 315 (ref NY 577648)

## Planetrees Roman Wall
Northumberland

A 15-metre (49 feet) length of later narrow Wall on earlier broad foundations, marking the junction between the two wall types.

### HOW TO FIND US

**Direction:** 1 mile SE of Chollerford on B6318

**Train:** Hexham 5½ miles

**Bus:** Stagecoach in Cumbria AD122 Carlise – Hexham (Jun-Sep plus Suns Apr, May & Oct); also Tyne Valley/Kimberleys 880/2 from Hexham, to within ¾ mile

MAP OS Map 43 (ref NY 929696)

## Poltross Burn Milecastle
Cumbria

One of the best preserved milecastles on Hadrian's Wall, Poltross includes an oven, a stair to the rampart walk, and the remains of its north gateway.

### HOW TO FIND US

**Direction:** On minor road E of Banks village. Immediately SW of Gilsland village, by old railway station

P

Parking (near the Station Hotel).

MAP OS Map 43 (ref NY 634662)

## Sewingshields Wall
Northumberland

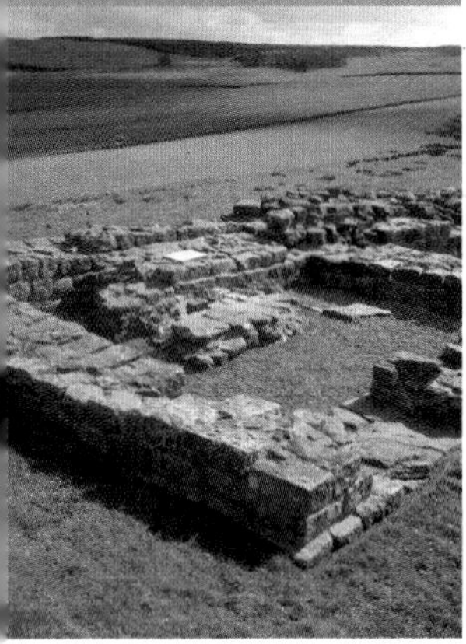

A length of Wall with milecastle remains, impressively sited along the Whin Sill, commanding fine views of many prehistoric and later earthworks to the north.

### HOW TO FIND US

**Direction:** N of B6318; 1½ miles E of Housesteads Fort

**MAP** OS Map 43 (ref NY 805702)

## Temple of Mithras, Carrawburgh
Northumberland

A fascinating temple near Carrawburgh fort to the god beloved by Roman soldiers, with facsimiles of altars found during excavation. Sited like many Mithraic temples near a military base, it was founded in the 3rd century, and eventually desecrated, probably by Christians. Nearby was the still more popular well shrine of the water-nymph Coventina.

### HOW TO FIND US

**Direction:** 3¾ miles W of Chollerford, on B6318. 1 mile NE of Greenhead, off B6318

P

**MAP** OS Map 43 (ref NY 859711)

## Vindolanda Fort
Northumberland

An extensively excavated fort and much-studied civilian settlement.

Owned and managed by Vindolanda Charitable Trust.

### ENTRY

| | |
|---|---|
| Adult | £4.95 |
| Concession | £4.10 |
| Child | £3.00 |
| Family | £14.00 |

10% discount for EH members

### OPENING TIMES

| | |
|---|---|
| 12 Feb-31 Mar, daily | 10am-5pm |
| 1 Apr-30 Sep, daily | 10am-6pm |
| 1 Oct-13 Nov, daily | 10am-5pm |

See website for winter opening

### HOW TO FIND US

**Direction:** 1¼ miles SE of Twice Brewed; on minor road off B6318

**Train:** Bardon Mill 2 miles

**Bus:** Stagecoach in Cumbria AD122 Carlise - ⇌ Hexham (Jun-Sep plus Suns Apr, May & Oct)

**Tel:** 01434 344277

www.vindolanda.com

**MAP** OS Map 43 (ref NY 771664)

## Walltown Crags
Northumberland

## Walltown Crags

One of the best places of all to see the Wall, dramatically snaking and diving along the crags of the Whin Sill.

### HOW TO FIND US

**Direction:** 1 mile NE of Greenhead, off B6318

**MAP** OS Map 43 (ref NY 674663)

## Willowford Wall, Turrets and Bridge
Cumbria

A fine 914 metre (2,999 feet) stretch of Wall, including two turrets and impressive bridge remains beside the River Irthing.

### HOW TO FIND US

**Direction:** W of minor road, ¾ mile W of Gilsland

♿

**MAP** OS Map 43 (ref NY 627664)

## Winshields Wall
Northumberland

The highest point on the Wall, in rugged country with spectacular views.

### HOW TO FIND US

**Direction:** W of Steel Rigg car park; on minor road off B6318

**MAP** OS Map 43 (ref NY 742676)

Tynemouth Priory and Castle – see page 253

# North East

'In these north parts, men say commonly they will have no Prince but a Percy'

Letter to Queen Elizabeth I, 1569

www.english-heritage.org.uk/northeast

# Properties See individual listings for details

### Durham
Auckland Castle Deer House
Barnard Castle
Bowes Castle
Derwentcote Steel Furnace
Egglestone Abbey
Finchale Priory

### Northumberland
Aydon Castle
Belsay Hall, Castle and Gardens
Berwick-upon-Tweed Barracks
Berwick-upon-Tweed Castle
Berwick-upon-Tweed Main Guard
Berwick-upon-Tweed Ramparts
Black Middens Bastle House
Brinkburn Priory
Dunstanburgh Castle
Edlingham Castle
Etal Castle
Lindisfarne Priory
Norham Castle
Prudhoe Castle
Warkworth Castle and Hermitage

### Redcar and Cleveland
Gisborough Priory

### Tyne and Wear
Bessie Surtees House
Hylton Castle
St Paul's Monastery
Tynemouth Priory and Castle

### Hadrian's Wall
See page 228

Comprehensive map of our sites Page 275

Above: (top left to right) Lindisfarne Priory, Tynemouth Priory and Castle, Belsay Hall, Castle and Gardens, (bottom left to right) Dunstanburgh Castle, Viking Stone at Lindisfarne Priory and (right) Finchale Priory.



# A Long Way From London

Before the advent of modern transport, the counties which make up English Heritage's North East region were a very long way from London both in time and spirit. Even galloping non-stop on relays of horses, the messenger carrying the news of Queen Elizabeth's death in 1603 took two days and a night to reach Northumberland. The area's remoteness and dangerous proximity to the Scots border meant that the monarchs of England must exercise power here by deputy. Thus the Bishops of Durham enjoyed quasi-royal rights in their 'County Palatine of Durham', while further north the 'wardenships of the Marches' (or borderlands) were frequently held by one or other of the great noble families of Percy and Neville.

The drawback was that these northern magnates did not always agree, either with each other or with the London government. So though the history of English Heritage's north-eastern castles often includes warfare with Scots invaders, there were also times when they were disputed between rival English forces. Between 1462 and 1464, during the Wars of the Roses, **Norham Castle** began in Yorkist hands, was unsuccessfully besieged by Lancastrians and Scots, and then betrayed to the Lancastrians before being retaken by the Yorkists. **Dunstanburgh Castle** changed hands three times before finally succumbing to the threat of the Yorkist 'great guns named Newcastle, London, Dijon the Brazen Gun and Richard the Bombard': and the great Percy stronghold of **Warkworth Castle** suffered the indignity of becoming the headquarters of their Neville rivals.

Nor did warfare between Englishman and Englishman end with the coming of the Tudors. In 1569, for once united in their support for Catholicism and Mary Queen of Scots, the Percy Earl of Northumberland and the Neville Earl of Westmoreland rose against Queen Elizabeth. Warkworth Castle and **Barnard Castle** (after a siege) were both garrisoned by the rebels, before the bloody suppression of the rising by royal forces. Thereafter the Percies never really recovered their princely power: but their memory remains not only at Warkworth and the much-disputed **Prudhoe Castle** (wherein they built a fine new mansion in the early 19th-century), but also in their exquisite little chantry chapel at **Tynemouth Priory and Castle**. The future lay not with castles but with the new-style bastioned artillery fortifications, of which much the finest examples in England are **Berwick-upon Tweed Castle and Ramparts**.

## Auckland Castle Deer House
Durham

A charming Gothic Revival 'eyecatcher' built in 1760 in the park of the Bishops of Durham. It provided deer with shelter and food, and had grounds for picnics and rooms for enjoying the view.

Managed by the Church Commissioners for England.

### OPENING TIMES

**House as per park opening times**

| | |
|---|---|
| 1 Apr-30 Sep, daily | 10am-6pm |
| 1 Oct-20 Mar, daily | 10am-4pm |
| Closed | 24-26 Dec and 1 Jan |

### HOW TO FIND US

**Direction:** Located in Auckland Park, Bishop Auckland; N of town centre on A68

**Train:** Bishop Auckland 1 mile

MAP Page 275 (5G)
OS Map 305 (ref NZ 216304)

## Aydon Castle
Northumberland – NE45 5PJ

One of the finest and most unaltered examples of a 13th-century English manor house, Aydon Castle stands in a secluded woodland setting. It was originally built as an undefended residence, but almost immediately fortified on the outbreak of Anglo-Scottish warfare. Nevertheless it was pillaged and burnt by the Scots

Aydon Castle

in 1315, seized by English rebels two years later, and again occupied by Scots in 1346. In the 18th century Aydon became a farmhouse, remaining so until 1966.

### NON-MEMBERS

| | |
|---|---|
| Adult | £3.50 |
| Concession | £2.60 |
| Child | £1.80 |

### OPENING TIMES

| | |
|---|---|
| 1 Apr-30 Sep, Thu-Mon | 10am-5pm |

### HOW TO FIND US

**Direction:** 1 mile NE of Corbridge, on minor road off B6321 or A68

**Train:** Corbridge 4 miles – approach via bridle path from W side of Aydon Rd, immediately N of Corbridge bypass

Tel: 01434 632450

OVP

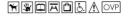

Disabled access (ground floor only).

Dogs on leads (restricted areas only).

MAP Page 275 (4F)
OS Map 316 (ref NZ 001663)

## Barnard Castle
Durham

Set on a high rock above the River Tees, imposing Barnard Castle was the stronghold of the Balliol family. Taking its name from Bernard de Balliol, who rebuilt it in the 12th century,

Barnard Castle

it includes a fine great hall and a dominating round-towered keep. Unsuccessfully besieged by the Scots in 1216, it was confiscated when John de Balliol, briefly King of Scotland, was deposed by Edward I. It last saw action during the Northern Rising against Queen Elizabeth in 1569, surrendering to 5,000 rebels, and was partly dismantled in 1630 to furnish materials for Sir Henry Vane's new Raby Castle.

### NON-MEMBERS

| | |
|---|---|
| Adult | £4.00 |
| Concession | £3.00 |
| Child | £2.00 |

### OPENING TIMES

| | |
|---|---|
| 1 Apr-30 Sep, daily | 10am-6pm |
| 1-31 Oct, daily | 10am-4pm |
| 1 Nov-20 Mar, Thu-Mon | 10am-4pm |
| Closed | 24-26 Dec and 1 Jan |

### HOW TO FIND US

**Direction:** In Barnard Castle town

**Bus:** Arriva 75/6 Darlington – Barnard Castle (passes close to Darlington)

**Tel:** 01833 638212

OVP

MAP Page 275 (6G)
OS Map 31 (ref NZ 049165)

## Belsay Hall, Castle and Gardens
See feature – Page 244

## Berwick-upon-Tweed Barracks and Main Guard
Northumberland – TD15 1DF

Berwick Barracks, among the first in England to be purpose-built, were begun in 1717 to the design of the distinguished architect Nicholas Hawksmoor. Today the Barracks hosts a number of attractions, including 'By Beat of Drum' – an exhibition on the life of the British infantryman. While there, visit the King's Own Scottish Borderers Museum, the Contemporary Art Gallery and the Berwick Borough Museum.

The Main Guard is a Georgian Guard House near the quay: it displays 'The Story of a Border Garrison Town' exhibition.

The Main Guard is managed by Berwick Civic Society.

### NON-MEMBERS

**Barracks**

| | |
|---|---|
| Adult | £3.40 |
| Concession | £2.60 |
| Child | £1.70 |

### OPENING TIMES

**Barracks**

| | |
|---|---|
| 1 Apr-30 Sep, daily | 10am-5pm |
| 1-31 Oct, daily | 10am-4pm |
| 1 Nov-20 Mar | Call site for details |
| Closed | 24-26 Dec and 1 Jan |

**Main Guard**

Tel: 01289 330 430 for details

## Berwick-upon-Tweed Barracks and Main Guard

### HOW TO FIND US

**Direction:** On the Parade, off Church St in town centre

**Train:** Berwick-upon-Tweed ¼ mile

**Bus:** From surrounding areas

**Tel:** 01289 304493

OVP

Disabled access (Main Guard).

Dogs on leads (restricted areas only).

Parking (in town).

**MAP Page 275 (1F) OS Map 346 (Barracks ref NU 001531, Main Guard ref NU 000525)**

## Berwick-upon-Tweed Castle and Ramparts
Northumberland – TD15 1DF

The remains of a medieval castle crucial to Anglo-Scottish warfare, superseded by the most complete and breathtakingly impressive bastioned town defences in England, mainly Elizabethan but updated in the 17th and 18th centuries. Surrounding the whole historic town, their entire circuit can be walked.

### OPENING TIMES

Any reasonable time

### HOW TO FIND US

**Direction:** The castle is adjacent to Berwick-upon-Tweed railway station. The ramparts surround the town (accessed at various points)

**Train:** Berwick-upon-Tweed, adjacent

**Bus:** From surrounding areas

Disabled access (Ramparts). Parking (Ramparts).

**Note:** Steep hidden drops. Dangerous after dark.

**MAP Page 275 (1F) OS Map 346 (ref NT 993534)**

## Bessie Surtees House
Tyne and Wear – NE1 3JF

These two five-storey 16th and 17th-century merchants' houses are fine examples of Jacobean domestic architecture, with some splendid period interiors. The Surtees house is best known as the scene of the elopement of Bessie with John Scott, later Lord Chancellor of England. An exhibition illustrating the history of the houses is on the first floor.

### OPENING TIMES

| | |
|---|---|
| All year round, Mon-Fri | 10am-4pm |
| Closed | Bank Hols and 24 Dec-3 Jan |

### HOW TO FIND US

**Direction:** 41-44 Sandhill, Newcastle upon Tyne

**Train:** Newcastle ½ mile

**Metro:** Central ½ mile

**Bus:** From surrounding areas

**Tel:** 0191 269 1200

**MAP Page 275 (4G) OS Map 88 (ref NZ 2563NW)**

## Bishop Auckland Deer House
See Auckland Castle Deer House – Page 242

# Belsay Hall, Castle and Gardens

Northumberland – NE20 0DX

Belsay has something for everyone. A fine medieval castle, enlarged into a mansion in the 17th century; the imposing Greek Revival villa which was built later; and the outstanding, plant-rich gardens linking the two buildings.

Belsay Castle

The whole ensemble is the creation of the Middleton family, over more than seven centuries. First came the castle, still dominated by its massive 14th-century 'peel tower', one of the best surviving examples in England. Though built as a refuge at a time of endemic Anglo-Scottish warfare, it was also designed to impress: its first-floor great chamber still displays rare traces of elaborate medieval wall-paintings.

Following the coming of peace under James I, a column-entranced mansion wing was added to the castle in 1614: here the family lived until Christmas Day 1817, when they moved into Belsay Hall.

Belsay Hall, now displayed without furnishings, revealing the fine craftsmanship of its construction, is an austerely Classical Greek Revival villa. Begun in 1807, it was designed by Sir Charles Monck (formerly Middleton), a man inspired by Ancient Greece, and the buildings he had seen on his honeymoon in Athens, particularly the Temple of Theseus. It had nevertheless a comfortable and up-to-date interior, arranged round its amazing central two-storey 'Pillar Hall.'

The vast gardens which provide a magnificent setting for castle and hall are also largely the work of Sir Charles Monck. His rugged and romantic Quarry Garden, created where stone was cut for his hall, has ravines, pinnacles and sheer rock faces inspired by the quarries of Sicily. His grandson Sir Arthur Middleton, likewise a pioneering plantsman, further embellished the Quarry with a wider range of exotic species, as well as adding the Winter Garden, Yew Garden, and Magnolia Terrace.

Level paths and short grass make the gardens suitable for wheelchairs, and there are plenty of seats.

NEW FOR 2007

A major new contemporary arts exhibition, called **Picture House – Film, Art and Design at Belsay**, will open to the public at the beginning of May. Artists and designers will interpret the space at Belsay and fill the property with their dazzling creations.

Belsay Hall

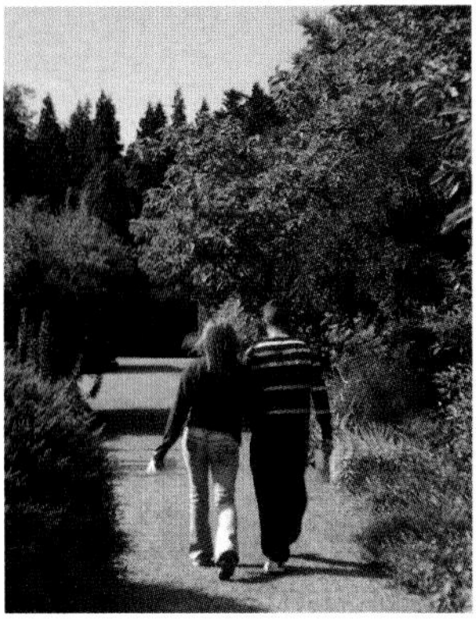

www.english-heritage.org.uk/belsayhall

## NON-MEMBERS

| | |
|---|---|
| Adult | £6.10 |
| Concession | £4.60 |
| Child | £3.10 |
| Family | £15.30 |

Different prices apply for Picture House exhibition, please see website for details.

## OPENING TIMES

| | |
|---|---|
| 1 Apr-30 Sep, daily | 10am-5pm |
| 1-31 Oct, daily | 10am-4pm |
| 1 Nov-20 Mar, Thu-Mon | 10am-4pm |
| Closed | 24-26 Dec and 1 Jan |

## HOW TO FIND US

**Direction:** In Belsay; 14 miles NW of Newcastle, on A696

**Train:** Morpeth 10 miles

**Bus:** Snaith's 808 from Newcastle; Munro's 131 Newcastle-Jedburgh

**Tel:** 01661 881636

**Local Tourist Information**
Morpeth: 01670 500700

E OVP

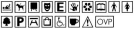

Disabled access (grounds, tea room and ground floor only; toilets).

Dogs on leads (restricted areas only).

Tearooms open daily Apr-Oct, Sat-Sun in Mar).

MAP Page 275 (3G)
OS Map 316 (ref NZ 086785)

## Black Middens Bastle House
Northumberland

A fortified farmhouse with thick stone walls, of a type distinctive to the troubled 16th-century Anglo-Scottish borders. The living quarters were only accessible at first floor level. Set in splendid walking country, on the Reivers Route cycle trail.

### OPENING TIMES
Any reasonable time

### HOW TO FIND US
**Direction:** 180 metres N of minor road, 7 miles NW of Bellingham; or along a minor road from A68

MAP Page 275 (3F)
OS Map 42 (ref NY 773900)

## Bowes Castle
Durham

The massive ruins of Henry II's 12th-century tower keep, set within the earthworks of a Roman fort guarding the strategic Stainmore pass over the Pennines.

### OPENING TIMES
Any reasonable time

### HOW TO FIND US
**Direction:** In Bowes Village off A66; 4 miles W of Barnard Castle town

**Bus:** Hodgson's 72, 574 from Barnard Castle

MAP Page 275 (6F)
OS Map 30/31 (ref NY 992135)

## Brinkburn Priory
Northumberland – NE65 8AR

The beautiful 12th-century church of the Augustinian priory of Brinkburn survives completely roofed and restored. Picturesquely set by a bend in the River Coquet, it is reached by a scenic 10-minute walk from the car park. Parts of the monastic buildings are incorporated into the elegant adjacent manor house.

### NON-MEMBERS

| | |
|---|---|
| Adult | £2.90 |
| Concession | £2.20 |
| Child | £1.50 |

### OPENING TIMES
1 Apr-30 Sep, Thu-Mon 10am-5pm

### HOW TO FIND US
**Direction:** 4½ miles SE of Rothbury, off B6344

**Train:** Acklington 10 miles

**Bus:** Arriva 146 Northumbria Coaches 516 Newcastle – Thropton (passing Morpeth) some from Morpeth with connections from Newcastle (passing Tyne & Wear Metro Haymarket) to within ½ mile.

**Tel:** 01665 570628

OVP

Picnic area (⅓ mile).

MAP Page 275 (3G)
OS Map 325 (ref NZ 116983)

## Derwentcote Steel Furnace
Durham

Built in the 1720s, Derwentcote is the earliest and most complete steel-making furnace in Britain. It produced high-grade steel for springs and cutting tools.

### OPENING TIMES
Please call for details

### HOW TO FIND US
**Direction:** 10 miles SW of Newcastle, on A694; between Rowland's Gill and Hamsterley

**Train:** Metro Centre, Gateshead, 7 miles

**Bus:** Go North East 45/6 Newcastle – Consett

**Tel:** 0191 269 1200 (Mon-Fri)

Dogs on leads (restricted areas only).

MAP Page 275 (4G)
OS Map 307 (ref NZ 130566)

## Dunstanburgh Castle
Northumberland – NE66 3TT

Dramatic Dunstanburgh Castle was built at a time when relations between King Edward II and his most powerful baron, Earl Thomas of Lancaster, had become openly hostile. Lancaster began the fortress in 1313, and

## Dunstanburgh Castle

the latest archaeological research carried out by English Heritage indicates that he built it on a far grander scale than was hitherto recognised, perhaps more as a symbol of his opposition to the king than as a military stronghold. The innovative gatehouse, for instance, competed with the new royal castles in Wales.

The earl failed to reach Dunstanburgh when his rebellion was defeated, being taken and executed in 1322. Thereafter the castle passed eventually to John of Gaunt, who strengthened it against the Scots by converting the great twin towered gatehouse into a keep. The focus of fierce fighting during the Wars of the Roses, it was twice besieged and captured by Yorkist forces, but subsequently fell into decay. Its impressive ruins now watch over a headland famous for seabirds.

Owned by The National Trust, maintained and managed by EH. Free to NT members.

### NON-MEMBERS

| | |
|---|---|
| Adult | £2.90 |
| Concession | £2.20 |
| Child | £1.50 |

### OPENING TIMES

| | |
|---|---|
| 1 Apr-30 Sep, daily | 10am-5pm |
| 1-31 Oct, daily | 10am-4pm |
| 1 Nov-20 Mar, Thu-Mon | 10am-4pm |

### HOW TO FIND US

**Direction:** 8 miles NE of Alnwick; on footpaths from Craster or Embleton – 1½ miles flat coastal walk

**Train:** Chathill (U), not Sun, 5 miles from Embleton, 7 miles from Castle; Alnmouth, 7 miles from Craster, 8¼ miles from Castle

## Dunstanburgh Castle

**Bus:** Arriva 401, 501 Alnwick – Belford with connections from Berwick-upon-Tweed and Newcastle (passing Metro Haymarket); alight Craster, 1½ miles

**Tel:** 01665 576231

OVP

Parking (in Craster village; approx 1½ miles walk. A charge is payable).

Nearest toilets located in Craster.

New guidebook.

MAP Page 275 (2G)
OS Map 332 (ref NU 257219)

## Edlingham Castle
Northumberland

The riverside ruins, principally the solar tower, of a manor house progressively fortified against the Scots during the 14th century.

Managed by the Parochial Church Council of St John the Baptist, Edlingham, with Bolton Chapel.

### OPENING TIMES

Any reasonable time

### HOW TO FIND US

**Direction:** At E end of Edlingham village, on minor road off B6341; 6 miles SW of Alnwick

**Train:** Alnmouth 9 miles

Note: waterproof footwear is recommended.

MAP Page 275 (2G)
OS Map 332 (ref NU 116092)

## Egglestone Abbey
Durham

The charming ruins of a small monastery of Premonstratensian 'white canons', picturesquely set above a bend in the River Tees near Barnard Castle. Remains include much of the 13th-century church and a range of living quarters, with traces of their ingenious toilet drainage system.

### OPENING TIMES

| | |
|---|---|
| Daily | 10am-6pm |

### HOW TO FIND US

**Direction:** 1 mile S of Barnard Castle, on a minor road off B6277

**Bus:** Arriva 79 Richmond – Barnard Castle; 75/6 Darlington – Barnard Castle (passes close to Darlington), then 1½ miles

MAP Page 275 (6G)
OS Map 31 (ref NZ 062151)

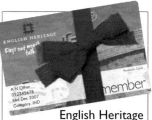

## Etal Castle
Northumberland – TD12 4TN

Etal was built in the mid-14th century by Robert Manners as a defence against Scots raiders, in a strategic position by a ford over the River Till. It fell to James IV's invading Scots army in 1513, immediately before their catastrophic defeat at nearby Flodden. An award-winning exhibition tells the story of Flodden, and the Anglo-Scottish border warfare which ended with the accession of James I in 1603.

### NON-MEMBERS

| | |
|---|---|
| Adult | £3.50 |
| Concession | £2.60 |
| Child | £1.80 |
| Family | £8.80 |

### OPENING TIMES

| | |
|---|---|
| 1 Apr-30 Sep, daily | 11am-4pm |

### HOW TO FIND US

**Direction:** In Etal village, 10 miles SW of Berwick

**Train:** Berwick-upon-Tweed 10½ miles

**Bus:** Border Villager 267 Berwick-upon-Tweed – Wooler

**Tel:** 01890 820332

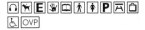

Audio (the audio tour guides visitors around the castle and the exhibition). Dogs on leads (restricted areas only). Toilets (in village).

MAP Page 275 (1F)
OS Map 339 (ref NT 925393)



## Finchale Priory
Durham – DH9 5SH

The very extensive remains of a 13th-century priory, founded on the site of a retired pirate's hermitage. Part of it later served as a holiday retreat for the monks of Durham Cathedral. Beautifully sited by the River Wear, it can be reached from Durham via a delightful riverside and woodland walk.

### NON-MEMBERS

| | |
|---|---|
| Adult | £2.50 |
| Concession | £1.90 |
| Child | £1.30 |

### OPENING TIMES

Please call for details
Tel: 01913 866 528

### HOW TO FIND US

**Direction:** 3 miles NE of Durham; on minor road off A167

**Train:** Durham 5 miles

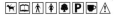

Parking (on south side of river; charge applicable).

Tearoom (not managed by EH).

MAP Page 275 (4G)
OS Map 308 (ref NZ 296471)

## Gisborough Priory
Redcar and Cleveland

The ruins of an Augustinian priory founded by the Bruce family, afterwards Kings of Scotland. They are dominated by the dramatic skeleton of the 14th-century church's east end.

Managed by Redcar and Cleveland Borough Council.

### NON-MEMBERS

| | |
|---|---|
| Adult | £1.10 |
| Concession | £0.75 |
| Child | £0.55 |

### OPENING TIMES

| | |
|---|---|
| 1 Apr-30 Sep, Tue-Sun | 9am-5pm |
| 1 Oct-20 Mar, Wed-Sun | 9am-5pm |
| Closed | 24 Dec-1 Jan |

### HOW TO FIND US

**Direction:** In Guisborough town, next to the parish church

**Train:** Marske 4½ miles

**Bus:** Arriva X56, 65, 93, 765 from Middlesbrough (passes close to Middlesbrough)

**Tel:** 01287 633801

Toilets (in town).

MAP Page 275 (6H)
OS Map 26/306 (ref NZ 617160)

## Hadrian's Wall
See page 228

## Hylton Castle
Tyne and Wear

The distinctive and highly decorative gatehouse-tower of a castle built by the wealthy Sir William Hylton, shortly before 1400. Originally containing four floors of self-contained family accommodation, its entrance front displays royal and family heraldry, including Richard II's white hart badge.

Managed by Sunderland City Council.

### OPENING TIMES
**Any reasonable time (grounds only)**

### HOW TO FIND US
**Direction:** 3¾ miles W of Sunderland

**Train:** Seaburn 2½ miles

**Bus:** From surrounding areas

Disabled access (grounds only).

Parking (in town centre).

**MAP Page 275 (4H)**
**OS Map 308 (ref NZ 358588)**

## Lindisfarne Priory
See feature – Page 250

## Norham Castle
Northumberland – TD15 2JY

Commanding a vital ford over the River Tweed, Norham was one of the strongest of the border castles, and the most often attacked by the Scots. Besieged at least 13 times – once for nearly a year by Robert Bruce – it was called 'the most dangerous and adventurous place in the country'. But even its powerful 12th-century keep and massive towered bailey walls could not resist James IV's heavy cannon, and it fell to him in 1513, shortly before his defeat at Flodden. The extensive 16th-century rebuilding which followed, adapting the fortress for its own artillery, is still clearly traceable.

### NON-MEMBERS

| | |
|---|---|
| Adult | £2.90 |
| Concession | £2.20 |
| Child | £1.50 |

### OPENING TIMES
**Admission limited. Please call 01289 304493 for details**

### HOW TO FIND US
**Direction:** In Norham village; 6 miles SW of Berwick-upon-Tweed, on minor road off B6470 (from A698)

**Train:** Berwick-upon-Tweed 7½ miles

**Bus:** Travelsure/Munro 23 Berwick-upon-Tweed – Kelso

Disabled access (excluding keep).

**MAP Page 275 (1F)**
**OS Map 339 (ref NT 906476)**

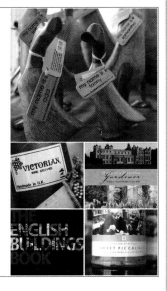

# Lindisfarne Priory Northumberland – TD15 2RX

Lindisfarne Priory on Holy Island was one of the most important centres of early Christianity in Anglo-Saxon England. It is still a place of pilgrimage today, the dramatic approach across the causeway adding to the fascination of the site.

The West Front

Viking stone, 9th century grave

St Aidan founded the monastery in AD 635, but St Cuthbert, Prior of Lindisfarne, is the most celebrated of the priory's holy men. After many missionary journeys, and 10 years as a hermit on lonely Farne Island, he reluctantly became Bishop before retiring to die on Farne in 687. Buried in the priory, his remains were transferred to a pilgrim shrine there after 11 years, and found still undecayed – a sure sign of sanctity.

From the end of the 8th century, the isolated island with its rich monastery was easy prey for Viking raiders. In 875 the monks left, carrying Cuthbert's remains, which after long wanderings were enshrined in Durham Cathedral in 1104, where they still rest. Only after that time did Durham monks re-establish a priory on Lindisfarne: the evocative ruins of the richly decorated priory church they built in c. 1150 still stand, with their famous 'rainbow arch' – a vault-rib of the now-vanished crossing tower. The small community lived quietly on Holy Island until the suppression of the monastery in 1537.

The museum has been refurbished, offering a clear and lively interpretation of the story of St Cuthbert and the development of Lindisfarne Priory.

View of West Front and surroundings

The causeway floods at high tide, so it is very important to check the tide times before crossing.

**www.english-heritage.org.uk/lindisfarnepriory**



## NON-MEMBERS

| | |
|---|---|
| Adult | £3.90 |
| Concession | £2.90 |
| Child | £2.00 |

## OPENING TIMES

| | |
|---|---|
| 1 Apr-30 Sep, daily | 9.30am-5pm |
| 1-31 Oct, daily | 9.30am-4pm |
| 1 Nov-31 Jan, Sat-Mon | 10am-2pm |
| 1 Feb-20 Mar, daily | 10am-4pm |
| Closed | 24-26 Dec and 1 Jan |

## HOW TO FIND US

**Direction:** On Holy Island, only reached at low tide across causeway; tide tables at each end, or details from tourist info

**Train:** Berwick-upon-Tweed 14 miles, via causeway

**Bus:** Travelsure 477 from Berwick-upon-Tweed (passes close to ⇄ Berwick-upon-Tweed); times vary with tides

**Tel:** 01289 389200

**Tourist Information Centre**
01289 330733

OVP

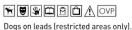

Dogs on leads (restricted areas only).

**MAP Page 275 (1G)**
**OS Map 340 (ref NU 126417)**

## Prudhoe Castle
Northumberland – NE42 6NA

Begun between 1100 and 1120 to defend a strategic crossing of the River Tyne against Scottish invaders, Prudhoe Castle has been continuously occupied for over nine centuries. After two sieges during the 1170s – the Scots attackers reportedly declaring 'as long as Prudhoe stands, we shall never have peace' – the mighty stone keep and a great hall were added, followed in about 1300 by two strong towers. Passing from its original Umfraville owners to the powerful Percies in 1398, it was again updated with a fashionable new great hall.

### Prudhoe Castle

Even after its last military action against the Scots in 1640, Prudhoe's importance as the centre of a great landed estate continued. Early in the 19th century the Percies restored it, building a fine new manor house within its walls. All these developments are now vividly interpreted in a family-friendly exhibition including site finds, helping visitors to explore and understand the extensive remains of this formidable and long-lived fortress.

### NON-MEMBERS

| | |
|---|---|
| Adult | £3.50 |
| Concession | £2.60 |
| Child | £1.80 |

### OPENING TIMES

1 Apr-30 Sep, Thu-Mon 10am-5pm

### HOW TO FIND US

**Direction:** In Prudhoe, on minor road off A695

**Train:** Prudhoe ¼ mile

**Bus:** From surrounding areas

**Tel:** 01661 833459

OVP

Dogs on leads (restricted areas only).

MAP Page 275 (4G)
OS Map 316 (ref NZ 091634)

## St Paul's Monastery, Jarrow
Tyne and Wear

The home of the Venerable Bede, chronicler of the beginnings of English Christianity, Jarrow has become one of the best-understood Anglo-Saxon monastic sites. The Anglo-Saxon church – with the oldest dedication stone in the country, dated AD 685 – partly survives as the chancel of the parish church. English Heritage members also receive a discount on the entry fee to the nearby Bede's World Museum.

Managed by Bede's World.

### OPENING TIMES

Monastery ruins any reasonable time

### HOW TO FIND US

**Direction:** In Jarrow, on minor road N of A185; follow signs for Bede's World

**Metro:** Bede ¾ miles

**Bus:** Go North East 527 Newcastle – South Shields

**Tel:** 01914 897052

MAP Page 275 (4H)
OS Map 316 (ref NZ 339652)

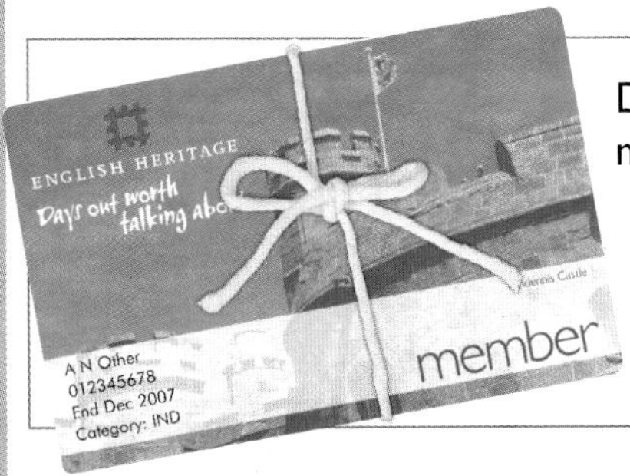


**Don't forget your membership card**

when you visit any of the properties listed in this handbook.

# Tynemouth Priory and Castle Tyne and Wear – NE30 4BZ

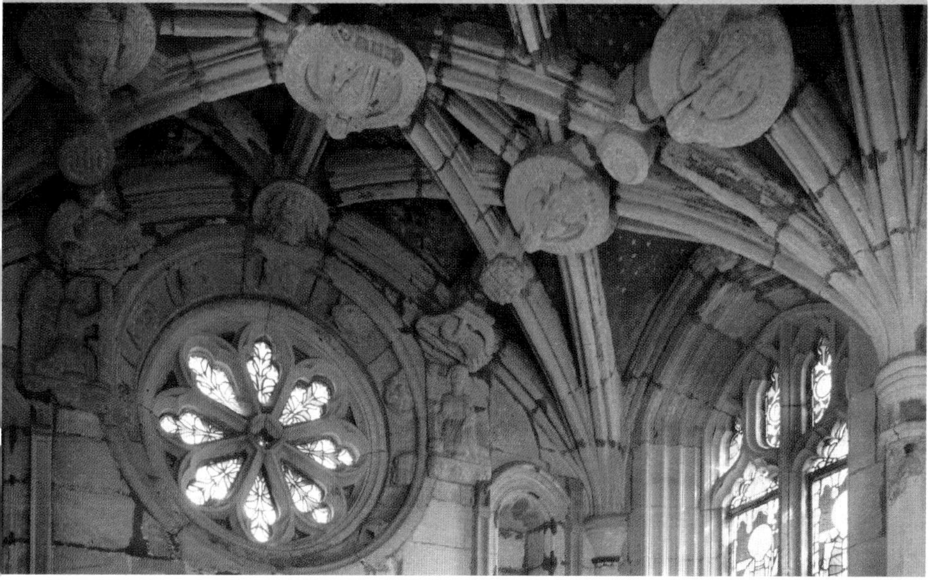

Set in an almost impregnable position on a steep headland between the river and the North Sea, Tynemouth has always been as much a fortress as a religious site.

Here stood a 7th-century Anglian monastery, burial place of Oswin, sainted king of Northumbria. After its destruction by Danish raiders, the present Benedictine priory was refounded on its site in c. 1090.

The towering east end of the priory church, built in c. 1200 with slender lancet windows and soaring arches, still survives almost to its full height, dominating the headland. Beyond it stands a small but complete and exceptionally well-preserved chapel, with a rose window and an ornately-sculpted roof vault, built in the mid-15th century as a chantry for the souls of the powerful Percy family, Earls of Northumberland.

Enclosing both headland and monastery, and still surviving in part, were the strong walls which once made Tynemouth among the largest fortified areas in England, and an important bastion against the Scots. Probably begun by Edward I in 1296, they were strengthened and updated in the 15th century. Thus when the priory's 19 monks surrendered Tynemouth to Henry VIII in 1539, it was immediately adopted as a royal castle. Thereafter the fortress-headland continued to play its centuries-old part in coastal defence, both against Napoleon and during the two World Wars. The restored magazine of its gun battery can be seen at weekends.

www.english-heritage.org.uk/tynemouthcastle

## NON-MEMBERS

| | |
|---|---|
| Adult | £3.50 |
| Concession | £2.60 |
| Child | £1.80 |
| Family | £8.80 |

## OPENING TIMES

| | |
|---|---|
| 1 Apr-30 Sep, daily | 10am-5pm |
| 1-31 Oct, daily | 10am-4pm |
| 1 Nov-20 Mar, Thu-Mon | 10am-4pm |
| Closed | 24-26 Dec and 1 Jan |

**Gun Battery:** Access limited, please ask site staff for details

## HOW TO FIND US

**Direction:** In Tynemouth, near North Pier

**Metro:** Tynemouth ½ mile

**Bus:** From surrounding areas

**Tel:** 0191 257 1090

OVP

Disabled access (priory only).

New guidebook.

MAP Page 275 (4H)
OS Map 316 (ref NZ 373694)

# Warkworth Castle and Hermitage

Northumberland – NE65 0UJ

The magnificent cross-shaped keep of Warkworth, crowning a hilltop rising steeply above the River Coquet, dominates one of the largest, strongest and most impressive fortresses in northern England. The castle's most famous owners were the Percy family, whose lion badge can be seen carved on many parts of their stronghold. Wielding almost kingly power in the north, their influence reached its apogee under the first Earl of Northumberland and his son 'Harry Hotspur', hero of many Border ballads as the bane of Scots raiders and a dominant character in Shakespeare's *Henry IV*. Having helped to depose Richard II, these turbulent 'kingmakers' both fell victim to Henry IV: the next three Percy Earls likewise died violent deaths.

Still roofed and almost complete, the uniquely-planned keep dates mainly from the end of the 14th century. It presides over the extensive remains of a great hall, chapel, fine gatehouse and a virtually intact circuit of towered walls.

Half a mile from the castle, tucked away by the Coquet and accessible only by boat, stands a much more peaceful building: the late medieval cave Hermitage and chapel of a solitary holy man.

There are free tours of the Duke's Rooms in the castle keep on Wed, Sun and Bank Holidays from 1 April to 30 September.

**www.english-heritage.org.uk/warkworthcastle**

## NON-MEMBERS

| | |
|---|---|
| **Castle:** | |
| Adult | £3.50 |
| Concession | £2.60 |
| Child | £1.80 |
| Family | £8.80 |
| **Hermitage:** | |
| Adult | £2.50 |
| Concession | £1.90 |
| Child | £1.30 |

## OPENING TIMES

| | |
|---|---|
| **Castle:** | |
| 1 Apr-30 Sep, daily | 10am-5pm |
| 1-31 Oct, daily | 10am-4pm |
| 1 Nov-20 Mar, Sat-Mon | 10am-4pm |
| Closed | 24-26 Dec and 1 Jan |
| **Hermitage:** | |
| 1 Apr-30 Sep, Wed, Sun & Bank Hols | 11am-5pm |

## HOW TO FIND US

**Direction:** In Warkworth; 7½ miles S of Alnwick, on A1068

**Train:** Alnmouth 3½ miles

**Bus:** Arriva 518 Newcastle – Alnwick

**Tel:** 01665 711423

P OVP

Audio tours (also available for the visually impaired and those with learning difficulties).

Disabled access (limited access only).

Dogs on leads (restricted areas only).

MAP Page 275 (2G)

OS Map 332 (ref NU 247058)

# Other historic attractions

Discounted entry to our members (discounts may not apply on event days)





## Bede's World Museum
Tyne and Wear – NE32 3DY

Adjacent to St Paul's Monastery (see p.252). A significant site which houses excavated artefacts and celebrates the extraordinary life of the Venerable Bede. A recreated Anglo-Saxon farm with buildings and animals.

Managed by Bede's World.

### ENTRY

| | |
|---|---|
| Adult | £4.50 |
| Concession | £3.00 |
| Child | £3.00 |
| Family (2+2) | £10.00 |

50% discount for EH members

Discount does not extend to EH Corporate Partners

### OPENING TIMES

1 Apr-31 Oct

| | |
|---|---|
| Mon-Sat | 10am-5.30pm |
| Sun | 12pm-5.30pm |

1 Nov-31 Mar

| | |
|---|---|
| Mon-Sat | 10am-4.30pm |
| Sun | 12pm-4.30pm |

Last admission 1 hr before closing

Closed Good Friday. Please call for Christmas opening hours

**Direction:** 2 miles from A19 Tyne Tunnel

**Tel:** 0191 489 2106

www.bedesworld.co.uk

MAP Page 275 (4H)
OS Map 316 (ref NZ 388654)

## The Bowes Museum
Co Durham – DL12 8NP

An inspirational day for all the family, with fascinating collections, a romantic history and beautiful grounds. Exhibitions for 2007 are based on antique lace and 'Watercolours and Drawings from The Collection of Queen Elizabeth the Queen Mother'. Please call for details.

### ENTRY

| | |
|---|---|
| Adult | £7.00 |
| Concession | £6.00 |
| Children | Free (under 16) |

10% off normal admission charge to EH members

Discount does not extend to EH Corporate Partners

### OPENING TIMES

| | |
|---|---|
| Open daily | 11am-5pm |
| Closed | 25-26 Dec and 1 Jan |

**Direction:** In Barnard Castle, off A66

**Tel:** 01833 690606

www.thebowesmuseum.org.uk

MAP Page 275 (5G)
OS Map 31 (ref NZ 056163)

## Chesters Walled Garden
Northumberland – NE46 4BQ

Historic two-acre walled garden famous for herbs and flower filled borders, organically grown. A haven of peace, scent and colour.

## Chesters Walled Garden

### ENTRY

£3.00

Discount for English Heritage members, please call for details.

Discount does not extend to EH Corporate Partners

### OPENING TIMES

| | |
|---|---|
| Mid-Mar-31 Oct daily | 10am-5pm |

**Direction:** ¼ mile W of Chollerford, off B6318

**Tel:** 01434 681483

www.chesterswalledgarden.co.uk

MAP Page 275 (4F)
OS Map 43 (ref NY 906703)

## Segedunum Roman Fort, Baths and Museum
Tyne and Wear – NE28 6HR

Remains of a Roman fort at the eastern end of Hadrian's Wall. Interactive museum, viewing tower and reconstructions of a bath house and Wall section.

Managed by Tyne and Wear Museums.

### ENTRY

| | |
|---|---|
| Adult | £3.95 |
| Concession | £2.25 |
| Children | Free (16 and under) |

10% discount for EH members

Discount does not extend to EH Corporate Partners

### OPENING TIMES

| | |
|---|---|
| 1 Apr-31 Oct, daily | 10am-5pm |
| 1 Nov-31 Mar, daily | 10am-3pm |

**Direction:** In Wallsend

**Tel:** 0191 236 9347

www.twmuseums.org.uk

MAP Page 275 (4H)
OS Map 316 (ref NZ 300660)

# Other Historic Attractions

**The Isle of Man, Wales and Scotland**

In addition to free admission to English Heritage properties featured in this handbook, members of English Heritage are also entitled to free or reduced-price entry to a host of other historic attractions in Scotland, Wales and on the Isle of Man. Entry is discounted in the first year of membership and free in subsequent years.

## Manx National Heritage

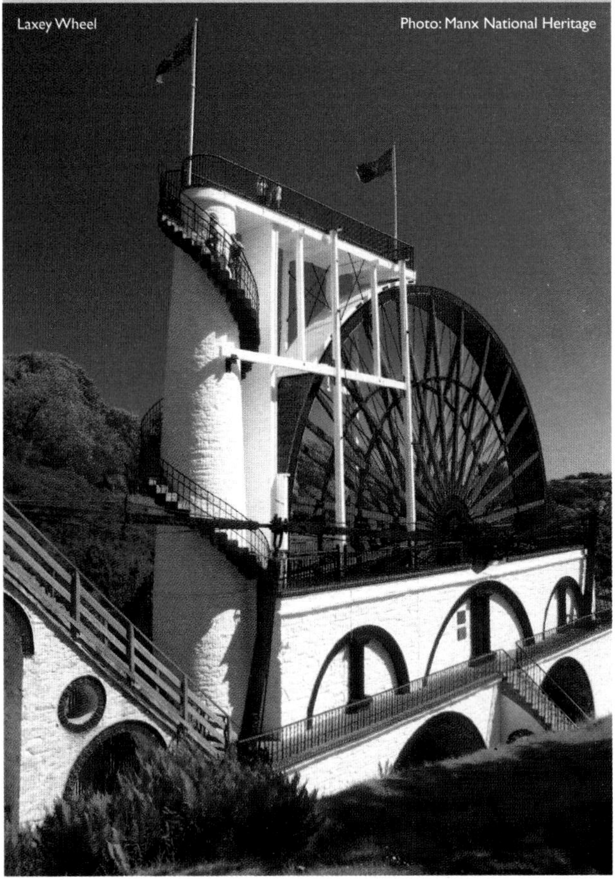

Laxey Wheel Photo: Manx National Heritage

English Heritage members can gain half-price admission to Manx National Heritage attractions during the first year of membership and free entry in subsequent years. All members must present a valid membership card on admission (members should note that Manx National Heritage only permit free admission to English Heritage members and children aged 4 years and under).

### Isle of Man

- Castle Rushen – Castletown
- Cregneash Folk Village – Cregneash
- The Grove – Ramsey
- House of Manannan – Peel
- Laxey Wheel and Mines Trail – Laxey
- Manx Museum – Douglas
- Nautical Museum – Castletown
- Niarbyl Café & Visitor Centre – Dalby
- Old Grammar School – Castletown
- Old House of Keys – Castletown
- Peel Castle – Peel
- Rushen Abbey – Ballasalla
- Sound Visitor Centre – Port St Mary

**For more details, please contact: Manx National Heritage, Kingswood Grove, Douglas, Isle of Man IM1 3LY.**

**Please call 01624 648000 or visit the Manx National Heritage website at www.storyofmann.com**

# Cadw: Welsh Historic Monuments

English Heritage members can gain half-price admission to Cadw attractions during the first year of membership and free entry in subsequent years.

Beaumaris Castle, Anglesey
Tel: 01248 810361

Blaenavon Ironworks, Nr Pontypool, Torfaen
Tel: 01495 792615

Caerleon Roman Fortress, Caerleon, Newport
Tel: 01633 422518

Caernarfon Castle, Caernarfon, Gwynedd
Tel: 01286 677617

Caerphilly Castle, Caerphilly
Tel: 02920 883143

Carreg Cennen Castle, Nr Trapp, Carmarthenshire
Tel: 01558 822291

Castell Coch, Cardiff
Tel: 02920 810101

Chepstow Castle, Chepstow, Monmouthshire
Tel: 01291 624065

Cilgerran Castle, Nr Cardigan, Ceredigion
Tel: 01239 621339

Conwy Castle, Conwy
Tel: 01492 592358

Criccieth Castle, Nr Criccieth, Gwynedd
Tel: 01766 522227

Dolwyddelan Castle, Dolwyddelan, Gwynedd
Tel: 01690 750366

Harlech Castle, Harlech, Gwynedd
Tel: 01766 780552

Kidwelly Castle, Kidwelly, Carmarthenshire
Tel: 01554 890104

Laugharne Castle, Laugharne, Carmarthenshire
Tel: 01994 427906

Oxwich Castle, Oxwich, Swansea
Tel: 01792 390359

Plas Mawr, Conwy
Tel: 01492 580167

Raglan Castle, Nr Raglan, Monmouthshire
Tel: 01291 690228

Rhuddlan Castle, Rhuddlan, Denbighshire
Tel: 01745 590777

Rug Chapel and Llangar Church, Corwen, Denbighshire
Tel: 01490 412025

St Davids Bishop's Palace, St Davids, Pembrokeshire
Tel: 01437 720517

Strata Florida Abbey, Pontrhydfendigaid, Ceredigion
Tel: 01974 831261

Tintern Abbey, Tintern, Monmouthshire
Tel: 01291 689251

Tretower Court and Castle, Tretower, Powys
Tel: 01874 730279

Valle Crucis Abbey, Nr Llangollen, Denbighshire
Tel: 01978 860326

Weobley Castle, Nr Llanrhidian, Swansea
Tel: 01792 390012

White Castle, Nr Abergavenny, Monmouthshire
Tel: 01600 780380

**For more details on Cadw, write to: Plas Carew, Unit 5/7 Cefn Coed, Parc Nantgarw, Cardiff CF15 7QQ**

**Please call 01443 336000 or visit the Cadw website at www.cadw.wales.gov.uk**

# Historic Scotland

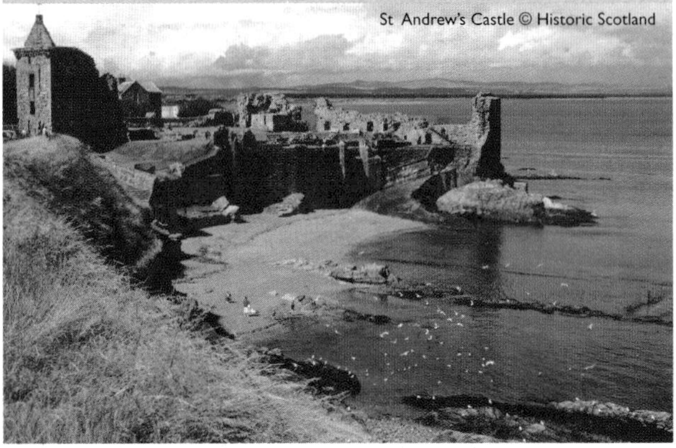

St Andrew's Castle © Historic Scotland

English Heritage members can gain half-price admission to Historic Scotland attractions during the first year of membership and free entry in subsequent years.

Aberdour Castle and Garden, Aberdour, Fife
Tel: 01383 860519

Arbroath Abbey, Angus
Tel: 01241 878756

Argyll's Lodging, Stirling, Central
Tel: 01786 431319

Balvenie Castle, Dufftown, Grampian
Tel: 01340 820121

Bishop's and Earl's Palaces, Kirkwall, Orkney
Tel: 01856 871918

The Black House, Arnol, Lewis, Western Isles
Tel: 01851 710395

Blackness Castle, Firth of Forth, Edinburgh and Lothians
Tel: 01506 834807

Bonawe Historic Iron Furnace, Taynuilt, Argyll
Tel: 01866 822432

Bothwell Castle, Bothwell, Greater Glasgow
Tel: 01698 816894

Broch of Gurness, Aikerness, Orkney
Tel: 01856 751414

Brough of Birsay, NW of Kirkwall, Orkney
Tel: 01856 841 815

Caerlaverock Castle, Nr Dumfries, Dumfries and Galloway
Tel: 01387 770244

Cairnpapple Hill, Torphichen, Edinburgh and Lothians
Tel: 01506 634622

Calanais Standing Stones, Isle of Lewis, Western Isles
Tel: 01851 621422

Cardoness Castle, Nr Gatehouse of Fleet Dumfries and Galloway
Tel: 01557 814427

Castle Campbell, Dollar Glen, Central
Tel: 01259 742408

Corgarff Castle, Nr Strathdon, Grampian
Tel: 01975 651460

Craigmillar Castle, Edinburgh and Lothians
Tel: 0131 6614445

Craignethan Castle, Lanark, Greater Glasgow
Tel: 01555 860364

Crichton Castle, Nr Pathhead, Edinburgh and Lothians
Tel: 01875 320017

Crossraguel Abbey, Nr Maybole, Greater Glasgow
Tel: 01655 883113

Dallas Dhu Historic Distillery, Nr Forres, Grampian
Tel: 01309 676548

Dirleton Castle and Gardens, Dirleton, Edinburgh and Lothians
Tel: 01620 850330

Doune Castle, Doune, Central
Tel: 01786 841742

Dryburgh Abbey, Nr Melrose, Borders
Tel: 01835 822381

Duff House, Banff, Grampian
Tel: 01261 818 181

Dumbarton Castle, Dumbarton, Greater Glasgow
Tel: 01389 732167

Dunblane Cathedral, Dunblane, Central
Tel: 01786 823 388

Dundonald Castle, Dundonald, Greater Glasgow
Tel: 01563 851489

Dundrennan Abbey, Nr Kirkcudbright, Dumfries and Galloway
Tel: 01557 500262

Dunfermline Palace and Abbey, Dunfermline, Fife
Tel: 01383 739026

Dunstaffnage Castle, Nr Oban, Argyll
Tel: 01631 562465

Edinburgh Castle, Edinburgh and Lothians
Tel: 0131 225 9846

Edzell Castle and Garden, Edzell, Angus
Tel: 01356 648631

Elcho Castle, Nr Bridge of Earn, Perthshire
Tel: 01738 639998

Elgin Cathedral, Elgin, Grampian
Tel: 01343 547171

Fort George, Nr Ardersier village, Highlands
Tel: 01667 460232

Glasgow Cathedral, Glasgow
Tel: 0141 552 6891

Glenluce Abbey, Nr Glenluce, Dumfries and Galloway
Tel: 01581 300541

Hackness Martello Tower and Battery, Hoy, Orkney
Tel: 01856 701727

## Historic Scotland

Above: (left) Inchmahome Priory, (centre top) New Abbey Corn Mill, (centre bottom) Edinburgh Castle and (right) Urquhart Castle.




Hermitage Castle,
Nr Newcastleton, Borders
**Tel:** 01387 376222

Huntingtower Castle, Nr Perth,
Perthshire
**Tel:** 01738 627231

Huntly Castle, Huntly, Grampian
**Tel:** 01466 793191

Inchcolm Abbey, Firth of Forth,
Fife
**Tel:** 01383 823332

Inchmahome Priory,
Lake of Menteith, Central
**Tel:** 01877 385294

Iona Abbey and Nunnery,
Island of Iona, Central
**Tel:** 01681 700512

Jarlshof Prehistoric and Norse
Settlement, Sumburgh Head,
Shetland
**Tel:** 01950 460112

Jedburgh Abbey and Visitor
Centre, Jedburgh, Borders
**Tel:** 01835 863925

Kildrummy Castle Nr Alford,
Grampian
**Tel:** 01975 571331

Kinnaird Head Castle, Lighthouse
and Museum, Fraserburgh,
Grampian
**Tel:** 01346 511022

Kisimul Castle, Isle of Barra,
Western Isles
**Tel:** 01871 810313

Linlithgow Palace, Linlithgow,
Edinburgh and Lothians
**Tel:** 01506 842896

Lochleven Castle, Lochleven,
Perthshire
**Tel:** 07778 040483

MacLellan's Castle, Kirkcudbright,
Dumfries and Galloway
**Tel:** 01557 331856

Maeshowe Chambered Cairn,
Nr Kirkwall, Orkney
**Tel:** 01856 761606

Meigle Sculptured Stone Museum,
Meigle, Angus
**Tel:** 01828 640612

Melrose Abbey, Melrose,
Borders
**Tel:** 01896 822562

New Abbey Corn Mill, New Abbey,
Dumfries and Galloway
**Tel: 01387 850260**

Newark Castle, Port Glasgow,
Greater Glasgow
**Tel:** 01475 741858

Rothesay Castle,
Rothesay, Isle of Bute
**Tel:** 01700 502691

St Andrew's Castle,
St Andrew's, Fife
**Tel:** 01334 477196

St Andrew's Cathedral,
St Andrew's, Fife
**Tel:** 01334 472563

St Serf's Church and Dupplin
Cross,
Dunning, Perthshire
**Tel:** 01764 684497

Seton Collegiate Church,
Nr Cockenzie, Edinburgh
and Lothians
**Tel:** 01875 813334

Skara Brae and Skaill House,
Nr Kirkwall, Orkney
**Tel:** 01856 841815

Smailholm Tower, Near
Smailholm, Borders
**Tel:** 01573 460365

Spynie Palace, Nr Elgin, Grampian
**Tel:** 01343 546358

Stirling Castle, Stirling, Central
**Tel:** 01786 450000

Sweetheart Abbey, New Abbey,
Dumfries and Galloway
**Tel:** 01387 850397

Tantallon Castle, Nr North
Berwick, Edinburgh and Lothians
**Tel:** 01620 892727

Threave Castle, Nr Castle Douglas,
Dumfries and Galloway
**Tel:** 07711 223101

Tolquhon Castle, Nr Aberdeen,
Grampian
**Tel:** 01651 851286

Urquhart Castle,
Drumnadrochit, Highlands
**Tel:** 01456 450551

**For more details on Historic Scotland, write to: Longmore House, Salisbury Place, Edinburgh EH9 1SH**

**Please call 0131 668 8999, email: hs.friends@scotland.gsi.gov.uk or visit the Historic Scotland website at www.historic-scotland.gov.uk**

# The Friends of Friendless Churches

St Andrew's Church, Woodwalton, Cambridgeshire by artist, Denis Clavreul.

## 50th Anniversary in 2007

The Friends own redundant but beautiful places of worship that would otherwise have been demolished or left to ruin. Founded by a proud Welshman Ivor Bulmer-Thomas in 1957 we now own 38 Grade II* and Grade I buildings in England and Wales. In 2007 we face major repair campaigns at Boveney in Buckinghamshire, Mundon in Essex and Woodwalton in Cambridgeshire (above), on all of which English Heritage has offered very useful grant aid.

We are a small, voluntary organisation which warmly welcomes visitors. We do not claim sophistication in terms of parking, toilets, attendants or shops, and access may require approach to a keyholder. Our churches are places for quiet study and contemplation.

Fifty years on, the need for us to campaign for historic churches is still vital. Help us make a difference by becoming a member or by getting involved with your local 'friendless church'.

FRIENDS OF FRIENDLESS CHURCHES

**THE FRIENDS OF FRIENDLESS CHURCHES**

St Ann's Vestry Hall, 2 Church Entry, London EC4V 5HB

**Tel:** 020 7236 3934

**Email:** office@friendsoffriendlesschurches.org.uk

**www.friendsoffriendlesschurches.org.uk**

**Registered charity no: 1113097**

Below left to right: Caldecote, Llanfigael St Baglan (photo by Ray Edgar) and stained-glass window at Matlock.

# The Churches Conservation Trust

'Lifelong learning', All Saints' Cambridge

The Churches Conservation Trust is the leading charity conserving England's most beautiful and historic churches which are no longer needed for regular worship. It promotes public enjoyment of these churches and encourages their use as an educational and community resource.

The Trust warmly welcomes all visitors, and invites them to discover and explore this fascinating and varied part of our national heritage. With over 335 churches throughout England, representing a microcosm of 1,000 years of English history, art and architecture, it can offer a very special lifelong learning experience for people of all ages and backgrounds.

There are hands-on workshops for students and families, teacher support and training, and dedicated education pages on the website featuring projects, lesson plans and downloadable notes on individual churches. Our publication *Exploring Churches*, and other education booklets produced in collaboration with English Heritage, provide curriculum-related activities. We also aim to increase adult visitors' understanding, appreciation and enjoyment through our guidebooks, and through family-focused activities during national learning events such as National Archaeology Days in July, Heritage Open Days in September and the Big Draw in October.

THE CHURCHES CONSERVATION TRUST

**THE CHURCHES CONSERVATION TRUST**

1 West Smithfield
London EC1A 9EE

**Tel:** 020 7213 0660
**Fax:** 020 7213 0678
**Email:** central@tcct.org.uk
**www.visitchurches.org.uk**

**Registered charity no: 258612**

# The Historic Chapels Trust

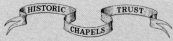

## Preserving places of worship in England

The trust was established to take into ownership redundant chapels and other places of worship in England which are of outstanding architectural and historic interest. Our mission is to secure for public benefit their preservation, repair and regeneration.

Below are 14 of the chapels in our care which you can visit. Please call the keyholder before visiting.

### London

The Dissenters' Chapel, Kensal Green Cemetery, London
Tel: 0207 602 0173

St George's German Lutheran Church, Tower Hamlets, London
Tel: 0207 481 0533

### South East

Cote Baptist Chapel, Oxfordshire
Tel: 01993 850421

### South West

Penrose Methodist Chapel, St Ervan, Cornwall
Tel: 01841 540737

Salem Chapel, East Budleigh, Devon
Tel: 01395 445236

### East of England

Walpole Old Chapel, Suffolk
Tel: 01986 798308

### Yorkshire

Farfield Friends Meeting House, West Yorkshire
Tel: 01756 710587

Todmorden Unitarian Church, West Yorkshire
Tel: 01706 813255

Wainsgate Baptist Church, West Yorkshire
Tel: 01422 843315

### North West

Shrine of Our Lady of Lourdes, Blackpool, Lancashire
Tel: 01253 302373

St Benet's Chapel, Netherton, Merseyside
Tel: 0151 520 2600

Wallasey Unitarian Church, Merseyside
Tel: 0151 639 9707

### North East

Biddestone RC Chapel, Northumberland
Tel: 01665 574420/01669 630270/01669 620230

Coanwood Friends Meeting House, Northumberland
Tel: 01434 321316

**For further information please visit our website www.hct.org.uk or telephone 0207 481 0533.**

# SOUTH WEST

Bristol
Cornwall
Devon
Dorset
Gloucester
Isles of Scilly
Somerset
Wiltshire

English Heritage Sites
Other Historic Attractions

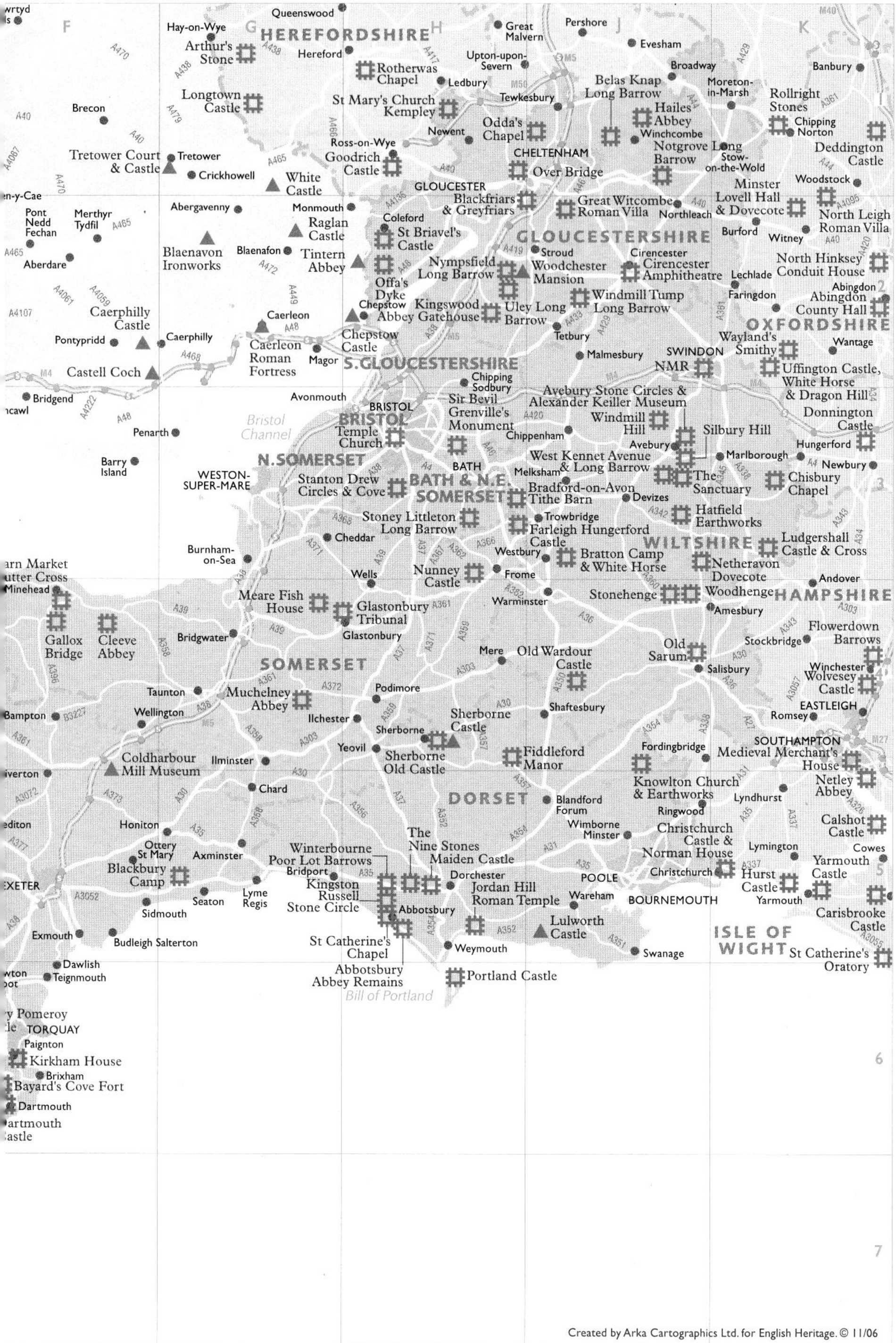


Created by Arka Cartographics Ltd. for English Heritage. © 11/06

A
B
C
D
E
1
2
3
4
5
6
7
Royal Leamington Spa
Warwick
Daventry
Althorp
NORTHAMPTON
78, Derngate
Bushmead Priory
St. N
WARWICKSHIRE
Stratford-upon-Avon
M40
M1
BEDFORDSHIRE
Sandy
Pershore
Evesham
Towcester
Newport Pagnell
MILTON KEYNES
BEDFORD
Biggleswade
Houghton House
Banbury
Brackley
Broadway
Moreton-in-Marsh
Buckingham
Bletchley
De Grey Mausoleum
Wrest Park
Belas Knap Long Barrow
Hailes Abbey
Winchcombe
Rollright Stones
Chipping Norton
Deddington Castle
BUCKINGHAMSHIRE
Letchworth
Dunstable
Stevenage
LUTON
CHELTENHAM
Stow-on-the-Wold
Bicester
Notgrove Long Barrow
Minster Lovell Hall & Dovecote
Woodstock
North Leigh Roman Villa
HER
Old Gorhambury House
Northleach
Great Witcombe Roman Villa
Burford
Aylesbury
Wendover
Berkhamsted Castle
Roman Wall
GLOUCESTERSHIRE
Witney
Rycote Chapel
Tring
St. Albans
Cirencester
North Hinksey Conduit House
OXFORD
Thame
Berkhamsted
HEMEL HEMPSTEAD
Cirencester Amphitheatre
Lechlade
Amersham
Windmill Tump Long Barrow
Faringdon
Abingdon County Hall
Abingdon
HIGH WYCOMBE
OXFORDSHIRE
Apsley House
Kenwo
Wayland's Smithy
Wantage
Didcot
Wallingford
Marlow
Kensal Green Cemetery
Malmesbury
SWINDON
NMR
Uffington Castle, White Horse & Dragon Hill
M4
Maidenhead
SLOUGH
Wellington Ar
Albert Memorial
Henley-on-Thames
Windmill Hill
Avebury Stone Circles & Alexander Keiller Museum
Donnington Castle
READING
Windsor
Chiswick House
Chippenham
Silbury Hill
Marble Hill House
Avebury
West Kennet Avenue & Long Barrow
Marlborough
Newbury
Bracknell
Coombe Conduit
The Sanctuary
Hungerford
Chisbury Chapel
BERKSHIRE
Aldermaston
Silchester Roman City Walls & Amphitheatre
Devizes
Hatfield Earthworks
WOKING
CAMBERLEY
Leatherhead
M25
WILTSHIRE
Ludgershall Castle & Cross
BASINGSTOKE
Fleet
Aldershot
GUILDFORD
Dorking
Bratton Camp & White Horse
Netheravon Dovecote
Farnham Castle Keep
Farnham
Waverley Abbey
Stonehenge
Woodhenge
Andover
SURREY
Amesbury
HAMPSHIRE
Alton
Stockbridge
Flowerdown Barrows
Northington Grange
CRAWLEY
Old Sarum
Itchen Abbas Roman Villa
Haslemere
Horsham
Salisbury
Winchester
Old Wardour Castle
Wolvesey Castle
Bishop's Waltham Palace
Petersfield
Midhurst
Petworth
EASTLEIGH
Romsey
Weald & Downland Open Air Museum
WEST SUSSE
SOUTHAMPTON
M27
Fordingbridge
Medieval Merchant's House
Southwick Priory
Fishbourne Roman Palace
Boxgrove Priory
Bramber Castle
Knowlton Church & Earthworks
Netley Abbey
Titchfield Abbey
Portchester Castle
Fontwell
Arundel
Lyndhurst
FAREHAM
Hove
Ringwood
CHICHESTER
WORTHING
Wimborne Minster
Christchurch Castle & Norman House
Calshot Castle
PORTSMOUTH
Royal Garrison Church
Marlipin Museum
Lymington
Fort Cumberland
Bognor Regis
Cowes
Hayling Island
Hurst Castle
Selsey
POOLE
Christchurch
Ryde
King James's & Landport Gates
BOURNEMOUTH
Yarmouth
Newport
Yarmouth Castle
Fort Brockhurst
Wareham
Carisbrooke Castle
Sandown
Osborne House
ISLE OF WIGHT
Shanklin
Swanage
St Catherine's Oratory
Ventnor
Appuldurcombe House

# LONDON AND SOUTH EAST

Berkshire
Buckinghamshire
East Sussex
Hampshire
Isle of Wight
Kent
Oxfordshire
Surrey
West Sussex

⌗ English Heritage Sites
▲ Other Historic Attractions

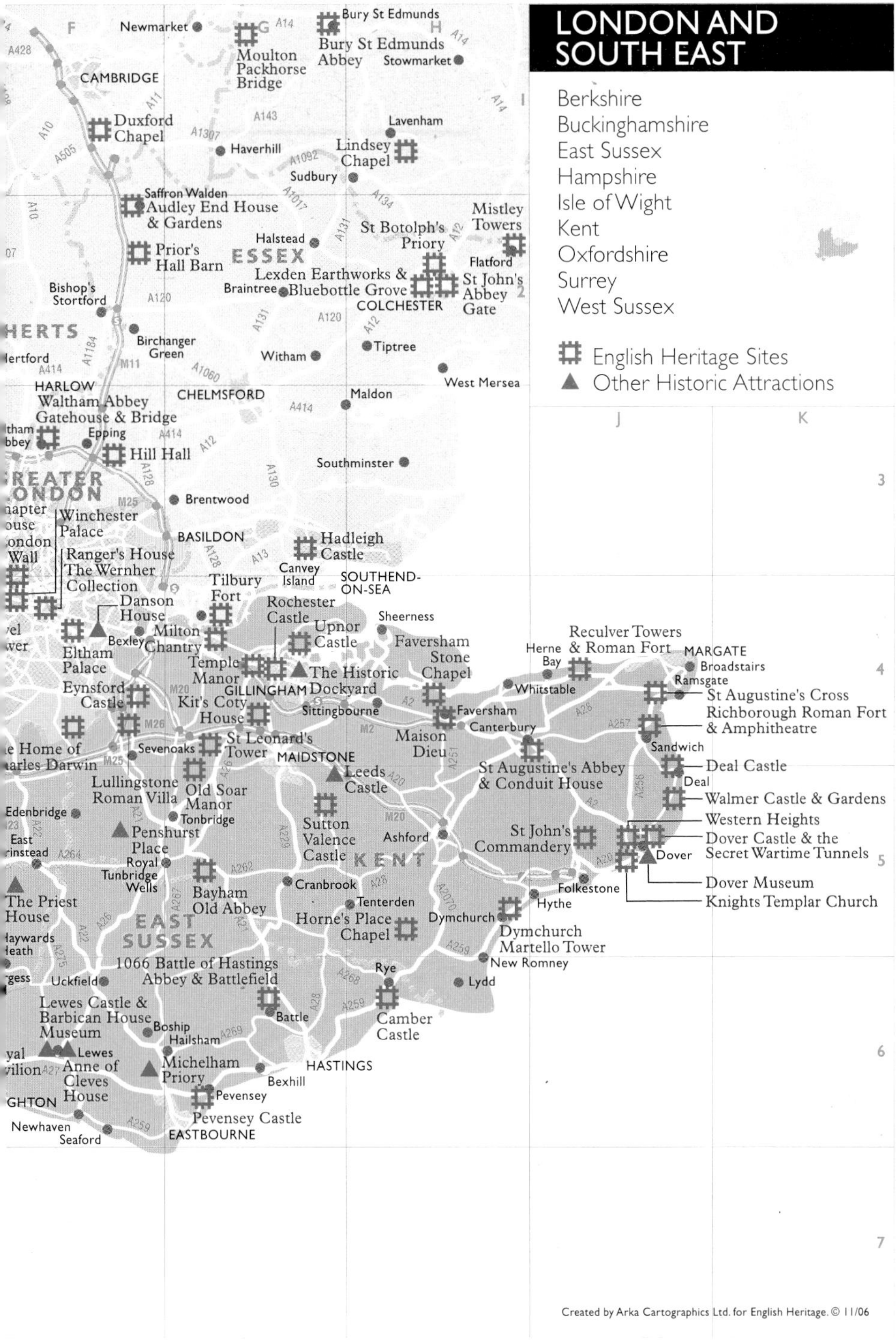


Created by Arka Cartographics Ltd. for English Heritage. © 11/06

# EAST OF ENGLAND

Bedfordshire
Cambridgeshire
Essex
Hertfordshire
Norfolk
Suffolk

⌗ English Heritage Sites
▲ Other Historic Attractions

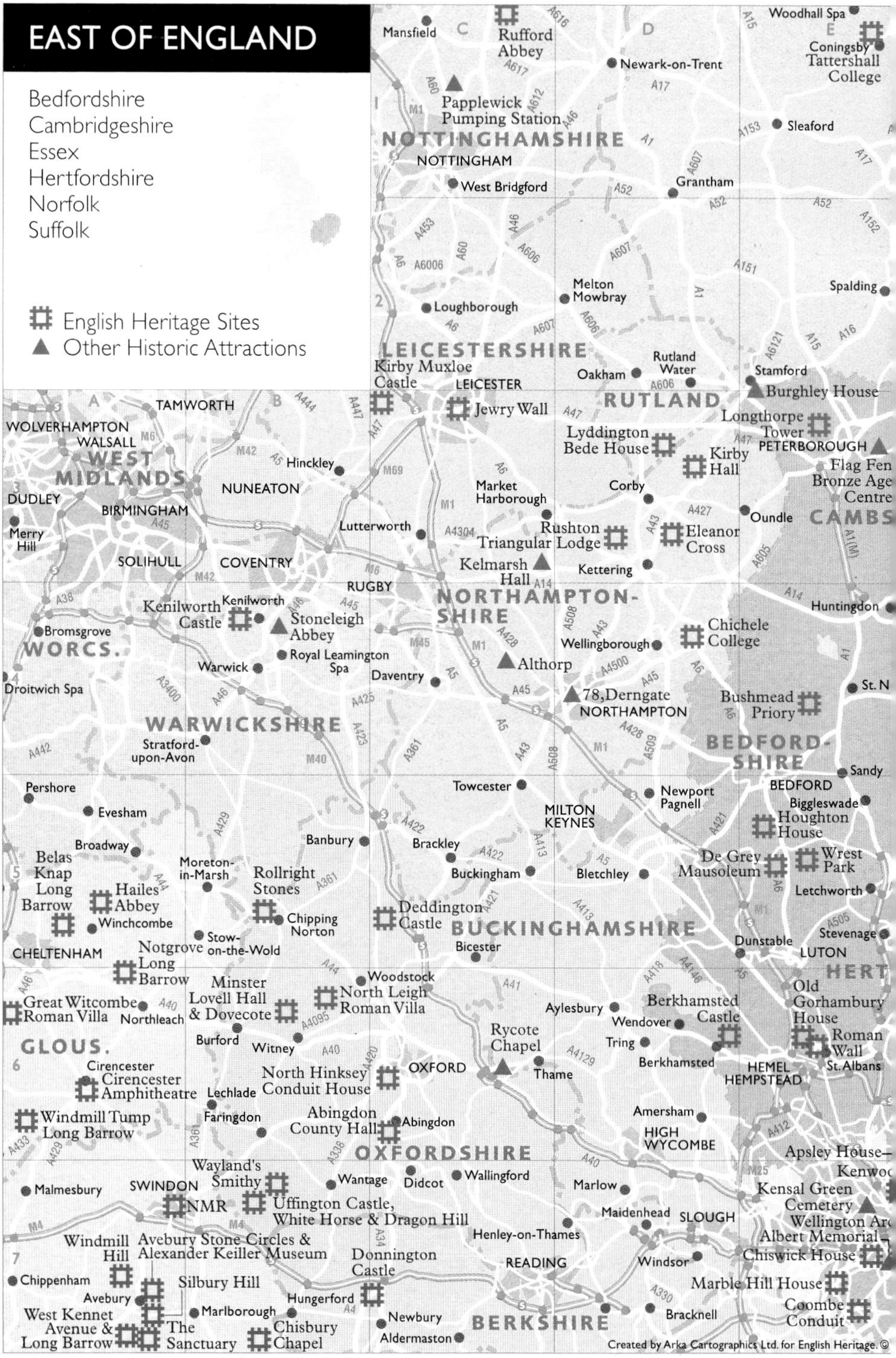

F
G
H
J
K
1
2
3
4
5
6
7
Sibsey Trader Windmill
Boston
Hunstanton
The Wash
Wells-next-the-Sea
Blakeney Guildhall
Creake Abbey
Binham Priory
Binham Market Cross
Holt
Baconsthorpe Castle
Sheringham
Cromer
Mundesley
North Walsham
Aylsham
Fakenham
Castle Rising Castle
Long Sutton
King's Lynn
Castle Acre Bailey Gate
Castle Acre Castle
Castle Acre Priory
North Elmham Chapel
Hoveton
Hemsby
Great Yarmouth Row Houses & Greyfriars' Cloisters
Caister Roman Site
Great Yarmouth
Time & Tide Museum
Cow Tower
NORWICH
East Dereham
Wisbech
Downham Market
Swaffham
NORFOLK
Berney Arms Windmill
Burgh Castle
Loddon
Wymondham
March
Grimes Graves
Attleborough
St Olave's Priory
LOWESTOFT
Thetford Warren Lodge
Weeting Castle
Thetford Priory
Brandon
Thetford
Bungay
Beccles
Kessingland
CAMBRIDGESHIRE
Chatteris
Isleham Priory Church
Ely
Church of the Holy Sepulchre
Diss
Halesworth
Southwold
SUFFOLK
Denny Abbey & the Farmland Museum
Bury St Edmunds Abbey
Saxtead Green Post Mill
Framlingham Castle
Leiston Abbey
Newmarket
Moulton Packhorse Bridge
Bury St Edmunds
Stowmarket
Aldeburgh
CAMBRIDGE
Woodbridge
Orford Castle
Orford
Duxford Chapel
Lavenham
Lindsey/ St James's Chapel
Haverhill
IPSWICH
Sudbury
Saffron Walden
Audley End House & Gardens
Mistley Towers
Felixstowe
Felixstowe Museum
Landguard Fort
St Botolph's Priory
Prior's Hall Barn
Halstead
ESSEX
Flatford
Harwich
Lexden Earthworks & Bluebottle Grove
St John's Abbey Gate
Braintree
COLCHESTER
Bishop's Stortford
Walton-on-the-Naze
HERTS.
Frinton-on-Sea
Birchanger Green
Tiptree
Witham
Clacton-on-Sea
West Mersea
HARLOW
CHELMSFORD
Maldon
Waltham Abbey Gatehouse & Bridge
Epping
Hill Hall
Southminster
Brentwood
GREATER LONDON
Islington
London Wall
BASILDON
Hadleigh Castle
Winchester Palace
Tilbury Fort
Canvey Island
SOUTHEND-ON-SEA
Greenwich
Eltham Palace
Bexley
Milton Chantry
Rochester Castle
Sheerness
Upnor Castle
Faversham Stone Chapel
Reculver Towers & Roman Fort
Ranger's House The Wernher Collection
Temple Manor
Chatham Historic Dockyard
Herne Bay
MARGATE
Broadstairs
Ramsgate
Eynsford Castle
Whitstable
St Augustine's Cross
A52
A149
A148
A1065
A140
A1101
A47
A10
A1122
A134
A1075
A11
A1067
A1151
A1062
A146
A143
A144
A145
A12
A142
A1123
A1066
A14
A1120
A1094
A1152
A143
A1307
A505
A1092
A1017
A131
A120
A133
A1184
M11
A414
A1060
A128
A130
M25
A13
M20
A2

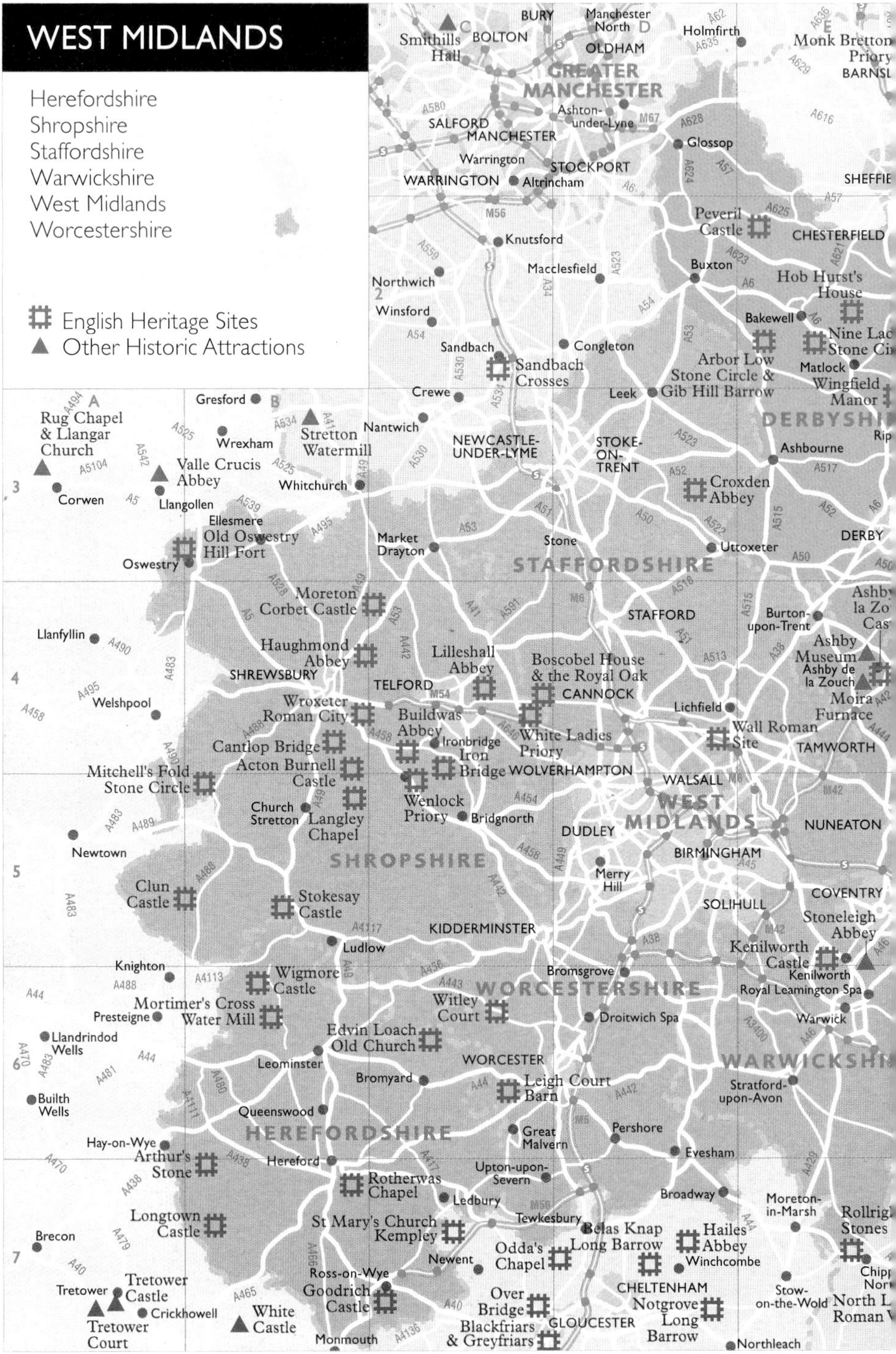
WEST MIDLANDS
Herefordshire
Shropshire
Staffordshire
Warwickshire
West Midlands
Worcestershire
English Heritage Sites
Other Historic Attractions
Smithills Hall
BOLTON
BURY
Manchester North
OLDHAM
Holmfirth
Monk Bretton Priory
BARNSL
GREATER MANCHESTER
SALFORD
MANCHESTER
Ashton-under-Lyne
Glossop
Warrington
WARRINGTON
Altrincham
STOCKPORT
SHEFFIE
Peveril Castle
CHESTERFIELD
Knutsford
Macclesfield
Buxton
Hob Hurst's House
Northwich
Winsford
Bakewell
Nine Lad Stone Ci
Sandbach
Congleton
Sandbach Crosses
Arbor Low Stone Circle & Gib Hill Barrow
Matlock
Wingfield Manor
Crewe
Leek
DERBYSHI
Rug Chapel & Llangar Church
Gresford
Wrexham
Stretton Watermill
Nantwich
NEWCASTLE-UNDER-LYME
STOKE-ON-TRENT
Ashbourne
Valle Crucis Abbey
Corwen
Llangollen
Whitchurch
Croxden Abbey
Ellesmere
Old Oswestry Hill Fort
Oswestry
Market Drayton
Stone
Uttoxeter
DERBY
STAFFORDSHIRE
Moreton Corbet Castle
STAFFORD
Burton-upon-Trent
Ashby la Zo Cas
Llanfyllin
Haughmond Abbey
Lilleshall Abbey
Boscobel House & the Royal Oak
Ashby Museum
Ashby de la Zouch
SHREWSBURY
TELFORD
CANNOCK
Lichfield
Moira Furnace
Welshpool
Wroxeter Roman City
Buildwas Abbey
Ironbridge
White Ladies Priory
Wall Roman Site
TAMWORTH
Cantlop Bridge
Acton Burnell Castle
Iron Bridge
WOLVERHAMPTON
WALSALL
Mitchell's Fold Stone Circle
Church Stretton
Langley Chapel
Wenlock Priory
Bridgnorth
WEST MIDLANDS
NUNEATON
DUDLEY
Newtown
SHROPSHIRE
BIRMINGHAM
Merry Hill
Clun Castle
Stokesay Castle
SOLIHULL
COVENTRY
Stoneleigh Abbey
KIDDERMINSTER
Ludlow
Kenilworth Castle
Kenilworth
Knighton
Wigmore Castle
Bromsgrove
WORCESTERSHIRE
Royal Leamington Spa
Mortimer's Cross Water Mill
Witley Court
Presteigne
Droitwich Spa
Warwick
Llandrindod Wells
Edvin Loach Old Church
Leominster
WORCESTER
WARWICKSHI
Bromyard
Leigh Court Barn
Stratford-upon-Avon
Builth Wells
Queenswood
HEREFORDSHIRE
Great Malvern
Pershore
Hay-on-Wye
Arthur's Stone
Hereford
Evesham
Upton-upon-Severn
Rotherwas Chapel
Ledbury
Broadway
Moreton-in-Marsh
Rollrig Stones
Longtown Castle
St Mary's Church Kempley
Tewkesbury
Belas Knap Long Barrow
Hailes Abbey
Brecon
Winchcombe
Newent
Odda's Chapel
Tretower Castle
Tretower
Ross-on-Wye
Goodrich Castle
CHELTENHAM
Stow-on-the-Wold
Over Bridge
Notgrove Long Barrow
North L Roman
Crickhowell
White Castle
Tretower Court
Blackfriars & Greyfriars
GLOUCESTER
Monmouth
Northleach

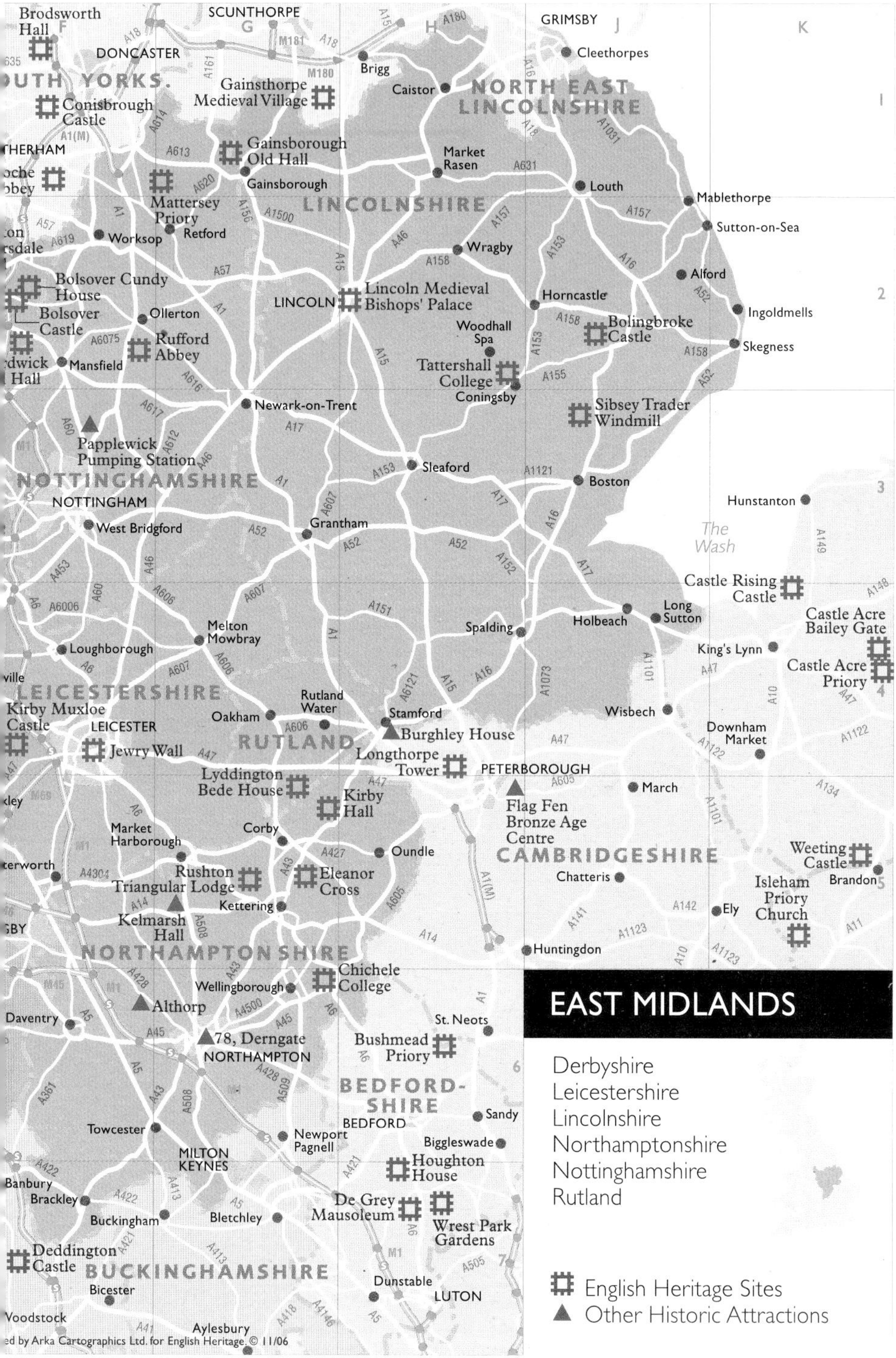


# EAST MIDLANDS

Derbyshire
Leicestershire
Lincolnshire
Northamptonshire
Nottinghamshire
Rutland

English Heritage Sites
▲ Other Historic Attractions

NORTH WEST (Bottom)
Cheshire
Greater Manchester
Lancashire
Merseyside
English Heritage Sites
Other Historic Attractions
CUMBRIA
LANCASHIRE
MERSEYSIDE
GREATER MANCHESTER
CHESHIRE
Maryport
Cockermouth
Workington
WHITEHAVEN
Egremont
Keswick
Castlerigg Stone Circle
Penrith Castle
PENRITH
Mayburgh Henge
Brougham Castle
Clifton Hall
Countess Pillar
King Arthur's Round Table
Appleby-in-Westmorland
Ullswater
Shap Abbey
Brough Castle
Brough
Bowes Castle
Seatoller Barn
Ravenglass & Eskdale Railway
Hardknott Roman Fort
Grasmere
Ambleside
Ambleside Roman Fort
Waterhead
Windermere
Hawkshead
Coniston
Kirkby Stephen
Tebay
Sellafield
Ravenglass
Muncaster Castle
Ravenglass Roman Bath House
Broughton-in-Furness
Stott Park Bobbin Mill
Kendal
Sedbergh
Hawes
Aysgarth Falls
Bootle
Millom
Ulverston
Holker Hall
Grange-over-Sands
Kirkby Longsdale
Horton-in-Ribblesdale
Furness Abbey
Bow Bridge
BARROW-IN-FURNESS
Piel Castle
Piel Island
Warton Old Rectory
Carnforth
Ingleton
High Bentham
Clapham
Morecambe
Morecambe Bay
Lancaster
Settle
Grassington
Malham
Skipton
Fleetwood
Garstang
Sawley Abbey
Barnoldswick
Cleveleys
Clitheroe
Pendle Heritage Centre
Whalley Abbey Gatehouse
BLACKPOOL
BURNLEY
Accrington
Hebden Bridge
Lytham St.Anne's
PRESTON
BLACKBURN
Oswaldtwistle
Goodshaw Chapel
Rawtenstall
Todmorden
SOUTHPORT
Chorley
Smithills Hall
ROCHDALE
Ormskirk
BURY
Manchester North
BOLTON
OLDHAM
Formby
BOOTLE
KIRKBY
ST. HELENS
St Helens
SALFORD
MANCHESTER
Ashton-under-Lyne
Glossop
St George's Hall
LIVERPOOL
Warrington
STOCKPORT
BIRKENHEAD
Runcorn
WIDNES
WARRINGTON
Altrincham
Norton Priory Museum & Gardens
RUNCORN
ELLESMERE PORT
Knutsford
Neston
Salt Museum
Northwich
Macclesfield
Flint
CHESTER
Winsford
Mold
Chester Castle
Chester Roman Amphitheatre
Beeston Castle
Sandbach
Sandbach Crosses
Congleton
Crewe
Leek
Gresford
Wrexham
Stretton Watermill
Nantwich
NEWCASTLE-UNDER-LYME
STOKE-ON-TRENT
Valle Crucis Abbey
Whitchurch
Llangollen
Llandudno
Rhos-on-Sea
Conwy
Colwyn Bay
Conwy Castle
Plas Mawr
Rhyl
Prestatyn
Rhuddlan Castle
Denbigh
Ruthin
Betws-y-Coed
Dolwyddelan Castle
Rug Chapel & Llangar Church
Blaenau Ffestiniog
Corwen
Created by Arka Cartographics Ltd. for English Heritage. © 11/06

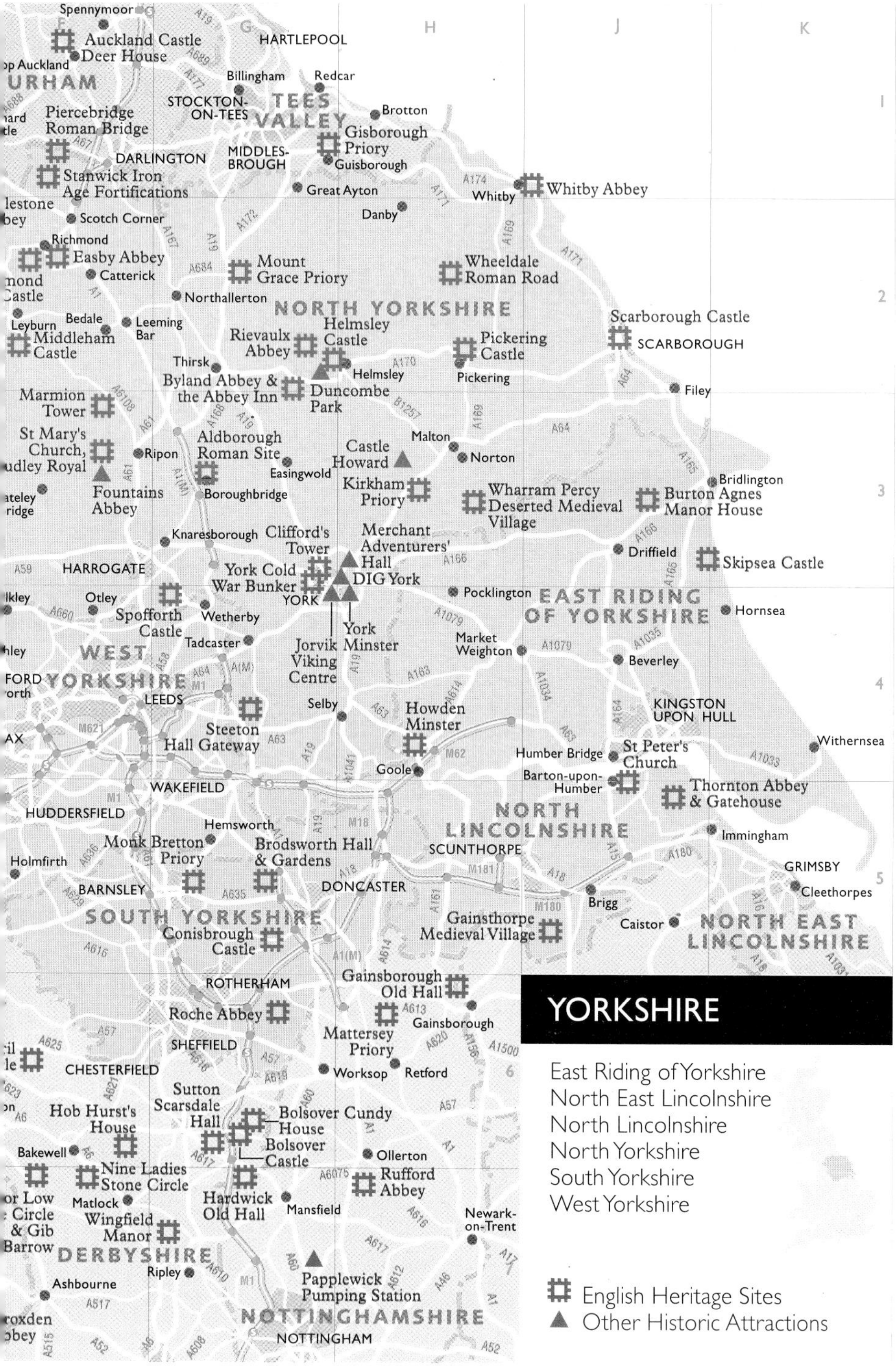


## YORKSHIRE

East Riding of Yorkshire
North East Lincolnshire
North Lincolnshire
North Yorkshire
South Yorkshire
West Yorkshire

English Heritage Sites
▲ Other Historic Attractions

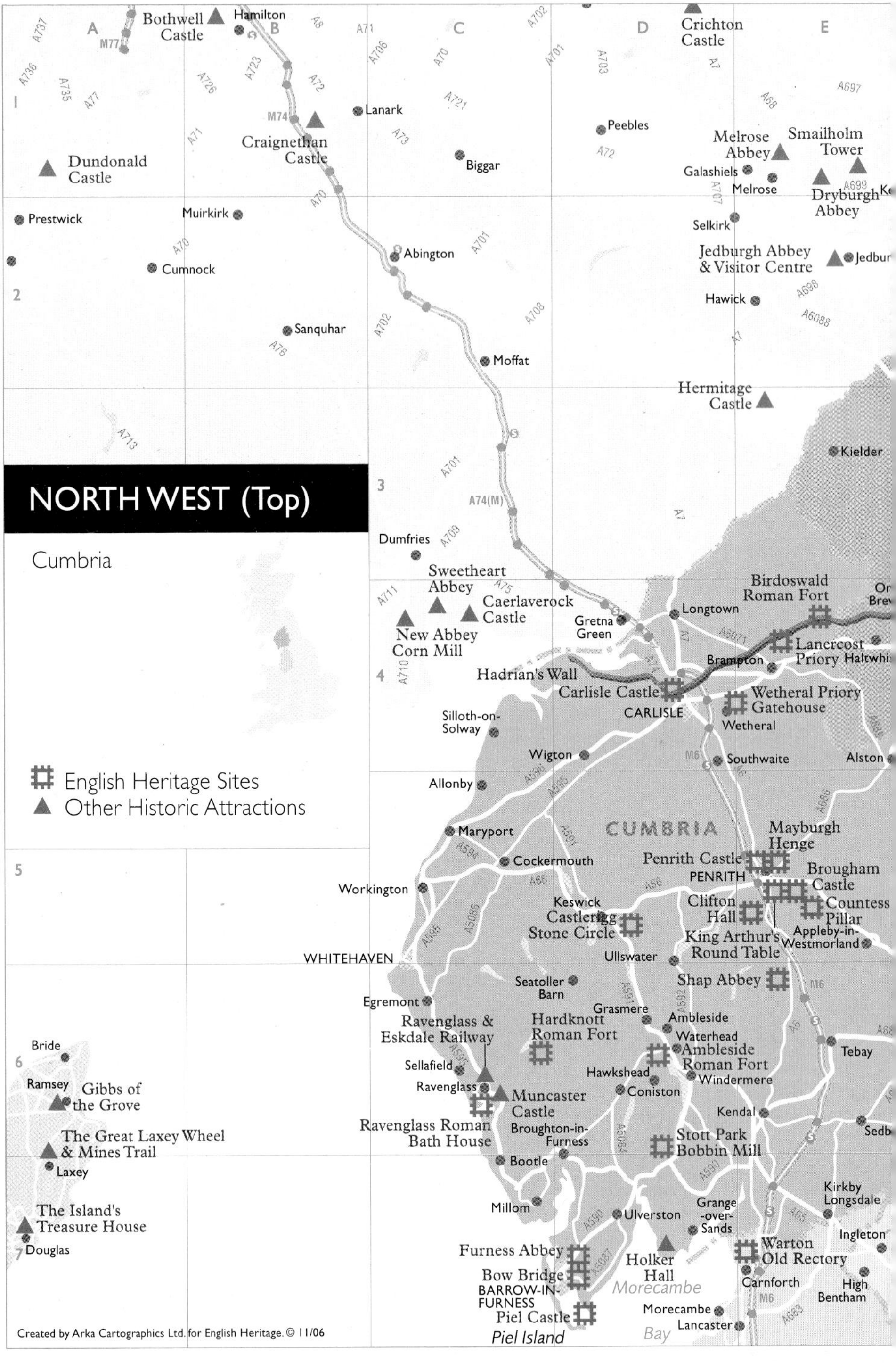
NORTH WEST (Top)
Cumbria
English Heritage Sites
Other Historic Attractions
Bothwell Castle
Hamilton
Crichton Castle
Lanark
Craignethan Castle
Peebles
Melrose Abbey
Smailholm Tower
Galashiels
Melrose
Dryburgh Abbey
Dundonald Castle
Biggar
Prestwick
Muirkirk
Selkirk
Abington
Jedburgh Abbey & Visitor Centre
Cumnock
Hawick
Sanquhar
Moffat
Hermitage Castle
Kielder
Dumfries
Sweetheart Abbey
Caerlaverock Castle
Birdoswald Roman Fort
New Abbey Corn Mill
Gretna Green
Longtown
Lanercost Priory
Brampton
Hadrian's Wall
Carlisle Castle
CARLISLE
Wetheral Priory Gatehouse
Wetheral
Silloth-on-Solway
Wigton
Southwaite
Alston
Allonby
CUMBRIA
Maryport
Mayburgh Henge
Cockermouth
Penrith Castle
PENRITH
Brougham Castle
Workington
Clifton Hall
Countess Pillar
Keswick
Castlerigg Stone Circle
King Arthur's Round Table
Appleby-in-Westmorland
WHITEHAVEN
Ullswater
Seatoller Barn
Shap Abbey
Egremont
Grasmere
Ravenglass & Eskdale Railway
Hardknott Roman Fort
Ambleside
Waterhead
Ambleside Roman Fort
Tebay
Bride
Sellafield
Hawkshead
Windermere
Ramsey
Gibbs of the Grove
Ravenglass
Coniston
Muncaster Castle
Kendal
Ravenglass Roman Bath House
Broughton-in-Furness
The Great Laxey Wheel & Mines Trail
Stott Park Bobbin Mill
Laxey
Bootle
Kirkby Longsdale
Millom
Grange-over-Sands
The Island's Treasure House
Ulverston
Ingleton
Douglas
Furness Abbey
Holker Hall
Warton Old Rectory
Bow Bridge
BARROW-IN-FURNESS
Morecambe
Carnforth
High Bentham
Piel Castle
Morecambe
Lancaster
Piel Island
Bay
Created by Arka Cartographics Ltd. for English Heritage. © 11/06

NORTH EAST
County Durham
Northumberland
Tyne & Wear
Tees Valley
English Heritage Sites
Other Historic Attractions
NORTHUMBERLAND
TYNE & WEAR
DURHAM
TEES VALLEY
NORTH YORKSHIRE
Berwick-upon-Tweed Barracks & Main Guard
Berwick-upon-Tweed Castle & Ramparts
Lindisfarne Priory
Etal Castle
Belford
Seahouses
Adderstone
Wooler
Dunstanburgh Castle
Craster
Alnwick
Edlingham Castle
Warkworth Castle & Hermitage
Rothbury
Amble
Brinkburn Priory
Otterburn
ASHINGTON
Morpeth
Newbiggin-by-the-Sea
Chesters Roman Fort
Belsay Hall Castle & Gardens
Blyth
Bessie Surtees House
Chesters Bridge Abutment
Whitley Bay
Tynemouth Priory & Castle
NEWCASTLE UPON TYNE
Segedunum Roman Fort
Aydon Castle
Prudhoe Castle
St Paul's Monastery
GATESHEAD
Bede's World Museum
Hexham
Prudhoe
Corbridge Roman Town
SUNDERLAND
Hylton Castle
Derwentcote Steel Furnace
Beamish
Consett
Finchale Priory
Peterlee
Stanhope
DURHAM
HARTLEPOOL
Spennymoor
Auckland Castle Deer House
Bishop Auckland
Billingham
Redcar
Bowes Museum
Barnard Castle
Piercebridge Roman Bridge
STOCKTON-ON-TEES
Brotton
Gisborough Priory
Guisborough
Barnard Castle
DARLINGTON
MIDDLESBROUGH
Bowes Castle
Bowes
Stanwick Iron Age Fortifications
Great Ayton
Whitby
Whitby Abbey
Egglestone Abbey
Scotch Corner
Danby
Richmond
Reeth
Easby Abbey
Mount Grace Priory
Wheeldale Roman Road
Catterick
Richmond Castle
Northallerton
Hawes
Aysgarth Falls
Leyburn
Bedale
Leeming Bar
Helmsley Castle
Scarborough Castle
Rievaulx Abbey
Middleham Castle
Pickering Castle
SCARBOROUGH
Thirsk
Helmsley
Pickering
Byland Abbey & the Abbey Inn
Duncombe Park
Filey
Marmion Tower
St Mary's Church, Studley Royal
Ripon
Aldborough Roman Site
Castle Howard
Malton
Burton Agnes Manor House
Fountains Abbey
Easingwold
Wharram Percy Deserted Medieval Village
Settle
Grassington
Pateley Bridge
Boroughbridge
Kirkham Priory
Malham

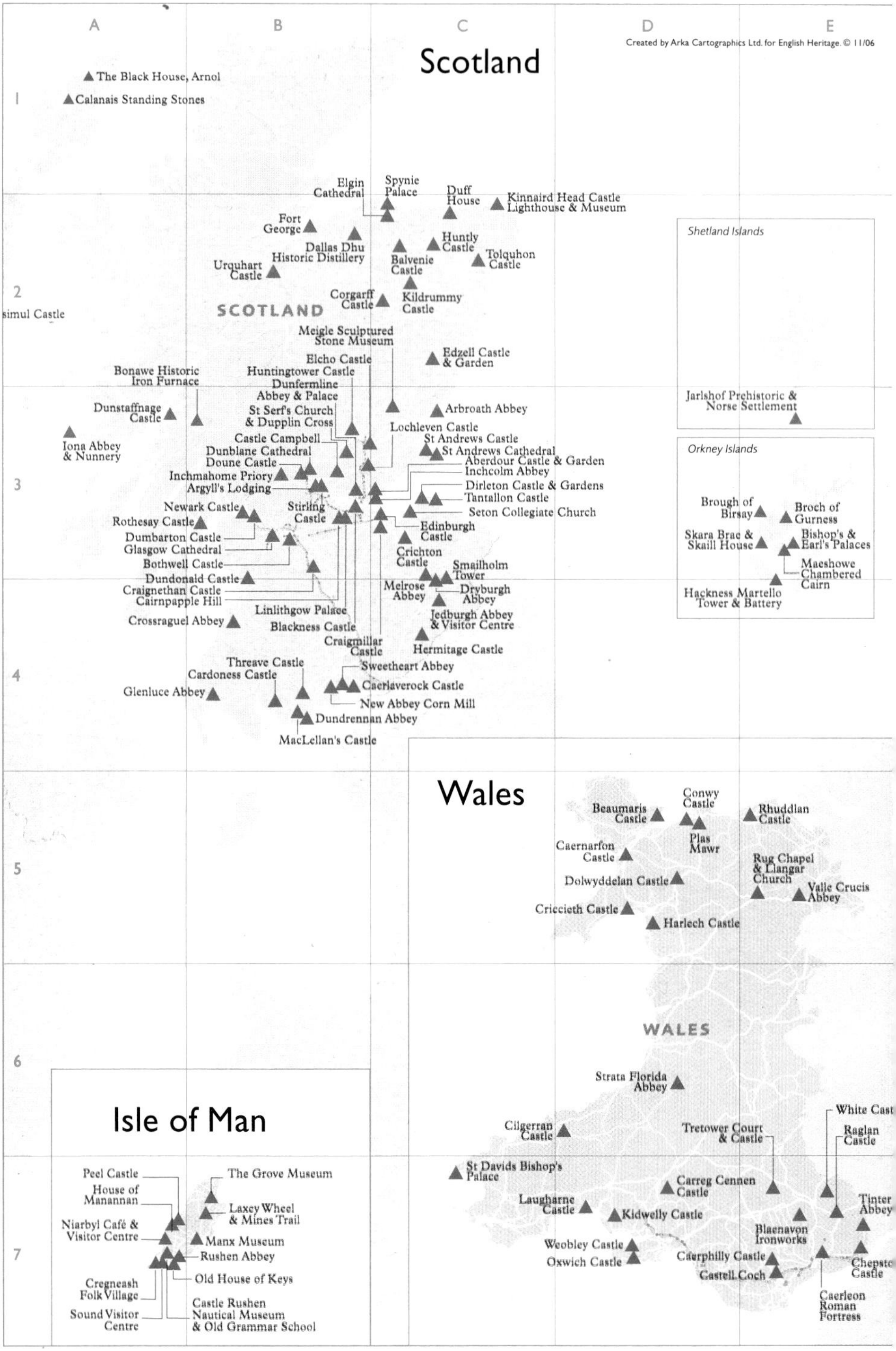
Scotland
Created by Arka Cartographics Ltd. for English Heritage. © 11/06
A
B
C
D
E
1
2
3
4
5
6
7
The Black House, Arnol
Calanais Standing Stones
Elgin Cathedral
Spynie Palace
Duff House
Kinnaird Head Castle Lighthouse & Museum
Fort George
Dallas Dhu Historic Distillery
Huntly Castle
Tolquhon Castle
Balvenie Castle
Urquhart Castle
Corgarff Castle
Kildrummy Castle
simul Castle
SCOTLAND
Meigle Sculptured Stone Museum
Edzell Castle & Garden
Elcho Castle
Huntingtower Castle
Bonawe Historic Iron Furnace
Dunfermline Abbey & Palace
Dunstaffnage Castle
St Serf's Church & Dupplin Cross
Arbroath Abbey
Lochleven Castle
Iona Abbey & Nunnery
Castle Campbell
St Andrews Castle
Dunblane Cathedral
St Andrews Cathedral
Doune Castle
Aberdour Castle & Garden
Inchmahome Priory
Inchcolm Abbey
Argyll's Lodging
Dirleton Castle & Gardens
Newark Castle
Stirling Castle
Tantallon Castle
Seton Collegiate Church
Rothesay Castle
Edinburgh Castle
Dumbarton Castle
Glasgow Cathedral
Crichton Castle
Bothwell Castle
Smailholm Tower
Dundonald Castle
Craignethan Castle
Melrose Abbey
Dryburgh Abbey
Cairnpapple Hill
Linlithgow Palace
Jedburgh Abbey & Visitor Centre
Crossraguel Abbey
Blackness Castle
Craigmillar Castle
Hermitage Castle
Threave Castle
Sweetheart Abbey
Cardoness Castle
Caerlaverock Castle
Glenluce Abbey
New Abbey Corn Mill
Dundrennan Abbey
MacLellan's Castle
Shetland Islands
Jarlshof Prehistoric & Norse Settlement
Orkney Islands
Brough of Birsay
Broch of Gurness
Skara Brae & Skaill House
Bishop's & Earl's Palaces
Maeshowe Chambered Cairn
Hackness Martello Tower & Battery
Wales
Beaumaris Castle
Conwy Castle
Rhuddlan Castle
Plas Mawr
Caernarfon Castle
Rug Chapel & Llangar Church
Dolwyddelan Castle
Valle Crucis Abbey
Criccieth Castle
Harlech Castle
WALES
Strata Florida Abbey
White Cast
Cilgerran Castle
Tretower Court & Castle
Raglan Castle
St Davids Bishop's Palace
Carreg Cennen Castle
Tintern Abbey
Laugharne Castle
Kidwelly Castle
Blaenavon Ironworks
Weobley Castle
Oxwich Castle
Caerphilly Castle
Chepstow Castle
Castell Coch
Caerleon Roman Fortress
Isle of Man
Peel Castle
The Grove Museum
House of Manannan
Laxey Wheel & Mines Trail
Niarbyl Café & Visitor Centre
Manx Museum
Rushen Abbey
Old House of Keys
Cregneash Folk Village
Castle Rushen
Sound Visitor Centre
Nautical Museum & Old Grammar School

**English Heritage Members' & Visitors' Handbook 2007/8**

For English Heritage: Dan Wolfe, Kate Linnell, Kathryn Steele-Childe, Tersia Mountford, Charles Kightly.

Design and Publishing: Ledgard Jepson Ltd

For Ledgard Jepson Ltd: David Exley, Craig Hebditch, Wayne Gilbert, Bev Turbitt, Andrea Rollinson.

Print: St Ives.

Transport Information: Barry Doe.